CLOSERS

Also by Mike Tronnes

Literary Las Vegas

CLOSERS

Great American Writers on the Art of Selling

Edited by Mike Tronnes

ST. MARTIN'S PRESS
NEW YORK

Production Editor: David Stanford Burr

Designer: Nancy Resnick

Library of Congress Cataloging-in-Publication Data

Closers : great American writers on the art of selling / edited by Mike Tronnes.
p. cm.
ISBN 0-312-18068-3
1. Sales personnel–Literary collections. 2. Selling–Literary collections. 3. American literature–20th century. I. Tronnes, Mike.
PS509.S2C58 1998
810.8'0352381–dc21 97-36530
CIP

First Edition: April 1998

10 9 8 7 6 5 4 3 2 1

To Jessica,

thanks for your
keen eye and warm heart

Contents

Acknowledgments		ix
Introduction		xi
Thomas Bontly	from *The Competitor*	1
Erskine Caldwell	*Handsome Brown's Day Off*	18
John Cheever	*The Autobiography of a Drummer*	26
Harry Crews	from *The Mulching of America*	30
Rick DeMarinis	*The Smile of a Turtle*	42
Peter De Vries	*Through a Glass Darkly*	49
William Saroyan	*Harry*	53
Raymond Carver	*Collectors*	60
Philip K. Dick	*Sales Pitch*	67
Michael Dorris	*Jeopardy*	82
Seymour Epstein	*My Brother's Keeper*	98
Edna Ferber	from *Roast Beef Medium*	108
M. F. K. Fisher	*The Unswept Emptiness*	119
Richard Ford	from *Independence Day*	128

David Mamet	from *Glengarry Glen Ross*	149
Ron Hansen	*Can I Just Sit Here For a While?*	158
Richard Price	from *Ladies' Man*	173
Sinclair Lewis	from *Elmer Gantry*	185
Phillip Lopate	from *The Rug Merchant*	199
William Price Fox	*200,000 Dozen Pairs of Socks*	209
Jack Matthews	*The Story Mac Told*	222
Arthur Miller	from *Death of a Salesman*	238
Lucia Nevai	*Likely Houses*	244
Flannery O'Connor	*Good Country People*	253
John O'Hara	*How Can I Tell You?*	273
J. F. Powers	*Blue Island*	280
Christopher Zenowich	*Think Big*	293
John Updike	from *Rabbit Is Rich*	308
Thomas Wolfe	*The Company*	322
Eudora Welty	*Death of a Traveling Salesman*	332

Permissions 345

ACKNOWLEDGMENTS

Special thanks to Lynette Lamb and Tony Goshko

Thanks to Cal Morgan, Dana Albarella, Jennifer Shepard, and everyone else at St. Martin's Press, and also to Holden Brooks, John Diebel, Adam Dolgins, Gordon Flagler, Van Foreman, Shelley Holl, Elizabeth Larsen, Carolyn Larson, Rob Levine, Eric Lindbom, Karla Miller. Tom McKusick, John Schultz, Chris Waddington, Bill White, Brad Zellar, everyone in the Tronnes and Strom families, and the helpful staff at the downtown branch of the Minneapolis Public Library, especially Helen Burke, Wendy Adamson, Katie Weiblen and Mike McCabe. Also, thanks to the publishers, agents, and authors who helped me to secure the rights to the articles. And finally, thanks to Chris Calhoun, without whose hard work, there would be no copies of *Closers* to open.

INTRODUCTION

Selling may be the defining activity of American society. On any given day, the number of sales messages that we are exposed to each day runs into the thousands. Fine-tuned by focus groups and targeted with scientific precision, most of these pitches are delivered impersonally, in the form of marketing or advertising. *Closers* is about a different kind of sales pitch—the pitch that is delivered in person, face-to-face—the kind that you can't tune out. More about the art of selling than the science, *Closers* brings together many of America's most important writers as they lend their literary voices to a subject long at the heart of our commercial culture. The writing spans an evolving century of selling and the products range from the stereotypical—cars, real estate, and vacuum cleaners—to the obscure—gravestones, chinchillas, and robots. But in these stories, the product is just a foot in the door for exploring the inherent conflict between buyer and seller and examining the lives and motivations of each.

Most of us have sold something at one time or another, and all of us know people who sell for a living, yet when we think of the profession, the images that come most readily to mind are those based in fiction. Although our lives are an endless stream of buying and selling, our perceptions of salespeople and our ambivalent relationships with them, are defined as much by books, plays, movies, and television as by our own experiences. Willy Loman, a man out of time in *Death of a Salesman,* the sleazy real estate hucksters in *Glengarry Glen Ross,* fast-talking car dealers and desperate door-to-door salesmen–characters who are always on the move and often on the make. *Closers* introduces you to these smooth and not-so-smooth operators–the foot soldiers of our bottom-line culture–while at the same time exploring our contradictory attitudes about them.

Some of us enjoy our work, and for others it's just a way to make a living. The stories in *Closers* reveal the degree to which this distinction is magnified among salespeople. Some are in the game because they love it–the energy of the sell, the opportunity to reinvent and reaffirm themselves with each new prospect, and the exhilaration of the close. There's always something on the line and selling affords them the possibility to come out of every encounter as a winner. For others, selling is nothing more than selling out. Society looks askance at the profession, and for many salespeople, there's little pride in telling people what they do for a living. Still, the money is good, and where your passions don't pay the rent, selling often does. But the tools of the trade–a glad hand and a welcoming smile–do not fit some salespeople as well as others. For many, this necessary affectation leads to inner conflict and becomes a rich source of personal drama that is equal parts tragedy and comedy. *Closers* beautifully articulates and clarifies this internal debate between selling and selling out.

Today, as marketing and selling come together, the distinction between who is and who isn't a salesperson is less clearly defined than ever. What is clear, is that the most common stereotype, the traveling salesman–once a very visible figure in the community and often a link to the outside world–is fading into the landscape, and its subset, the door-to-door salesman, is vanishing altogether. No longer is a pedestrian army necessary–or even welcome–to move product. The electronically delivered sales pitch can cut through the security systems and into the gated communities in a way that even the fastest-talking salesman never could. When he was researching *Elmer Gantry,* Sinclair Lewis posed as a door-to-door Bible salesman. Today, he would take a job hawking Bibles on QVC or the Christian Broadcasting Network. Many of the stories in *Closers* speak to a time when the salesman's persuasive techniques were as important in creating demand as a fifteen-second television spot is today. These stories serve to illustrate what has been largely lost in today's electronic marketplace—the personality and humanity that embody the art of selling.

—MIKE TRONNES

CLOSERS

Thomas Bontly

from *The Competitor*

10:30 a.m.

"Shoes for these three," the woman said. She came up to the seats in long-legged strides, her three girls trailing behind her like ducklings. Her eyes were hidden behind dark glasses with sparkly frames, and it made Marty vaguely uncomfortable not to see her eyes.

"What kind of shoes would you like for them, ma'am?" he asked, taking his slip-stick from its perch on the edge of the sock bar.

"Something practical," the woman said. "They go through shoes like nobody's business." Marty put her age at about thirty-five, maybe older. Her hair was bleached that pinkish gray shade that seemed popular lately, and her lipstick was almost orange. She was wearing Bermudas, and her legs were good and nicely tanned, but the blue veins were starting to show and there was a smudge of dirt on each knee, as if she had just come from gardening. She lit a cigarette and puffed quickly, holding it away from her with each quick, affected drag.

Marty bent down beside the smallest girl, took off her sandal, and ignoring the torrent of sand that poured out and across his knees, measured her foot.

"I want patent leather," the little girl said.

"Don't be ridiculous," the woman said, between puffs.

"Then penny loafers," the little girl said.

"Definitely not," the woman said. "They ruin your feet. You'll get a tie shoe and like it." Puff–puff.

"How about saddle shoes?" Marty asked, hoping for a compromise.

"Oh, yes! Saddle shoes!" the little girl said. "Please, mommy, can I have saddle shoes?"

"May I," the woman said automatically. "Who's going to polish them?"

"I will," the little girl said. "I promise! Please, mommy? If I can't have saddles, then I don't want anything!"

The woman puffed, sighed, and looked at Marty in mock despair. "Saddle shoes," she said.

That was all Marty needed to identify the type. A pose of authority and sophistication, but not enough patience–really, not enough interest–to resist. After eighteen years of selling, Marty knew all the types and how to deal with them. From here on in it was automatic.

"How about you girls?" he asked, measuring the other two.

"We want those new bubble saddles, those red and white ones," the older girl said.

"Oh, God," the woman said, "not those honey. They don't give you enough support. Do they?" She was looking to Marty for confirmation. Marty considered it a cheap trick–that type always tried it when they lost interest. Push the disciplining of their children off on him. He dealt with it accordingly.

"That was last year," he said. "We have a new line this year. Much better for support. Re-enforced arch and steel shank–let me show them to you."

"I want bubble saddles too," the little girl said, but Marty was already moving away from them and pretended not to hear. A man was standing in the foyer, looking at the window displays. Jack Ryan, working the front section right across from Marty, was keeping his eye on the door, but Marty out-maneuvered him by going up to the counter as if to check something in his sales book, and when the door opened he cut easily in front of Jack, rushing up from the seats, and said, "Yessir! Can I help you?"

"I'd like a pair of shoes, I guess," said the man.

Ryan put his knuckles into Marty's spine and went back to his customers. "Just step right over here to my section," Marty said. The man followed him meekly. Marty sat him down and measured his foot.

"It's usually a ten D," the man said.

"Right you are," Marty said, snapping shut the stick. It had read eleven B, but eleven B was a damn hard size to find around this store. You had to save what few you had for those who knew their size. "Something in black?" Marty asked.

"Yeah, kinda dressy," the man said. He was the baggy sweater, pipe-smoking type. They were easy to please. They didn't like to haggle.

Marty stopped briefly with the teenage girl, who was stupidly fondling a pair of black baby-heels and biting her lip in an agony of indecision.

"You won't make up your mind that way," Marty said. "Walk around on them some. Get the feel of 'em. I'll be right back now."

He ducked into the stock alley and headed for the saddle shoes. Hank Grady rushed down the aisle in a whirlwind of arms and legs, scraps of tissue paper swirling behind him, that look of rapture—"suspended asininity"—on his face. Marty flattened himself against the shelves and Hank charged on by.

Saddle shoes, Marty said to himself. Bubble saddles. Three, six and eight. Three, six and eight. Bubble saddles, bubble saddles. . . .

Andy was standing before the saddle shoes, scanning the boxes. "This dumb broad," he said. "She doesn't know what the hell she wants."

"So tell her what she wants," Marty said. "You're the salesman, aren't you?" He had to jump to reach the eight.

"Yeah, sure—she doesn't even speak my language," Andy said.

Marty dodged back onto the salesfloor just as Ryan grabbed two teenagers at the door. You bastard, he thought. Cutting between the seats on his way to the men's department, he nearly collided with Hank, headed back to the stock alley. Roy was contemplating the selection of boy's shoes. He pulled out a three ninety-nine oxford.

"Show 'em the five ninety-nine," Marty said. "It's practically the same thing."

He hurried on to the men's department, picked out a good style for the pipe and sweater man—plain toe with a rubber heel, they always wanted rubber heels—and started back. Roy was still standing before the boy's department, comparing the three ninety-nine and five ninety-nine.

"You know, they *are* the same," he said.

"Okay, okay–get the lead out, huh?" Marty said.

Hank brushed past him again, his arms full of shoes, with shoes stuffed in his pockets and tucked under his belt.

"Here ya are, folks," Hank said, descending on his customers. "Shoes for everybody–you, and you–try these on for size, will you? Here we are, shoes, shoes, shoes–"

Marty reached his section, slipped the black plain-toe on the man and proceeded to the woman and her three ducklings.

"The new bubble saddle," he said. "Notice the improvement–much sturdier through the arch and instep–" He bent the shoe double and waved it beneath the woman's nose. She nodded wisely, trying to pretend she recognized a difference. Marty slipped the shoes on the girls, had them stand up and checked the size. His strong, experienced fingers probed and tested–the arch, the instep, the ball of the foot and the little toe. He took a certain pride in his ability to fit shoes properly, and in his principle of never mis-fitting children. There was almost a craftsmanship in fitting shoes, and Marty sometimes thought that he took more pleasure in that than in racking up a high total. It gave his job a certain dignity, somehow.

"This one needs a narrower width," he told the woman. "The other two are fine."

Now back to the man.

"How's that sir? Feels good, huh?"

"Fine–how do they wear?"

"Like a million. Shine up real nice, too."

"Okay, I'll take 'em."

Easy as pie. On the way up to the counter Marty said, "How about some polish for those?"

"No thanks, I've got a closet-full at home."

"Ah, but we've got some new stuff–just came in last week–much easier to apply. Let me show you–"

The shoes and polish written up on slips, Marty went back to his seats. A few more like those, and he'd have it made. He was off to a very good start. Twelve sales, still in their first hour. And if he could keep grabbing the men's shoes away from Grady and Ryan, his average would be considerably higher than the usual four bucks a sale. Of course, he could always get off to a good start. Mornings were his best time. It was the afternoons that gave him trouble, that wore away his strength, sapped him of energy and nibbled away at his presence of mind. In the afternoons he didn't stand a chance with young, tough men like Jack Ryan. That was why he had to pour it on now.

Somehow, an old lady had wandered into his section. Marty saw Ryan grinning at him across the seats, where he was trying Italian loafers–eight ninety-nine–on his pair of teenagers. The bastard.

"And what can we do for you today, ma'am?" he asked the old lady.

"Well, I'd like a pair of walking shoes," the old lady said.

"All righty, let's see what we can do," Marty said, taking off her heavy shoe and trying to measure her foot. The bunion and toes were so swollen and misshapen with age he could barely fit the stick on her foot. It would be inaccurate anyway. About an eight double-E, he thought. They had two of them in the store, both wedgies.

"I'd like something nice and soft–for walking," the old lady said. "Do you know what I mean? An old-fashioned walking shoe, that's what I want."

"No spike heels for you today, then?" Marty asked, smiling at her. She was a nice old lady, with rosy cheeks.

"Oh, Lord," she said, laughing, "those things!"

"Say, mister," the woman with the three girls called, "I have a lot of shopping to do today, if you don't mind."

"Coming right up, ma'am," Marty said. He ducked into the alley and headed for the saddle shoes. Three B, he thought. Three B, three B, three B–

Andy was still there, or had gone and come back.

"You still working on the same customer?"

"Hell, this ignorant plebeian dopey bitch," Andy said.

"Get rid of her," Marty said. "Turn her over to Roy or Gene. You can't spend all day on one customer."

He slipped out of the alley and ducked around to the backroom. Somebody had brought more coffee. He paused long enough to remove the paper cover and let it sit while he hunted down the wedgies. He was just digging them out of their dusty, well-worn box when the backdoor opened and Renaldo came in. Marty glanced at the Ardsley clock. It was ten-forty.

"Well, this is a hell of a nice time to come to work," Marty said. He noticed that Renaldo wasn't marked up.

"Am I late?" Renaldo said innocently. "Well, fancy that. Something must've gone wrong with my watch." He went over to the mirror above the workbench and ran his comb through thick black curls, sweeping wavey sides to a perfect ducktail, teasing a forelock so that it coiled across his low forehead. Marty regarded him with distaste. His suit was padded at the shoulders. The material was woven with glossy threads that gave it a purplish, greenish sheen. When he took off the coat he revealed beltless, thigh-tight trousers slung low across his lean hips. Their cuffless ends broke above the shiny black Italian loafers with viciously pointed toes. Marty had never seen clothes just like them before, except on the teenage punks that hung around Capitol Street on Saturday nights—and Renaldo was no teenager.

"I suppose you were out cattin' again last night," Marty said, edging his voice with sarcasm. "Must be rough when Georgia's husband comes to town."

"Man, she ain't the only pussy in town," Renaldo said. "Not even in this hicksville. You oughta come along some night, amigo—I'd show you where the real stuff hangs out." He grinned at Marty in the mirror. He had a dimpled, toothy grin that struck Marty as obscene—like a peddler of smutty pictures offering his wares. "Now there's one bar—you wouldn't believe it, amigo—all the snatch in that bar. Good stuff, too, you know? Just the way I like 'em. 'Bout thirty or thirty-five—you don't want to mess around with these kids, you know, these flashy little jobs you see on the street. Pure trouble and not much technique, anyway. No, you gotta get 'em nice and ripe—like avocadoes, so they squish when you squeeze 'em."

"No thanks," Marty said. "I'd sooner shack up in a leper colony than touch any of your broads."

"Old married man like you," Renaldo said, "you oughta get out once in awhile. You must get pretty stale. You oughta get some fresh stuff once in awhile—it would perk you up. Even your wife would thank me for it. Just like vitamins, amigo. Mmmmmm—bueno!"

He began adjusting the already perfect four-in-hand of his pink knit tie, then picked a shoehorn out of the junk on the bench and slipped it into his back pocket.

"Just a minute," Marty said. "I've got a little job for you before you start selling."

"Job!" Renaldo said. "Amigo, you must be kiddin'. This is like the big rumble–you need your ace on the floor, man."

"Yeah, well you shoulda thought of that before you came waltzing in here forty minutes late," Marty said. "Now I want that workbench straightened up so we can use it. Throw away that old display unit, put away those signs and price tags, hang up those tools and sort out that polish. I want it all shaped up–and *pronto, amigo.*"

Renaldo let his eyes harden for a moment, and Marty met their gaze as well as he could. Insolent little bastard, he thought, I could break him in two. Still, it was a relief when Renaldo's stare broke into a broad, dimpled grin.

"Si, amigo. As you command." He exaggerated his Spanish accent, mockingly. "The workbench, she shall be cleaned. And pronto!"

He turned to it with a show of vigorous industry. Marty felt cheated as he hurried back to the salesfloor. He hadn't done it right, somehow. He hadn't really asserted himself. Even when he did take orders, Renaldo was insubordinate. Insubordinate. The military sound of the word pleased him. Cocky little bastard never will get anyplace in this outfit, Marty thought, until he learns to take orders.

He shoved the bubble saddle on the little girl's foot.

"Socks, four pair for a dollar today," he told the woman.

"Sorry, I haven't time today," she said, heading for the counter with her ducklings in tow.

Marty had to hurry to keep up with her long strides. "Four pair for a dollar. That's worth a minute, isn't it? You won't find a better buy in town."

"Well, let's see them," the woman said.

He left her at the counter with the shoes and three packs of socks, cut over to the door and was just in time to nose out Grady and Ryan for a family of six. They made angry noises as he led the family back to his section. Feeling better, he measured up the girl and three boys–one of them was large enough for a man's shoe–and went back to the old lady. She was scowling at her wedgies.

"I don't want no wedgies," she said firmly. "I want a–a whachamacallit–one of those Cuban heels."

"Oh, I'm sorry," Marty said, "we don't carry those anymore. Not since Castro. The State Department asked us not to. Economic retaliation, you might say."

The old lady took him seriously. "I didn't know," she said meekly.

He went back to the teenage girl. She had finally decided on a pair of black flats with a white bow on the front. Marty showed her a matching handbag. The girl said she didn't have enough money with her, but she would ask her mother if she could come back for it. Marty wrote up a sales slip for the purse and left it behind the counter, just in case she really did come back. That way he'd be sure to get credit for the sale, whoever waited on her.

The influx of customers had temporarily died down. Grady still had three and Ryan two. Roy, Gene, and Andy were up by the door, waiting for the customers straggling across the foyer, arguing about whose turn it was. The old lady was getting restless, and Marty didn't want to bother with her anymore.

"I got to have a Cuban heel," she said, "Castro or no Castro."

"Well, I'll tell you what," Marty said. "I'll ask the man in charge of that department to see what he can do. Mr. Ryan? Would you step over here for a moment, please?"

Jack made a face, but he came.

"See what you can do for this lady," Marty said. "She'd like a Cuban heel."

"Oh, I'm sorry," Jack said, in his most condescending tone, "no Cuban heels. But if you want a good old-fashioned shoe—you know, like they used to make—we have a brand new line based on the good old styles. It's called the 'Comfort-plus But No Fancy Foolishness Shoe.' Big advertisement last month in the *Ladies Home Journal*—maybe you saw it?"

"No, I never saw any such," the old lady said, looking Jack over suspiciously.

"Well, I'll just have to show it to you," Jack said. He managed to kick Marty's shin as he headed for the backroom. He was gone a long time. Marty took care of his family, then picked up two more sales by diving through the cluster of salesmen at the door to grab the customers as they came in. According to the company rule book, the assistant manager was supposed to have his pick of customers, but Marty had nothing but scorn for those assistants who relied on the rules to run a big total. He always took his chances with the rest of the crew, confident he could hold his own, and he knew Eddie wanted it that way. Nothing dampened the competitive spirit of a store so much as an assistant manager insisting on his privileges. Marty was the old pro—the standard by which they could measure their own success. He could play it rough, but he couldn't hide behind the rules.

Now his seats were empty again, save for the old lady who seemed to have fallen asleep over her wedgies. Marty went on to the backroom. His coffee was cold, and he took it down in a swallow. Jack was at the workbench, doctoring up a pair of ancient Cuban heels. Marty noticed that Renaldo hadn't done much to the workbench. He'd moved things around a little, but it was still a mess.

"Where the hell did you ever find those old dogs?" Marty asked.

"In the furnace room," Jack said. "We stuck 'em back there last fall, remember?" He took one of the wooden shoe forms off the rack and jammed it down into the shoe, then twisted the long metal handle. The form expanded and began to bulge out the sides of the shoes.

"Better use the bunion-stretcher, too," Marty said.

"And the toe-stretcher," Jack said, "and put in an arch support, and pad the heel, and put an extra hole in the ankle strap. Christ, I'm practically making her a new shoe."

"Well, that's our policy," Marty said. "If we ain't got the size, we make it."

"Don't know why the hell I didn't kick her out of here," Jack said. "I must be goin' soft in the head, spendin' this much time on a lousy three ninety-nine. Damn you for a rotten crook, Hansen."

"Don't worry, Jack," Marty said. "I'll see the scout-master gives you a merit badge for this."

He dodged the stream of profanity Ryan flung at him and went back on the salesfloor. Business was picking up. All the salesmen were busy, and customers were lined three deep at the up-front counter, waiting to pay for their shoes. Georgia was nowhere in sight.

Marty went behind the counter and rang up cash until the jam-up was cleared away. There were customers waiting for him in his section, but he couldn't leave the counter unattended. He ducked around the corner and into the stock alley. At the end, by the socks and polish, Georgia and Renaldo were talking. Renaldo had his hand on Georgia's bare shoulder, caressing the smooth white flesh.

"I can't, honey, really," Georgia said. "Not while Archie's here—maybe next week—"

She saw Marty coming down the aisle and blushed, pulling her shoulder away from Renaldo's hand. Marty saw the red imprint of his fingers.

"Okay, what the hell is this?" he asked.

Renaldo turned on Marty with a defiant glare that lasted just long enough to stop Marty in his tracks—then suddenly broke into his obscene grin. It was all very deliberate, Marty thought, like something he'd seen in some cheap gangster film.

"I'm just helping this dumb chick get some shoe polish," he said. "She sure is slow about it. Come on, Georgia baby, the store's still open for business, you know."

"Okay, I'll get it for her," Marty said. "You get the hell out on the salesfloor."

"You mean you really want me to sell shoes, amigo?" Renaldo asked. "I thought maybe you were gettin' a little worried about the competition, what with yesterday's totals. Was the workbench cleaned to your satisfaction? You want I should maybe sweep the floor first? Anything to give you a break, amigo."

"Just get the hell out there," Marty said. "I've had enough of your goddamn wising-off for one day."

Renaldo gave Georgia a broad wink, brushed past Marty, and executed a short dance step down the aisle. "To-the-sales-floor—cha-cha-cha," he said, pausing at the exit to grin back at Marty. Then he was gone. Marty wiped his moist palms on the side of his trousers.

"Now what polish did you want?" he asked Georgia.

She avoided his eyes. "Cordovan, black, and tan. We'll need a box of each—they're on the top shelf."

Marty brought over the step ladder and climbed up. He wrestled the small heavy boxes off their shelf and handed them down to Georgia. Reaching up to take them, Georgia's arms pushed her breasts together, and Marty saw them swell above her low-cut summer dress. Soft, rich creamy flesh. Long white throat and smooth white shoulders beneath swirling, falling dark hair. A tiny gold earring on a tiny white lobe. Blue eyes, long lashes, parted lips—a brief pink flame of tongue as she took the weight of the heavy box. Marty's knees were shaking when he came down from the ladder.

He bent over the boxes and broke them open with his knuckles, striking the heavy tape and driving through. He ripped back the lids. Then he stacked them up and lifted them.

"This all you need?"

"Yes, I think it will do for now."

"Okay," Marty said. "Now, look–it's none of my business what the hell games you wanna play after hours, but keep away from that grease-ball while you're here at the store. Understand?"

He didn't wait for an answer, but carried the boxes up to the counter, then hurried over to his section.

Insubordinate bastard, he thought, running down sizes. Just trying to see how much he can get away with. Thinks he's got me on the run just because I was setting up displays for two hours yesterday and the bastard got a few more sales than I did. To hell with him. And her, too. What do I care? None of my affair. Just so she stays where she belongs and takes care of her customers, damn it.

Another lull, and Marty went back to the office. Eddie was sitting at his desk, going through the mail. Marty paused in the doorway, lit up a cigarette, and imagined himself saying, "Chief–I know it's not up to me to tell you who you ought to have workin' for you, but I'm getting pretty fed up–I've had about as much as I can take–it's bad business, if you ask me–"

Eddie tossed the last letter into the wastepaper basket and swung his chair around.

"Biggest goddamn day of the year," he said. "Biggest goddamn day, and your buddy Stanley decides its time to look for 'greener pastures.' "

Stanley. Marty had almost forgotten. "He's no buddy of mine," he said. "I just gave him a ride to the bus station."

"If you had any brains, you'd a locked him up in the broom closet," Eddie said. "Biggest goddamned day, and here we are short-handed!"

"Well, I tried to talk him into staying," Marty said. "But hell, chief, he hasn't been selling enough lately to matter much, anyway. We can take up the slack easy enough. Grady's got half his section, and Andy's got the other half. And Grady could handle it by himself . . . he usually did, anyway."

"Well–" Eddie had to agree, but he still wanted to grumble–"it was a hell of damn dirty trick, anyway. Lousy thing to do after the chance I gave him. I knew from the start he was worthless. And just because he was a Polsky–that's got nothing to do with it. Anyway, he was a Chicago Polsky. They're nothin' but Bohunks and Sheenies anyway."

He swung his swivel chair around and glared at his desk. "And if he thinks I'm sending him his paycheck, he's got another think coming. Let him come back and ask for it, if he's got the guts."

Marty had expected that. He'd warned Stanley, but Stanley had said he hadn't made enough last week to worry about, anyway.

"Oh, well, it's some world, ain't it?" Eddie said, lighting up a cigarette. "Hell of a hard way to make a livin'."

"That's for sure," Marty said. He perched on the edge of the desk, at Eddie's elbow. "Say, chief–"

"I'm sorry I popped off at you just now," Eddie said. "I know it wasn't your fault. As a matter of fact, old buddy, I've been meaning to tell you for some time now what a hell of a bang-up job I think you've been doing for me around here."

Marty was taken by surprise. "Oh, well, hell–"

"No–no, I know it's not easy, ramrodding this crew," Eddie said. "Especially with a couple of real pros like Grady and Ryan in there puttin' on the pressure. This is one of the hardest batch of guys I think I've ever seen, Marty–but between the two of us, we keep 'em pretty well shaped up, don't we?"

"Yeah, I guess so," Marty said. "But I've been wanting to talk to you about that, chief–"

"Well, I don't mind telling you," Eddie said, "I think you're a damn fine assistant, Marty. And I've been wanting to talk to you, too. Now we've been together two years, old buddy, and now and then we've talked about your chances of getting a store of your own–you've been around this outfit quite some time now, haven't you? How long has it been? Ten, twelve years?"

"Eighteen, in October," Marty said.

"Is that right," Eddie said. "Well, you're sure as hell due for one. Don't know why you haven't got a store of your own by now. Hard telling how the big boys think, sometimes."

Marty thought that Eddie probably did know why he had never gotten a store of his own. Most of the old-timers in the district knew. Years ago, Marty had had the misfortune to incur the wrath of the district manager. Now he was stranded in the ranks, and it was no accidental over-sight. In spite of his years of service, in spite of his proven ability, Marty had been passed over again and again. It was a long, miserable story, and if Eddie chose to feign ignorance of it, Marty had no objections.

"Well, here's what's on my mind," Eddie said. "Now there are two ways to get a store in this outfit. One way is Ryan's—you make a real name for yourself as a hotshot salesman. Ryan's a young man—he can do it that way. But looking at it realistically now, Marty, you're a little beyond that stage. Now don't get me wrong, buddy—I don't say you can't sell shoes, because you sure as hell can. Why, I remember when I was just breaking into this outfit—you were top dog then. Everybody was talking about you, like they're talking about Ryan now. That's one reason I wanted you for my assistant. An assistant that can't hold his own with the men ain't worth a damn in my book. He's gotta be able to keep their respect. But my point is just this—as good as you still are, you just can't powerhouse your way into a store anymore. You've just got too much mileage."

Marty didn't really consider himself an old man. Sure, he had been in the business eighteen years—but he was only sixteen when he started. Still, there were times when he felt old, especially on those long, hard afternoons. Whatever it was that made for a good salesman, it was burned out of you fast in an outfit like Friendly's.

"Now, I'll tell you what old Eddie's got up his sleeve," Eddie said, that shrewd look coming into his blue eyes. "You know the district manager is takin' over a post in New York in the next couple of months, and you know I'm up for his job. Now, if I can get that job, Marty, I'll be in a pretty damn good position to see you get any store you like in this whole damn district. You want this store? With me in the district office, it's yours."

Marty had heard hints to that effect before, but he had never expected an open promise. Something must be in the wind, he thought. Eddie's onto something, or he wouldn't bring this up now. Eddie always knew what was going on in the district before anyone else. That was one reason why he was in the front running for the district manager's job.

"Jeez, chief, that's very—"

Eddie waved him off. "That's all right, Marty, that's all right. I think you'd make a damn fine manager. But first I've got to get that district managership, don't I? Well, that's where you come in, ole buddy. Now, there's style shows in Chicago next month, and the annual sales convention in Detroit in November. I've got to make it to those things, ole buddy—that's my big chance to meet some of the big boys and let 'em give ole Eddie the once-over. I mean, if we're gonna be realistic about this Marty, it's politics that gets the good jobs in this racket—it's all a matter of politics. And I can't campaign from a desk full of inventory sheets, now can I? I've got to get some of this damn bookwork off my hands so I can maneuver. Now, I know you're carrying more than your load already, and I appreciate that. You've been damn fine about giving a hand here and there. But I'm afraid I'm just gonna have to ask you for a little bit more. Until this thing is settled, I'm gonna need all you can give me, ole buddy. But ole Eddie will make it worth your while, I promise you that. You scratch my back, I scratch yours. And there you have it—the one rule for getting anywhere in this business. You scratch my back, I'll scratch yours. So what do you say? Is it a deal?"

Marty didn't hesitate. "Sure chief—a deal."

They shook hands.

"Well, that's a load off my mind," Eddie said. "Marty, you're a real pal. And like I told you—I don't expect you to outrun Grady and Ryan. Grady's got all week to rest up on that high school teachin' job of his, and Ryan's got too many years on you. But you can keep your head up with the rest, can't you? You see, if you're gonna take over this store, you've gotta be able to command the respect of this crew. And if you should start turning up at the hind tit, that would make it pretty rough for giving orders, wouldn't it?"

"I can do it all right," Marty said. "Yesterday was just an accident. I was setting up those displays half the afternoon—"

"Hell, Marty, no alibis—that's not necessary. I understand all that. You've got your hands full. I just thought I'd mention it. So you knew it already, so okay. Just do your best, and I know that'll be good enough. You've got a lot of heart, ole buddy. You stay in there swingin'. Now that's the main thing in this racket, isn't it? Like the song says, 'you gotta have heart.' "

"Well, I'll give 'em all a run for their money today," Marty said.

"Atta boy," Eddie said, slapping his thigh. "That's the way I like to hear you talk. All heart. And I can count on you, and you can count on me. Together, ole buddy, we can pull this thing out of the fire, believe-you-me."

Marty was already leaving the office when Eddie said, "Oh—and one more thing, Marty. Damn nuisance, but I have to make a luncheon this noon. I'm on the fund-raising committee for the Businessmen's Club, of all the damn things. I don't see how I can get out of it. It'll take about two hours, at most. Can you hold things down while I'm gone?"

"Sure," Marty said.

"And I'm expecting a long distance call from D.M., too. He said he'd call sometime today—I think maybe something's gonna break. If I'm out, tell him I've just run out to replace a light bulb or something, huh?"

"Sure," Marty said. It wouldn't be the first time he'd lied to the district manager for Eddie. Eddie was always going to luncheons that lasted most of the afternoon. He often got a mild sunburn at them.

"Atta boy, Marty," Eddie said.

Back at his section:

"Mister, I've been sitting here for twenty minutes—would you *please* wait on me?" Bright green eyes, magnified by thick glasses, glared up at Marty through the frizzled strands of a cheap permanent. Marty could see specks of dandruff on the glasses.

"Certainly, ma'am. What would you like?"

"You got any cheap sandals on sale?"

"I'm sorry, our summer season is over now."

"Well I know it is—that's why I asked if you had any on sale. That's when you have all the sales, ain't it? After the season is all over?"

There were three crates of left-over sandals in the backroom. Marty decided that, for a buck ninety-nine, they weren't worth the trip.

"Our sale was last week," he said. "We sold every last pair."

"Oh, darn!" The huge green eyes were furious. "Didn't you advertise? I never heard about it."

"Yes ma'am. Both newspapers and television spots."

"Well, I never saw them."

Marty started to move on to the next customer, but the woman reached out to grab his sleeve. "Well I've got to have some shoes. What's on sale now?"

Marty politely but firmly removed his sleeve from her grasp. "Nothing's on sale now, ma'am. This is the start of a brand new season and it's all brand new stock at our regular prices. Perhaps you'd like to look at the styles in the window–"

"Just show me something," she said. "Something cheap."

Marty bent to measure her boney foot. A heavy stench rose up to greet him. "Something inexpensive," he said. "Low heels? Dark color? Hard sole?"

"Yeah, just keep 'em cheap," she said.

In the stock alley, Marty scanned the stock. Renaldo waltzed by. "My-o-my, isn't that a sweetie-pie you've got there. I bet you're hot for her, hey amigo? Mmmmm–bueno!"

Andy came running up, out of breath. "What the hell do we have in a nurse's oxford–she wants a crepe sole wedgie with five eyelets and a soft nap and a built-in arch support."

"That's number 63789," Marty said. "Fit her a size narrow, they run wide."

Ryan and Grady, both charging in from the salesfloor, collided in the doorway. "Jesus Christ, Grady," Jack cried, "get them damn long legs outa my way, will you?"

"Up yours, buddy," Grady yelled over his shoulder, already halfway up to the stock alley, grabbing boxes from the shelves as he went.

Marty picked out a black flat and a tan one, both two ninety-nine. Then, just for the hell of it, he took out a three ninety-nine. Maybe he could push her up a buck or two. Customers like that, the ones that tried to push you–you just had to push them back.

Oh, hell, Marty thought. Push, push, push. For eighteen years, nothing but push. No wonder I feel like an old man. Maybe I wasn't cut out for this racket.

Maybe he wasn't cut out for it? Well, this was a nice time to discover it, after eighteen years. And what else had there been for him to do? Selling shoes was all he knew. Marty looked down the long, narrow stock alley, already cluttered with discarded shoeboxes and scraps of tissue paper. He heard the rising hum of voices on the salesfloor, the ring of the cash register, the moan of the radio as adolescent voices mutilated old standards. I've got to get busy, he thought.

He lit a cigarette and took several quick drags at the salesfloor entrance. Now there was Eddie–good old Eddie. And maybe this was his chance, at long last. A store of his own. All he had to do was keep pushing. Just a little while longer pushing, and then, maybe–

From his position just inside the stock alley, Marty could see the front door. A man was just crossing the foyer. Hank Grady was advancing along the far side of the salesfloor. Marty took a last deep drag and crushed his cigarette underfoot. Running the length of the salesfloor, moving quietly and swiftly along the wall, he cut between the sock bar and the up-front counter, ploughed through Andy and Gene, sent Gene into the counter with his elbow, and cut in front of the windmill arms and legs of Hank Grady to come to a stop before the door just as it swung open.

"Yessir," Marty said. "Can I help you?"

Erskine Caldwell

Handsome Brown's Day Off

Ma went up the street to the next corner after breakfast to talk to Mrs. Howard about the Sycamore Ladies' Improvement Society meeting, and the last thing she said before she left was for Handsome Brown to have the dishes washed and dried and the dishcloths rinsed and hung out to dry in the sun before she got back. It was Handsome's day off, although he had never had a day off, even though he had worked for us ever since he was eleven years old, because something always seemed to happen that kept him from going away somewhere and loafing for a whole day. Handsome always liked to take his time doing the dishes, no matter whether it was just a regular day like all the others, or whether it was really his day off, because he knew every day always turned out in the end to be the same as any other, anyway; and he generally managed to find a good excuse for not doing the dishes any sooner than he had to. That morning after Ma had gone up to Mrs. Howard's, he said he was hungry; he went into the kitchen and cooked himself a skilletful of hog-liver scrapple.

My old man was sprawled on the back porch steps dozing in the sun, just as he did every morning after breakfast when he had the chance, because he said a nap after breakfast always made him feel a lot better for the remainder of the day. Handsome took a long time to eat the scrapple, as he knew he had the dishes to do when he finished, and he was still sitting in a chair hunched over the cook-stove eating out of the skillet when somebody knocked on our front door. Since both Pa and Handsome were busy, I went around to the side of the house to find out who it was.

When I got to the front yard, I saw a strange-looking girl, about eighteen or twenty years old, standing at the door with her face pressed against the screen trying to see inside. She was carrying a square tan bag made like a small suitcase, and she was bare-headed with long brown hair curled on the ends. I knew right away I'd never seen her anywhere before, and I thought she was a stranger trying to find the house of somebody in town she had come to visit. I watched her until she put her hand on the latch and tried to open the screen door.

"Who do you want to see?" I asked her, going as far as the bottom step and stopping.

She turned around as quick as a flash.

"Hello, sonny," she said, coming to the edge of the porch. "Is your father at home?"

"Pa's taking a nap on the back porch," I told her. "I'll go tell him."

"Wait a second!" she said excitedly, running down the steps and grabbing me by the arm. "You show me where he is. That'll be a lot better."

"What do you want to see him about?" I asked, wondering who she was if she really knew my old man. "Are you looking for somebody's house?"

"Never mind, sonny," she smiled. "You take me to him."

We walked around the side of the house and went through the gate into the backyard. Every time the girl took a step a big wave of perfume blew off of her and her stockings began sagging under her knees. My old man was sound asleep with his mouth hanging open and the back of his head resting on the top step. He always sprawled out that way when he was sleeping in the sun, because he said it was the only way he could feel comfortable while he dozed. I could see Handsome standing in the kitchen and looking out at us through the screen door while he ate the scrapple from the skillet.

The girl put down her suitcase, pulled her stockings up under her garters, and tiptoed to where my old man was sprawled over the steps.

Then she got down beside him and put both hands over his eyes. I could see Handsome stop eating just when he had raised a spoonful of scrapple halfway to his mouth.

"Guess who!" the girl cried.

My old man jumped sort of sidewise, the way he generally did when Ma woke him up when he wasn't expecting it. He didn't leap clear off the steps though, because almost as soon as he sat up, the girl pushed his head back and kept him from seeing anything at all. I could see his nose flare open and shut like a hound sniffing a coon up a tree when he got a whiff of the perfume.

"Guess who!" she said again, laughing out loud.

"I'll bet it ain't Martha," Pa said, feeling her arms all the way up to her elbows.

"Guess again!" she said, teasing him.

My old man flung her hands away and sat up wild-eyed.

"Well, I'll be dogged!" my old man said. "Who in the world are you?"

The girl got up from the steps, still laughing, and went for her suitcase. While all three of us watched to see what she was going to do, she opened the lid and took out an armful of brand new neckties. She had more ties than a store.

Pa rubbed the sleep out of his eyes and took a good look at the girl while she was bending over the suitcase.

"This would look wonderful on you," she said, picking out a tie made of bright green and yellow cloth. She went over to where he sat and looped it around his neck. "It was made for you!"

"For me?" Pa said, looking up and sniffing the perfume that floated all around her.

"Of course," she said, turning her head sideways and taking a good look at Pa and the tie. "It couldn't suit you better."

"Lady," Pa told her, "I don't know what you're up to, but whatever it is, you're wasting your time at it. I ain't got no more use for a necktie than a pig has with a side-saddle."

"But it's such a beautiful tie," she said, dropping the armful of ties into her suitcase and coming up closer to my old man. "It just suits your complexion."

She sat down close beside him on the step and began tieing a knot in the tie. They sat there beside each other until my old man's face turned red all over. The perfume had drifted all over the place by that time.

"Well, what do you know about that!" Pa said, looking as though he didn't know what he was saying. "Who'd have ever thought a necktie would've suited my complexion!"

"Let's see you in a mirror," she told him, patting the tie against his chest. "When you look at yourself in a mirror, you'll know you can't get along without that tie. Why, it's perfect on you!"

My old man cut his eyes around and glanced up the street towards Mrs. Howard's house on the corner.

"There's a mirror inside," he said, talking in a low voice as though he didn't want anybody else to hear him.

"Come on, then," the girl said, pulling him by the arm.

She picked up her suitcase and went inside with my old man right behind her. After they were inside Handsome came out of the kitchen and we hurried to the far side of the house where we could look through one of the windows.

"What did I tell you?" the girl said. "Didn't I tell you it was a beauty? I'll bet you never had a tie like that in all your life before."

"I reckon you're right, at that," Pa said. "It's sure a beauty, all right. It sort of sets me off, don't it?"

"Of course," she said, standing behind my old man and looking over his shoulder into the mirror. "Here, let me tie a better knot in it for you."

She went around in front of my old man and drew the knot tighter under his chin. Then she just stood there with her hands on his shoulders and smiled up at him. My old man stopped looking at himself in the mirror and looked at her. Handsome began getting fidgety.

"Mis' Martha'll be coming home almost any minute now," he said. "Your Pa ought to take care. There's liable to be a big fuss if Mis' Martha comes home while he's standing in there like that fooling around with that necktie. I wish I had them dishes all done so I could go and take my day off before Mis' Martha gets back."

My old man leaned over and smelled the air over the girl's head and put his arms around her waist.

"How much do you get for it?" he asked her.

"Fifty cents," she told him.

Pa shook his head from side to side.

"I ain't got fifty cents to my name," he said sadly.

"Oh, now, come on and loosen up," she said, shaking him hard. "Fifty cents isn't anything at all."

"But I just ain't got it," he told her, getting a tighter grip around her waist. "I just ain't, that's all."

"Don't you know where you can get it?"

"Not exactly."

Handsome groaned.

"I wish your Pa would stop messing around over that old necktie like that," he said. "I just know ain't nothing good's going to come out of it. I feel in my bones that something bad's going to come along, and it looks like I'm always the one who gets in trouble when something like that happens. I declare, I wish my day off had started long before that girl came here with them neckties."

The girl put her arms around my old man's neck and squeezed herself up against him. They stood that way for a long time.

"I think maybe I could get me a half-a-dollar somewheres," my old man told her. "I've just been thinking about it. I feel maybe I can, after all."

"All right," she said, taking her arms down and backing away. "Hurry and get it."

"Will you wait right here till I come back?" he asked.

"Of course. But don't stay away too long."

My old man started backing towards the door.

"You wait right here where you are," he told her. "Don't budge a single inch from this room. I'll be back before you know it."

In barely any time at all he came running out on the back porch.

"Handsome!" he shouted. "Handsome Brown!"

Handsome groaned as if he were getting ready to die.

"What you want with me on my day off, Mr. Morris?" he said, sticking his head around the corner of the house.

"Never mind what I want," Pa told him, hurrying down the steps. "You come on with me like I tell you. Hurry up, now!"

"What we aiming to do, Mr. Morris?" Handsome said. "Mis' Martha told me to be sure and do them dishes in the kitchen before she got back. I can't do nothing else but that when she done told me to do it."

"The dishes can wait," my old man said. "They'll get dirty after we eat off them the next time, anyway." He grabbed Handsome by the sleeve and pulled him towards the street. "Get a hustle on and do like I tell you."

We went down the street with Handsome trotting to keep up. When we got to Mr. Tom Owens' house, we turned into the yard. Mr. Owens was hoeing witch grass out of his garden.

"Tom," Pa shouted over the fence, "I've decided to let Handsome work for you a day like you wanted. He's ready to start in right away!"

He pushed Handsome inside Mr. Owens' garden and made him hurry up between the rows of cabbages and turnips to where Mr. Owens was.

"Give Handsome the hoe, Tom," Pa said, taking it away from Mr. Owens and shoving it at Handsome.

"But, Mr. Morris, ain't you clear forgot about this being my day off?" Handsome said. "I declare, I just naturally don't want to hoe that old witch grass, anyway."

"Shut up, Handsome," Pa said, turning and shaking him hard by the shoulder. "Mind your own business."

"But I is minding my own business, Mr. Morris," Handsome said. "Ain't it my business when I have a day off coming to me?"

"You've got a whole lifetime ahead of you to take a day off in," Pa told him. "Now, start grubbing out that witch grass like I told you."

Handsome raised the hoe and let the blade fall on a bunch of witch grass. The growth was so wiry and tough that the hoe blade bounced a foot off the ground when it struck it.

"Now, Tom," Pa said, turning around, "give me the fifty cents."

"I ain't going to pay him till he does a day's work," Mr. Owens said, shaking his head. "Suppose he don't do a half-a-dollar's worth of work? I'd be cheating myself if I went and paid out the money and then found out he wasn't worth it."

"You don't have to worry about that part of it," Pa said. "I'll see to it that you get your money's worth out of Handsome. I'll be back here ever so often just to stand over him and see to it that he's doing the work like he ought to for the pay he's getting."

"Mr. Morris, please, sir?" Handsome said, looking at Pa.

"What is it, Handsome?" he asked.

"I don't want to have to hoe this old witch grass, please, sir. I want my day off."

Pa gave Handsome a hard look and pointed at the hoe with his foot.

"Now, just give me the fifty cents, Tom," he said.

"What makes you in such a big hurry to collect the pay before the work's done?"

"I've got something that has got to be settled right away. Now, if you'll just hand me the money, Tom—"

Mr. Owens watched Handsome hitting the witch grass with the blade for a while, and then he put his hand into his overalls pocket and took out a handful of nails, screws, and small change. He hunted through the pile until he had picked out half-a-dollar in nickels and dimes.

"This'll be the last time I'll ever hire that colored boy to do anything for me if he don't do a good hard day's work," he told Pa.

"You won't regret hiring Handsome," Pa said. "Handsome Brown's one of the hardest workers I ever seen anywhere."

Mr. Owens handed Pa the money and put the rest of the pile back into his pocket. As soon as my old man had the money, he started for the gate.

"Mr. Morris, please, sir?" Handsome said.

"What do you want now, Handsome?" Pa shouted back at him. "Don't you see how busy I am?"

"Could I get off sort of early this afternoon and have a little bit of my day off?"

"No!" Pa shouted back. "I don't want to hear no more talk about taking a day off, anyway. You don't never see me taking a day off, do you?"

My old man was in such a hurry by that time that he didn't wait to say anything more even to Mr. Owens. He hurried back up the street and ran into the house. He latched the screen door on the way in.

The girl was sitting on the bed folding neckties one by one and laying them in her suitcase. She looked up when Pa ran into the room.

"Here's the money, just like I said!" he told her. He sat down on the bed beside her and dropped the nickels and dimes into her hand. "It didn't take me no time at all to collect it."

The girl put the money in her purse, folded some more ties, and pulled her stockings up around her knees.

"Here's your tie," she said, picking the bright green and yellow one up from the bed and putting it into Pa's hand. The tie fell on the floor at his feet.

"But, ain't you going—" he said, surprised, looking at her hard.

"Ain't I going to do what?" she said right back.

My old man stared at her with his mouth hanging open. She bent over and folded the rest of the ties and put them into the suitcase.

"Well, I thought maybe you'd put it around my neck and tie it again like you did just a little while ago," he said slowly.

"Listen," she said. "I made the sale, didn't I? What else do you want for fifty cents? I've got this whole town to cover between now and night. How many sales do you think I'd make if I spent all my time tieing neckties around people's necks after I'd already made me a sale?"

"But—but—I thought—" my old man stammered.

"You thought what?"

"Well, I kind of thought maybe you'd—I thought maybe you'd want to tie it around my neck again—"

"Oh, yeah?" she laughed.

She got up and slammed the cover on her suitcase. My old man sat where he was, watching her while she picked it up and walked out of the room. The front door slammed and we could hear her running down the steps. In no time at all she was all the way down the street in front of Mr. Owens' house and was turning into his yard.

My old man sat on the bed for a long time looking at the green and yellow necktie on the floor. After a while he stood up and kicked it with all his might across the room, and then he went out on the back porch and sat down on the steps where he could stretch out in the sun again.

John Cheever

The Autobiography of a Drummer

I was born in Boston in 1869. My family had lived in Boston and had been schoolmasters and shipmasters there ever since anyone could remember. We were poor and my mother was a widow. She ran a boarding house. My other brother and sister worked and I prepared to go to work as soon as I had finished grammar school. I decided to go into the shoe business and I decided to be a commercial traveler. I wanted to be a commercial traveler as other men want to be doctors and generals and presidents.

When I was twelve years old I left school and got a job as an office boy in a big boot and shoe firm. My salary for the first year was one hundred dollars. Then I was promoted to an entry clerk and my salary for the next year was two hundred dollars. Jobs were not easy to get then and I had to work hard to hold my job. When I went to work the streets were empty and when I came home from work the streets were dark and empty. Finally I got a chance to learn the construction end of the business in a shoe factory in Lynn. I went there and lived in a cheap boarding house and learned how shoes were made. I still know how shoes are made. I can tell the price and sometimes the manufacture of nearly every pair of shoes I see; although sometimes it makes me sick to look at them, they are so cheap. Well, I worked there for five years and in 1891 my salary had grown to seven hundred dollars. That was the year I was given my first chance to sell on the road.

I will never forget that as long as I live. I took a train from Boston to New York and from New York to Baltimore. I like to travel in trains. (Whenever I have spent my vacations in the country I walk down to the depot each day to see the one train come through.) I had a new suit and a new grip and a sample case and a new pair of shoes. The shoes hurt like hell. I've never worn new shoes on a trip since then. My wallet was full of expense money. I like money too. Whenever I have money in my pocket and whenever I'm taking a train for another city it always seems as though my life were beginning. When I got on that train it seemed as if my life were beginning.

That time I went down to Baltimore, as I have said. I came into Baltimore late one afternoon. I took a sample room at the Carrollton Hotel. There was running water in the room but no bath. The rates were four dollars a day including four big meals if you wanted them. The man who took your hat at the entrance of the dining room, I remember, never gave you a check, but he always returned the right hat to each guest. A ten-cent tip was plenty. The waiters were courteous and distinguished looking. The dining room was on the second floor. I stayed there two days and I made enough to cover my expenses and salary at a little under the estimated selling cost of the home office. When I got back the boss congratulated me.

That was my first success and that was the beginning of a lot of success. My mother had since died and my brother and sister had married. I didn't see much of my mother at the end of her life and I have always regretted this. I didn't have much interest in what my brother and sister were doing. I had my own life. It kept me busy all of the time. Every sign I looked at and every color and shape I saw and even the rain and the snow reminded me of sales talk and shoes. I began to get a reputation. I worked with that firm until 1894 and then I had a better offer out in Syracuse, so I went out there. I was making three thousand dollars a year then. I always traveled by the fastest trains and I had all of my clothes made by a good tailor and I stayed in expensive hotels. I had a lot of friends and a lot of women. The time went quickly. My salary grew larger by a thousand dollars every year.

Those years on the road were the best years and they didn't seem to have any end. I often sold two carloads of shoes over a glass of whiskey. Half of the time I had more money than I knew what to do with. I was successful. I was more successful than I had ever imagined I would be; even when I was twelve years old. I spent all of those years in trains and clubs and hotels. My territory was changed at intervals so that at one time or another I have covered every section of the United States. I know the United States and I love the United States. I can repeat the names of its towns now in hundreds like the names of women and I know the hotels and the timetables and even its train smoke smells sweet to me.

I had ten suits of clothing and twenty pairs of shoes and two sailboats, which I kept in Boston and raced whenever I was in that city. I gambled on the horses at all the big tracks and played Canfield and craps and roulette. I was a Mason and an honorary member of the Elks and I had two large insurance premiums.

My sales record varied as conditions changed, but my income stayed close to ten thousand. It was down on some seasons and way up on others. Droughts, heavy rains, fashions, deaths, scraps between partners, all had their effects on the business but it was fundamentally the same business I had been learning since I was twelve years old. If you lost one customer you could always get another. Buying was done by individuals for individual firms. The shoes I sold were expensive and beautiful. The business also had a seasonal lift because men wore boots in the winter and oxfords in the summer, and nobody ever wore oxfords in the winter. If they did they were crazy.

In 1925 my salary began to decrease, going from ten thousand to eight thousand. I was working for a firm in Rockland then, with my headquarters at the Hotel Statler in Detroit. At the end of that year the firm went out of business. They were beginning to feel the trend in fashion toward inexpensive shoes. They were wise to get out of it when they did and not to hang around like the rest of us suckers.

At the beginning of the next year I went on the road for a firm in Lynn, but they liquidated after I had been with them for nine months. All of the wise men were getting out of the business and forgetting about it. But I couldn't get out of it and I couldn't forget it. I was fifty-seven years old. I was growing old. I couldn't remember anything but trains and hotels and shoes.

After that I tried to find another firm that manufactured the kind of shoes I was used to handling but I couldn't find one. They were all selling out or liquidating. Finally I went on the road selling cheap shoes for a firm in Weymouth, Massachusetts. This was the first time in my life that I had ever sold cheap shoes and I hated to do it. You had to sell a thousand pairs to make what you could make on a hundred pairs in the old days. My sales hardly covered my commission and salary and expenses. I worked hard and I sold a lot of shoes but I couldn't make any profit. It was like trying to stop it from raining with my two hands. In those last years I never made more than three thousand dollars.

After that all of my trips went in the red. Methods of doing business had changed, faster than I could change. Chain stores and stores owned by manufacturers took the place of stores owned by individuals. Cheap shoes took the place of expensive shoes. Railway fares went up and hotel rates didn't get any lower. The few independent dealers who remained did not buy enough to pay the expenses of selling them. Hand-to-chin buying, we call it. On my sixty-second birthday I was without work. I have not worked since. I am growing old. My insurance policy has lapsed. My money has gone. My brother and my sister are dead. My friends are dead. The world that I know how to walk and talk and earn a living in, has gone. The sound of the traffic below the window of this furnished room reminds me of that.

We have been forgotten. Everything we know is useless. But when I think about the days on the road and about what I have done and what has been done to me, I hardly ever think about it with any bitterness. We have been forgotten like old telephone books and almanacs and gas-lights and those big yellow houses with cornices and cupolas that they used to build. That is all there is to it. Although sometimes I feel as if my life had been a total loss. I feel it in the morning sometimes when I'm shaving. I get sick as if I had eaten something that didn't agree with me and I have to put down the razor and support myself against the wall.

HARRY CREWS

from *The Mulching of America*

The air was a shimmering of heat, and it felt to Hickum Looney as though with every step he took the weight of the sun on the top of his balding head and his thin shoulders became heavier. The long sidewalk in front of him was so hot that it shook and undulated in his eyes and made them feel cracked and gritty.

There was nothing unusual about that, though. Just another ordinary August day in Miami. Hickum had suffered through twenty-five years of such summers, and if he could survive five more, he could walk away from the only job he'd ever known—if he did not count the three years he had spent as a supply technician in the air force.

And he had never counted those years a job. He'd spent every hour of every working day in an air-conditioned office filing copies of supply requisitions. Those were pleasant, comfortable days, the kind of days during which a man could let his mind float where it would while he stood over an open file drawer, daydreaming and fantasizing, and no one would care because no one would notice whether he was actually filing anything or not.

He went into the air force a private and he came out a private. He never got any letters of commendation, but he never got any turds in his personnel file, either. Any way he figured it, it was an easy ride. And he did not know how much he had liked it until his hitch was up and he was a civilian again, looking for a job, and ended up as a door-to-door salesman for a company named Soaps For Life, and realized before the first month was out that he did not like being a door-to-door salesman talking to people day in and day out about soap.

It wasn't that he hated it, or anything nearly that strong. He just had never been able to make himself care for it very much, which he thought was worse than the promotions he had deserved in the air force but never got. Nor did he want to learn more about selling soap than he already knew, which he felt must be about as much as any sane man ought to know about anything, nor did he want to talk about it nonstop when two or more salesmen of Soaps For Life got together, which the Boss had gone to some trouble to let all the salesmen know was precisely what was expected of them.

The real horror of the whole thing was that Hickum had taken this job twenty-five years ago with the intention of quitting it the following week and going to work as an apprentice in a sheet metal shop. All he had to do was wait seven days for the sheet metal job to come open and he could kiss the door-to-door business good-bye. But it didn't work out that way. The morning before he was to start as an apprentice, a butane gas tank had blown up and left nothing of the sheet metal shop but flat ground and grieving widows.

He knew he ought to count himself lucky not to have been there when the tank blew up. But all he could seem to think of was that he had lost a job. In some screwy way he did not understand, it seemed to him that he had always missed every good job he had had a chance for. Except for Soaps For Life. So he had obsessively clung to it for a quarter of a century now, always secretly wishing he was doing something else.

One of the worst parts of having the job was going to the annual sales convention and listening to the harelipped little man who had founded the Company and who invariably spent three podium-pounding hours telling his salesmen–every one of whom, with the exception of Hickum Looney, seemed to want to be just like him–how he had single-handedly built his company. Over and over, he would hammer through his success story: one-man-and-one-dream-and-one-case-of-soap-samples-and-one-long-street-that-never-ended-until-that-one-man-and-that-one-dream-had-become-an-empire. *"Shoe leather,"* the little man would scream, *"shoe leather is the secret."*

Again and again during the interminable speech that at times seemed deranged and half out of control, the little man hopped about the stage as though he had hot coals in his shoes, often raising his hands above his head in what could have been surrender or supplication, and screamed: "You nink I nare if I not a narenip?"

He might not care, but God, did he have a harelip! It was by far the worst one Hickum had ever seen.

"My narenip was given na me by Nod!" Hysterical applause made him smile, and the smile would always show a single enormous, square, and badly stained tooth in the center of his face. Then he would raise his hands for silence. "Nu nink I non't know what people nall me? I know! I know plenty! But, now listen! I may be kind of strange and warped . . ." In this part of the speech, he often went into a kind of frenzied jitterbug: head snapping, arms flapping, and knees pumping like pistons. "Can nu near me? Can nu near me, brothers?"

After each question there was a responsive roar that shook the walls of the convention center: *Yes,* they could hear him. Then the Boss would abruptly become very still. When his voice came out of his mouth, it would come in a whisper, and yet the whisper reached every man and woman present. And that voice, so quiet and yet so strongly surging, gave them all gooseflesh.

"I am most awfully ugly. But! *Near me now!* I am standing in a nousand dollars' worth of suit!"

The roar of approval seemed it would take the plaster off the walls.

"Nand I may have wists and nurns in me na make a rattlesnake crazy. But I still drive a Cadillac car. Ne biggest Cadillac car nay build. Nand I got a nelephone in nat Cadillac, got it right by my knee. Nand finally, finally, I trade for me a new Cadillac car every year!"

It was then that the salesmen got loose and crazy, some of them bashing their heads together in an ecstasy of enthusiasm and longing. Hickum never felt like bashing heads with another salesman at the annual convention, and certainly he never felt ecstatic with joy by anything the Boss said from the podium. Hickum thought this to be some failing in himself that he could not identify. Nonetheless, he never doubted it was somehow his fault.

But if he dropped dead this very instant on the short flagstone walk leading to the house of his prospect of the day—a modest yellow cinder block house with a white roof—he would be recorded in the annals of the Company with an asterisk identifying him as one of the top salesmen it ever had. If it hadn't been for the Boss, Hickum would have been the champion salesman at Soaps For Life. But it was the Boss who held all selling records. Year after year, he remained unbeatable. So if Hickum Looney didn't feel an urge to bash heads every year at the convention, why didn't he at least feel a convulsive jolt of accomplishment? Why instead did he carry a cold fury and dread at the center of his chest, where he had always supposed his heart to be?

He knew why. Of course he did. He could not easily or graciously accept being second best. The Boss had somehow taught him to accept nothing less than being a winner and then—year after year—refused to allow him to win. This was the first day of August, the month of the contest for Salesman of the Year. Whoever sold the most soap this month would win a Cadillac, a trip to Disney World in Orlando, Florida, and $2,000 spending money.

There was only one problem. The Boss always entered the contest each year himself, always in a different part of the country, and he always won. To ensure it was absolutely honest, the Boss's completed sales forms were entrusted to an old and honorable CPA firm, which verified the accuracy of the sales. For the twenty-five years Hickum Looney had worked for the Company, the Boss had been the undisputed champion salesman. And finally, in a gesture that the Boss called magnificently generous, but a gesture that humbled and humiliated his salesmen all the same, humbled and humiliated them as nothing else in their lives could, he took the sum total of the winnings—the car, the trip, the spending money—and divided all of it evenly among his salesmen across the country. In all the years Hickum had been with Soaps For Life, the share for each salesman had never exceeded $4. Last year, Hickum's check had been for $3.36.

And yet every year, including last year, Hickum had fought his heart out to win. And in spite of himself, in spite of not wanting to bash heads with his fellow salesmen at the convention when the Boss spoke, he fully intended to walk the leather off as many pairs of shoes as it took to win. The Boss always told his men to think of the contest as a learning experience because, he said, that was why he had started it in the first place, and he also told them he always entered the contest himself to demonstrate to them that he was not asking the salesmen to do anything he would not and could not do himself. It was to strengthen the bond between them.

Hickum Looney shook his head violently to get rid of the unthinkable notion of strengthening the bond between himself and the little demented harelip. He had to make himself focus on the Selling Mode and at the same time try to get himself into it. The founder of the Company, known universally as the Boss, demanded that all his salesmen focus their concentration on getting into the Selling Mode before ever approaching the first prospect at the beginning of each working day. But even after all these years Hickum Looney still did not know exactly what that meant. He must be doing something right, though, because it was rare when one entire order book was not full, or nearly so, when he got back to the office in the evening.

He loosened his tie and tried to look haunted and full of stress. For a salesman to give a potential customer the impression that he was haunted and full of stress was called simply the Look in the Official Sales Manual. When he felt everything was as it should be for him to make a quick sale, he walked up to the little yellow cinder block house and rang the bell. He had a habit of counting after the first ring of the doorbell or knock on the door.

"One hippopotamus, two hippopotamus, three hippopotamus . . ."

If nobody appears or he did not hear somebody moving behind the door by the time he got to *thirty hippopotamus,* he usually went back to *one hippopotamus* and counted to *twenty hippopotamus* before he rang or knocked again. But there were often times when he simply walked away. It all depended on what his instincts dictated that he do. He trusted his instincts and he trusted signs, and always tried to trust whatever signs he thought he saw or what his instincts were trying to tell him.

He had counted back to *fifteen hippopotamus* when the wooden door behind the screen eased open a little. He had heard no footsteps, no bolt sliding in a lock, no sound of hinges turning, nothing at all. There was no light in the room behind the door, which had slowly closed now to about six inches. The person, dim as a ghost behind the screen wire, was the size of a jockey with a cap of closely cropped gray hair twisted into wild tufts. Hickum had no idea if it was a man or a woman. But then one of the person's hands reached up and patted the twisted tufts of hair and then dropped and held a tiny gold locket suspended from a gold chain. The hand was full of blue veins under translucent skin marked with liver spots. It was a woman. No question in his mind at all.

"Good day, madam. My name's Hickum Looney and I represent Soaps For Life. Our headquarters are in Atlanta, Georgia, but we've got representation for our product in every state in the Union. The company that I represent makes exactly what you need, no matter what that need might be. I know that makes me sound just about too beautiful and too good for your ordinary citizen to accept. But all the representatives of Soaps For Life are one of a kind. Yes, madam, one of a kind. You might have seen our thirty-minute infomationals on television."

As Hickum talked, he watched one of the old lady's nearly fleshless hands float slowly but steadily upward and latch the screen door before floating in the same slow and steady way back to her side.

When he heard the latch fall into place, he looked down and rubbed the toe of his shoe in her welcome mat and said: "Aw, now how come you to do that, ma'am?"

"Because you might be a crazy person," said the little old lady in a dry rasping voice, "with murder in his heart and rape on his mind. Don't you read the papers? Happens every day."

Hickum smiled broadly. He always did when he was in the Selling Mode. It didn't matter at all what the prospect said to him. She'd need a hatchet to get the Selling Smile (treated at length in the Sales Manual) off his face, now that he was in the Selling Mode.

"I try never to dispute a lady," said Hickum, "but you are flat wrong is what you are. I come from a long line of honest, hard-working people. Back in east Tennessee my mother was a Hickum, so I got her maiden name. And Looney? My daddy's a Looney. Up in east Tennessee it's enough Hickums and Looneys to fight a war. Matter of fact it was a war between the Looneys and the Hickums off and on for nearly a hundred years, so the story goes. But then they got started marrying each other and such, as men and women are subject to do, and that kind of cooled things down, if you know what I mean."

"I do not believe I would care to know what you mean now or any other time," said the little old lady. She had taken a half step back into the room and Hickum could hardly see her through the screen door.

Her cap of gray hair bobbed and weaved in a way that made her head seem to move, in the deep shadowy light, as if free of a body.

"I don't believe I understand," said Hickum.

"Well, a fool can see you don't understand a whole lot," she said. "If you understood much of anything at all, you wouldn't be standing on my porch at my front door at this time of the morning holding a suitcase full of soap and expecting to be let into my house. That's the way us girls get raped, you know, strangers showing up on our doorstep carrying suitcases made out of tin and wanting to use our phones."

"I do not want to use your phone, ma'am. I never said one single word about using a phone of yours."

"They mostly never do, but that don't mean a thing." She clicked her false teeth in a little rhythm like castanets.

Hickum glanced down at his metal briefcase and then back to the old lady, who was growing more indistinct and harder to see as she moved deeper into the room. The old ones were usually either the easiest or the most difficult to sell. They had only a few years left and they weren't risking anything by opening the door for the wrong reason. On the other hand, nearly all of them were desperately lonely. That's the kind all the salesmen at Soaps For Life tried to search out when they could. Most people seemed not to notice it, but a salesman could not help but notice how many of the old ones were so desperately lonely they would let the devil through the front door if he promised to talk to them.

Hickum sighed. This was what door-to-door selling was all about. Anybody could sell who could somehow manage to get inside the house. Failed salesmen always got shut out on the steps before they could make their presentation. A man who could never find a way to make his presentation could never make a sale. But there was always a way to handle getting on the inside, and top-of-the-line door-to-door men like Hickum Looney always knew that, and given enough time, he could always find a way to go in.

Hickum lifted the metal briefcase and smiled for all he was worth. "Don't you think this is just a little small to be a suitcase?"

In a tight little voice that sounded like an infuriated schoolteacher, she said: "I try not to think of that which is of no concern to me."

"But this is your concern. This box holds life everlasting."

If someone had a gun to his head, Hickum Looney could not have explained why he had said his box held life everlasting. He didn't even know what such a statement might mean, or if it meant anything at all. But there was no denying that some days he was more creative than others. He had suspected for a long time now that the habit of meeting strangers at their doors, a habit stretching back over his entire working life, had taught him instinctively what to say. In any event, he had found out early on that simply saying something like that would not move the product, just as smelling good would never sell a bar of soap. Everybody that sold anything seemed to sing the same tired song. And no doubt that was why the Sales Manual had a whole chapter demonstrating that a good salesman could play a customer like a banjo: Pluck the right string, get the right sound, and get a sale. A door-to-door man simply had to find the string that said: *I'll buy.*

But there was no single string, no single tune, no single song a door-to-door man could use that would sell everybody. That was the Boss's great secret. Or he said it was. Read the customer like a road map and you'll go straight to his heart. That was what the Boss said he had built his company on, his company and his selling record, year in and year out. And where was the evidence to prove him wrong? He had his suit and his Cadillac car and men all over the country ready to follow him anywhere he led. What didn't he have? What?

The little lady came rushing out of the shadows until her nose was nearly pressed against the screen door. Her tiny eyes were black and shiny as a bird's.

"Everlasting? Did you say *life everlasting?* Young man, you keep on talking like that and sure as I'm standing here lightning will strike my house. And I'm not insured against lightning, and on top of that, I'm not even a Christian."

"Madam, could you unlatch the screen door? I wasn't raised to talk to a lady through a screen door."

"What was that you said?"

Hickum knew she had heard him, but he repeated it anyway, adding: "And I can just look at you and tell you're not the sort to have conversations through a screen door, either. Anybody can see that's way yonder too trashy for a lady like you."

She caught her bony little chin in her hand and seemed to think on that for a moment. "It's what's wrong with the world today, people doing business through screen doors. But you can't be too careful, am I right?"

"Right as rain. *Careful* is the watchword."

She squinted her eyes as though to see him better. "*Careful* is the watch . . . what?"

"Word," he said.

"Word? Is that what you said?"

Hickum had not been paying enough attention to what he had been saying. He had to stay focused or he would let himself slip onto automatic pilot and lose her after he already had her moving in his direction.

He nodded his head and said, "Yes, madam. I believe *watchword* is what I said."

"You've started spinning your wheels. You better quit while you're still ahead."

"No doubt the gospel truth. Yes, indeed, I . . ."

But even as he was talking, her hand drifted up and unlatched the door.

Without making a move, Hickum said: "You're a very wise lady. Not many in this old world's going to put one over on you. Noosirree!"

"You can count on it, buster. My face may be red but I wasn't born yesterday," she said.

Hickum gave the Hearty Company Laugh, and at the same time he eased the door open, not knowing if she would allow it or not. She did, though. She left it open while she kept her eye on his metal briefcase as he moved slowly to a low coffee table and set it down on its side.

He straightened up and put one of the Company's Looks on his face, a look that the manual called *the truth can be awful.*

He looked closely at her, judged her age as best he could, and said: "Let me ask you this, madam. Do you suffer from swelling of the joints? Night sweats? Failing eyesight? Thinning hair? Difficulty falling asleep? Or find it hard waking up?"

Was there a goddamn woman her age in the whole sorry country who didn't suffer from at least one of the ailments he'd named?

"I don't know as I go around having conversations with total strangers about what I have and what I don't." But her voice had a tremor in it when she spoke, and Hickum knew he had caught the scent of blood spoor, the sweet fragrance of old mortality. And he had known for a long time now that getting mortality into the game could never hurt, no matter what game a man was playing.

"That's more gospel truth right there," he said. "People nowadays don't seem to know what's public and what's private. They just go ahead and tell anything and everything."

The old woman watched him but said nothing. Hickum focused his smile on her with ultimate intensity, and then winked, which made her head snap back as if she'd been slapped.

"I told you my name at the door, Hickum Looney, remember? Don't believe I got yours."

"Don't believe I gave it," she said.

Hickum Looney clasped his hands and remained standing. Every blind in the house was drawn, making the room very dark. She either didn't have any air-conditioning or did not have it on. He had to wait for his eyes to adjust before he could see very clearly. First dimly and then in sharp detail, Hickum saw a man standing in a corner of the room, and it made him jump and grunt as though he had been struck in the stomach. It was a God's own wonder that it didn't make him scream and bolt for the door, leaving the briefcase behind, so badly did it unnerve him. But squinting harder showed it to be not a man but rather a rubber aspidistra plant. It was very old and very tired and the thick leaves were gray with a thin layer of dust. But it looked for all the world like an old man wearing a ruined hat.

"What's that?" she said. She had stopped on the other side of the coffee table and not taken her eyes off the briefcase.

"What's what?"

"You grunted," she said.

"Why would I grunt?"

"How would I know? Why'd you show up at my door with a suitcase full of soap?"

"Briefcase," he said.

"What?"

"That on the table there is not a suitcase, it's a briefcase."

"Full of soap?" she said.

"Full of soap."

"You still grunted."

"Not me. Not today."

She regarded him for a moment and then said, "If that was not a grunt I heard, maybe we better leave it alone and get on with the business at hand, because if what you say is true, I may be on the edge of the last deep hole and just about to slide in."

He said: "You're too hard on yourself. You're still a fine figure of a woman."

"I'll tell you, buddy boy, you make a move on me and I'll dial nine-one-one so fast it'll make your head swim. They've got a place for salesmen gone bad."

He dropped his eyes to her hands, joined over her stomach by twisted, large-jointed fingers. Then he called on a voice that was deep with authority, a voice that had been given him by the Boss, along with the soap, the metal briefcase, the Manual for Presentation of Products, and everything else that had made him the salesman he had become.

He pulled himself up but restrained his desire to go all the way to tiptoe, tilted his chin upward, and called on the voice that the Company Manual insisted would open the gates of heaven themselves. "I am an honorable man doing an honorable job with an honorable product. Now, would you please sit down, Mizz . . . , sit down, Mizz . . . ?"

"Ida Mae," she said in a curiously subdued voice hardly more than a whisper.

". . . sit down, Mizz Ida Mae. There are other of God's children waiting."

"Waiting?" she said, her eyes going wide to show red broken veins at their edges.

"For me," he said, still in the Company voice, "for me and the soap to save them."

The business about soap and God's children waiting for him to save them was something that had only occurred to him once he got inside the house. It just seemed to go with the decor, with the dusty aspidistra plant wearing a hat, or something that looked like a hat, in the corner of the living room, crushed, dry, and hopeless. But now that the lie had come to him, there was nothing to do but see what he could squeeze out of it. The Boss would have been pleased that he noticed it and, further, that he planned to milk it.

He snapped the hasps in the front of his briefcase and lifted the lid.

It was lined in red velvet. Round jars were held in round slots. Each jar had a different-colored lid on it. And on each lid of each jar was a single letter, each letter drawn in elaborate Germanic script.

Slowly, she traced out each of the letters with a rigid, thick-jointed finger. As she touched each letter there in the dim little room, she pronounced each of them as soft as breathing: "S-A-I-P-P-U-A-K-I-V-I-K-A-U-P-P-I-A-S."

Rick DeMarinis

The Smile of a Turtle

Cobb knows the cooped housewives need him. A new breed of degenerate (de-gents, Cobb calls them) has been making the headlines. A door-to-door salesman with a sharp yen for the average, haggard, wide-beam housewife. Cobb saw it in the *Times* yesterday morning. This degent peddling a glass knife guaranteed to slice overripe tomatoes. College educated guy at that. Nice, trim, clean-cut, good suit from Bullock's or Macy's, and this normally cautious housewife *lets him in.* He demonstrated his glass knife on her. Sliced her, diced her, iced her. Then went out to his Volvo to jerk off. Bad news. The bad old world is full of it, but Cobb's product promises freedom from such bad dreams. He holds the three-inch chrome-plated cylinder up to the cracked (but still chained) door so that the lady can see it clearly. His blond, unlined face looks harmless and sincere and deeply concerned about Home Security. It's his business, and Cobb has been working the hot neighborhoods of West L.A. all morning this burning day in early August.

"You need this device, ma'am," Cobb says, sincere as the Eagle Scout he once was. "Every housewife in L.A. needs it. A simple demonstration will make this abundantly clear. The de-gents, ma'am, are everywhere." He says "ma'am" in the soft southern way to slow her trotting heart. But the gadget sells itself. And it's a bargain at five dollars. Ten would be fair and most would pay twenty, but all he wants is the price of a movie ticket. Isn't home security worth at least that much—the price of, say, *Friday the 13th Part Three* or *Dressed to Kill?*

She opens the door a hair wider, hooked. Cobb looks like her kid brother, or her old high school boyfriend, or maybe the nice boy who delivers the paper. All-American Cleancut. He looks harmless as a puppy. There's even something cuddly about him, something you could *pet.* A dancing prickle of heat glides across the nape of her neck and into her hair line.

Cobb is working on projecting these positive vibes. He feels that he's able, now, to radiate serious alpha waves. His boss, Jake the Distributor, has this theory. He thinks every man and woman is an animal at heart. We respond, he says, to the animal in each other. We see it in our little unconscious moves and gestures. We see it in our eyes. The trick, says Jake the Distributor, is to identify *your* personal animal and let the pure alpha waves flow out of it. This is how you become your proper self. This is how you become a world-class salesman. Jake the Distributor has studied the subject in depth. "You," he said to Cobb, "are obviously a turtle." He said this at a big sales meeting and everyone laughed. Turtle, what good is a turtle, Cobb thought, humiliated, and, as if answering his thoughts, someone hollered, "Soup! Soup!" and they all laughed at him and among the laughers he identified the barking hyenas and dogs, the hooting chimps and gibbons, and the softly hissing turtles.

Cobb bought Jake the Distributor's theory. He made a study of turtles. The Chinese had some definite ideas about them, for instance. On the plus side, turtles are careful and shy, fond of warm mud, and ready to leave a bad scene at the first sign of trouble. On the minus side, they are shifty, shiftless, and dirty-minded. They think about getting it morning, noon, and night. They are *built* for getting it. Even their tails help out. The turtle tail is prehensile during the act. It holds the female close and tight and there's no way she can detach herself once things get under way. Turtles can screw ten, fifteen times a day and not lose interest.

But Jake the Distributor says, Emphasize the positive and you will make your fortune. Keep your fingernails clean and clipped. Wash up several times a day—you can develop a bad stink walking the neighborhoods all day long. Change your shorts. Use a strong underarm spray. Don't touch yourself out of habit in the area of your privates while in the process of making a pitch. Keep a good shine on your shoes. Keep your nap up. Hair trimmed and combed. Teeth white, breath sweet, pits dry. Groom, groom, groom.

It's the brace-and-bit, though, that tends to do major harm to his first good impression. This can't be helped—tools of the trade. Cobb tries to hold it down behind his leg. But she's seen it and is holding her breath. So he starts his pitch, talking fast. "It's called Cyclops, ma'am," he says. (Southern, says Jake the Distributor, don't forget to sound southern. They *trust* southern. Sound New York and you are dead meat in the street. Sound L.A. and you get no pay. Think genteel, southern Mississippi. Think graceful Georgia. But do not think Okie. Talk Okie and they will pee their drawers. Bike gangs are Okie. Bible salesmen are weirdo Okie. Think magnolia blossoms and mint juleps. Think *Gone With the Wind.* Make them think they are Scarlett O'Hara.) "The *Farrago* Cyclops, ma'am," Cobb explains. "Charles V. Farrago being the name of the gentleman who invented it and who currently holds the exclusive manufacturing rights. Yes, there are many cheap imitations, ma'am, but there is only one Farrago Cyclops!"

She stands there blinking in the crack of the chained door. She's a *mouse,* Cobb begins to realize. Thirty-five to forty, afraid of sudden moves and noise, bright outdoor light always a threat, for there are hawks, there are cats. Her house is dark inside, like a cave chewed into wood by quick, small teeth. She is wearing a gray housecoat and she is nibbling something—a piece of cheese!—and Cobb almost grins in her face, pleased that he's identified her secret animal so perfectly.

He fights back his knowing smile, for the smile of a turtle is a philosophical thing. It tends to put things into long-term perspective. It makes the recipient think: there's more to this situation than I presently understand. It will give the recipient a chill. A mouse will run from such a smile, though in nature mice and turtles are not enemies. But, Cobb thinks, we are not in nature. This is L.A., this is the world. He masters the smile and muscles it back to where it came from.

"Here you go, ma'am," he says. "Take it. Try it." She receives it gingerly, as if it were a loaded gun with a hair trigger. *Microtus pennsylvanicus,* Cobb thinks, mouse, and that is what she surely was meant to be, down to the cream cheese marrow of her small bones. He begins to think of her as "Minnie."

Cobb kneels down suddenly on her welcome mat. Stitched into a sisal mat are the letters of a Spanish word, *bienvenido.* He crouches down as low as he can get. Neighborhood children freeze with curiosity on their skateboards. The heat leans down through the perpetually grainy sky. In the north, the annual arsonists have set fire to the brushy hills once again. In the east, flash floods. Rapists, stranglers, and slashers roam the jammed tract-house valleys. Santa Ana wind, moaning in the TV antennas, spills over the mountains from the desert, electrifying the air. The ionized air lays a charge on the surface of his skin, the hair of his arms stands up stiff and surly, as if muscled, and his brain feels tacked into its casing. His back is soaked with sweat and his pits are swampy.

"Sometimes these de-gents will ring the bell, ma'am," he says, "and then drop down to all fours like this, hoping that the lady occupant, such as yourself, will make the fatal mistake of opening the door to see what's going on even though she didn't see anybody in the peephole. Some of these de-gents are real weasels, take my word for it. But the Farrago Cyclops will expose them, due to the fish-eye lens system." And he can see now that she is suddenly gripped by the idea of the sort of *weasel* who would ring her bell and then hide on the doorstep, waiting to spring.

"The worst is sure to happen, ma'am," he says gravely, "sooner or later, because of the nature of the perverted mind in today's world. This is a proven fact, known to most as Murphy's Law." Cobb makes a movement with his wrist, suggesting a weapon. Sledge, ax, awl, ice pick, the rapist's long razor. He shows her some crotch bulge, the possible avenger in there, coiled to strike. "You *can* see me, ma'am?" he asks. She gives one nod, her face crimped up as she peers into the Cyclops. "That's it, ma'am," says Cobb, doing Georgia, doing 'Bama. "Hold it level to the ground, as if it was already in place in your door."

"You sort of look funny," she says. "Oblong. Or top-heavy."

"It's the lens, ma'am. Fish eye. It puts a bend in the world, but you get to see more of it that way."

Cobb stands up and makes a quick pencil mark on the door. "Right about here, I guess. What are you, ma'am, about five foot one?" She nods. "Husband gone most of the day? His work take him out of town a lot?" She looks like a fading photograph of herself. Cobb stops his grin before it crawls into his lips. He raises the brace-and-bit, pauses just long enough to get her consent, which she gives by stepping backward a few inches and turning her head slightly to one side, a gesture of acquiescence, and Cobb scores the flimsy laminated wood with the tip of the bit and starts the hole, one inch in diameter, right on the pencil mark, level with her wide open eyes. He leans on the brace and cranks. The wood is tract-house cheap, false-grain oak, so thin that a child of nine could kick a hole in it.

To see how fast her door can be penetrated unsettles her and so Cobb tries to calm her down with a brief outline of the Charles V. Farrago success story. Rags to riches in the Home Security field. From shop mechanic to multimillionaire. From Cedar Rapids to Carmel by the Sea. The undisputed king of home surveillance devices. A genius by any standard. Cobb carries a photograph of Charles V. Farrago and promises to show it to the woman as soon as he drills out her door. In the photograph, taken some twenty or thirty years ago, Farrago has a big round head and a smile that seems two hands across with more teeth in it than seem possible. He has shrewd little eyes that preside above the smile like twin watchdogs.

Cobb tells the woman other stories. He tells her about the woman, housewife like herself, who had oil of vitriol pumped up her nose through one of those old fashioned door-peepers. Knock knock, and she opened the little peeper to see who was there and it was a de-gent. Splat. Blinded for life and horribly disfigured all for the want of a proper doorstep surveillance device. Blue crater where once was her nose, upper lip a leather flap, eyes milky clouds. The reason? No *reason*. There never is a reason. It was a prank. The de-gent chemistry student had seen *Phantom of the Opera* on TV. It was Halloween in Denver or Salt Lake or Omaha. A few years ago. He told the police: "I just had this big urge to melt a face, you know?"

Cobb tells her the one about the naked de-gent who knocked on a peeperless door and said, "Parcel Post!" He made love to his victim with a gardening tool right in front of her little kids. He left a red hoofprint on her shag carpet and that's how the cops caught him: his right foot only had two toes and the print looked like it had been left there by a goat. The *Times* called him "The Goatfoot Gasher."

The grumbling bit chews through the last lamination of veneer and Cobb reaches around the still-chained door to catch the curls of blond wood which he puts into his shirt pocket. Do not leave an unsightly mess, says Jake the Distributor. Be neat as a pin. Cobb inserts the Cyclops gently and with a little sigh into the tight hole then screws on the locking flange. "Let's give it a try, ma'am," he says.

She closes the door and Cobb goes out to the sidewalk. He stands still long enough for her to get used to the odd shapes the fish-eye lens produces, then starts to move down the sidewalk in big sidesteps. Then he reverses direction, moving in sidesteps to the other extreme of her vision. He approaches the house on the oblique, crossing the lawn, dropping behind a shrub, reemerging on hands and knees, moving swiftly now like a Dirty Dozen commando toward the welcome mat. He knows what she is seeing, knows how the lens makes him look heavy through the middle, pinheaded, legs stubby, his shined shoes fat as seals, the mean unsmiling lips, the stumpy bulge at the apex of his fat thighs, the neighborhood curving around him like a psychopathic smirk.

"It really works," she says, showing as much enthusiasm as she feels she can afford when Cobb reappears at the door, brushing off his knees and smiling like a helpful Scout. She slips a five-dollar bill through the cracked door and Cobb notices that it has been folded into a perfect square the size of a stamp.

"Satisfaction fully guaranteed, ma'am," he says, unfolding, meticulously, the bill. A fragrance, trapped in the bill for possibly years, makes his nostrils flare.

Cobb winks and the woman allows herself a coo of gratitude. Turtle and mouse rapport, Cobb thinks, pleased. This is what you strive for, says Jake the Distributor. Cross the species lines. This is the hallmark of the true salesman. Make them think you are just like them, practically *kin,* though we know that this is basically laughable.

This is Cobb's tenth sale this morning. He keeps one dollar and fifteen cents out of every five. On good days he'll sell fifty. But today won't be a good day—for sales, at least. Too hot. He feels as if there's this big unfair hand in the sky that's been lowering all morning, pushing him down. He needs a break. He needs to cool off, wash up—a nice shower would do it—he needs to get out of his swampy shirt, air his pits and the steaming crotch of his slacks. He wants to use her john, but he knows her mouse heart will panic if he asks. Instead, he asks if he can use her phone. "Need to check in," he explains, his voice decent, a fellow human being making a reasonable request, a finely honed act. She fades a bit, but she is not a swift thinker and can't find a way to say no pleasantly. Cobb has his Eagle Scout glow turned up full blast. His boy-like vulnerability is apparent in the bend of his spine, put there by the unfair bone-warping hand that presses down on him from the dirty sky, trying to make him crawl again, but he is through crawling today and is ready to lay claim to the small things of this world that should be his, but are not. The woman slides the chained bolt out of its slot and opens the door wide in jerky, indecisive increments.

"Oh, lady," he says, his voice relaxing now into its natural cadence. "You're the angel of mercy in the flesh. Really." And Cobb, hard thin lips flexed in a triumphant V, walks in.

Peter De Vries

Through a Glass Darkly

I have a mackintosh that is the apple of my eye, two topcoats, and a smoked melton, yet when a plugger in a clothing store recently detained me with a quick-change skit in which he whipped off a raglan, turned it inside out, and whipped it on again, with a hanky-panky on its behalf as a garment suitable for wet days, I bought it. Why? Because I am unable to rescue myself from demonstrators. Once my attention has been speared by a pitchman paring a potato with a trick knife, I stand mesmerized by the lengthening peel, powerless to move on till the operation is over and I have plunked down my quarter. I have thought of hiring an analyst to clean my coils, but the matter isn't really complicated enough for that. I'll give a few more examples of my trouble and then say what I think is at the bottom of it.

Not long ago, I was sauntering up Seventh Avenue in the Forties when a rap on the window of a store I was passing brought my head around in a reflex. Behind the glass, a man in a barber's tunic buttered his palms with a pomade called Lustrine and ground it into the noodle of a Latin youth seated before him on a three-legged stool. The stooge had dark, liquid eyes, which sought mine with a look of mute patience, as though for me alone was he taking this drubbing. When it was over and his locks were being combed into glossy undulations, I stepped inside for my trial size.

Later that week, a man in a tan duster banged a wand imperiously on a store pane in the East Thirties, alerting me and a middle-aged couple. He directed our attention to the skeleton of a human foot and then pointed to a printed sign alleging that the bones had been mangled by unscientific shoes. The couple moseyed along, but I was inside in a trice. A man in quasi-surgical garb shucked off my brogans and led me in stocking feet to a fluoroscope, which laid bare the dismal secrets of my own metatarsals. Ten minutes later I hobbled out scientifically shod, carrying my former footgear under my arm.

It was a few months later that another unguarded moment—one in the basement of a downtown emporium—brought me suddenly face to face with a bull-necked man on a dais who, having taken a spraddled stance, pulled the legs of a pair of denim pants in opposite directions till I thought he would pop, then gave up with a good-natured laugh, thus acknowledging himself hopelessly bested by the workmanship in the crotch. Some other shoppers who had paused went on, leaving me stranded. The man strained at the dungarees a second time and a third, his eyes reproaching me for my apparent immunity to reasonable proof. Something had to give, and it was me—four ninety-eight.

So it goes. I have the feeling these birds can spot me, or can spot the gelatinous type. I once read that suckers have their affliction written clearly in their features, so I decided to try the experiment of concealing as much of mine as possible one recent Saturday afternoon. I donned the reversible raglan, turning the collar up around my ears, drew on a soft hat, pulling it well down over one eye, and swaddled myself up to and including the chin in a heavy woollen muffler, leaving little visible of my face but my nose and a single eye. Even my gait was altered, for my scientifically constructed shoes had substantially deranged one foot.

Thus dressed, I strolled up Sixth Avenue clenching an unlighted cigar and humming an air from "Die Fledermaus." Just short of Central Park, I heard the familiar clatter of a stick on glass. It was in a drugstore window on my immediate right. I stopped but didn't turn. Deliberately, I struck a match on my thumbnail, set fire to the cigar, and puffed till I stood in a dense cloud of smoke. The rap came again, this time more insistently. I inhaled a deep lungful and let it out leisurely, snapping the match into the gutter. A third summons sounded, prolonged and peremptory. I swung to.

A man in a laboratory jacket stood in the window. He drew my attention crisply to a chart down which digestive organs meandered in color. Having, by deftly flipping the pages of a folio on an easel, enumerated the ills that lay in wait for me if they had not already begun secretly to waste me, he picked up a bottle filled with purple liquid and shook it to a bright froth, holding up three fingers to indicate that I was to take this three times a day. I nodded and went inside.

These instances will suffice to illustrate the compulsion. As for elucidating it, I will have to relate an incident in my past in which it is most likely rooted. This involves an interval when I was myself, very briefly, a demonstrating salesman. I graduated from college in 1931, the year that marked the depth of the depression. You took anything you could get, those days. I took a job selling pressure cookers, which were then being promoted on a wide scale for the first time. The company I worked for emphasized group demonstrations. You cooked a meal in the kitchen of a woman who had called in her friends or neighbors for the occasion, they ate it, and you signed up as many of the women as you could. I was given a short course in operating the pressure cooker and sent into the field. This was in Chicago in the summer.

My first prospect was a widow named Mrs. Tannenbaum, whom I knew slightly. She agreed to gather a group of housewives for a bridge supper, which I was to fix. I arrived about four-thirty on the day of the demonstration, lugging the pressure cooker, in its leather case, and a pot roast under one arm. We were to have potatoes with the pot roast, of course, and I had told Mrs. Tannenbaum I thought carrots would be nice. We had used carrots in class. Mrs. Tannenbaum supplied the vegetables.

The ladies clustered in the kitchen while I ran through the fine points of the cooker for them, got the roast on, and set the valve. Then I shooed them to their bridge tables and peeled my potatoes and scraped my carrots. Mrs. Tannenbaum shut the kitchen door, leaving me alone. I got my vegetables on, and then strayed out to the back porch and sat down on a glider with a magazine, to wait for the meal to be done. A little later, as I was thumbing through the magazine, an acrid odor reached my nostrils. I hurried in to the stove. I have since been at pains to forget the incident to the point of no longer clearly knowing what a pressure cooker looks like, but as I recall it, instead of closing the valve I had left it open, thus dissipating the steam, boiling all the water away, and burning everything, including the roast, to a crisp.

I stood, stricken, in the middle of the kitchen, debating what to do. A shred of laughter floated in above the hubbub at the front of the house. I lifted the smoking pot off the stove, tiptoed out the back door, down the stairs, along the walk beside the garage, to the alley, and dropped the whole works, cooker and all, into the garbage can. I set the lid back on the can and stole up the alley to the street, where I broke into a trot.

The recollection of that occurrence has haunted me ever since. I never showed up at the pressure-cooker office again and I never saw Mrs. Tannenbaum again—except that I still see her in my mind's eye, standing flabbergasted in the empty kitchen, her hungry and baffled guests around her. I don't know whether that or the vision of myself creeping away behind the garages is the more oppressive. Like Lord Jim, I carry down the years the adhesive memory of cowardice, but mine, unlike his, is a cowardice without scope.

Thus, at the bottom of my constant purchases of paring knives and trial sizes is a quest for absolution. I have an expiatory urge that makes me secretly *want* situations in which I become a customer, an at times almost voluptuous desire for the buyer-seller relation, so that I can punish myself by being symbolically identified with my victims of that afternoon, especially Mrs. Tannenbaum. In fact, I try to *outdo* Mrs. Tannenbaum as a victim, because she didn't actually buy, while I do, in a sacrificial gesture that must be repeated, over and over again.

William Saroyan

Harry

This boy was a worldbeater. Everything he touched turned to money, and at the age of fourteen he had over six hundred dollars in the Valley Bank, money he had made by himself. He was born to sell things. At eight or nine he was ringing door bells and showing housewives beautiful colored pictures of Jesus Christ and other holy people—from the Novelty Manufacturing Company, Toledo, Ohio—fifteen cents each, four for a half dollar. "Lady," he was saying at that early age, "this is Jesus. Look. Isn't it a pretty picture? And only fifteen cents. This is Paul, I think. Maybe Moses. You know. From the Bible."

He had all the houses in the foreign district full of these pictures, and many of the houses still have them, so you can see that he exerted a pretty good influence, after all.

After a while he went around getting subscriptions for *True Stories Magazine.* He would stand on a front porch and open a copy of the magazine, showing pictures. "Here is a lady," he would say, "who married a man thirty years older than her, and then fell in love with the man's sixteen-year-old son. Lady, what would *you* have done in such a fix? Read what this lady did. All true stories, fifteen of them every month. Romance, mystery, passion, violent lust, everything from A to Z. Also editorials on dreams. They explain what your dreams mean, if you are going on a voyage, if money is coming to you, who you are going to marry, all true meanings, scientific. Also beauty secrets, how to look young all the time."

In less than two months he had over sixty married women reading the magazine. Maybe he wasn't responsible, but after a while a lot of unconventional things began to happen. One or two wives had secret love affairs with other men and were found out by their husbands, who beat them or kicked them out of their houses, and a half dozen women began to send away for eye-lash beautifiers, bath salts, cold creams and things of that sort. The whole foreign neighborhood was getting to be slightly immoral. All the ladies began to rouge their lips and powder their faces and wear silk stockings and tight sweaters.

When he was a little older, Harry began to buy used cars, Fords, Maxwells, Saxons, Chevrolets and other small cars. He used to buy them a half dozen at a time in order to get them cheap, fifteen or twenty dollars each. He would have them slightly repaired, he would paint them red or blue or some other bright color, and he would sell them to high school boys for three and four times as much as he had paid for them. He filled the town with red and blue and green used automobiles, and the whole countryside was full of them, high school boys taking their girls to the country at night and on Sunday afternoons, and anybody knows what that means. In a way, it was a pretty good thing for the boys, only a lot of them had to get married a long time before they had found jobs for themselves, and a number of other things happened, only worse. Two or three girls had babies and didn't know who the other parent was, because two or three fellows with used cars had been involved. In a haphazard way, though, a lot of girls got husbands for themselves.

Harry himself was too busy to fool around with girls. All he wanted was to keep on making money. By the time he was seventeen he had earned a small fortune, and he looked to be one of the best-dressed young men in town. He got his suits wholesale because he wouldn't think of letting anyone make a profit on him. It was his business to make the profits. If a suit was marked twenty-seven fifty, Harry would offer the merchant twelve dollars.

"Don't tell *me,*" he would say. "I know what these rags cost. At twelve dollars you will be making a clean profit of two dollars and fifty cents, and that's enough for anybody. You can take it or leave it."

He generally got the suit for fifteen dollars, alterations included. He would argue an hour about the alterations. If the coat was a perfect fit and the merchant told him so, Harry would think he was being taken for a sucker, so he would insist that the sleeves were too long or that the shoulders were too loose. The only reason merchants tolerated him at all was that he had the reputation of being well-dressed, and to sell him a suit was to get a lot of good free advertising. It would bring a lot of other young fellows to the store, fellows who would buy suits at regular prices.

Otherwise, Harry was a nuisance. Not only that, the moment he made a purchase he would begin to talk about reciprocity, how it was the basis of American business, and he would begin to sell the merchant earthquake insurance or a brand new Studebaker. And most of the time he would succeed. All sorts of business people bought earthquake insurance just to stop Harry talking. He chiseled and he took for granted chiseling in others, so he always quoted chisel-proof prices, and then came down to the regular prices. It made his customers feel good. It pleased them to think that they had put one over on Harry, but he always had a quiet laugh to himself.

One year the whole San Joaquin valley was nearly ruined by a severe frost that all but wiped out a great crop of grapes and oranges. Harry got into his Studebaker and drove into the country. Frost-bitten oranges were absolutely worthless because the Board of Health wouldn't allow them to be marketed, but Harry had an idea. He went out to the orange groves, and looked at the trees loaded with fruit that was now worthless. He talked to the farmers and told them how sorry he was.

Then he said:

"But maybe I can help you out a little. I can use your frost-bitten oranges . . . for hog and cattle feed. Hogs don't care if an orange is frost-bitten, and the juice is good for them the same way it's good for people . . . vitamines. You don't have to do anything. I'll have the oranges picked and hauled away, and I'll give you a check for twenty-five dollars, spot cash."

That year he sent over twenty truck loads of frost-bitten oranges to Los Angeles for the orange-juice stands, and he cleaned up another small fortune.

Everyone said he could turn anything into money. He could figure a way of making money out of anything. When the rest of the world was down in the mouth, Harry was on his toes, working on the Los Angeles angle of disposing of bad oranges.

He never bothered about having an office. The whole town was his office, and whenever he wanted to sit down, he would go up to the eighth floor of Cory Building and sit in M. Peters' office, and chew the rag with the attorney. He would talk along casually, but all the time he would be finding out about contracts, and how to make people come through with money, and how to attach property, and so on. A lot of people were in debt to him, and he meant to get his money.

He had sold electric refrigerators, vacuum cleaners, radios, and a lot of other modern things to people who couldn't afford to buy them, and he had sold these things simply by talking about them, and by showing catalogue pictures of them. The customer had to pay freight and everything else. All Harry did was talk and sell. If a man couldn't pay cash for a radio, Harry would get five dollars down and a note for the balance, and if the man couldn't make his payments, Harry would attach the man's home, or his vineyard, or his automobile, or his horse, or anything else the man owned. And the amazing thing was that no one ever criticised him for his business methods. He was very smooth about attaching a man's property, and he would calmly explain that it was the usual procedure, according to law. What was right was right.

No one could figure out what Harry wanted with so much money. He already had money in the bank, a big car, and he wasn't interested in girls; so what was he saving up all the money for? A few of his customers sometimes asked him, and Harry would look confused a moment, as if he himself didn't know, and then he would come out and say:

"I want to get hold of a half million dollars so I can retire."

It was pretty funny, Harry thinking of retiring at eighteen. He had left high school in his first year because he hadn't liked the idea of sitting in a class room listening to a lot of nonsense about starting from the bottom and working up, and so on, and ever since he had been on the go, figuring out ways to make money.

Sometimes people would ask him what he intended to do after he retired, and Harry would look puzzled again, and finally he would say, "Oh, I guess I'll take a trip around the world."

"Well, if he does," everyone thought, "he'll sell something everywhere he goes. He'll sell stuff on the trains and on the boats and in the foreign cities. He won't waste a minute looking around. He'll open a catalogue and sell them foreigners everything you can think of."

But things happen in a funny way, and you can never tell about people, even about people like Harry. Anybody is liable to get sick. Death and sickness play no favorites; they come to all men. Presidents and kings and movie stars, they all die, they all get sick.

Even Harry got sick. Not mildly, not merely something casual like the flu that you can get over in a week, and be as good as new again. Harry got T. B. and he got it in a bad way, poor kid.

Well, the sickness got Harry, and all that money of his in the Valley Bank didn't help him a lot. Of course he did try to rest for a while, but that was out of the question. Lying in bed, Harry would try to sell life insurance to his best friends. Harry's cousin, Simon Gregory, told me about this. He said it wasn't that Harry really wanted more money; it was simply that he couldn't open his mouth unless it was to make a sales talk. He couldn't carry on an ordinary conversation because he didn't know the first thing about anything that didn't have something to do with insurance, or automobiles, or real estate. If somebody tried to talk politics or maybe religion, Harry would look irritated, and he would start to make a sales talk. He even asked Simon Gregory how old he was, and when Simon said that he was twenty-two, Harry got all excited.

"Listen, Simon," he said, "you are my cousin, and I want to do you a favor. You haven't a day to lose if you intend to be financially independent when you are sixty-five. I have just the policy you need. Surely you can afford to pay six dollars and twenty-seven cents a month for the next forty-three years. You won't be able to go to many shows; but what is more important, to see a few foolish moving pictures, or to be independent when you are sixty-five?"

It almost made Simon bawl to hear Harry talking that way, sick as he was.

The doctor told Harry's folks that Harry ought to go down to Arizona for a year or two, that it was his only hope, but when they talked the matter over with Harry, he got sore and said the doctor was trying to get him to spend his money. He said he was all right, just a cold in the chest, and he told his folks to ask the doctor to stay away. "Get some other doctor," he said. "Why should I go down to Arizona?"

Every now and then we would see Harry in town, talking rapidly to someone, trying to sell something, but it would be for only a day or two, and then he would have to go back to bed. He kept this up for about two years, and you ought to see the change that came over that poor boy. It was really enough to make you feel rotten. To look at him you would think he was the loneliest person on earth, but the thing that hurt most was the realization that if you tried to talk to him, or tried to be friendly toward him, he would turn around and try to sell you life insurance. That's what burned a man up. There he was dying on his feet, and still wanting to sell healthy people life insurance. It was too sad not to be funny.

Well, one day (this was years ago) I saw Simon Gregory in town, and he looked sick. I asked him what the trouble was, and he said Harry had died and that he had been at the bedside at the time, and now he was feeling rotten. The things Harry talked about, dying. It was terrible. Insurance, straight to the end, financial independence at sixty-five.

Harry's photograph was in *The Evening Herald,* and there was a big story about his life, how smart Harry had been, how ambitious, and all that sort of thing. That's what it came to, but somehow there was something about that crazy jackass that none of us can forget.

He was different, there is no getting away from it. Nowadays he is almost a legend with us, and there are a lot of children in this town who were born after Harry died, and yet they know as much about him as we do, and maybe a little more. You would think he had been some great historical personage, somebody to talk to children about in order to make them ambitious or something. Of course most of the stories about him are comical, but just the same they make him out to be a really great person. Hardly anyone remembers the name of our last mayor, and there haven't been any great men from our town, but all the kids around here know about Harry. It's pretty remarkable when you bear in mind that he died before he was twenty-three.

Whenever somebody fails to accomplish some unusual undertaking in our town, people say to one another, "Harry would have done it." And everybody laughs, remembering him, the way he rushed about town, waking people up, making deals. A couple of months ago, for example, there was a tight-wire walker on the stage of the Hippodrome Theatre, and he tried to turn a somersault in the air and land on the tight-wire, but he couldn't do it. He would touch the wire with his feet, lose his balance, and leap to the stage. Then he would try it over again, from the beginning, music and all, the drum rolling to make you feel how dangerous it was. This acrobat tried to do the trick three times and failed, and while he was losing his balance the fourth time, some young fellow away back in the gallery hollered out as loud as he could, "Get Harry. Harry is the man for the emergency." Then everybody in the theatre busted out laughing. The poor acrobat was stunned by the laughter, and he began to swear at the audience in Spanish. He didn't know about our town's private joke.

All this will give you an idea what sort of a name Harry made for himself, but the funniest stories about him are the ones that have to do with Harry in heaven, or in hell, selling earthquake insurance, and automobiles, and buying clothes cheap. He was a worldbeater. He was different. Everybody likes to laugh about him, but all the same this whole town misses him, and there isn't a man who knew him who doesn't wish that he was still among us, tearing around town, talking big business, making things pop, a real American go-getter.

RAYMOND CARVER

Collectors

I was out of work. But any day I expected to hear from up north. I lay on the sofa and listened to the rain. Now and then I'd lift up and look through the curtain for the mailman.

There was no one on the street, nothing.

I hadn't been down again five minutes when I heard someone walk onto the porch, wait, and then knock. I lay still. I knew it wasn't the mailman. I knew his steps. You can't be too careful if you're out of work and you get notices in the mail or else pushed under your door. They come around wanting to talk, too, especially if you don't have a telephone.

The knock sounded again, louder, a bad sign. I eased up and tried to see onto the porch. But whoever was there was standing against the door, another bad sign. I knew the floor creaked, so there was no chance of slipping into the other room and looking out that window.

Another knock, and I said, Who's there?

This is Aubrey Bell, a man said. Are you Mr. Slater?

What is it you want? I called from the sofa.

I have something for Mrs. Slater. She's won something. Is Mrs. Slater home?

Mrs. Slater doesn't live here, I said.

Well, then, are you Mr. Slater? the man said. Mr. Slater . . . and the man sneezed.

I got off the sofa. I unlocked the door and opened it a little. He was an old guy, fat and bulky under his raincoat. Water ran off the coat and dripped onto the big suitcase contraption thing he carried.

He grinned and set down the big case. He put out his hand.

Aubrey Bell, he said.

I don't know you, I said.

Mrs. Slater, he began. Mrs. Slater filled out a card. He took cards from an inside pocket and shuffled them a minute. Mrs. Slater, he read. Two-fifty-five South Sixth East? Mrs. Slater is a winner.

He took off his hat and nodded solemnly, slapped the hat against his coat as if that were it, everything had been settled, the drive finished, the railhead reached.

He waited.

Mrs. Slater doesn't live here, I said. What'd she win?

I have to show you, he said. May I come in?

I don't know. If it won't take long, I said. I'm pretty busy.

Fine, he said. I'll just slide out of this coat first. And the galoshes. Wouldn't want to track up your carpet. I see you do have a carpet, Mr. . . .

His eyes had lighted and then dimmed at the sight of the carpet. He shuddered. Then he took off his coat. He shook it out and hung it by the collar over the doorknob. That's a good place for it, he said. Damn weather, anyway. He bent over and unfastened his galoshes. He set his case inside the room. He stepped out of the galoshes and into the room in a pair of slippers.

I closed the door. He saw me staring at the slippers and said, W. H. Auden wore slippers all through China on his first visit there. Never took them off. Corns.

I shrugged. I took one more look down the street for the mailman and shut the door again.

Aubrey Bell stared at the carpet. He pulled his lips. Then he laughed. He laughed and shook his head.

What's so funny? I said.

Nothing. Lord, he said. He laughed again. I think I'm losing my mind. I think I have a fever. He reached a hand to his forehead. His hair was matted and there was a ring around his scalp where the hat had been.

Do I feel hot to you? he said. I don't know, I think I might have a fever. He was still staring at the carpet. You have any aspirin?

What's the matter with you? I said. I hope you're not getting sick on me. I got things I have to do.

He shook his head. He sat down on the sofa. He stirred at the carpet with his slippered foot.

I went to the kitchen, rinsed a cup, shook two aspirin out of a bottle.

Here, I said. Then I think you ought to leave.

Are you speaking for Mrs. Slater? he hissed. No, no, forget I said that, forget I said that. He wiped his face. He swallowed the aspirin. His eyes skipped around the bare room. Then he leaned forward with some effort and unsnapped the buckles on his case. The case flopped open, revealing compartments filled with an array of hoses, brushes, shiny pipes, and some kind of heavy-looking blue thing mounted on little wheels. He stared at these things as if surprised. Quietly, in a churchly voice, he said, Do you know what this is?

I moved closer. I'd say it was a vacuum cleaner. I'm not in the market, I said. No way am I in the market for a vacuum cleaner.

I want to show you something, he said. He took a card out of his jacket pocket. Look at this, he said. He handed me the card. Nobody said you were in the market. But look at the signature. Is that Mrs. Slater's signature or not?

I looked at the card. I held it up to the light. I turned it over, but the other side was blank. So what? I said.

Mrs. Slater's card was pulled at random out of a basket of cards. Hundreds of cards just like this little card. She has won a free vacuuming and carpet shampoo. Mrs. Slater is a winner. No strings. I am here even to do your mattress, Mr. . . . You'll be surprised to see what can collect in a mattress over the months, over the years. Every day, every night of our lives, we're leaving little bits of ourselves, flakes of this and that, behind. Where do they go, these bits and pieces of ourselves? Right through the sheets and into the mattress, *that's* where! Pillows, too. It's all the same.

He had been removing lengths of the shiny pipe and joining the parts together. Now he inserted the fitted pipes into the hose. He was on his knees, grunting. He attached some sort of scoop to the hose and lifted out the blue thing with wheels.

He let me examine the filter he intended to use.

Do you have a car? he asked.

No car, I said. I don't have a car. If I had a car I would drive you someplace.

Too bad, he said. This little vacuum comes equipped with a sixty-foot extension cord. If you had a car, you could wheel this little vacuum right up to your car door and vacuum the plush carpeting and the luxurious reclining seats as well. You would be surprised how much of us gets lost, how much of us gathers, in those fine seats over the years.

Mr. Bell, I said, I think you better pack up your things and go. I say this without any malice whatsoever.

But he was looking around the room for a plug-in. He found one at the end of the sofa. The machine rattled as if there were a marble inside, anyway something loose inside, then settled to a hum.

Rilke lived in one castle after another, all of his adult life. Benefactors, he said loudly over the hum of the vacuum. He seldom rode in motorcars; he preferred trains. Then look at Voltaire at Cirey with Madame Châtelet. His death mask. Such serenity. He raised his right hand as if I were about to disagree. No, no, it isn't right, is it? Don't say it. But who knows? With that he turned and began to pull the vacuum into the other room.

There was a bed, a window. The covers were heaped on the floor. One pillow, one sheet over the mattress. He slipped the case from the pillow and then quickly stripped the sheet from the mattress. He stared at the mattress and gave me a look out of the corner of his eye. I went to the kitchen and got the chair. I sat down in the doorway and watched. First he tested the suction by putting the scoop against the palm of his hand. He bent and turned a dial on the vacuum. You have to turn it up full strength for a job like this one, he said. He checked the suction again, then extended the hose to the head of the bed and began to move the scoop down the mattress. The scoop tugged at the mattress. The vacuum whirred louder. He made three passes over the mattress, then switched off the machine. He pressed a lever and the lid popped open. He took out the filter. This filter is just for demonstration purposes. In normal use, all of this, this *material*, would go into your bag, here, he said. He pinched some of the dusty stuff between his fingers. There must have been a cup of it.

He had this look to his face.

It's not my mattress, I said. I leaned forward in the chair and tried to show an interest.

Now the pillow, he said. He put the used filter on the sill and looked out the window for a minute. He turned. I want you to hold onto this end of the pillow, he said.

I got up and took hold of two corners of the pillow. I felt I was holding something by the ears.

Like this? I said.

He nodded. He went into the other room and came back with another filter.

How much do those things cost? I said.

Next to nothing, he said. They're only made out of paper and a little bit of plastic. Couldn't cost much.

He kicked on the vacuum and I held tight as the scoop sank into the pillow and moved down its length—once, twice, three times. He switched off the vacuum, removed the filter, and held it up without a word. He put it on the sill beside the other filter. Then he opened the closet door. He looked inside, but there was only a box of Mouse-Be-Gone.

I heard steps on the porch, the mail slot opened and clinked shut. We looked at each other.

He pulled on the vacuum and I followed him into the other room. We looked at the letter lying face down on the carpet near the front door.

I started toward the letter, turned and said, What else? It's getting late. This carpet's not worth fooling with. It's only a twelve-by-fifteen cotton carpet with no-skid backing from Rug City. It's not worth fooling with.

Do you have a full ashtray? he said. Or a potted plant or something like that? A handful of dirt would be fine.

I found the ashtray. He took it, dumped the contents onto the carpet, ground the ashes and cigarets under his slipper. He got down on his knees again and inserted a new filter. He took off his jacket and threw it onto the sofa. He was sweating under the arms. Fat hung over his belt. He twisted off the scoop and attached another device to the hose.

He adjusted his dial. He kicked on the machine and began to move back and forth, back and forth over the worn carpet. Twice I started for the letter. But he seemed to anticipate me, cut me off, so to speak, with his hose and his pipes and his sweeping and his sweeping. . . .

I took the chair back to the kitchen and sat there and watched him work. After a time he shut off the machine, opened the lid, and silently brought me the filter, alive with dust, hair, small grainy things. I looked at the filter, and then I got up and put it in the garbage.

He worked steadily now. No more explanations. He came out to the kitchen with a bottle that held a few ounces of green liquid. He put the bottle under the tap and filled it.

You know I can't pay anything, I said. I couldn't pay you a dollar if my life depended on it. You're going to have to write me off as a dead loss, that's all. You're wasting your time on me, I said.

I wanted it out in the open, no misunderstanding.

He went about his business. He put another attachment on the hose, in some complicated way hooked his bottle to the new attachment. He moved slowly over the carpet, now and then releasing little streams of emerald, moving the brush back and forth over the carpet, working up patches of foam.

I had said all that was on my mind. I sat on the chair in the kitchen, relaxed now, and watched him work. Once in a while I looked out the window at the rain. It had begun to get dark. He switched off the vacuum. He was in a corner near the front door.

You want coffee? I said.

He was breathing hard. He wiped his face.

I put on water and by the time it had boiled and I'd fixed up two cups he had everything dismantled and back in the case. Then he picked up the letter. He read the name on the letter and looked closely at the return address. He folded the letter in half and put it in his hip pocket. I kept watching him. That's all I did. The coffee began to cool.

It's for a Mr. Slater, he said. I'll see to it. He said, Maybe I will skip the coffee. I better not walk across this carpet. I just shampooed it.

That's true, I said. Then I said, You're sure that's who the letter's for?

He reached to the sofa for his jacket, put it on, and opened the front door. It was still raining. He stepped into his galoshes, fastened them, and then pulled on the raincoat and looked back inside.

You want to see it? he said. You don't believe me?

It just seems strange, I said.

Well, I'd better be off, he said. But he kept standing there. You want the vacuum or not?

I looked at the big case, closed now and ready to move on.

No, I said, I guess not. I'm going to be leaving here soon. It would just be in the way.

All right, he said, and he shut the door.

Philip K. Dick

Sales Pitch

Commute ships roared on all sides, as Ed Morris made his way wearily home to Earth at the end of a long hard day at the office. The Ganymede-Terra lanes were choked with exhausted, grim-faced businessmen; Jupiter was in opposition to Earth and the trip was a good two hours. Every few million miles the great flow slowed to a grinding, agonized halt; signal-lights flashed as streams from Mars and Saturn fed into the main traffic-arteries.

"Lord," Morris muttered. "How tired can you *get?*" He locked the autopilot and momentarily turned from the control-board to light a much-needed cigarette. His hands shook. His head swam. It was past six; Sally would be fuming; dinner would be spoiled. The same old thing. Nerve-wracking driving, honking horns and irate drivers zooming past his little ship, furious gesturing, shouting, cursing . . .

And the ads. That was what really did it. He could have stood everything else—but the ads, the whole long way from Ganymede to Earth. And on Earth, the swarms of sales robots; it was too much. And they were everywhere.

He slowed to avoid a fifty-ship smashup. Repair-ships were scurrying around trying to get the debris out of the lane. His audio-speaker wailed as police rockets hurried up. Expertly, Morris raised his ship, cut between two slow-moving commercial transports, zipped momentarily into the unused left lane, and then sped on, the wreck left behind. Horns honked furiously at him; he ignored them.

"Trans-Solar Products greets you!" an immense voice boomed in his ear. Morris groaned and hunched down in his seat. He was getting near Terra; the barrage was increasing. "Is your tension-index pushed over the safety-margin by the ordinary frustrations of the day? Then you need an Id-Persona Unit. So small it can be worn behind the ear, close to the frontal lobe—"

Thank God, he was past it. The ad dimmed and receded behind, as his fast-moving ship hurtled forward. But another was right ahead.

"Drivers! Thousands of unnecessary deaths each year from interplanet driving. Hypno-Motor Control from an expert source-point insures your safety. Surrender your body and save your life!" The voice roared louder. "Industrial experts say—"

Both audio ads, the easiest to ignore. But now a visual ad was forming; he winced, closed his eyes, but it did no good.

"Men!" an unctuous voice thundered on all sides of him. "Banish internally-caused obnoxious odors *forever.* Removal by modern painless methods of the gastrointestinal tract and substitution system will relieve you of the most acute cause of social rejection." The visual image locked; a vast nude girl, blonde hair disarranged, blue eyes half shut, lips parted, head tilted back in sleep-drugged ecstasy. The features ballooned as the lips approached his own. Abruptly the orgiastic expression on the girl's face vanished. Disgust and revulsion swept across, and then the image faded out.

"Does this happen to you?" the voice boomed. "During erotic sex-play do you offend your love-partner by the presence of gastric processes which—"

The voice died, and he was past. His mind his own again, Morris kicked savagely at the throttle and sent the little ship leaping. The pressure, applied directly to the audio-visual regions of his brain, had faded below spark point. He groaned and shook his head to clear it. All around him the vague half-defined echoes of ads glittered and gibbered, like ghosts of distant video-stations. Ads waited on all sides; he steered a careful course, dexterity born of animal desperation, but not all could be avoided. Despair seized him. The outline of a new visual-audio ad was already coming into being.

"You, mister wage-earner!" it shouted into the eyes and ears, noses and throats, of a thousand weary commuters. "Tired of the same old job? Wonder Circuits Inc. has perfected a marvelous long-range thoughtwave scanner. Know what others are thinking and saying. Get the edge on fellow employees. Learn facts, figures about your employer's personal existence. Banish uncertainty!"

Morris' despair swept up wildly. He threw the throttle on full blast; the little ship bucked and rolled as it climbed from the traffic-lane into the dead zone beyond. A shrieking roar, as his fender whipped through the protective wall—and then the ad faded behind him.

He slowed down, trembling with misery and fatigue. Earth lay ahead. He'd be home, soon. Maybe he could get a good night's sleep. He shakily dropped the nose of the ship and prepared to hook onto the tractor beam of the Chicago commute field.

"The best metabolism adjuster on the market," the salesrobot shrilled. "Guaranteed to maintain a perfect endocrine-balance, or your money refunded in full."

Morris pushed wearily past the salesrobot, up the sidewalk toward the residential-block that contained his living-unit. The robot followed a few steps, then forgot him and hurried after another grim-faced commuter.

"All the news while it's news," a metallic voice dinned at him. "Have a retinal vidscreen installed in your least-used eye. Keep in touch with the world; don't wait for out-of-date hourly summaries."

"Get out of the way," Morris muttered. The robot stepped aside for him and he crossed the street with a pack of hunched-over men and women.

Robot-salesmen were everywhere, gesturing, pleading, shrilling. One started after him and he quickened his pace. It scurried along, chanting its pitch and trying to attract his attention, all the way up the hill to his living-unit. It didn't give up until he stooped over, snatched up a rock, and hurled it futilely. He scrambled in the house and slammed the doorlock after him. The robot hesitated, then turned and raced after a woman with an armload of packages toiling up the hill. She tried vainly to elude it, without success.

"Darling!" Sally cried. She hurried from the kitchen, drying her hands on her plastic shorts, bright-eyed and excited. "Oh, you poor thing! You look so tired!"

Morris peeled off his hat and coat and kissed his wife briefly on her bare shoulder. "What's for dinner?"

Sally gave his hat and coat to the closet. "We're having Uranian wild pheasant; your favorite dish."

Morris' mouth watered, and a tiny surge of energy crawled back into his exhausted body. "No kidding? What the hell's the occasion?"

His wife's brown eyes moistened with compassion. "Darling, it's your birthday; you're thirty-seven years old today. Had you forgotten?"

"Yeah," Morris grinned a little. "I sure had." He wandered into the kitchen. The table was set; coffee was steaming in the cups and there was butter and white bread, mashed potatoes and green peas. "My golly. A real occasion."

Sally punched the stove controls and the container of smoking pheasant was slid onto the table and neatly sliced open. "Go wash your hands and we're ready to eat. Hurry—before it gets cold."

Morris presented his hands to the wash slot and then sat down gratefully at the table. Sally served the tender, fragrant pheasant, and the two of them began eating.

"Sally," Morris said, when his plate was empty and he was leaning back and sipping slowly at his coffee. "I can't go on like this. Something's got to be done."

"You mean the drive? I wish you could get a position on Mars like Bob Young. Maybe if you talked to the Employment Commission and explained to them how all the strain—"

"It's not just the drive. *They're right out front.* Everywhere. Waiting for me. All day and night."

"Who are, dear?"

"Robots selling things. As soon as I set down the ship. Robots and visual-audio ads. They dig right into a man's brain. They follow people around until they die."

"I know." Sally patted his hand sympathetically. "When I go shopping they follow me in clusters. All talking at once. It's really a panic—you can't understand half what they're saying."

"We've got to break out."

"Break out?" Sally faltered. "What do you mean?"

"We've got to get away from them. They're destroying us."

Morris fumbled in his pocket and carefully got out a tiny fragment of metal-foil. He unrolled it with painstaking care and smoothed it out on the table. "Look at this. It was circulated in the office, among the men; it got to me and I kept it."

"What does it mean?" Sally's brow wrinkled as she made out the words. "Dear, I don't think you got all of it. There must be more than this."

"A new world," Morris said softly. "Where they haven't got to, yet. It's a long way off, out beyond the solar system. Out in the stars."

"Proxima?"

"Twenty planets. Half of them habitable. Only a few thousand people out there. Families, workmen, scientists, some industrial survey teams. Land free for the asking."

"But it's so—" Sally made a face. "Dear, isn't it sort of underdeveloped? They say it's like living back in the twentieth century. Flush toilets, bathtubs, gasoline driven cars—"

"That's right." Morris rolled up the bit of crumpled metal, his face grim and dead-serious. "It's a hundred years behind times. None of this." He indicated the stove and the furnishings in the living room. "We'll have to do without. We'll have to get used to a simpler life. The way our ancestors lived." He tried to smile but his face wouldn't cooperate. "You think you'd like it? No ads, no salesrobots, traffic moving at sixty miles an hour instead of sixty million. We could raise passage on one of the big trans-system liners. I could sell my commute rocket . . ."

There was a hesitant, doubtful silence.

"Ed," Sally began. "I think we should think it over more. What about your job? What would you do out there?"

"I'd find something."

"But *what?* Haven't you got that part figured out?" A shrill tinge of annoyance crept into her voice. "It seems to me we should consider that part just a little more before we throw away everything and just—take off."

"If we don't go," Morris said slowly, trying to keep his voice steady, "they'll get us. There isn't much time left. I don't know how much longer I can hold them off."

"Really, Ed! You make it sound so melodramatic. If you feel that bad why don't you take some time off and have complete inhibition check? I was watching a vidprogram and I saw them going over a man whose psychosomatic system was much worse than yours. A much older man."

She leaped to her feet. "Let's go out tonight and celebrate. Okay?" Her slim fingers fumbled at the zipper of her shorts. "I'll put on my new plastirobe, the one I've never had nerve enough to wear."

Her eyes sparkled with excitement as she hurried into the bedroom. "You know the one I mean? When you're up close it's translucent but as you get farther off it becomes more and more sheer until–"

"I know the one," Morris said wearily. "I've seen them advertised on my way home from work." He got slowly to his feet and wandered into the living room. At the door of the bedroom he halted. "Sally–"

"Yes?"

Morris opened his mouth to speak. He was going to ask her again, talk to her about the metal-foil fragment he had carefully wadded up and carried home. He was going to talk to her about the frontier. About Proxima Centauri. Going away and never coming back. But he never had a chance.

The doorchimes sounded.

"Somebody's at the door!" Sally cried excitedly. "Hurry up and see who it is!"

In the evening darkness the robot was a silent, unmoving figure. A cold wind blew around it and into the house. Morris shivered and moved back from the door. "What do you want?" he demanded. A strange fear licked at him. "What is it?"

The robot was larger than any he had seen. Tall and broad, with heavy metallic grippers and elongated eye-lenses. Its upper trunk was a square tank instead of the usual cone. It rested on four treads, not the customary two. It towered over Morris, almost seven feet high. Massive and solid.

"Good evening," it said calmly. Its voice was whipped around by the night wind; it mixed with the dismal noises of evening, the echoes of traffic and the clang of distant street signals. A few vague shapes hurried through the gloom. The world was black and hostile.

"Evening," Morris responded automatically. He found himself trembling. "What are you selling?"

"I would like to show you a fasrad," the robot said.

Morris' mind was numb; it refused to respond. What was a *fasrad?* There was something dreamlike and nightmarish going on. He struggled to get his mind and body together. "A what?" he croaked.

"A fasrad." The robot made no effort to explain. It regarded him without emotion, as if it was not its responsibility to explain anything. "It will take only a moment."

"I–" Morris began. He moved back, out of the wind. And the robot, without change of expression, glided past him and into the house.

"Thank you," it said. It halted in the middle of the living room. "Would you call your wife, please? I would like to show her the fasrad, also."

"Sally," Morris muttered helplessly. "Come here."

Sally swept breathlessly into the living room, her breasts quivering with excitement. "What is it? Oh!" She saw the robot and halted uncertainly. "Ed, did you order something? Are we buying something?"

"Good evening," the robot said to her. "I am going to show you the fasrad. Please be seated. On the couch, if you will. Both together."

Sally sat down expectantly, her cheeks flushed, eyes bright with wonder and bewilderment. Numbly, Ed seated himself beside her. "Look," he muttered thickly. "What the hell is a fasrad? *What's going on?* I don't want to buy anything!"

"What is your name?" the robot asked him.

"Morris." He almost choked. "Ed Morris."

The robot turned to Sally. "Mrs. Morris." It bowed slightly. "I'm glad to meet you, Mr. and Mrs. Morris. You are the first persons in your neighborhood to see the fasrad. This is the initial demonstration in this area." Its cold eyes swept the room. "Mr. Morris, you are employed, I assume. Where are you employed?"

"He works on Ganymede," Sally said dutifully, like a little girl in school. "For the Terran Metals Development Co."

The robot digested this information. "A fasrad will be of value to you." It eyed Sally. "What do you do?"

"I'm a tape transcriber at Histo-Research."

"A fasrad will be of no value in your professional work, but it will be helpful here in the home." It picked up a table in its powerful steel grippers. "For example, sometimes an attractive piece of furniture is damaged by a clumsy guest." The robot smashed the table to bits; fragments of wood and plastic rained down. "A fasrad is needed."

Morris leaped helplessly to his feet. He was powerless to halt events; a numbing weight hung over him, as the robot tossed the fragments of table away and selected a heavy floor lamp.

"Oh dear," Sally gasped. "That's my best lamp."

"When a fasrad is possessed, there is nothing to fear." The robot seized the lamp and twisted it grotesquely. It ripped the shade, smashed the bulbs, then threw away the remnants. "A situation of this kind can occur from some violent explosion, such as an H-Bomb."

"For God's sake," Morris muttered. "We–"

"An H-Bomb attack may never occur," the robot continued, "but in such an event a fasrad is indispensable." It knelt down and pulled an intricate tube from its waist. Aiming the tube at the floor it atomized a hole five feet in diameter. It stepped back from the yawning pocket. "I have not extended this tunnel, but you can see a fasrad would save your life in case of attack."

The word *attack* seemed to set off a new train of reactions in its metal brain.

"Sometimes a thug or hood will attack a person at night," it continued. Without warning it whirled and drove its fist through the wall. A section of the wall collapsed in a heap of powder and debris. "That takes care of the thug." The robot straightened out and peered around the room. "Often you are too tired in the evening to manipulate the buttons on the stove." It strode into the kitchen and began punching the stove controls; immense quantities of food spilled in all directions.

"Stop!" Sally cried. "Get away from my stove!"

"You may be too weary to run water for your bath." The robot tripped the controls of the tub and water poured down. "Or you may wish to go right to bed." It yanked the bed from its concealment and threw it flat. Sally retreated in fright as the robot advanced toward her. "Sometimes after a hard day at work you are too tired to remove your clothing. In that event–"

"Get out of here!" Morris shouted at it. "Sally, run and get the cops. The thing's gone crazy. *Hurry.*"

"The fasrad is a necessity in all modern homes," the robot continued. "For example, an appliance may break down. The fasrad repairs it instantly." It seized the automatic humidity control and tore the wiring and replaced it on the wall. "Sometimes you would prefer not to go to work. The fasrad is permitted by law to occupy your position for a consecutive period not to exceed ten days. If, after that period–"

"Good God," Morris said, as understanding finally came. "You're the fasrad."

"That's right," the robot agreed. "Fully Automatic Self-Regulating Android (Domestic). There is also the fasrac (Construction), the fasram (Managerial), the fasras (Soldier), and the fasrab (Bureaucrat). I am designed for home use."

"You–" Sally gasped. "You're for sale. You're selling yourself."

"I am demonstrating myself," the fasrad, the robot, answered. Its impassive metal eyes were fixed intently on Morris as it continued, "I am sure, Mr. Morris, you would like to own me. I am reasonably priced and fully guaranteed. A full book of instructions is included. I cannot conceive of taking *no* for an answer."

At half past twelve, Ed Morris still sat at the foot of the bed, one shoe on, the other in his hand. He gazed vacantly ahead. He said nothing.

"For heaven's sake," Sally complained. "Finish untying that knot and get into bed; you have to be up at five-thirty."

Morris fooled aimlessly with the shoelace. After a while he dropped the shoe and tugged at the other one. The house was cold and silent. Outside, the dismal night-wind whipped and lashed at the cedars that grew along the side of the building. Sally lay curled up beneath the radiant-lens, a cigarette between her lips, enjoying the warmth and half-dozing.

In the living room stood the fasrad. It hadn't left. It was still there, was waiting for Morris to buy it.

"Come on!" Sally said sharply. "What's wrong with you? It fixed all the things it broke; it was just demonstrating itself." She sighed drowsily. "It certainly gave me a scare. I thought something had gone wrong with it. They certainly had an inspiration, sending it around to sell itself to people."

Morris said nothing.

Sally rolled over on her stomach and languidly stubbed out her cigarette. "That's not so much, is it? Ten thousand gold units, and if we get our friends to buy one we get a five per cent commission. All we have to do is show it. It isn't as if we had to *sell* it. It sells itself." She giggled. "They always wanted a product that sold itself, didn't they?"

Morris untied the knot in his shoelace. He slid his shoe back on and tied it tight.

"What are you doing?" Sally demanded angrily. "You come to bed!" She sat up furiously, as Morris left the room and moved slowly down the hall. "Where are you going?"

In the living room, Morris switched on the light and sat down facing the fasrad. "Can you hear me?" he said.

"Certainly," the fasrad answered. "I'm never inoperative. Sometimes an emergency occurs at night: a child is sick or an accident takes place. You have no children as yet, but in the event—"

"Shut up," Morris said, "I don't want to hear you."

"You asked me a question. Self-regulating androids are plugged in to a central information exchange. Sometimes a person wishes immediate information; the fasrad is always ready to answer any theoretical or factual inquiry. Anything not metaphysical."

Morris picked up the book of instructions and thumbed it. The fasrad did thousands of things; it never wore out; it was never at a loss; it couldn't make a mistake. He threw the book away. "I'm not going to buy you," he said to it. "Never. Not in a million years."

"Oh, yes you are," the fasrad corrected. "This is an opportunity you can't afford to miss." There was calm, metallic confidence in its voice. "You can't turn me down, Mr. Morris. A fasrad is an indispensable necessity in the modern home."

"Get out of here," Morris said evenly. "Get out of my house and don't come back."

"I'm not your fasrad to order around. Until you've purchased me at the regular list price, I'm responsible only to Self-Regulating Android Inc. Their instructions were to the contrary; I'm to remain with you until you buy me."

"Suppose I never buy you?" Morris demanded, but in his heart ice formed even as he asked. Already he felt the cold terror of the answer that was coming; there could be no other.

"I'll continue to remain with you," the fasrad said; "eventually you'll buy me." It plucked some withered roses from a vase on the mantel and dropped them into its disposal slot. "You will see more and more situations in which a fasrad is indispensable. Eventually you'll wonder how you ever existed without one."

"Is there anything you can't do?"

"Oh, yes; there's a great deal I can't do. But I can do anything *you* can do—and considerably better."

Morris let out his breath slowly. "I'd be insane to buy you."

"You've got to buy me," the impassive voice answered. The fasrad extended a hollow pipe and began cleaning the carpet. "I am useful in all situations. Notice how fluffy and free of dust this rug is." It withdrew the pipe and extended another. Morris coughed and staggered quickly away; clouds of white particles billowed out and filled every part of the room.

"I am spraying for moths," the fasrad explained.

The white cloud turned to an ugly blue-black. The room faded into ominous darkness; the fasrad was a dim shape moving methodically about in the center. Presently the cloud lifted and the furniture emerged.

"I sprayed for harmful bacteria," the fasrad said.

It painted the walls of the room and constructed new furniture to go with them. It reinforced the ceiling in the bathroom. It increased the number of heat-vents from the furnace. It put in new electrical wiring. It tore out all the fixtures in the kitchen and assembled more modern ones. It examined Morris' financial accounts and computed his income tax for the following year. It sharpened all the pencils; it caught hold of his wrist and quickly diagnosed his high blood-pressure as psychosomatic.

"You'll feel better after you've turned responsibility over to me," it explained. It threw out some old soup Sally had been saving. "Danger of botulism," it told him. "Your wife is sexually attractive, but not capable of a high order of intellectualization."

Morris went to the closet and got his coat.

"Where are you going?" the fasrad asked.

"To the office."

"At this time of night?"

Morris glanced briefly into the bedroom. Sally was sound asleep under the soothing radiant-lens. Her slim body was rosy pink and healthy, her face free of worry. He closed the front door and hurried down the steps into the darkness. Cold night wind slashed at him as he approached the parking lot. His little commute ship was parked with hundreds of others; a quarter sent the attendant robot obediently after it.

In ten minutes he was on his way to Ganymede.

The fasrad boarded his ship when he stopped at Mars to refuel.

"Apparently you don't understand," the fasrad said. "My instructions are to demonstrate myself until you're satisfied. As yet, you're not wholly convinced; further demonstration is necessary." It passed an intricate web over the controls of the ship until all the dials and meters were in adjustment. "You should have more frequent servicing."

It retired to the rear to examine the drive jets. Morris numbly signalled the attendant, and the ship was released from the fuel pumps. He gained speed and the small sandy planet fell behind. Ahead, Jupiter loomed.

"Your jets aren't in good repair," the fasrad said, emerging from the rear. "I don't like that knock to the main brake drive. As soon as you land I'll make extensive repair."

"The Company doesn't mind your doing favors for me?" Morris asked, with bitter sarcasm.

"The Company considers me your fasrad. An invoice will be mailed to you at the end of the month." The robot whipped out a pen and a pad of forms. "I'll explain the four easy-payment plans. Ten thousand gold units cash means a three per cent discount. In addition, a number of household items may be traded in—items you won't have further need for. If you wish to divide the purchase in four parts, the first is due at once, and the last in ninety days."

"I always pay cash," Morris muttered. He was carefully resetting the route positions on the control board.

"There's no carrying charge for the ninety day plan. For the six month plan there's a six per cent annum charge which will amount to approximately—" It broke off. "We've changed course."

"That's right."

"We've left the official traffic lane." The fasrad stuck its pen and pad away and hurried to the control board. "What are you doing? There's a two unit fine for this."

Morris ignored it. He hung on grimly to the controls and kept his eyes on the viewscreen. The ship was gaining speed rapidly. Warning buoys sounded angrily as he shot past them and into the bleak darkness of space beyond. In a few seconds they had left all traffic behind. They were alone, shooting rapidly away from Jupiter, out into deep space.

The fasrad computed the trajectory. "We're moving out of the solar system. Toward Centaurus."

"You guessed it."

"Hadn't you better call your wife?"

Morris grunted and notched the drive bar farther up. The ship bucked and pitched, then managed to right itself. The jets began to whine ominously. Indicators showed the main turbines were beginning to heat. He ignored them and threw on the emergency fuel supply.

"I'll call Mrs. Morris," the fasrad offered. "We'll be beyond range in a short while."

"Don't bother."

"She'll worry." The fasrad hurried to the back and examined the jets again. It popped back into the cabin buzzing with alarm. "Mr. Morris, this ship is not equipped for inter-system travel. It's a Class D four-shaft domestic model for home consumption only. It was never made to stand this velocity."

"To get to Proxima," Morris answered, "we need this velocity."

The fasrad connected its power cables to the control board. "I can take some of the strain off the wiring system. But unless you rev her back to normal I can't be responsible for the deterioration of the jets."

"The hell with the jets."

The fasrad was silent. It was listening intently to the growing whine under them. The whole ship shuddered violently. Bits of paint drifted down. The floor was hot from the grinding shafts. Morris' foot stayed on the throttle. The ship gained more velocity as Sol fell behind. They were out of the charted area. Sol receded rapidly.

"It's too late to vid your wife," the fasrad said. "There are three emergency-rockets in the stern; if you want, I'll fire them off in the hope of attracting a passing military transport."

"Why?"

"They can take us in tow and return us to the Sol system. There's a six hundred gold unit fine, but under the circumstances it seems to me the best policy."

Morris turned his back to the fasrad and jammed down the throttle with all his weight. The whine had grown to a violent roar. Instruments smashed and cracked. Fuses blew up and down the board. The lights dimmed, faded, then reluctantly came back.

"Mr. Morris," the fasrad said, "you must prepare for death. The statistical probabilities of turbine explosion are seventy-thirty. I'll do what I can, but the danger-point has already passed."

Morris returned to the viewscreen. For a time he gazed hungrily up at the growing dot that was the twin star Centaurus. "They look all right, don't they? Prox is the important one. Twenty planets." He examined the wildly fluttering instruments. "How are the jets holding up? I can't tell from these; most of them are burned out."

The fasrad hesitated. It started to speak, then changed his mind. "I'll go back and examine them," it said. It moved to the rear of the ship and disappeared down the short ramp into the thundering, vibrating engine chamber.

Morris leaned over and put out his cigarette. He waited a moment longer, then reached out and yanked the drives full up, the last possible notch on the board.

The explosion tore the ship in half. Sections of hull hurtled around him. He was lifted weightless and slammed into the control board. Metal and plastic rained down on him. Flashing incandescent points winked, faded, and finally died into silence, and there was nothing but cold ash.

The dull *swish-swish* of emergency air-pumps brought consciousness back. He was pinned under the wreckage of the control board; one arm was broken and bent under him. He tried to move his legs but there was no sensation below his waist.

The splintered debris that had been his ship was still hurling toward Centaurus. Hull-sealing equipment was feebly trying to patch the gaping holes. Automatic temperature and gray feeds were thumping spasmodically from self-contained batteries. In the viewscreen the vast flaming bulk of the twin suns grew quietly, inexorably.

He was glad. In the silence of the ruined ship he lay buried beneath the debris, gratefully watching the growing bulk. It was a beautiful sight. He had wanted to see it for a long time. There it was, coming closer each moment. In a day or two the ship would plunge into the fiery mass and be consumed. But he could enjoy this interval; there was nothing to disturb his happiness.

He thought about Sally, sound asleep under the radiant-lens. Would Sally have liked Proxima? Probably not. Probably she would have wanted to go back home as soon as possible. This was something he had to enjoy alone. This was for him only. A vast peace descended over him. He could lie here without stirring, and the flaming magnificence would come nearer and nearer . . .

A sound. From the heaps of fused wreckage something was rising. A twisted, dented shape dimly visible in the flickering glare of the viewscreen. Morris managed to turn his head.

The fasrad staggered to a standing position. Most of its trunk was gone, smashed and broken away. It tottered, then pitched forward on its face with a grinding crash. Slowly it inched its way toward him, then settled to a dismal halt a few feet off. Gears whirred creakily. Relays popped open and shut. Vague, aimless life animated its devastated hulk.

"Good evening," its shrill, metallic voice grated.

Morris screamed. He tried to move his body but the ruined beams held him tight. He shrieked and shouted and tried to crawl away from it. He spat and wailed and wept.

"I would like to show you a fasrad," the metallic voice continued. "Would you call your wife, please? I would like to show her a fasrad, too."

"Get away!" Morris screamed. "Get away from me!"

"Good evening," the fasrad continued, like a broken tape. "Good evening. Please be seated. I am happy to meet you. What is your name? Thank you. You are the first persons in your neighborhood to see the fasrad. Where are you employed?"

Its dead eye-lenses gaped at him empty and vacant.

"Please be seated," it said again. "This will take only a second. Only a second. This demonstration will take only a—"

Michael Dorris

Jeopardy

The backseat and floor of my blue '89 Buick LeSabre are awash in industry pamphlets and reprints, the mess a result of my stopping too quickly at too many red lights. Next to me on the passenger side slumps a trash bag full of empty Hardee's and Burger King wrappings, their contents consumed on the fly. I have this idea to recycle–inspired by a panicky talk show I tuned in on the long drive from Billings to Bozeman–but all that happens is greater accumulation. That's the sum of good intentions.

On this Friday morning at the end of a long week my schedule puts me into Kalispell, a spic-and-span town at the northwest tip of Nowhere, Montana, beautiful to look at but cold, and I don't mean only climate-cold, either. All the docs are clustered in two or three professional buildings, cement-block forts with Muzak and back issues of *People* in waiting rooms guarded by blond, Charlie's Angels–haired women. I check my list: my first stop is Dee Dee, about whom I have noted in the margin: "Kid with allergy. Likes Dairy Queen blizzard (tropical?). 6."

The "6" refers to the minutes of chitchat it usually takes to admit me to the inner sanctum. I get paid by the number of scrips–physician signatures acknowledging our conversations–that I collect, not by time spent or volume of orders. It all boils down to human contact, though the verbal conversation is pretty much one way, me to her, with her replies made in eyebrows, sighs, shrugs, and head movements.

"Lots of pollen around, huh? Hey, maybe your little boy . . . That's not him in the frame on your desk? I can't believe how he's grown. No. . . . Maybe he could try this new inhaler. It's a miracle worker. Just remember, you don't know where you got it, right, because I could get in major trouble and it's just because we're friends, you know, and I had allergies myself as a kid. Sure I do. Three puffs a day this time of year, and not a wheeze. Don't mention it, I just hope it helps him, because that's what counts, that's why I'm in this business, to help people. And if you could just get me in to see the physician for five minutes, max, I want to tell him about this product, not yet commercially available–amazing stuff, really, the cutting edge. I'm positive he'd want to know about it direct, not hear it from his competition or from a patient who had read about it in *Time* or somewhere. Well, not yet, but they've assigned a science reporter. I'll just sit over here and straighten out my schedule–I've got more appointments than I can handle and I just wish all of them were . . . No, whenever, no problem, no hurry. Forget I'm here, but if he has three minutes, I'll be quick. Cross my heart. So . . . hey, are you still using that old pen from my last visit? That's kind of sentimental. I'm touched. But let me give you a new one. Take one for your son too. Good, two. Kids lose things. Tell me about it."

I check my watch. Six minutes flat.

And then I sit, not watching Dee Dee not watch me, and read an article about John Travolta's happy marriage. Every once in a while I make a point of catching Dee Dee's eye, and salute. Meanwhile she waves in a procession of strep throats and backaches, varicose veins and odd pains in the chest. I make a game of guessing the ailment as well as the amount of consult time by focusing on the mouths: indignant-grim versus scared-grim, ready-to-be-mad versus ready-to-cry. I'm the only cheerful presence–besides Dee Dee's hair–in the room, the only healthy delegate in a convention of germs. Still, inside an hour, I'm out the front door with three signatures.

Next on the list comes Lisa, the mother type. She presides over a whole clinic of potential scrip-signers, all stacked neatly behind a single swinging half-door. Ducks in a row, fish in a barrel. Those docs are so overworked with Medicaids that they're glad for the diversion, actually ask questions about the product to keep me talking. They see my face and head for Mr. Coffee like kids who'd rather play at cleaning their rooms than do their homework, or people so bored that they sit around their houses waiting for Jehovah's Witnesses to drop by. The answer to a rep's prayer. With them it isn't getting your toe in the door, it's escaping before dark, not a dilemma I often encounter and not one I'm complaining about either.

Sympathy's the key to Lisa's lock, as it is with a lot of them. You open your heart wide enough, she presses the buzzer under her desk and it's Hello Sesame. The challenge is keeping the story straight. What sad tale did I use last time? Which detail made her pupils tighten, her neck muscles tense to attention? With the pity freaks my life has to be soap opera, and believe me, these women have a memory. Lisa almost trips me up halfway through today's installment of My Unfair Divorce.

"I thought you said you'd been happily married for four years before you got the boot," she challenges, her face balled up into a loose fist. "Now, suddenly, it's three."

Call her Perry Mason.

"Well, it's both, I guess." I'm thinking fast. "See, I don't like to admit it but we lived together for a year before we actually tied the knot." This is a calculation on my part, a hope that Lisa, the romantic, will forgive shacking up more than she will gross exaggeration.

She shakes her head in a disapproval that's more interested than serious. "They do that now."

I nod, sharing her despair at the decline of morals. "*Her* idea," I confess, seizing sudden inspiration and running with it. "I'm the old-fashioned type."

I hold up my left hand to show I still wear a ring, even separated. I let that band of gold speak volumes about the kind of guy I am.

Lisa's eyes approve, though I notice that her ring finger's bare. In unrequited love with one of the docs is my bet, one of those men whose wives don't understand the pressures of the medical profession, Lisa's specialty.

"What did you say her name was?"

Great. A test. I flip through my mental Rolodex. Betsy? Maria? Luanne? How did I read Lisa the first time? Not ethnic, certainly, so Maria's out, but am I married up or down? Am I left for a rich boy or for a bum?

"Betsy?" I venture. Betsy the bitch whose father had opposed our marriage because I wasn't good enough for her. Betsy, who even now, while I'm out trying to make an honest dollar, is probably sipping a gin and tonic at the country club with the pro after her tennis lesson.

"That's right," Lisa recalls. Bingo. "Well, you hang in there, honey. One of these days you're going to meet a girl who'll appreciate you. I promise."

Right, I think, and then what? How many visits of happily ever after before you get bored? No way. So I sigh, sorry for myself but brave, uncomplaining.

"I'm staying with my dad now," I add for good measure. You can't beat the truth for authentic details. "He's been kind of low since he was laid off his job. Watches 'Jeopardy' three times a day on the satellite dish, even tapes it."

Lisa nods. I'm a good son, too. There's no end to my virtue.

"I know they're looking forward to seeing you." She gestures toward the examining rooms with her chin, trying to cheer me up. "It won't be long. I'll arrange it so they're all free at the same time. Why should *you* have to wait?"

The end of the day I reserve for Patt. She's not bad-looking in a kind of white starched way. I could imagine her taking off her glasses, shaking out her hair, unlacing her shoes. We have this flirt thing going, the game being that I'm chasing and she's holding me at bay, just barely. One of these days, if I don't watch out, she'll decide to take me up on dinner, whatever.

"So, is the divorce final?" she wants to know first thing, giving me a wink. "No more Maria?" Her fingers caress the sample box of lavender bath beads, the exact size and shape of Som-U-Rest, the sleeping pill I represent on the side.

"Maria who?" With Patt I sort of sit on the edge of her desk, my thigh brushing the telephone so she has to consciously avoid touching me if a call comes in.

"Then why still the ring? You carrying a torch?"

I look at my finger. Damn. "Can I be honest?"

That snags her. It's almost too easy.

"See, in my profession I meet a lot of women, some of them lonely."

Patt could imagine.

"Well, you understand, a man on the road. Some might think I'm looking for a one-night stand, which I'm not, but all those jokes about traveling salesmen? It's a, you know, occupational stereotype."

Patt snorts, warning me I am pushing this maybe too far.

"I can read your mind," I inform her. "You think because I kid around with you I do it with everybody, right? That I come on to all the women I meet?"

"Well . . . ?" Patt sees the trap, but plows ahead anyway.

I close my eyes, open them, then speak slowly, as though revealing something that isn't easy to admit. "Truth, okay? The ring's protection. It says, 'Sorry, taken,' which avoids misunderstanding. Hey, listen to me. Now you'll think I spill my life story to everybody. It isn't even that interesting."

"No," Patt automatically objects. "No, it is, really."

"Don't be nice, all right? It's just with you I feel I can be . . . what? Myself?"

She doesn't move, expecting me to go on. Instead I let the silence grow, wait her out. Finally she reaches over, touches my hand where it rests on my leg.

"I told you, don't be nice."

"I'm not being nice," Patt says. "I hear you, is all."

A woman and her little boy come through the door from the examining rooms. Patt and I both sit up straighter, as though caught in the act.

"He says to squeeze us in next Tuesday," the woman tells Patt, who searches the book for a free fifteen minutes.

"Tuesday he's solid."

"He *said,*" the woman insists.

"I'll have to do some shuffling." Patt's not a bit pleased with the physician's disregard for her careful appointment keeping. She looks up at me, Mr. Reasonable, not asking for a thing of her that's hard. "Why don't you run in while I make a couple of calls," she suggests, and glances at the clock. "Maybe we can continue this conversation later. If you're free."

I give her a look like, are you kidding?

Of course by the time I come out, my samples bag a little lighter, Patt has remembered an engagement she can't get out of. I grab my shirt, try to hold my breaking heart in one piece, but the fact is I'm relieved at the prospect of a quiet night at the Outlaw Inn, writing up my report, filing my receipts. After a day of smiling, being whoever people need me to be, I'm ready to grab a bite, call Dad, do some work, then crash in front of the in-room HBO.

The Outlaw is big, two indoor pools big, with an instant-cash machine in the lobby, the accommodations of choice for Salt Lake City–based Delta crews on a layover and for businessmen like myself, even though it does come on a bit strong. Each building has a theme—the roundup, Indians, bank robberies, what have you—that leaks from the halls into the individual guest rooms, and the restaurant menu features "a taste of Montana," which means huckleberries dumped into everything from breast of chicken to Irish coffee.

First thing after check-in, I try Dad to see how he's making out. He and I have become one of those can't live with him/can't live without him relationships after batching it together for a year. I let the phone go five rings before I bag it and head for the lounge. Probably he stayed late at the library, boning up for the next "Jeopardy" open-call contestants' competition. I figure a couple or three B & B's have my name on them after the day I've put in.

The Branding Iron is Friday-full. I stand in the entrance and let my eyes adjust to the smoky light while I check for a familiar face. You do this job long enough and you meet people, on the road like yourself. Sure enough, sitting alone in a booth there's Jim Dohene, a rep for a medical supplies concern out of Denver.

As I head across the room, I inventory what facts I've stored about his life: married, no kids; about thirty-five thousand dollars a year; drives an Olds; not too bad in the sack.

The last time I saw him was Spokane a year ago. We both had a few drinks and started trading war stories, tales only a fellow rep would understand the full significance of, and over the course of an hour or two, each of us taking turns standing another round, we built what I can only call a sense of trust between us. Then, one thing led to another, as it sometimes will do.

On the road, trust makes or breaks you. You have to know the odds when you hear a lead about a doc or a secretary, because it can backfire in a major way. Somebody might say: "Take the aggressive tack with that one. She folds like an accordion." Or, "Be sure to call him by his first name. He hates that formal crap." If the advice is accurate, it's time-saving, important to know. It could be three, four personal visits before you psyched it out for yourself. But if it's a curve ball, if she says, "Fuck you, buddy" when you get pushy, or he goes, "I spent eight years and a hundred thousand bucks to be addressed as *doctor* except by my closest friends," it's damage that can't easily be repaired.

Jim, I recall as I squeeze his shoulder, waking him up from wherever his mind has wandered, is okay. He clued me that Kathi in Missoula was a sucker for chocolate, and my next swing through Montana I scored three scrips in thirty minutes.

"What's happening, stranger?" I say in greeting. "Still raking it in with that new line of double-carbon prescription forms?"

"God, the word gets out." Jim pats my hand, good sign number one. "Such as you left a trail of artificially mellow desk clerks in Great Falls last time you passed through. What do you use, a stun gun?"

"That isn't what she called it this afternoon." I make a face, thinking of Patt. "But what can I say? Some products sell themselves." I drop into the seat opposite and blow a kiss to the waitress to get her attention.

"I guess that's why you're here alone."

"Doesn't mean I have to leave that way." I raise my shoulders, hold up my palms, and provide him an easy out if he wants it. "And anyway, they never stay the night. I guess the husband would catch on."

"In your dreams. What's that new pill you're dealing got in it, anyway?"

We small talk like that back and forth, ironing out the kinks, giving us each time. Jim gets to the tape before me.

"So," he asks, pairing up two significant facts of my life at the same moment. "You still unattached, and how's your dad doing?"

I give him credit. No wonder he pulls in the bucks.

"Sorry to say, and okay, considering," I answer.

Jim shakes his head, understanding.

"I just tried to call him, but no answer," I continue, deciding to tackle the second point first. This early in the evening there's no need to rush if we both want to go there. "Probably out on the town."

"Party animal." Jim nods, raises his margarita. "Must run in the family."

Number two. I take his meaning, clink glasses. "So, been through Spokane lately?"

Jim pauses his drink in midair, cocks his head as if searching his memory banks, then puts his glass to his lips and takes a deep swallow.

"Spokane, Spokane, Spokane?" He gives his I've-just-made-a-sale smile. "I can't remember the last good night's sleep I had in that town."

"You can't, huh?"

"Let's see. Wait a minute, wait a minute, it's coming back to me, kind of in a hangover haze. The Sheraton, right?"

Beneath the table our knees bump. I signal the waitress. "Mine," I tell Jim. "I've got some catch-up to play."

He settles back into his seat. Now that we both know where we're headed, we can relax.

"So, your dad . . ."

"I'm not going to kid you. He's obsessed. I tried to get him on Prozac, but no. He'd rather follow his dream to land a spot on a quiz program, to show the world how smart he is."

"He needs to get out, meet people," Jim says. "Have some fun."

"Life's too short not to," I agree, and lay a ten down on the table to wait for our drinks. "You grab the opportunity when it presents itself or it passes you standing still."

Jim nods. He buys that theory one hundred percent and is ready and able to prove it.

"Which building they put you in?" I ask. "You a cowboy tonight?"

"Everybody's a cowboy in Montana after the sun goes down. It's a state of mind. You eat yet or what?"

I glance at my watch and see it's only eight-thirty. Too early to head upstairs, and we're both still way too sober anyhow. "Well, I had this hot date," I say. "But we must have got our signals crossed."

Jim pushes the menu in my direction. "I'd recommend the trout. It was fresh . . . once. So who did you see today?"

"I started with Dee Dee."

"Her kid's nose still a faucet?"

Later in the dark, kept awake by Jim's snores, I punch in Dad's number by touch, counting each of the little buttons and hoping I don't make a mistake and wake up a stranger in the middle of the night. I don't plan to talk when he answers, just hear his "Hello" to make sure he made it home all right, and then hang up. I let the damn thing ring a long time. Maybe he unplugged the phone, got absentminded, and left it that way. Maybe he covered it with a pillow and is sleeping too soundly. Maybe he stashed it in the refrigerator again.

Dad lets the details slide. An idea man, he calls himself, always one step ahead, but in fact he usually has too many plans going at once.

"I should have been an architect," he informs me the night before I left. We're sitting on the couch, naturally watching his "Jeopardy," his steady beat since he was force-retired from the TV station.

"You don't have the patience," I tell him. The woman in the middle is beating the two-time champ. She's on a roll, marching down World Georgraphy toward the $1,000 square. Alex Trebek smiles as she buzzes in again.

"I love that blueprint paper," Dad says. His eyes stay fixed on the screen, ready. "All you need is a ruler and the right kind of eraser. Supplies you can carry in your back pocket, stuff you can work with out of your own home."

The Daily Double is under the $600 and the woman goes for broke, her whole stash of $3,100. She's nervous and eager, like a person high above a pool on a springboard, thinking out a half-gainer. The answer box swings around: "Belgian Congo."

"What is Zaire?" Dad shouts.

The woman licks her upper lip, juggling countries. The other two contestants are rooting against her.

"You just have to learn the symbols," Dad continues on his other track. "Windows, closets. The doors are drawn half-open to show the direction of their swing. You can mock in the landscaping, everything. You're your own boss. All that matters is your imagination, and that gets better and better with experience."

"Zaire," the woman announces at last, pleased with her memory. When there's no applause from the studio audience she looks unsure. "It *is* Zaire," she insists hopelessly. Alex shakes his head. He's sorry.

"In Double Jeopardy the answer has to be in the form of a question," he reminds her. The woman's money screen blips. Wipeout.

"A pool is nothing," Dad says. "Four lines at right angles."

"Who's this house for, anyway?" I ask him.

"Not my grandchildren, that's for damn sure."

I tense up, ready to go another round, but this time he only winks at me, nods toward the hallway. "Thirsty?"

"I could."

"Get me one too, while you're up." He's tricky.

I push myself out of my chair, go to the kitchen, open the refrigerator. Meanwhile I hear Dad switch channels to the station, Channel 7, that let him go. He does that from time to time, hoping to see snow, but when I come back into the living room empty-handed, everything on-screen appears normal, except there's no sound, thanks to the mute button. Ed Finley, about whom Dad has some strong negative emotions, is standing in front of a weather map pointing to a red lightning bolt in the vicinity of Ohio and working his mouth, talking and smiling, his little pig eyes as desperate as ever.

"We're all out of beer but the phone was in there."

"They could get a trained seal to do that." Dad points his thumb toward Ed. "Hold a stick in its mouth, clap with its flippers. Did I tell you how much take-home he gets?"

Ed Finley was not in Dad's corner when it counted, despite their long professional association on opposite sides of the #2 camera. Now, as I watch, the weatherman opens a large umbrella decorated with happy faces, meaning rain tomorrow.

"The telephone?" I ask.

Dad sighs, switches back to "Jeopardy," now in the last write-down question phase.

"It got on my nerves," Dad says, irritated. "I let it cool off."

The topic is the U.S. Presidency and the answer is Harry Truman's vice president. The three contestants screw up their faces, chew on their magic pencils, wait for inspiration. Finally, as the theme music winds down, they each scribble on the pads in front of them, but without conviction. You can tell the Zaire woman has done it again, bet over her head.

"Who is Alben W. Barkley?" Dad yells at the TV. "I win."

One after another the contestants come up with zero, except for the woman. She learned her lesson after all and has held back a dollar, and that gets her a ticket to tomorrow's show. The way she crows you'd think she's won the Publishers Clearing House sweepstakes instead of guessing Al Smith and losing $1,600.

* * *

I wake up alone in my bed still wearing my half-buttoned shirt. The TV is on, sun is pouring through the space where the blinds don't quite meet, and a line of light shows under the bathroom door. I listen for the sound of the shower.

"You in there?" I call. No answer. The room feels empty, though I have no recollection of Jim leaving. I have some difficulty even remembering what we got into last night.

I roll onto my stomach, reach for the phone, and dial Dad. The digital clock reads seven-twelve. After ten rings I give up and stare at the receiver as if it can tell me where the fuck he is. "I should call somebody." I must say this aloud, because I hear my own advice. I try to think of logical explanations: the lines are down, he's brushing his teeth, I forgot to use the correct area code. I dial his number again, listen to the ring while I get out of bed, dig my address book out of my case, and look up Dad's neighbor, Mrs. Kelsey.

"I'm overreacting," I explain when I tell her why I'm calling, "but if you could just check?"

"The newspaper was on his porch last night," she whispers, ominously proven right in her suspicions. "Still folded."

"I'll hang on," I tell her. "I'll wait while you go knock."

It's almost ten o'clock by the time I get done talking with the ambulance and the coroner and a funeral home whose name popped into my head. There's nothing left for me to do before I head back to Tacoma except report in to the district manager and have her cancel the rest of my appointments.

When I've finished all the business, I suddenly can't catch my breath. A panic rises in me, steady as water running into a tub, and I think I'm going to pass out. Somehow this is a familiar feeling—asthma, my chest squeezing shut. It comes back to me: I'd wake up like this and Dad would appear next to my bed with a brown grocery bag. He'd bunch it around a small opening and make me breathe into it while he counted. One, two, three, four, four and a half, five. By the time I got to ten I was back in control.

I look around the room and all I can find is a plastic laundry sack in a bureau drawer. It will have to do. I gather the opening into a tunnel, blow inside until my lungs are empty, hold them that way, then draw in slowly. Again. I see the sides of the bag move, expand and contract with the force of my oxygen. I don't know how many times I do this, but when I stop I don't need the bag anymore, and I have an idea.

I ask the motel operator for Jim's room.

"I'm sorry, sir. Mr. Dohene checked out a little over two hours ago."

I imagine Jim all brushed and neat. He's nobody I think of from one month to the next, so why can't I let it go? If we run into each other again and we're both free and in the mood, fine. If not, no biggie. Still, I call his company in Denver, pretend I'm a relative who needs to know his schedule.

"Is this a medical emergency or a personal matter?" the receptionist inquires, following procedure before releasing information. She might have to explain her reasons to Jim or to her boss and is covering her ass.

"A death," I say. For some reason I use my salesman's voice, the one that gets me through the door to the inner offices, the one they can't resist.

"Just one moment, please."

She smells a practical joke or worse, another rep trying to beat her guy to an appointment. She'll bump the call up the line to someone used to saying "no." I can tell the truth, some part of it. Jim and I are old friends who had dinner, a few drinks. Fast-forward through the part about wearing each other out all night and get to the punch line: I just heard that my dad passed away six hundred miles from here and I don't want to be alone, okay?

While I wait, listening to the piped music playing over the receiver in between recorded commercials for the company's products, mentally rehearsing my story, I glance around the room. Towels everywhere, my shorts still where Jim tossed them behind the chair, the ice bucket full of water, my sample case open on the floor.

"Screw it," I say into the phone. If I need comfort, I'll prescribe it for myself. I reach for my appointment book and dial Patt's office before I remember that today's Saturday. What's her last name? Higgins? No, that's Lisa. Jones, Smith, Robinson. Peters! Double T double P is how I've stored it in my memory. I locate the Kalispell directory and scroll down the possibilities. No Patt or P, but wait, there is: Bob and Patt, on Seventh Street South. Bob?

I recognize her voice right off when she finally answers.

"Guess who?" I say. "Just wondering if your previous engagement is out of the way."

There's a long pause and for a minute I think she doesn't place me. "It's Don," I remind her. "From yesterday."

"Hi, *Sally,*" Patt answers, bearing down on the name. "Hey, I can't talk now. Bob and I are in the middle of something, if you know what I mean."

"How about later? Just to, you know, talk?"

"Mmmm. That's too bad. Can I call you back, like on *Monday* or something?"

"I'm only in town today, but I could wait around for you."

"Great. Talk to you after the weekend."

"You don't even know where I'm staying. I'm—"

"Sally, I've really got to run. Say hello to Rick."

Dial tone. Okay. I turn to Higgins, and there she is, Lisa. No disguise. I imagine her reaction to my news, all sympathy and concern. She'll want me to come to dinner, probably, and maybe I'll take her up on it. I don't have to be in Tacoma until tomorrow.

"Lisa, it's Don Banta." I identify myself right off.

"Who?"

"Don. We talked at your office? I used to be married to Betsy?" I'm proud of myself for recalling this detail with no prompting.

"Who?"

"I'm a drug rep."

"Oh. Right, right. The one who lives with his father. I'm sorry. At the end of the week I leave the office at the office. What can I do for you?"

"Well, I was hoping you were free. For lunch? There's something I want your advice about."

"My advice?"

"I don't want to go into it over the phone."

"That sounds mysterious, but it won't work out for today. I'm running my kids to ten things at once: piano, gymnastics, skating, a birthday party."

Kids. "I assumed you were single."

"Only in my prayers. But really, if you want to tell me what you need, maybe there's something–*Teresa, give that to her!* This place is a zoo."

"No, that's great. You're busy. I'll catch you the next time through."

"Okay, if you're sure. Bye-bye."

That leaves only Dee Dee, and her line's busy. While I wait to try again I can't keep my mind off Dad. He drives me nuts. He gets these projects started and then drops them when he loses interest. Sometimes I don't even know until afterwards, and then by accident, like when I was walking down a side street downtown one early evening on my way to scope out a new bar, Aunt Fred's, and what do I see in a storefront window? A polished headstone, a life-size example of what can be ordered from a mason, according to the sign, for under a thousand dollars. It rests on a nest of black velvet, and is elevated so that the inscription catches the eye.

CHARLES WILLIAM BANTA
At Rest
1919–1986

"Can I help you?" the clerk asks when I walk through the door. He's no more than twenty-five, Italian good-looking, dark eyes, and far enough away from death to sell it with a clear conscience. I circle the slab of granite.

"A fine piece of work," he encourages. His voice is deeper than you'd expect.

Either the name or the dates alone could be a coincidence, but both?

"Johnny," the young man identifies himself and holds out his hand for me to shake.

"Johnny," I say. "Charlie Banta is my dad."

Johnny, still grinning, tries to place the name. I nod toward the stone and watch him read.

"Oh, shit."

"Johnny, I've got to ask you: what's going on?"

He looks around for another customer, glances over at the phone to make sure it isn't ringing.

"I didn't do the sale," he says at last. "It happened before I started working here."

"But you know the story."

"I heard about it. This older guy—I mean, your father—comes in one day and orders a stone, for himself he claims. Wants top of the line, the best engraving. Makes a down payment of two hundred dollars, so the owner—Curtis?—goes ahead and places the order. It comes back a month later, we call the . . . your dad . . . and he says he's changed his mind. Curtis was totally pissed. Talked about small-claims court but it was too much of a hassle. So for revenge he sends the rock back to have the year of death carved in, then sticks it in the window. Sick, huh?"

It was Dad all over.

"Do you, does he, live in the neighborhood? I guess he'd be pretty upset to see it, but it's been here all this time, at least a year, and—"

"He hasn't seen it, and if he did, he'd laugh or want a commission for the use of his name," I say. Johnny in his embarrassment has developed a great blush, which makes him look even better. "And me, I'm on my way over to a place I heard about. Aunt Fred's?"

Johnny gives a half-smile, relieved and something more.

"I guess it's cool if you're still into disco."

"Not necessarily."

Dee Dee must have just gotten off the phone because she's there on the first ring.

"Doctor Anderson?"

"It's Don Banta," I tell her. "I represent Allied Pharmaceuticals."

"You're the one who gave me that sample for Jeremy."

I figure Jeremy must be the kid in the photo on her desk.

"The same."

"Amazing."

"What is amazing?"

"Mr. Banta, you may very well have saved my son's life this morning."

I had been leaning back against the pillows, but sit up straight at this announcement.

"He had an attack about four, the worst one ever. I used his old prescription, I patted his chest, but nothing helped. Finally I called 911 but while I was waiting for the ambulance his lips started to go blue and suddenly I remembered that inhaler and what you called it: a miracle worker. I needed a miracle. It was still in my purse."

"What happened?"

"What happened is it calmed him down." Dee Dee's voice is strained with exhaustion. "I can't believe you're calling me. It's like you knew."

"He's all right now?"

"Mr. Banta, my family owes you a big one. If ever—*if ever*—there's anything . . ."

I close my eyes and I feel the chain of things: Dad to me, me to Dee Dee, Dee Dee to her kid. There's purposes we don't suspect, side paths we don't venture but a few steps down, and yet there's a give-and-take that leads forward, a surprise when we don't even know we need it. For the first time in a while I remember I'm a part of the flow, more than I admit, a river that can best be witnessed from very far away.

"It's like you knew all along," Dee Dee repeats for the lack of anything else to add.

"I . . ." I begin, but then the words stick. My fingers curl tight around the receiver and I stare at my packed suitcase where it waits by the door.

"Are you there?" Dee Dee wants to know. "Hello? Mr. Banta?"

I don't answer, I don't have one thing to say, and after a moment, the line goes dead.

Seymour Epstein

My Brother's Keeper

Almost the very instant Mr. Kent walked into the office, Miriam felt the irritation of his presence. Physically there was nothing disturbing about him. He was of medium height, slight in build, but the smile that hung on his lips had that angle of false ingratiation she particularly despised.

"Mr. Simon, please," he said.

"Do you have an appointment?" Miriam asked.

"No-o. I didn't know that was necessary."

"Mr. Simon usually sees by appointment," Miriam said, untruthfully. Mr. Simon saw, if at all, by whim. She took the card he extended between two fingers. It bore the name of Vincent Kent, and, in the lower left-hand corner, the name of the company. She didn't recognize it.

"Salesman?" she asked.

The smile became even more angular.

"If I could see Mr. Simon, I'd be better able to tell."

Miriam was used to every type of approach: coyness, bluster, charm. She preferred directness. The man who gave his card and announced the purpose of his call had, at least, the benefit of her neutrality.

"What sort of merchandise do you sell?" she asked.

"Well, no merchandise really. I represent a trade journal. This company's trade, I might add."

At that point, Mr. Kent raised his hand and rubbed the knuckle of his forefinger against the side of his nose. It was a violent gesture, done with such force that it left the contacted flesh red. It was obviously something he couldn't control. Miriam dropped her eyes.

"Just a moment," she said. "I'll find out if Mr. Simon can see you."

Mr. Simon, when he read the card, made a clucking noise of disapproval.

"Why do you bother me with such things? You know how busy I am. What is he selling?"

Miriam told him, and Mr. Simon closed his eyes in martyrdom. The world was a circle of time-consuming enemies, and it was precisely for such sorties that he depended upon Miriam.

"Since when . . ."

"All you have to do is say no." Miriam cut him off, a sharp edge in her own voice. She was, besides the receptionist, Mr. Simon's secretary and confidante—one of those work-horse factotums you find in most small businesses. Because of her value, Mr. Simon had come to recognize and respect the well-defined borders of her patience. Asked in a businesslike way (she did not even require the common amenities) there was no labor she would not perform, but Mr. Simon had to take his dramatics elsewhere. She simply wouldn't put up with them.

"O. K.," sighed Mr. Simon. "I'll see"—he picked up the card—"Mr. Kent in a few minutes. That's what I'm here for, I guess. To see salesmen. Tell him to wait."

Miriam walked back to the reception desk. She was more angry with herself than with Mr. Simon or the spastic stranger in the hall. She knew her job too well not to realize that she had been derelict. Dozens like Mr. Kent had been eased out of the place without Mr. Simon ever knowing of their call. If anything, it was that uncontrollable gesture that threw her off guard. It destroyed the man's poise in so sudden a flash that she could not help feeling sorry for him.

(Once she had turned away a salesman in a rather brusque way, and he had answered her rudeness with matching politeness. When he rang for the elevator, she noticed the shining mechanism that substituted for a hand. For days after, she inflicted a penance on herself. She left exposed her wound of remorse, denying it the relief of forgetfulness.)

Mr. Kent was standing where she had left him, hat in hand.

"Mr. Simon will see you in a few minutes," she said. "Please have a seat."

"Thank you."

He didn't move. Miriam glanced up at him. She judged his age to be in the mid-forties. He might have been good-looking once, but now his features were marked with that flabbiness which characterized a long illness or a too sudden loss of weight. Encased in their swollen pouches, his blue eyes retained an expression of pointless humor, such as people adopt when they have no self-assurance. Miriam had the uncomfortable feeling that he knew exactly what had gone on in Mr. Simon's office.

"Salesmen are a nuisance, aren't they?" he said, in a tone of deprecation. His hand flashed again, and the knuckle dug into the side of his nose. He tried to convert the spasm into something ordinary. He lowered his hand slightly and pretended to cough. "Still," he said, "we all have to make a living."

Miriam nodded curtly, not knowing how to react. She wished he would sit down and occupy himself with a magazine. She opened her book of shorthand notes as a cue, but it was lost on Mr. Kent.

"I haven't been selling terribly long," he went on. His lips pursed into a disagreeably coaxing smile. "I have the feeling that you guessed that, Miss . . ."

"Fisher," said Miriam. She began to type, deliberately leaving his question unanswered. A waist-high glass partition separated them and through it, in the upper part of her vision, she watched the blue material of his suit. She waited for it to move out of sight. When it did not, she looked up once again, prepared for cold finality.

He wasn't looking at her. His gaze inclined upward towards something his thoughts had projected, and his slack mouth and squinting eyes gave him the appearance of a man recalling a recent grief. From that angle, Miriam perceived for the first time the debased refinement of his features. Roughly she could sketch in the sort of college he had attended, the background that had lost its cohesion, the assumptions that had withered or fled beyond his grasp. He was no salesman—that was obvious. His presence here was probably one in a series of desperate little moves made in secrecy and killing embarrassment.

Aware of Miriam's appraising look, Mr. Kent blinked and assumed his artificial smile. His hand went once again to his face, but this time it fluttered nervously over mouth and chin and fell away to his side.

"What sort of man is Mr. Simon?" he asked.

"A businessman," Miriam answered, concentrating on the carriage of her machine.

"I see," said Mr. Kent, pleasantly. "I think I know what you mean. The no-nonsense type. Straight to the point. That's my difficulty. I digress. It's my one failing. Perhaps you can tell me how to stick to the point. You must see many salesmen."

Miriam shrugged slightly. The impending interview with Mr. Simon took on the proportions of disaster. She would have liked to take Mr. Kent by the arm and lead him to the elevator. "Take a tip from me," she would say. "Spare yourself the pain. You won't get an order anyway. Good-bye—and forget about being a salesman. Go back to your family in New Haven, or wherever you come from."

"I'm afraid I know very little about sales technique," she said.

Mr. Kent moved closer and rested an elbow on the glass partition. "I'll let you in on a secret," he said. "I'm not a salesman. Not really. When I took the job, I didn't think there'd be much to it. After all, selling is talking, and I do that fairly well. The trouble is that I talk about the wrong things. Or rather, I don't talk about the right things forcefully enough. No conviction, if you know what I mean."

"Then why sell?" Miriam asked.

"Well, I have to," he said. His voice lost its affability. A petulant note crept into it. "What else in the world is there for a man to do who hasn't a trade or profession? Nothing! Quite literally nothing! Believe me, I've tried. Of course, I have friends, but I wouldn't dream of imposing on them. Rather influential people, too. I think you'd recognize them, but I'd rather not mention names." Mr. Kent dropped his arm from the partition and dug that cruel knuckle into his flesh. "I have the reputation of being a drinker," he said. His easy manner returned, and he smiled in an aggravatingly superior way. "You can reform the habit but never the reputation. Which is a bit unfair, don't you agree, Miss . . . ?"

"Fisher," said Miriam. "Why don't you have a seat, Mr. Kent? Read a magazine."

Mr. Kent winked at her. "I'll do that," he said. But as he turned toward the chair, Mr. Simon came out of his office. He stood there, potbellied, sour, his sandy tufts stiff with truculence.

"Mr. Kent," he called, in a flat, uninviting voice.

Mr. Kent paled and fell into the posture of a brave man walking alone to the bullet-riddled wall. Some resource of nerve supported the smile that remained pinned to his lips as he passed Miriam on his way into Mr. Simon's office.

Miriam tried to work, but she could do nothing but wait for the unimaginable sound sure to be produced by so odd a contact. But nothing happened. Their voices seeped out to her with the alternate consistency of enamel and sandpaper, and at the end of ten minutes Mr. Kent emerged, zipping the top of his leather briefcase.

"Thank you, Mr. Simon," he said, shaking hands. "You've been *most* kind. Naturally I don't expect you to make up your mind immediately, but, if I may, I'd like to drop back in a few days."

Mr. Simon nodded with his head, his shoulders, his whole body. He seemed to be saying yes to everything, particularly to Mr. Kent's imminent departure. With one final nod, he ducked back into his office.

Mr. Kent paused at Miriam's desk. "Not bad," he said. "I may have a sale here." He rested his briefcase on the edge of the desk, and both hands on top of the briefcase. He leaned toward Miriam, bringing within range of her senses the spicy-sweet odor of shaving lotion. All his pale features sagged downward in an expression of weary anxiety. "What do you think?" he asked. "I mean, you know Mr. Simon. Is he the sort that says no outright if he means no?"

Miriam made a gesture with her hands and shrugged her shoulders. The well-oiled mechanism of the routine lie was suddenly full of grit. "There's no telling," she said, with a frown.

Mr. Kent nodded, blinked, and again maltreated the side of his nose. An abstract look returned to his eyes.

"Be nice if it came through," he murmured. It was a fiberless wish, uttered without determination or real desire—rather as a child wishes for an impossible toy. He floated off to some mountain peak of vagueness and from that vast distance regarded Miriam.

"Yes," said Miriam, crisply. She felt an urge to snap her fingers before his face and shout, "Hey, wake up!"

Slowly, laboriously, Mr. Kent made his way back.

"Listen," he said, with a quick glance toward Mr. Simon's office, "I've *got* to get an order. I've *got to.* That silly ass of a sales manager will surely get me sacked if I don't come up with something pretty soon. He's already dropped a hint. See if you can't persuade your charming Mr. Simon to place an ad. The whole thing doesn't amount to a hill of beans, but it would mean a great deal to me." His voice dropped to an even lower register. It became almost a whisper. "Frankly," he said, "I'm at my last ditch. In the past year I've run through more jobs than you can shake a stick at. I just wouldn't have the strength to start again if I flubbed this one."

He backed away and concentrated a look of profound reliance on Miriam. They might have been childhood friends, long lovers come at last to the test of their affection. "You can believe this or not," he declared solemnly, "but I haven't had a drink since I took this job. If I get over this hurdle, I'll be all right. If I don't . . ." He made a tight-lipped grimace.

Stunned with this gratuitous load of confidence, Miriam stared at the man as he walked to the elevator and rang. The wildly unexpected can sometimes deprive one of speech, and Miriam sat there mouth agape, as if someone had dashed in and deposited an infant on her desk. The elevator came and with one foot inside Mr. Kent delivered a parting adjuration.

"I'm depending on you," he said, and disappeared.

With the sound of the closing elevator door, Mr. Simon thrust out of his office like a turtle out of its shell. He walked straight to Miriam's desk, his brow wrinkled with vindication and rebuke. He planted himself before Miriam and performed an alarmingly accurate parody of Mr. Kent's knuckle-to-nose reflex. Then, with upthrust arms and eyebrows, he silently called upon Heaven to witness his ordeal. Still wordless and shaking his head, he stumped back to his office.

Miriam flipped over the page of her notebook and stared at the squiggles blankly. A little blaze of fury started up within her, but it quickly subsided and she began to type.

* * *

Mr. Kent's first appearance was on a Tuesday. On Friday of that same week, Miriam came back from lunch to find him sitting in the outer office, thumbing through a magazine. His presence shocked her. She had not exactly dismissed him from her mind, but her intuitive thought was that she had seen the last of him. He was of that type that wanders in every so often, sets the office on its ear, accomplishes nothing, and is never heard from again. Persistence was the last thing she expected from Mr. Kent.

His smile was archly familiar. "I'm told Mr. Simon won't be back until late this afternoon," he said.

"That's right," said Miriam, walking to her desk. "You should have called first."

Mr. Kent got up and followed her to the partition. He performed his little act, and Miriam felt a strong desire to slap his hand.

"Did you get a chance to talk to him?" he asked.

"I?" Miriam stared at him with astonished eyes. "About what?"

"About what!" he echoed, looking instantly aggrieved. "About placing an ad in the trade journal I represent. Surely you remember . . . ?"

Miriam sat down at her desk and gathered the scattered clips into a little heap. She became suddenly conscious of the fact that her shoes hurt dreadfully. She had met her friend Sally for lunch, and they had walked miles looking for something suitable for tropical climates. Sally was to be married in a few weeks. She and her husband were going to Bermuda. The world was a catherine wheel throwing off lovely flames. One must forgive Sally everything these days—even a little thoughtlessness. Miriam had hoped to get back to the assuaging rattle of her typewriter and work off the poison of envy that had dripped into her system. Mr. Kent, with his weird antics and despairing eye, was her mood made flesh. If he vanished that instant, she would never question the benevolent miracle.

"You'd better make it next week sometime," she said.

"Next week!" He ran his hand over his thin, blond hair. "I take it then you didn't even speak to him."

Miriam noticed that a drawer was open. She slammed it shut.

"Where did you ever get the idea that I was supposed to speak to him?" she snapped. Her head was pounding idiotically. "Look here, Mr. Kent, I only work here. I'm not an officer of the company."

"Oh, for God's sake!" he almost whined. "I've been to this kind of office long enough to know the power you gals exert. All I asked you to do was to put in a good word for me. Is that so much? I mean, after all, what kind of world is this anyway where one person won't lift a finger to help another!"

"Well! . . . *Well!*"

Unreasoning rage poured into Miriam from a hundred hidden sluiceways. Everything was swept into the flood. Her shapeless body; her stringy hair; her mother's soft, galling solicitude; the nightly riot of argument and television; that hideous, *hideous* vase in the foyer she would one day smash; the loneliness that pinched at her heart with relentless fingers; the whole pointless mess of living.

"And who are you that I should help you?" Her voice skidded and careened like something headed for a wreck. "Who helps me, I'd like to know? Who do you think you are coming in here and demanding that people should help you? You've got some nerve, that's all I've got to say! *Some damned . . . !*"

And madly, disgracefully, she was weeping. Two large drops fell on a typewritten page, glistened, and were absorbed. Miriam opened the bottom drawer of her desk and pulled out a tissue.

Mr. Kent withdrew deferentially. He examined the cuffs of his trousers; he rubbed his nose; he looked neither surprised nor contrite.

"I'll make it some other time," Miriam heard him say.

Fortunately her little reception room was separate from the rest of her office. The bookkeeper and the extra girl had not witnessed the scene. Miriam went to the washroom after Mr. Kent left and locked herself in for ten minutes. When she came out, she was wearing a little more powder and rouge than was her habit.

Mr. Simon returned to the office about four-thirty. As usual, his hat was on crooked and all his clothes looked dampened and crushed.

"Some letters," he threw at Miriam, in passing. "Five minutes."

She was used to it. Four-thirty to five, the easing-off period—it was anything but that for her. Mr. Simon's scattered senses came into focus at that hour. As he explained to her when she took the job twelve years ago, he didn't like a clock-watcher.

Straightening the things on her desk, Miriam realized with a drop of despair that she would speak about Mr. Kent. She couldn't say who she felt sorry for—herself, him. It was all one. They might inhabit different worlds, the histories of their grief might be written in foreign tongues, but for an instant each had given a cry of pain, and in that was a common shame. She chose the moment before Mr. Simon began his dictation.

"That salesman was in again," she said.

"What salesman?"

"The one who was in Tuesday. You know, the one who kept rubbing his nose."

Mr. Simon laced his fingers behind his head and cracked all his knuckles.

"That's nice," he said. "Did you throw him out?"

"You gave him permission to come back."

"*I* gave him permission! Are you crazy? What would I want that maniac around here for?"

Miriam shrugged. "I don't know. It's possible you were thinking of placing an ad. They tell me it's worthwhile advertising in trade journals."

Mr. Simon looked at her suspiciously. "He isn't a cousin of yours or something, is he?" he asked.

"Does he look like my cousin?"

Mr. Simon gave a deep sigh. "Do you want to get home tonight?" he asked, matter-of-factly. "I've got at least a half a dozen letters to get out tonight. If you want to talk about that nut, I'll telephone for sandwiches and we'll spend a nice evening chatting."

Miriam stared down at the blank page of her book.

"I'm waiting," she said.

Mr. Kent's third and last appearance occurred exactly one week after his first. It was Tuesday, late in the afternoon. The door-latch of the elevator clicked before opening, and Miriam was seized with a sickly premonition. That Mr. Kent should walk out and remove his hat like a well-bred mendicant seemed a proper epilogue of the whole sorry little tale.

"How's Miss Fisher?" he greeted her. The blue, pin-stripe suit he wore was probably the only presentable one he had. He had worn it all three times.

"I spoke to Mr. Simon," she said quickly. "He doesn't feel that we can devote any money to advertising at this time. I'm sorry."

"Ah," said Mr. Kent. His mouth hung open. "Oh."

He returned his hat to his head, settled it neatly, and turned toward the elevators. Midway there he halted and looked toward Miriam. "You and I, Miss Fisher . . ." he began, shaking his head. But he didn't complete his thought. He left it for Miriam to finish in the thousand different ways that conscience might suggest.

The elevator took an eternity to come. Waiting for the sound of the door, it was as though a weight pressed down on her, keeping her head bowed over her machine. And when the elevator did come, and the door opened and shut, Miriam still sat so, with lowered head, as though to look up and see the emptiness in the hall was more than she could bear.

Edna Ferber

from *Roast Beef Medium: The Business Adventures of Emma McChesney*

Simply Skirts

They may differ on the subjects of cigars, samples, hotels, ball teams and pinochle hands, but two things there are upon which they stand united. Every member of that fraternity which is condemned to a hotel bedroom, or a sleeper berth by night, and chained to a sample case by day agrees in this, first: That it isn't what it used to be. Second: If only they could find an opening for a nice, paying gents' furnishing business in a live little town that wasn't swamped with that kind of thing already they'd buy it and settle down like a white man, by George! and quit this peddling. The missus hates it anyhow; and the kids know the iceman better than they do their own dad.

On the morning that Mrs. Emma McChesney (representing T. A. Buck, Featherloom Petticoats) finished her talk with Miss Hattie Stitch, head of Kiser & Bloch's skirt and suit department, she found herself in a rare mood. She hated her job; she loathed her yellow sample cases; she longed to call Miss Stitch a green-eyed cat; and she wished that she had chosen some easy and pleasant way of earning a living, like doing plain and fancy washing and ironing. Emma McChesney had been selling Featherloom Petticoats on the road for almost ten years, and she was famed throughout her territory for her sane sunniness, and her love of her work. Which speaks badly for Miss Hattie Stitch.

Miss Hattie Stitch hated Emma McChesney with all the hate that a flat-chested, thin-haired woman has for one who can wear a large thirty-six without one inch of alteration, and a hat that turns sharply away from the face. For forty-six weeks in the year Miss Stitch existed in Kiser & Bloch's store at River Falls. For six weeks, two in spring, two in fall, and two in mid-winter, Hattie lived in New York, with a capital L. She went there to select the season's newest models (slightly modified for River Falls), but incidentally she took a regular trousseau with her.

All day long Hattie picked skirt and suit models with unerring good taste and business judgment. At night she was a creature transformed. Every house of which Hattie bought did its duty like a soldier and a gentleman. Nightly Hattie powdered her neck and arms, performed sacred rites over her hair and nails, donned a gown so complicated that a hotel maid had to hook her up the back, and was ready for her evening's escort at eight. There wasn't a hat in a grill room from one end of the Crooked Cow-path to the other that was more wildly barbaric than Hattie's, even in these sane and simple days when the bird of paradise has become the national bird. The buyer of suits for a thriving department store in a hustling little Middle-Western town isn't to be neglected. Whenever a show came to River Falls Hattie would look bored, pass a weary hand over her glossy coiffure and say: "Oh, yes. Clever little show. Saw it two winters ago in New York. This won't be the original company, of course." The year that Hattie came back wearing a set of skunk everyone thought it was lynx until Hattie drew attention to what she called the "brown tone" in it. After that Old Lady Heinz got her old skunk furs out of the moth balls and tobacco and newspapers that had preserved them, and her daughter cut them up into bands for the bottom of her skirt, and the cuffs of her coat. When Kiser & Bloch had their fall and spring openings the town came ostensibly to see the new styles, but really to gaze at Hattie in a new confection, undulating up and down the department, talking with a heavy Eastern accent about this or that being "smart" or "good this year," or having "a world of style," and sort of trailing her toes after her to give a clinging, Grecian line, like pictures of Ethel Barrymore when she was thin. The year that Hattie confided to some one that she was wearing only scant bloomers beneath her slinky silk the floor was mobbed, and they had to call in reserves from the basement ladies-and-misses-ready-to-wear.

Miss Stitch came to New York in March. On the evening of her arrival she dined with Fat Ed Meyers, of the Strauss Sans-silk Skirt Company. He informed her that she looked like a kid, and that that was some classy little gown, and it wasn't every woman who could wear that kind of thing and get away with it. It took a certain style. Hattie smiled, and hummed off-key to the tune the orchestra was playing, and Ed told her it was a shame she didn't do something with that voice.

"I have something to tell you," said Hattie. "Just before I left I had a talk with old Kiser. Or rather, he had a talk with me. You know I have pretty much my own way in my department. Pity if I couldn't have. I made it. Well, Kiser wanted to know why I didn't buy Featherlooms. I said we had no call for 'em, and he came back with figures to prove we're losing a good many hundreds a year by not carrying them. He said the Strauss Sans-silk skirt isn't what it used to be. And he's right."

"Oh, say–" objected Ed Meyers.

"It's true," insisted Hattie. "But I couldn't tell him that I didn't buy Featherlooms because McChesney made me tired. Besides, she never entertains me when I'm in New York. Not that I'd go to the theater in the evening with a woman, because I wouldn't, but–Say, listen. Why don't you make a play for her job? As long as I've got to put in a heavy line of Featherlooms you may as well get the benefit of it. You could double your commissions. I'll bet that woman makes her I-don't-know-how-many thousands a year."

Ed Meyers' naturally ruddy complexion took on a richer tone, and he dropped his fork hastily. As he gazed at Miss Stitch his glance was not more than half flattering. "How you women do love each other, don't you! You don't. I don't mind telling you my firm's cutting down its road force, and none of us knows who's going to be beheaded next. But–well–a guy wouldn't want to take a job away from a woman–especially a square little trick like McChesney. Of course she's played me a couple of low-down deals and I promised to get back at her, but that's business. But–"

"So's this," interrupted Miss Hattie Stitch. "And I don't know that she is so square. Let me tell you that I heard she's no better than she might be. I have it on good authority that three weeks ago, at the River House, in our town–"

Their heads came close together over the little, rose-shaded restaurant table.

At eleven o'clock next morning Fat Ed Meyers walked into the office of the T. A. Buck Featherloom Petticoat Company and asked to see old T. A.

"He's in Europe," a stenographer informed him, "spaing, and sprudeling, and badening. Want to see T. A. Junior?"

"T. A. Junior!" almost shouted Ed Meyers. "You don't mean to tell me *that* fellow's taken hold—"

"Believe *me.* That's why Featherlooms are soaring and Sans-silks are sinking. Nobody would have believed it. T. A. Junior's got a live wire looking like a stick of licorice. When they thought old T. A. was going to die, young T. A. seemed to straighten out all of a sudden and take hold. It's about time. He must be almost forty, but he don't show it. I don't know, he ain't so good-looking, but he's got swell eyes."

Ed Meyers turned the knob of the door marked "Private," and entered, smiling. Ed Meyers had a smile so cherubic that involuntarily you armed yourself against it.

"Hel-lo Buck!" he called jovially. "I hear that at last you're taking an interest in skirts—other than on the hoof." And he offered young T. A. a large, dark cigar with a fussy-looking band encircling its middle. Young T. A. looked at it disinterestedly, and spake, saying:

"What are you after?"

"Why, I just dropped in—" began Ed Meyers lamely.

"The dropping," observed T. A. Junior, "is bad around here this morning. I have one little formula for all visitors to-day, regardless of whether they're book agents or skirt salesmen. That is, what can I do for you?"

Ed Meyers tucked his cigar neatly into the extreme right corner of his mouth, pushed his brown derby far back on his head, rested his strangely lean hands on his plump knees, and fixed T. A. Junior with a shrewd blue eye.

"That suits me fine," he agreed. "I never was one to beat around the bush. Look here. I know skirts from the draw-string to the ruffle. It's a woman's garment, but a man's line. There's fifty reasons why a woman can't handle it like a man. For one thing the packing cases weigh twenty-five pounds each, and she's as dependent on a packer and a porter as a baby is on its mother. Another is that if a man has to get up to make a train at 4 A.M. he don't require twenty-five minutes to fasten down three sets of garters, and braid his hair, and hook his waist up the back, and miss his train. And he don't have neuralgic headaches. Then, the head of a skirt department in a store is a woman, ten times out of ten. And lemme tell you," he leaned forward earnestly, "a woman don't like to buy of a woman. Don't ask me why. I'm too modest. But it's the truth."

"Well?" said young T. A., with the rising inflection.

"Well," finished Ed Meyers, "I like your stuff. I think it's great. It's a seller, with the right man to push it. I'd like to handle it. And I'll guarantee I could double the returns from your Middle-Western territory."

T. A. Junior had strangely translucent eyes. Their luminous quality had an odd effect upon any one on whom he happened to turn them. He had been scrawling meaningless curlycues on a piece of paper as Ed Meyers talked. Now he put down the pencil, turned, and looked Ed Meyers fairly in the eye.

"You mean you want Mrs. McChesney's territory?" he asked quietly.

"Well, yes, I do," confessed Ed Meyers, without a blush.

Young T. A. swung back to his desk, tore from the pad before him the piece of paper on which he had been scrawling, crushed it, and tossed it into the wastebasket with an air of finality.

"Take the second elevator down," he said. "The nearest one's out of order."

For a moment Ed Meyers stared, his fat face purpling. "Oh, very well," he said, rising. "I just made you a business proposition, that's all. I thought I was talking to a business man. Now, old T. A.–"

"That'll be about all," observed T. A. Junior, from his desk.

Ed Meyers started toward the door. Then he paused, turned, and came back to his chair. His heavy jaw jutted out threateningly.

"No, it ain't all, either. I didn't want to mention it, and if you'd treated me like a gentleman, I wouldn't have. But I want to say to you that McChesney's giving this firm a black eye. Morals don't figure with a man on the road, but when a woman breaks into this game, she's got to be on the level."

T. A. Junior rose. The blonde stenographer who had made the admiring remark anent his eyes would have appreciated those features now. They glowed luminously into Ed Meyers' pale blue ones until that gentleman dropped his eyelids in confusion. He seemed at a disadvantage in every way, as T. A. Junior's lean, graceful height towered over the fat man's bulk.

"I don't know Mrs. McChesney," said T. A. Junior. "I haven't even seen her in six years. My interest in the business is very recent. I do know that my father swears she's the best salesman he has on the road. Before you go any further I want to tell you that you'll have to prove what you just implied, so definitely, and conclusively, and convincingly that when you finish you'll have an ordinary engineering blue-print looking like a Turner landscape. Begin."

Ed Meyers, still standing, clutched his derby tightly and began.

"She's a looker, Emma is. And smooth! As the top of your desk. But she's getting careless. Now a decent, hard-working, straight girl like Miss Hattie Stitch, of Kiser & Bloch's, River Falls, won't buy of her. You'll find you don't sell that firm. And they buy big, too. Why, last summer I had it from the clerk of the hotel in that town that she ran around all day with a woman named LeHaye–Blanche LeHaye, of an aggregation of bum burlesquers called the Sam Levin Crackerjack Belles. And say, for a whole month there, she had a tough young kid traveling with her that she called her son. Oh, she's queering your line, all right. These days are past when it used to be a signal for a loud, merry laugh if you mentioned you were selling goods on the road. It's a fine art, and a science these days, and the name of T. A. Buck has always stood for–"

Downstairs a trim, well-dressed, attractive woman stepped into the elevator and smiled radiantly upon the elevator man, who had smiled first.

"Hello, Jake," she said. "What's old in New York? I haven't been here in three months. It's good to be back."

"Seems grand t' see you, Mis' McChesney," returned Jake. "Well, nothin' much stirrin'. Whatcha think of the Grand Central? I understand they're going to have a contrivance so you can stand on a mat in the waiting-room and wish yourself down to the track an' train that you're leavin' on. The G'ints have picked a bunch of shines this season. T. A. Junior's got a new sixty-power auto. Genevieve–that yella-headed steno–was married last month to Henry, the shipping clerk. My wife presented me with twin girls Monday. Well, thank *you,* Mrs. McChesney. I guess that'll help some."

Emma McChesney swung down the hall and into the big, bright office. She paused at the head bookkeeper's desk. The head bookkeeper was a woman. Old Man Buck had learned something about the faithfulness of women employees. The head bookkeeper looked up and said some convincing things.

"Thanks," said Emma, in return. "It's mighty good to be here. Is it true that skirts are going to be full in the back? How's business? T. A. in?"

"Young T. A. is. But I think he's busy just now. You know T. A. Senior isn't back yet. He had a tight squeeze, I guess. Everybody's talking about the way young T. A. took hold. You know he spent years running around Europe, and he made a specialty of first nights, and first editions, and French cars when he did show up here. But now! He's changed the advertising, and designing, and cutting departments around here until there's as much difference between this place now and the place it was three months ago as there is between a hoop-skirt and a hobble. He designed one skirt—Here, Miss Kelly! Just go in and get one of those embroidery flounce models for Mrs. McChesney. How's that? Honestly, I'd wear it myself."

Emma McChesney held the garment in her two hands and looked it over critically. Her eyes narrowed thoughtfully. She looked up to reply when the door of T. A. Buck's private office opened, and Ed Meyers walked briskly out. Emma McChesney put down the skirt and crossed the office so that she and he met just in front of the little gate that formed an entrance along the railing.

Ed Meyers' mouth twisted itself into a smile. He put out a welcoming hand.

"Why, hello, stranger! When did you drive in? How's every little thing? I'm darned if you don't grow prettier and younger every day of your sweet life."

"Quit Sans-silks?" inquired Mrs. McChesney briefly.

"Why—no. But I was just telling young T. A. in there that if I could only find a nice, paying little gents' furnishing business in a live little town that wasn't swamped with that kind of thing already I'd buy it, by George! I'm tired of this peddling."

"Sing that," said Emma McChesney. "It might sound better," and marched into the office marked "Private."

T. A. Junior's good-looking back and semibald head were toward her as she entered. She noted, approvingly, woman-fashion, that his neck would never lap over the edge of his collar in the back. Then Young T. A. turned about. He gazed at Emma McChesney, his eyebrows raised inquiringly. Emma McChesney's honest blue eyes, with no translucent nonsense about them, gazed straight back at T. A. Junior.

"I'm Mrs. McChesney. I got in half an hour ago. It's been a good little trip, considering business, and politics, and all that. I'm sorry to hear your father's still ill. He and I always talked over things after my long trip."

Young T. A.'s expert eye did not miss a single point, from the tip of Mrs. McChesney's smart spring hat to the toes of her well-shod feet, with full stops for the fit of her tailored suit, the freshness of her gloves, the clearness of her healthy pink skin, the wave of her soft, bright hair.

"How do you do, Mrs. McChesney," said Young T. A. emphatically. "Please sit down. It's a good idea—this talking over your trip. There are several little things—now Kiser & Bloch, of River Falls, for instance. We ought to be selling them. The head of their skirt and suit department is named Stitch, isn't she? Now, what would you say of Miss Stitch?"

"Say?" repeated Emma McChesney quickly. "As a woman, or a buyer?"

T. A. Junior thought a minute. "As a woman."

Mrs. McChesney thoughtfully regarded the tips of her neatly gloved hands. Then she looked up. "The kindest and gentlest thing I can say about her is that if she'd let her hair grow out gray maybe her face wouldn't look so hard."

T. A. Junior flung himself back in his chair and threw back his head and laughed at the ceiling.

Then, "How old is your son?" with disconcerting suddenness.

"Jock's scandalously near eighteen." In her quick mind Emma McChesney was piecing odds and ends together, and shaping the whole to fit Fat Ed Meyers. A little righteous anger was rising within her.

T. A. Junior searched her face with his glowing eyes.

"Does my father know that you have a young man son? Queer you never mentioned it."

"Queer? Maybe. Also, I don't remember ever having mentioned what church my folks belonged to, or where I was born, or whether I like my steak rare or medium, or what my maiden name was, or the size of my shoes, or whether I take my coffee with or without. That's because I don't believe in dragging private and family affairs into the business relation. I think I ought to tell you that on the way in I met Ed Meyers, of the Strauss Sans-silk Skirt Company, coming out. So anything you say won't surprise me."

"You wouldn't be surprised," asked T. A. Junior smoothly, "if I were to say that I'm considering giving a man your territory?"

Emma McChesney's eyes—those eyes that had seen so much of the world and its ways, and that still could return your gaze so clearly and honestly—widened until they looked so much like those of a hurt child, or a dumb animal that has received a death wound, that young T. A. dropped his gaze in confusion.

Emma McChesney stood up. Her breath came a little quickly. But when she spoke, her voice was low and almost steady.

"If you expect me to beg you for my job, you're mistaken. T. A. Buck's Featherloom Petticoats have been my existence for almost ten years. I've sold Featherlooms six days in the week, and seven when I had a Sunday customer. They've not only been my business and my means of earning a livelihood, they've been my religion, my diversion, my life, my pet pastime. I've lived petticoats, I've talked petticoats, I've sold petticoats, I've dreamed petticoats—why, I've even worn the darned things! And that's more than any man will ever do for you."

Young T. A. rose. He laughed a little laugh of sheer admiration. Admiration shone, too, in those eyes of his which so many women found irresistible. He took a step forward and laid one well-shaped hand on Emma McChesney's arm. She did not shrink, so he let his hand slip down the neat blue serge sleeve until it reached her snugly gloved hand.

"You're all right!" he said. His voice was very low, and there was a new note in it. "Listen, girlie. I've just bought a new sixty-power machine. Have dinner with me to-night, will you? And we'll take a run out in the country somewhere. It's warm, even for March. I'll bring along a fur coat for you. H'm?"

Mrs. McChesney stood thoughtfully regarding the hand that covered her own. The blue of her eyes and the pink of her cheeks were a marvel to behold.

"It's a shame," she began slowly, "that you're not twenty-five years younger, so that your father could give you the licking you deserve when he comes home. I shouldn't be surprised if he'd do it anyway. The Lord preserve me from these quiet, deep devils with temperamental hands and luminous eyes. Give me one of the bull-necked, red-faced, hoarse-voiced, fresh kind every time. You know what they're going to say, at least, and you're prepared for them. If I were to tell you how the hand you're holding is tingling to box your ears you'd marvel that any human being could have that much repression and live. I've heard of this kind of thing, but I didn't know it happened often off the stage and outside of novels. Let's get down to cases. If I let you make love to me, I keep my job. Is that it?"

"Why–no–I–to tell the truth I was only–"

"Don't embarrass yourself. I just want to tell you that before I'd accept your auto ride I'd open a little fancy art goods and needlework store in Menominee, Michigan, and get out the newest things in Hardanger work and Egyptian embroidery. And that's my notion of zero in occupation. Besides, no plain, everyday workingwoman could enjoy herself in your car because her conscience wouldn't let her. She'd be thinking all the time how she was depriving some poor, hard-working chorus girl of her legitimate pastime, and that would spoil everything. The elevator man told me that you had a new motor car, but the news didn't interest me half as much as that of his having new twin girls. Anything with five thousand dollars can have a sixty-power machine, but only an elevator man on eight dollars a week can afford the luxury of twins."

"My dear Mrs. McChesney–"

"Don't," said Emma McChesney sharply. "I couldn't stand much more. I joke, you know, when other women cry. It isn't so wearing."

She turned abruptly and walked toward the door. T. A. Junior overtook her in three long strides, and placed himself directly before her.

"My cue," said Emma McChesney, with a weary brightness, "to say, 'Let me pass, sir!' "

"Please don't," pleaded T. A. Junior. "I'll remember this the rest of my life. I thought I was a statue of modern business methods, but after to-day I'm going to ask the office boy to help me run this thing. If I could only think of some special way to apologize to you–"

"Oh, it's all right," said Emma McChesney indifferently.

"But it isn't! It isn't! You don't understand. That human jellyfish of a Meyers said some things, and I thought I'd be clever and prove them. I can't ask your pardon. There aren't words enough in the language. Why, you're the finest little woman–you're–you'd restore the faith of a cynic who had chronic indigestion. I wish I–Say, let me relieve you of a couple of those small towns that you hate to make, and give you Cleveland and Cincinnati. And let me–Why say, Mrs. McChesney! Please! Don't! This isn't the time to–"

"I can't help it," sobbed Emma McChesney, her two hands before her face. "I'll stop in a minute. There; I'm stopping now. For Heaven's sake, stop patting me on the head!"

"Please don't be so decent to me," entreated T. A. Junior, his fine eyes more luminous than ever. "If only you'd try to get back at me I wouldn't feel so cut up about it."

Emma McChesney looked up at him, a smile shining radiantly through the tears.

"Very well. I'll do it. Just before I came in they showed me that new embroidery flounced model you just designed. Maybe you don't know it, but women wear only one limp petticoat nowadays. And buttoned shoes. The eyelets in that embroidery are just big enough to catch on the top button of a woman's shoe, and tear, and trip her. I ought to have let you make up a couple of million of them, and then watch them come back on your hands. I was going to tell you, anyway, for T. A. Senior's sake. Now I'm doing it for your own."

"For–" began T. A. Junior excitedly. And found himself addressing the backs of the letters on the door marked "Private," as it slammed after the trim, erect figure in blue.

M. F. K. Fisher

The Unswept Emptiness

When the wax-man came around the corner of the house Matey was feeling sorry and alone, and that is why she cried out so warmly, "Why, it's my friend the wax-man!"

"Matey, Matey," her little daughter said, in a dance of excitement, "a visitor for us!" And the three dogs were barking pleasurably, their tails like banners and the bitch too heavy and near her pup-time now to jump, wallowing like a happy tugboat in the wake of all the noise. Matey looked up with a quick smile, and because she was full of sorrow about many things and lonely too, for her husband was far away and she could feel him missing her and the two little girls and the dogs, she cried out, "Why, it's my friend the wax-man!"

She put down the trowel, and rubbed her hands stained with weeds and earth on the sides of her overalls, and as she climbed up the embankment toward the man she thought of what always happened when she saw him. It was the same problem every time, and even though he had not paid his annual visit to her for five years, since gas rationing began, it still gave her a familiar hysterical feeling not to be able to remember his name, and to know that when she finally did she would want to laugh. He sold wax and took orders for wax, the way people sold brushes. If he had sold brushes his name would not be Fuller, which would be logical, but Kent, which was also logical but in a less obvious way: Fuller brushes, Kent brushes, one made in America and one in England. But he sold waxes. But his name was not Johnson, which in the same way would be logical. So what was it?

Matey tried not to feel gigglish and hysterical. She knew that before it was too late she would recall the wax-name that was the right one for him, and that then she must have a reserve supply of self-control, so that she would not laugh in his face with relief and amusement.

She saw as she climbed up toward him that he looked generally the same as five years ago, holding his heavy black hat in one hand and his little suitcase full of samples in the other, standing motionless in the swirl of dogs and noise while the small girl hopped around.

"Hel*lo,*" Matey said, keeping her voice as it had been at first when he surprised her in her sorrow and loneliness, not wanting to hurt him by a quick change to normal politeness after that first warmth, for he had indeed come once more up the long rough dirt road to sell waxes to her. "I haven't seen you for a long time," she said, standing beside him.

"Who *is* this man, Matey?" her daughter asked in a gay excited voice, and the three dogs looked up at him gaily too, their tails still fluttering as they waited to know.

Matey felt the hysteria loom inside her. It is not Mr. Johnson, she said firmly, helpless to tell yet what the name would be, the logical name for her friend the wax-man. "This is my friend the wax-man, Sarah," she said, and then she felt shy and awkward, hoping once again as she always did that he would not find her rude to forget his right name, after his long ride up the hill.

"Oh," the little girl said, as if the answer were complete and deeply satisfying, and the dogs felt that too and sniffed courteously at his dusty black shoes, his creased pepper-and-salt trousers.

"No, I couldn't attend to my old customers during the war years," he said in his familiar gentle voice, and he was breathing in a guarded way, as if he tried not to puff.

"You're just in time," Matey said happily, as she always did to him whether it was true or not. It was ridiculous to infer that she was at this very moment almost out of the wax he had last sold her five years before, but it was so pleasant to see him unchanged and faithful, and to feel that she was one of his old customers, that she almost believed that the shelf in the broom-closet was indeed empty, and not well filled with bottles and jars of polish she had bought at the village hardware store. "I need *gallons* of stuff," she said.

She led the way through the patio to the side door, so as not to have the three of them tramping past the baby's room to waken her, and sank down in her familiar place upon the couch with Sarah tense with excitement beside her, while the wax-man dropped expertly upon one knee and flipped open the same suitcase, with the same wares fitted into it. It was as if five years had folded back upon themselves, like a portable silver drinking cup she once had that snapped back into a single ring, flat for her pocket, when she pressed it. Sarah was not her child born since last she bought wax from this same man, but perhaps just a neighbor visiting. There was no baby sleeping close by. She would give the order she always gave, and watch him write it on a pad on his knee, and some time before he left she would remember his name, as she had always done.

"Now this is a new product," he was saying, "which I have supplied to many of my old customers, really very nice for kitchens and," he hesitated, "for bathrooms too they all tell me, and you can see," and he deftly held out an advertisement pasted to a sheet of cardboard, "here it is in the *Saturday Evening Post* of three weeks ago, very well displayed too I may say, one of our new products which I feel is a real addition to our list, as you will see if I may just give you a teeny-weeny hint of it," and before Matey could stop him he had sprayed from the fat atomizer in his hand a little cloud.

"Pee-*ugh,*" Sarah said.

"Oh," Matey cried, "what is it?"

"We have Pineywoods, but this sample happens to be Arabian Nights," he murmured.

"Oh, it's simply awful," she said. "I'm sorry, but I simply can't stand it." She almost said, "It smells like a bad public toilet," and she almost called him Mr. Johnson. She began to feel impatient with her lagging memory, and a little hurt that he had shot this stink into the air, and beside her Sarah bounced nervously. Matey put one hand on her child's tiny knee, and said, "But I *do* need a lot of floor-oil and all that."

"Now here is something," he went on in his soft sleepy voice, "that I am recommending personally for a really high polish."

Matey laughed a little, because he always said that and then she always replied as she did now, "But these old floors! Rough pine! No use trying to polish them!" Then, as always, she looked at his remote thin face, knowing that he would glance very quickly, without any change of expression, at the floor at the end of the rug he was kneeling on, before he looked back at his sample.

Suddenly she was hot with discouragement, and almost overwhelmed by a rush of loneliness for her long-absent husband. If only he would unwind the red tape of discharge papers and such, and be home again, so that she would feel like a whole creature and be able to keep their house sparkling! If only he were home! Then there would be no dust, no murk of footprints on the oiled floors, no fluff of house-moss and dog hairs and untidiness under the piano. She leaned down in a welter of self-castigation and sniffed at the top of Sarah's head, and sure enough it smelled like the head of a hot dirty little girl. Ah, I should have washed her hair last Saturday, Matey thought morbidly. I am neglecting her. And she looked at the earth under her own fingernails, and then at her filthy old battered tennis-shoes sticking out from the faded overalls, and she felt unkempt and careless and desolate. When will he ever come home, she wondered, deep in a chasm of sadness.

"Absolutely no use," she said to the wax-man. "It's your good old floor-oil I need, gallons of it."

"This polish is really fine for furniture too," he went on softly. "I have always supplied it to my customers who value their antiques, you know." And he flicked his eyes imperturbably at the front of the walnut-secretary-from-Matey's-great-grandmother, all covered with smudges where the baby was learning to pull herself up.

Matey almost said, "Oh, Mr. Johnson, I've had *two* children since last you came! Yes, Mr. Johnson, I have *another* little girl, almost a year old! Such changes, Mr. Johnson!" But she did not. She said, "A pint of it, then. I think just a pint."

"Yes," he said gently. "Some of my best customers have always supplied themselves with it . . . Mrs. Huntington Logan, you must know her, such beautiful antiques, and Mrs. James S. Reed but of course you may not know her so far away always used it, and Mrs. J. Howard Burnham, so very *very* particular about her antiques. . . ." He put the sample back tidily, and marked the order-blank on his knee.

Matey wondered, as she always had done at this point in their meetings, how he could kneel so long. She had read once that his company gave all its salesmen special training in such gymnastics. He folded down so neatly, and then at the end he stood up without making even a crackle or snap in his knee-joints, which she was sure she could never in the world have done. Perhaps Sarah could, but certainly not she. "And then of course a gallon of the regular floor-oil, for these horrible old pine floors," she said. "No, *two* gallons, I think."

"Two, yes," he murmured, flicking his eyes with no change of expression at the dust-blurred floors.

Matey once more sank down in herself with misery, and thought of the gleaming parquetry of all his other old customers, the shimmer under the piano of Mrs. Huntington Logan, the shine under Mrs. James S. Reed's maple dining table, the black glitter of antique oak beams under antique Mrs. J. Howard Burnham's antique armoire. They all have husbands, she thought bitterly, husbands out of Washington forever, husbands home and with jobs. That is why they have polished floors, all right. That's it, Mr. Johnson. "Two gallons at *least,*" she said, laughing.

"I'll just mark down two," the wax-man said softly, licking the tip of his pencil. "I hope to be able to serve my regular old customers every six months now, since we no longer have rationing of gasoline. Two will suffice until my next visit."

In a daze, a glaze, of unhappiness Matey ordered two cans of wax for the icebox and the stove, and some liquid polish for the kitchen linoleum. They were goads to her, whips on her lazy slatternly back, sluttish hausfrau Matey. Never again will the wax-man oddly enough not called Johnson come here and see dustdustdust, smudges, smears, house-moss, she swore desolately. Never again, dear Mr. Johnson. She remembered as if it had been many years ago, five years ago perhaps, the light joy she had felt when he came this afternoon around the corner of the house, with all the barking and Sarah hopping excitedly among the dogs. How could she have felt so joyful, well knowing as she did that the house was filthy, *filthy?* How could she have been there in the sunlight, nonchalantly pulling weeds while the dust lay everywhere inside? Ah, if she could remember his name, then she would be more at peace with herself, she knew.

They stood up, the wax-man flipping shut his sample-case and Matey and Sarah as like as two peas, grimy and healthy, and while the two females waited on the terrace, so that perhaps the baby would not wake for a few more minutes, and the two dogs and the tub-like gravid bitch flounced and floundered about the man's legs, he went down to his old car for what had been ordered.

Matey held her checkbook and fountain pen. His name his name his name, she prayed, figuring ways to find out, in case the customary miracle did not happen and pop it into her mind. She would ask carelessly, "Shall I make it out to the company or to you?" . . . something like that. "Just what *are* your initials?" she would ask carelessly, laughingly.

Sarah said, "Matey, our old friend the wax-man is having troubles," and it was true: he stood halfway up the path with cans and cans of polish rolling out of his arms, and a look of dismay on his face at this inexpert unpracticed unaccustomed untidiness, so that they hurried down to him and Sarah went yelling and chasing after a round box of wax.

When everything was picked up and brought as far as the steps, Matey said, "Let's leave it all here, and my husband will help me," because even though she felt sure the wax-man knew that her husband would not be home for weeks-months-years she could not bear to have him come into the house again, for a nightmarish fear that he would fold down onto his knee and flick open his satchel and tell her once more about the clean sparkling gleaming homes of his other old customers.

"Now for the check," she said in a brisk voice that embarrassed her. What would happen? Would she have to ask his name? Would she remember, in a photo-finish? Was there still time for the familiar miracle, the name that was not as logical as it might at first seem, taken in conjunction with his profession as a wax-man, not as right as the name Johnson perhaps but still right, exotic, farfetched but right . . . ?

He slid a card onto the stone wall beside her checkbook, and then looked out across the valley, his back to her. He is discreet, she thought gratefully. He is a kind sensitive man. No wonder I welcomed him. The card, face down, said on its back "$12.56."

Matey filled in everything on her check but the name-line, and her stub and its name-line, and then asked in a voice that sounded a little too loud to her, "Shall I make it out to you? Would that be better?"

He did not turn, as she could tell without looking at him, but said very softly, "Please."

She turned over the card, still waiting to remember what it would say. And even as she read it she remembered too, so that there was surely not a half-second between the reading and the memory. Of course his name was Bee, Mr. J. M. Bee. It was unforgettable: Mr. Bee sells wax. What other man with what other name could ever sell wax but Mr. J. M. Bee? Real laughter, not helpless hysterical giggles, loomed in her, and all of a sudden she felt so full of relief that she wanted to cry out to him, "Oh, Mr. Bee! I am so happy that you came back, Mr. Bee! I missed you, these five years. I have always loved having you come up here on the hill. You have always been so nice, to come clear up here onto this dry rocky place, when most of your old customers have nice large shining houses on the flat of the valley, with lawns in front and no dogs and no children. I am really delighted to see you, especially today, Mr. Bee!"

She turned to him, waving the check like a flag. She felt young, triumphant, unconquerable. "Mr. Bee!" she cried.

He shrugged his shoulders in their neat pepper-and-salt suit, without turning toward her, and she stood looking with him at the far quiet valley, the two ridges of hills, one brown and one bluish behind it, and then the climbing jagged mountains and the final snow. Above the inaudible sound of the words her mind was still calling out so gaily she could hear a gobble of turkeys from a distant farm, and the droning hum of a tractor. She could hear, indeed she *did* hear, the little girl Sarah sigh once, close beside her, as if with a world-weariness, while the dogs sat in a silent row on the terrace wall, the bulging bitch in the middle, watching.

"Old Baldy," the wax-man said. There was still no immediate sound, and below in the valley the tractor and the turkeys made their small heartbeat into the thin clear air. "Old Baldy," he said again. "That old mountain always gets me, does something to me."

Matey still felt like telling him how much she liked him, because she was drunk with relief and amusement and well-being, at last to have his wonderful name safe in her mind. She thought in a flash that she would tell him about the name too, about her annual, semi-annual trauma or whatever it might be that made her suffer so, remembering

Fuller-Kent-Johnson and then always the final miracle of *Mr. Bee.* But he whirled around and looked sternly at her, and said in a harsh shocking voice, "Funny what these old mountains do to you, all right!"

Matey saw in amazement, in a kind of horror, that his pale grey eyes were thick with tears, and that his mouth, which she had never really looked at, was trembling and bluish over his even white false teeth. She saw that his neat clothes were very loose upon his frame. He was old. He was much more than five years older than he had been five years ago, she saw. And then she remembered what she must have seen subconsciously in the living room, how he had stood up from his jaunty expert kneeling: he had unfolded in painful sections, in a kind of repressed agony of balancing and posing, of trying to maintain the good old wax-company stance, the tried-and-true ageless salesman's limberness. Oh Mr. Bee, she thought, weak with compassion. She knew that she could not tell him now about the name. It would not ever be funny again for her. And now she would never forget it: that she knew.

He blinked unashamedly, and a tear ran down one cheek and he licked it up with his tongue and surprisingly smacked his lips, the way the baby did sometimes when a whole bean got into the smooth puree of beans. It probably tasted awful, Matey thought . . . like alum.

She held out the check to him. He folded it neatly, thanked her with a jerky bow, and turned away without any confusion for the way his face was streaked. It was as if blaming tears on a far snow-white mountain absolved him of weakness.

Matey and Sarah and the three dogs watched him walk stiffly down the steep path to his car.

"Goodbye, friend the wax-man," the little girl called.

He turned, and said in his new scratchy loud voice, "Glad to have served you again. Things have certainly changed all right. Faces in the valley have all changed. I tell you, I hardly know a soul. All the old customers have gone."

Matey thought wildly, *Not* Mrs. Logan and Mrs. Reed, *not* Mrs. J. Howard Burnham too! Oh Mr. Bee!

"Well," she said, grinning fatuously at his blind face, "I'm still here. I hope I'm always here. I love it here."

He turned noncommittally and got into his car.

Sarah waved as it coasted down the hill. The bitch ran heavily along the road after it for a few feet and then turned and walked with caution toward her bowl of water on the patio, the other dogs after her. Matey stood waiting to hear the baby cry for light and air and *la vie joyeuse* after a long nap.

Everything was pretty much as it had always been: the wax-man had come; she had ordered with her usual lavish disregard of present supplies, oppressed by the thought of his long loyal drive up the hilly road; she had suffered and then been rewarded by the inimitable coincidence that the wax-man's name was, as it had always been, Mr. Bee, an unforgettable name forgotten annually.

But five years were not annually. . . . Matey thought of the two new children and the coming puppies, and of the emptiness and the smudged outlines of her present life, the undusted floors and the unpolished nails and the unwashed heads of sweet babygirlhair, and then for a minute she rose above all that at the memory of blue-lipped Mr. Bee getting up so cautiously from the dirty rug of his last faithful old customer, and she was young and strong and happy and well-beloved. She knew that as fast as her husband could, he would come home to her. She knew that the floors would shine again, and the children's heads, and her own well-formed fingernails. But as she heard the cry she had been waiting for, the one full of hunger and sleep from the younger girl, she turned toward the far white mountain that had betrayed the wax-man into weeping, and for a minute or two she could easily have wept, herself.

Richard Ford

from *Independence Day*

My clients the Markhams, whom I'm meeting at nine-fifteen, are from tiny Island Pond, Vermont, in the far northeast corner, and their dilemma is now the dilemma of many Americans. Sometime in the indistinct Sixties, each with a then-spouse, they departed unpromising flatlander lives (Joe was a trig teacher in Aliquippa, Phyllis a plump, copper-haired, slightly bulgy-eyed housewife from the D.C. area) and trailered up to Vermont in search of a sunnier, less predictable *Weltansicht.* Time and fate soon took their unsurprising courses: spouses wandered off with other people's spouses; their kids got busily into drugs, got pregnant, got married, then disappeared to California or Canada or Tibet or Wiesbaden, West Germany. Joe and Phyllis each floated around uneasily for two or three years in intersecting circles of neighborhood friends and off-again, on-again *Weltansichts,* taking classes, starting new degrees, trying new mates and eventually giving in to what had been available and obvious all along: true and eyes-open love for each other. Almost immediately, Joe Markham—who's a stout, aggressive little bullet-eyed, short-armed, hairy-backed Bob Hoskins type of about my age, who played nose guard for the Aliquippa Fighting Quips and who's not obviously "creative"—started having good luck with the pots and sand-cast sculptures in abstract forms he'd been making, projects he'd only fiddled around with before and that his first wife,

Melody, had made vicious fun of before moving back to Beaver Falls, leaving him alone with his regular job for the Department of Social Services. Phyllis meanwhile began realizing she, in fact, had an untapped genius for designing slick, lush-looking pamphlets on fancy paper she could actually make herself (she designed Joe's first big mailing). And before they knew it they were shipping Joe's art and Phyllis's sumptuous descriptive booklets all over hell. Joe's pots began showing up in big department stores in Colorado and California and as expensive specialty items in ritzy mail order catalogues, and to both their amazement were winning prizes at prestigious crafts fairs the two of them didn't even have time to attend, they were so busy.

Pretty soon they'd built themselves a big new house with cantilevered cathedral ceilings and a hand-laid hearth and chimney, using stones off the place, the whole thing hidden at the end of a private wooded road behind an old apple orchard. They started teaching free studio classes to small groups of motivated students at Lyndon State as a way of giving something back to the community that had nurtured them through assorted rough periods, and eventually they had another child, Sonja, named for one of Joe's Croatian relatives.

Both of them, of course, realized they'd been lucky as snake charmers, given the mistakes they'd made and all that had gone kaflooey in their lives. Though neither did they view "the Vermont life" as necessarily the ultimate destination. Each of them had pretty harsh opinions about professional dropouts and trust-fund hippies who were nothing more than nonproducers in a society in need of new ideas. "I didn't want to wake up one morning," Joe said to me the first day they came in the office, looking like bedraggled, wide-eyed missionaries, "and be a fifty-five-year-old asshole with a bandanna and a goddamn earring and nothing to talk about but how Vermont's all fucked up since a lot of people just like me showed up to ruin it."

Sonja needed to go to a better school, they decided, so she could eventually get into an even better school. Their previous batch of kids had all trooped off in serapes and Sorels and down jackets to the local schools, and that hadn't worked out very well. Joe's oldest boy, Seamus, had already done time for armed robbery, toured three detoxes and was learning-disabled; a girl, Dot, got married to a Hell's Commando at sixteen and hadn't been heard from in a long time. Another boy, Federico, Phyllis's son, was making the Army a career. And so, based on these sobering but instructive experiences, they understandably wanted something more promising for little Sonja.

They therefore made a study of where schools were best and the lifestyle pretty congenial, and where they could have some access to NYC markets for Joe's work, and Haddam came at the top in every category. Joe blanketed the area with letters and résumés and found a job working on the production end for a new textbook publisher, Leverage Books in Highstown, a job that took advantage of his math and computer background. Phyllis found out there were several paper groups in town, and that they could go on making pots and sculptures in a studio Joe would build or renovate or rent, and could keep sending his work out with Phyllis's imaginative brochures, yet embark on a whole new adventure where schools were good, streets safe and everything basked in a sunny drug-free zone.

Their first visit was in March—which they correctly felt was when "everything" came on the market. They wanted to take their time, survey the whole spectrum, work out a carefully reasoned decision, make an offer on a house by May first and be out watering the lawn by the 4th. They realized, of course, as Phyllis Markham told me, that they'd probably need to "scale back" some. The world had changed in many ways while they were plopped down in Vermont. Money wasn't worth as much, and you needed more of it. Though all told they felt they'd had a good life in Vermont, saved some money over the past few years and wouldn't have done anything—divorce, wandering alone at loose ends, kid troubles—one bit differently.

They decided to sell their own new hand-built house at the first opportunity, and found a young movie producer willing to take it on a ten-year balloon with a small down. They wanted, Joe told me, to create a situation with no fallback. They put their furniture in some friends' dry barn, took over some other friends' cabin while they were away on vacation, and set off for Haddam in their old Saab one Sunday night, ready to present themselves as home buyers at somebody's desk on Monday morning.

Only they were in for the shock of their lives!

What the Markhams were in the market for—as I told them—was absolutely clear and they were dead right to want it: a modest three-bedroom with charm and maybe a few nice touches, though in keeping with the scaled-back, education-first ethic they'd opted for. A house with hardwood floors, crown moldings, a small carved mantel, plain banisters, mullioned windows, perhaps a window seat. A Cape or a converted saltbox set back on a small chunk of land bordering some curmudgeonly old farmer's cornfield or else a little pond or stream. Pre-war, or just after. Slightly out of the way. A lawn with maybe a healthy maple tree, some mature plantings, an attached garage possibly needing improvement. Assumable note or owner-finance, something they could live with. Nothing ostentatious: a sensible home for the recast nuclear family commencing life's third quartile with a kid on board. Something in the 148K area, up to three thousand square feet, close to a middle school, with a walk to the grocery.

The only problem was, and is, that houses like that, the ones the Markhams still google-dream about as they plow down the Taconic, mooning out at the little woods-ensconced rooftops and country lanes floating past, with mossy, overgrown stone walls winding back to mysterious-wondrous home possibilities in Columbia County—those houses are history. Ancient history. And those prices quit floating around at about the time Joe was saying good-bye to Melody and turning his attentions to plump, round-breasted and winsome Phyllis. Say 1976. Try four-fifty today if you can find it.

And I *maybe* could come close if the buyer weren't in a big hurry and didn't faint when the bank appraisal came in at thirty-under-asking, and the owner wanted 25% as earnest money and hadn't yet heard of a concept called owner-finance.

The houses I *could* show them all fell significantly below their dream. The current median Haddam-area house goes for 149K, which buys you a builder-design colonial in an almost completed development in not-all-that-nearby Mallards Landing: 1,900 sq ft, including garage, three-bedroom, two-bath, expandable, no fplc, basement or carpets, sited on a 50-by-200-foot lot "clustered" to preserve the theme of open space and in full view of a fiberglass-bottom "pond." All of which cast them into a deep gloom pit and, after three weeks of looking, made them not even willing to haul out of the car and walk through most of the houses where I'd made appointments.

Other than that, I showed them an assortment of older village-in houses inside their price window—mostly small, dark two-bedrooms with vaguely Greek facades, originally built for the servants of the rich before the turn of the century and owned now either by descendants of immigrant Sicilians who came to New Jersey to be stonemasons on the chapel at the Theological Institute, or else by service-industry employees, shopkeepers or Negroes. For the most part those houses are unkempt, shrunken versions of grander homes across town—I know because Ann and I rented one when we moved in eighteen years ago—only the rooms are square with few windows, low-ceilinged and connected in incongruous ways so that inside you feel as closed in and on edge as you would in a cheap chiropractor's office. Kitchens are all on the back, rarely is there more than one bath (unless the place has been fixed up, in which case the price is double); most of the houses have wet basements, old termite damage, unsolvable structural enigmas, cast-iron piping with suspicions of lead, subcode wiring and postage-stamp yards. And for this you pay full price just to get anybody to break wind in your direction. Sellers are always the last line of defense against reality and the first to feel their soleness threatened by mysterious market corrections. (Buyers are the second.)

On two occasions I actually ended up showing houses to *Sonja* (who's my daughter's age!) in hopes she'd see something she liked (a primly painted "pink room" that could be hers, a particularly nifty place to snug a VCR, some kitchen built-ins she thought were neat), then go traipsing back down the walk burbling that this was the place she'd dreamed of all her little life and her Mom and Dad simply had to see it.

Only that never happened. On both of these charades, as Sonja went clattering around the empty rooms, wondering, I'm sure, how a twelve-year-old is supposed to buy a house, I peeked through the curtains and saw Joe and Phyllis waging a corrosive argument inside my car—something that'd been brewing all day—both of them facing forward, he in the front, she in the back, snarling but not actually looking at each other. Once or twice Joe'd whip his head around, focus-in his dark little eyes as intent as an ape, growl something withering, and Phyllis would cross her plump arms and stare out hatefully at the house and shake her head without bothering to answer. Pretty soon we were out and headed to our next venue.

Unhappily, the Markhams, out of ignorance and pigheadedness, have failed to intuit the one gnostic truth of real estate (a truth impossible to reveal without seeming dishonest and cynical): that people never find or buy the house they say they want. A market economy, so I've learned, is not even remotely premised on anybody getting what he wants. The premise is that you're presented with what you might've thought you didn't want, but what's available, whereupon you give in and start finding ways to feel good about it and yourself. And not that there's anything wrong with that scheme. Why should you only get what you think you want, or be limited by what you can simply plan on? Life's never like that, and if you're smart you'll decide it's better the way it is.

My own approach in all these matters and specifically so far as the Markhams are concerned has been to make perfectly clear who pays my salary (the seller) and that my job is to familiarize them with our area, let them decide if they want to settle here, and then use my accumulated goodwill to sell them, in fact, a house. I've also impressed on them that I go about selling houses the way I'd want one sold to me: by not being a realty wind sock; by not advertising views I don't mostly believe in; by not showing clients a house they've already said they won't like by pretending the subject never came up; by not saying a house is "interesting" or "has potential" if I think it's a dump; and finally by not trying to make people believe in *me* (not that I'm untrustworthy—I simply don't invite trust) but by asking them to believe in whatever they hold dearest—themselves, money, God, permanence, progress, or just a house they see and like and decide to live in—and to act accordingly.

All told today, the Markhams have looked at forty-five houses—dragging more and more grimly down from and back to Vermont—though many of these listings were seen only from the window of my car as we rolled slowly along the curbside. "I wouldn't live in that particular shithole," Joe would say, fuming out at a house where I'd made an appointment. "Don't waste your time here, Frank," Phyllis would offer, and away we'd go. Or Phyllis would observe from the back seat: "Joe can't stand stucco construction. He doesn't want to be the one to say so, so I'll just make it easier. He grew up in a stucco house in Aliquippa. Also, we'd rather not share a driveway."

And these weren't bad houses. There wasn't a certifiable "fixer-upper," "handyman special," or a "just needs love" in the lot (Haddam doesn't have these anyway). I haven't shown them one yet that the three of them couldn't have made a damn good fresh start in with a little elbow grease, a limited renovation budget and some spatial imagination.

Since March, though, the Markhams have yet to make a purchase, tender an offer, write an earnest-money check or even see a house twice, and consequently have become despondent as we've entered the dog days of midsummer. In my own life during this period, I've made eight satisfactory home sales, shown a hundred other houses to thirty different people, gone to the Shore or off with my kids any number of weekends, watched (from my bed) the Final 4, opening day at Wrigley, the French Open and three rounds of Wimbledon; and on the more somber side, I've watched the presidential campaigns grind on in disheartening fashion, observed my forty-fourth birthday, and sensed my son gradually become a source of worry and pain to himself and me. There have also been, in this time frame, two fiery jetliner crashes far from our shores; Iraq has poisoned many Kurdish villagers, President Reagan has visited Russia; there's been a coup in Haiti, drought has crippled the country's midsection and the Lakers have won the NBA crown. Life, as noted, has gone on.

Meanwhile, the Markhams have begun "eating into their down" from the movie producer now living in their dream house and, Joe believes, producing porn movies using local teens. Likewise Joe's severance pay at Vermont Social Services has come and gone, and he's nearing the end of his piled-up vacation money. Phyllis, to her dismay, has begun suffering painful and possibly ominous female problems that have required midweek trips to Burlington for testing, plus two biopsies and a discussion of surgery. Their Saab has started overheating and sputtering on the daily commutes Phyllis makes to Sonja's dance class in Craftsbury. And as if that weren't enough, their friends are now home from their geological vacation to the Great Slave Lake, so that Joe and Phyllis are having to give thought to moving into the original and long-abandoned "home place" on their own former property and possibly applying for welfare.

Beyond all that, the Markhams have had to face the degree of unknown involved in buying a house—unknown likely to affect their whole life, even if they were rich movie stars or the keyboardist for the Rolling Stones. Buying a house will, after all, partly determine what they'll be worrying about but don't yet know, what consoling window views they'll be taking (or not), where they'll have bitter arguments and make love, where and under what conditions they'll feel trapped by life or safe from the storm, where those spirited parts of themselves they'll eventually leave behind (however overprized) will be entombed, where they might die or get sick and wish they were dead, where they'll return after funerals or after they're divorced, like I did.

After which all these unknown facts of life to come have then to be figured into what they still don't know about a house itself, right along with the potentially grievous certainty that they *will* know a *great* deal the instant they sign the papers, walk in, close the door and it's theirs; and then later will know even a great deal more that's possibly not good, though they want none of it to turn out badly for them or anyone they love. Sometimes I don't understand why anybody buys a house, or for that matter does anything with a tangible downside.

As part of my service to the Markhams, I've tried to come up with some stop-gap accommodations. Addressing that feeling of not knowing *is*, after all, my job, and I'm aware what fears come quaking and quivering into most clients' hearts after a lengthy, unsatisfactory realty experience: Is this guy a crook? Will he lie to me and steal my money? Is this street being rezoned C-I and he's in on the ground floor of a new chain of hospices or drug rehab centers? I know also that the single biggest cause of client "jumps" (other than realtor rudeness or blatant stupidity) is the embittering suspicion that the agent isn't paying any attention to your wishes. "He's just showing us what he hasn't already been able to unload and trying to make us like it"; or "She's never shown us anything like what we said we were interested in"; or "He's just pissing away our time driving us around town and letting us buy him lunch."

In early May I came up with a furnished condominium in a remodeled Victorian mansion on Burr Street, behind the Haddam Playhouse, complete with utilities and covered off-street parking. It was steep at $1,500, but it was close to schools and Phyllis could've managed without a second car if they'd stayed put till Joe started work. Joe, though, swore he'd lived in his last "shitty cold-water flat" in 1964, when he was a sophomore at Duquesne, and didn't intend to start Sonja off in some oppressive new school environment with a bunch of rich, neurotic suburban kids while the three of them lived like transient apartment rats. She'd never outlive it. He'd rather, he said, forget the whole shittaree. A week later I turned up a perfectly workable brick-

and-shingle bungalow on a narrow street behind Pelcher's—a bolt-hole, to be sure, but a place they could get into with some lease-to-buy furniture and a few odds and ends of their own, exactly the way Ann and I and everybody else used to live when we were first married and thought everything was great and getting greater. Joe, however, refused to even drive by.

Since early June, Joe has grown increasingly sullen and mean-spirited, as though he's begun to see the world in a whole new way he doesn't like and is working up some severe defense mechanisms. Phyllis has called me twice late at night, once when she'd been crying, and hinted Joe was not an easy man to live with. She said he'd begun disappearing for parts of the day and had started throwing pots at night over in a woman artist friend's studio, drinking a lot of beer and coming home after midnight. Among her other worries, Phyllis is convinced he might just forget the whole damn thing—the move, Sonja's schooling, Leverage Books, even their marriage—and sink back into an aimless nonconformist's life he lived before they got together and charted a new path to the waterfall. It was possible, she said, that Joe couldn't stand the consequences of real intimacy, which to her meant sharing your troubles as well as your achievements with the person you loved, and it seemed also possible that the act of trying to buy a house had opened the door on some dark corridors in herself that she was fearful of going down, though she thankfully seemed unready to discuss which these might be.

In so many sad words, the Markhams are faced with a potentially calamitous careen down a slippery socio-emotio-economic slope, something they could never have imagined six months ago. Plus, I know they have begun to brood about all the other big missteps they've taken in the past, the high cost of these, and how they don't want to make any more like that. As regret goes, theirs, of course, is not unusual in kind. Though finally the worst thing about regret is that it makes you duck the chance of suffering new regret just as you get a glimmer that nothing's worth doing unless it has the potential to fuck up your whole life.

A tangy metallic fruitiness filters through the Jersey ozone—the scent of overheated motors and truck brakes on Route 1—reaching clear back to the rolly back road where I am now passing by an opulent new pharmaceutical world headquarters abutting a healthy wheat field managed by the soil-research people up at Rutgers. Just beyond this is Mallards Landing (two ducks coasting-in on a colonial-looking sign made to resemble wood), its houses-to-be as yet only studded in on skimpy slabs, their bald, red-dirt yards awaiting sod. Orange and green pennants fly along the roadside: "Models Open." "Pleasure You Can Afford!" "New Jersey's Best-Kept Secret." But there are still long ragged heaps of bulldozered timber and stumps piled up and smoldering two hundred yards to one side, more or less where the community center will be. And a quarter mile back and beyond the far wall of third-growth hardwoods where no animal is native, a big oil-storage depot lumps up and into what's becoming thickened and stormy air, the beacons on its two great canisters blinking a red and silver *steer clear, steer clear* to the circling gulls and the jumbo jets on Newark approach.

When I make the final right into the Sleepy Hollow, two cars are nosed into the potholed lot, though only one has the tiresome green Vermont plate—a rusted-out, lighter-green Nova, borrowed from the Markhams' Slave Lake friends, and with a muddy bumper sticker that says ANESTHETISTS ARE NOMADS. A cagier realtor would've already phoned up with some manufactured "good news" about an unexpected price reduction in a previously out-of-reach house, and left this message at the desk last night as a form of torture and enticement. But the truth is I've become a little sick of the Markhams—given our long campaign—and have fallen into a not especially hospitable mood, so that I simply stop midway in the lot, hoping some emanations of my arrival will penetrate the flimsy motel walls and expel them both out the door in grateful, apologetic humors, fully ready to slam down their earnest money the instant they set eyes on this house in Penns Neck that, of course, I have yet to tell them about.

A thin curtain does indeed part in the little square window of room #7. Joe Markham's round, rueful face—which looks changed (though I can't say how)—floats in a small sea of blackness. The face turns, its lips move. I make a little wave, then the curtain closes, followed in five seconds by the banged-up pink door opening, and Phyllis Markham, in the uncomfortable gait of a woman not accustomed to getting fat, strides out into the midmorning heat. Phyllis, I see from the driver's seat, has somehow amplified her red hair's coppery color to make it both brighter and darker, and has also bobbed it dramatically into a puffy, mushroomy bowl favored by sexless older moms in better-than-average suburbs, and which in Phyllis's case exposes her tiny ears and makes her neck look shorter. She's dressed in baggy khaki culottes, sandals and a thick damask Mexican pullover to hide her extra girth. Like me, she is in her forties, though unclear where, and she carries herself as if there were a new burden of true woe on the earth and only she knows about it.

"All set?" I say, my window down now, cracking a smile into the new pre-storm breeze. I think about Paul's horse joke and consider telling it, as I said I would.

"He says he's not going," Phyllis says, her bottom lip slightly enlarged and dark, making me wonder if Joe has given her a stiff smack this morning. Though Phyllis's lips are her best feature and it's more likely Joe has gifted himself with a manly morning's woogling to take his mind off his realty woes.

I'm still smiling. "What's the problem?" I say. Paper trash and parking lot grit are kicking around on the hot breeze now, and when I peek in the rearview there's a dark-purple thunderhead closing fast from the west, toiling the skies and torquing up winds, making ready to dump a big bucket of rain on us. Not a good augury for a home sale.

"We had an argument on the way down." Phyllis lowers her eyes, then casts an unhappy look back at the pink door, as if she expects Joe to come bursting through it in camo gear, screaming expletives and commands and locking and loading an M-16. She takes a self-protective look at the teeming sky. "I wonder if you'd mind just talking to him." She says this in a clipped, back-of-the-mouth voice, then elevates her small nose and stiffens her lips as two tears teeter inside her eyelids. (I've forgotten how much Joe's gooby western PA accent has rubbed off on her.)

Most Americans will eventually transact at least some portion of their important lives in the presence of realtors or as a result of something a realtor has done or said. And yet my view is, people should get their domestic rhubarbs, verbal fisticuffs and emotional jugular-snatching completely out of the way *before* they show up for a house tour. I'm more or less at ease with steely silences, bitter cryptic asides, eyes rolled to heaven and dagger stares passed between prospective home buyers, signaling but not actually putting on display more dramatic after-midnight wrist-twistings, shoutings and real rock-'em, sock-

'em discord. But the client's code of conduct ought to say: Suppress all important horseshit by appointment time so I can get on with my job of lifting sagging spirits, opening fresh, unexpected choices, and offering much-needed assistance toward life's betterment. (I haven't said so, but the Markhams are on the brink of being written off, and I in fact feel a strong temptation just to run up my window, hit reverse, shoot back into the traffic and head for the Shore.)

But instead I simply say, "What would you like me to say?"

"Just tell him there's a great house," she says in a tiny, defeated voice.

"Where's Sonja?" I'm wondering if she's inside, alone with her dad.

"We had to leave her home." Phyllis shakes her head sadly. "She was showing signs of stress. She's lost weight, and she wet the bed night before last. This has been pretty tough for all of us, I guess." (She has yet to torch any animals, apparently.)

I reluctantly push open my door. Occupying the lot beside the Sleepy Hollow, inside a little fenced and razor-wire enclosure, is a shabby hubcap emporium, its shiny silvery wares nailed and hung up everywhere, all of it clanking and stuttering and shimmering in the breeze. Two old white men stand inside the compound in front of a little clatter-board shack that's completely armored with shiny hubcaps. One of them is laughing about something, his arms crossed over his big belly, swaying side to side. The other seems not to hear, just stares at Phyllis and me as if some different kind of transaction were going on.

"That's exactly what I was going to tell him anyway," I say, and try to smile again. Phyllis and Joe are obviously nearing a realty meltdown, and the threat is they may just dribble off elsewhere, feeling the need for an unattainable fresh start, and end up buying the first shitty split-level they see with another agent.

Phyllis says nothing, as if she hasn't heard me, and just looks morose and steps out of the way, hugging her arms as I head for the pink door, feeling oddly jaunty with the breeze at my back.

I half tap, half push on the door, which is ajar. It's dark and warm inside and smells like roach dope and Phyllis's coconut shampoo. "Howzit goin' in here?" I say into the gloom, my voice, if not full of confidence, at least half full of false confidence. The door to a lighted bathroom is open; a suitcase and some strewn clothes are on top of an unmade bed. I have the feeling Joe might be on the crapper and I may have to conduct a serious conversation about housing possibilities with him there.

Though I make him out then. He's sitting in a big plastic-covered recliner chair back in a shadowed corner between the bed and the curtained window where I saw his face before. He's wearing—I can make out—turquoise flip-flops, tight silver Mylar-looking stretch shorts and some sort of singlet muscle shirt. His short, meaty arms are on the recliner's arms, his feet on the elevated footrest and his head firmly back on the cushion, so that he looks like an astronaut waiting for the first big G thrust to drive him into oblivion.

"Sooou," Joe says meanly in his Aliquippa accent. "You got a house you want to sell me? Some dump?"

"Well, I do think I've got something you ought to see, Joe, I really do." I am just addressing the room, not specifically Joe. I would sell a house to anyone who happened to be here.

"Like what?" Joe is unmoving in his spaceship chair.

"Well. Like pre-war," I say, trying to bring back to memory what Joe wants in a house. "A yard on the side and in back and in front too. Mature plantings. Inside, I think you'll like it." I've never been inside, of course. My info comes from the rap sheet. Though I may have driven past with an agents' cavalcade, in which case you can pretty well guess about the inside.

"It's just your shitty job to say that, Bascombe." Joe has never called me "Bascombe" before, and I don't like it. Joe, I notice, has the beginnings of an aggressive little goatee encircling his small red mouth, which makes it seem both smaller and redder, as though it served some different function. Joe's muscle shirt, I also see, has *Potters Do It With Their Fingers* stenciled on the front. It's clear he and Phyllis are suffering some pronounced personality and appearance alterations—not that unusual in advanced stages of house hunting.

I'm self-conscious peeking in the dark doorway with the warm, blustery storm breeze whipping at my backside. I wish Joe would just get the hell on with what we're all here for.

"D'you know what *I* want?" Joe's begun to fiddle for something on the table beside him—a package of generic cigarettes. As far as I know, Joe hasn't been a smoker until this morning. He lights up now though, using a cheap little plastic lighter, and blows a huge cloud of smoke into the dark. I'm certain Joe considers himself a ladies' man in this outfit.

"I thought you came down here to buy a house," I say.

"What I want is for reality to set in," Joe says in a smug voice, setting his lighter down. "I've been kidding myself about all this bullshit down here. The whole goddamn mess. I feel like my whole goddamn life has been in behalf of bullshit. I figured it out this morning while I was taking a dump. You don't get it, do you?"

"What's that?" Holding this conversation with Joe is like consulting a cut-rate oracle (something I in fact once did).

"You think your life's leading someplace, Bascombe. You *do* think that way. But I saw myself this morning. I closed the door to the head and there I was in the mirror, looking straight at myself in my most human moment in this bottom-feeder motel I wouldn't have taken a whore to when I was in college, just about to go look at some house I would never have wanted to live in in a hundred years. Plus, I'm taking a fucked-up job just to be able to afford it. That's something, isn't it? There's a sweet scenario."

"You haven't seen the house yet." I glance back and see that Phyllis has climbed into the back seat of my car before the rain starts but is staring at me through the windshield. She's worried Joe's scotching their last chance at a good house, which he may be.

Big, noisy splats of warm rain all at once begin thumping the car roof. The wind gusts up dirty. It is truly a bad day for a showing, since ordinary people don't buy houses in a rainstorm.

Joe takes a big, theatrical drag on his generic and funnels smoke expertly out his nostrils. "Is it a Haddam address?" he asks (ever a prime consideration).

I'm briefly bemused by Joe's belief that I'm a man who believes life's leading someplace. I *have* thought that way other times in life, but one of the fundamental easements of the Existence Period is not letting whether it is or whether it isn't worry you—as loony as that might be. "No," I say, recollecting myself. "It's not. It's in Penns Neck."

"I see." Joe's stupid half-bearded red mouth rises and lowers in the dark. "Penns Neck. I live in Penns Neck, New Jersey. What does that mean?"

"I don't know," I say. "Nothing, I guess, if you don't want it to." (Or better yet if the bank doesn't want you to, or if you've got a mean Chapter 7 lurking in your portfolio, or a felony conviction, or too many late payments on your Trinitron, or happen to enjoy the services of a heart valve. In that case it's back to Vermont.) "I've shown you a lot of houses, Joe," I say, "and you haven't liked any of them. But I don't think you'd say I tried to force you into any of them."

"You don't offer advice, is that it?" Joe is still cemented to his lounge chair, where he obviously feels in a powerful command modality.

"Well. Shop around for a mortgage," I say. "Get a foundation inspection. Don't budget more than you can pay. Buy low, sell high. The rest isn't really my business."

"Right," Joe says, and smirks. "I know who pays your salary."

"You can always offer six percent less than asking. That's up to you. I'll still get paid, though."

Joe takes another drastic slag-down on his weed. "You know, I like to have a view of things from above," he says, absolutely mysteriously.

"Great," I say. Behind me, air is changing rapidly with the rain, cooling my back and neck as the front passes by. A sweet rain aroma envelops me. Thunder is rumbling over Route 1.

"You remember what I said when you first came in here?"

"You said something about reality setting in. That's all I remember." I'm staring at him impatiently through the murk, in his flip-flops and Mylar shorts. Not your customary house-hunting attire. I take a surreptitious look at my watch. Nine-thirty.

"I've completely quit becoming," Joe says, and actually smiles. "I'm not out on the margins where new discoveries take place anymore."

"I think that's probably too severe, Joe. You're not doing plasma research, you're just trying to buy a house. You know, it's my experience that it's when you don't think you're making progress that you're probably making plenty." This is a faith I in fact hold—the Existence Period notwithstanding—and one I plan to pass on to my son if I can ever get where he is, which at the moment seems out of the question.

"When I got divorced, Frank, and started trying to make pots up in East Burke, Vermont"—Joe crosses his short legs and cozies down authoritatively in his lounger—"I didn't have the foggiest idea about what I was doing. Okay? I was out of control, actually. But things just worked out. Same when Phyllis and I got together—just slammed into each other one day. But I'm not out of control anymore."

"Maybe you are more than you think, Joe."

"Nope. I'm *in* control way too much. That's the problem."

"I think you're confusing things you're already sure about, Joe. All this has been pretty stressful on you."

"But I'm on the verge of something here, I think. That's the important part."

"Of what?" I say. "I think you're going to find this Houlihan house pretty interesting." Houlihan is the owner of the Penns Neck property.

"I don't mean *that.*" He pops both his chunky little fists on the plastic armrests. Joe may be verging on a major disorientation here—a legitimate rent in the cloth. This actually appears in textbooks: Client abruptly begins to see the world in some entirely new way he feels certain, had he only seen it earlier, would've directed him down a path of vastly greater happiness—only (and this, of course, is the insane part) he inexplicably senses that way's still open to him; that the past, just this once, doesn't operate the way it usually operates. Which is to say, irrevocably. Oddly enough, only home buyers in the low to middle range have these delusions, and for the most part all they bring about is trouble.

Joe suddenly bucks up out of his chair and goes slappety-slap through the dark little room, taking big puffs on his cigarette, looking into the bathroom, then crossing and peeping out between the curtains to where Phyllis waits in my car. He then turns like an undersized gorilla in a cage and stalks past the TV to the bathroom door, his back to me, and stares out the frosted, louvered window that reveals the dingy motel rear alley, where there's a blue garbage lugger, full to brimming with white PVC piping, which I sense Joe finds significant. Our talk now has the flavor of a hostage situation.

"What do you think you mean, Joe?" I say, because I detect that what he's looking for, like anybody on the skewers of dilemma, is *sanction:* agreement from beyond himself. A nice house he could both afford and fall in love with the instant he sees it could be a perfect sanction, a sign some community recognizes him in the only way communities ever recognize anything: financially (tactfully expressed as a matter of compatibility).

"What I mean, Bascombe," Joe says, leaning against the doorjamb and staring pseudo-casually through the bathroom at the blue load lugger (the mirror where he's caught himself on the can must be just behind the door), "is that the reason we haven't bought a house in four months is that I don't *want* to goddamned buy one. And the reason for that is I don't want to get trapped in some shitty life I'll never get out of except by dying." Joe swivels toward me—a small, round man with hirsute butcher's arms and a little sorcerer's beard, who's come to the sudden precipice of what's left of life a little quicker than he knows how to cope with. It's not what I was hoping for, but anyone could appreciate his predicament.

"It *is* a big decision, Joe," I say, wanting to sound sympathetic. "If you buy a house, you own it. That's for sure."

"So are you giving up on me? Is that it?" Joe says this with a mean sneer, as if he's observed now what a shabby piece of realty dreck I am, only interested in the ones that sell themselves. He is probably indulging in the idyll of what it'd be like to be a realtor himself, and what superior genius strategies he'd choose to get his point across to a crafty, interesting, hard-nut-to-crack guy like Joe Markham. This is another well-documented sign, but a good one: when your client begins to see things as a realtor, half the battle's won.

My wish of course is that after today Joe will spend a sizable portion if not every minute of his twilight years in Penns Neck, NJ, and it's even possible he believes it'll happen, himself. My job, therefore, is to keep him on the rails—to supply sanction *pro tempore,* until I get him into a buy-sell agreement and cinch the rest of his life around him like a saddle on a bucking horse. Only it's not that simple, since Joe at the moment is feeling isolated and scared through no fault of anyone but him. So that what I'm counting on is the phenomenon by which most people will feel they're not being strong-armed if they're simply allowed to advocate (as stupidly as they please) the position opposite the one they're really taking. This is just another way we create the fiction that we're in control of anything.

"I'm not giving up on you, Joe," I say, feeling a less pleasant dampness on my back now and inching forward into the room. Traffic noise is being softened by the rain. "I just go about selling houses the way I'd want one sold to me. And if I bust my ass showing you property, setting up appointments, checking out this and that till I'm purple in the face, then you suddenly back out, I'll be ready to say you made the right decision if I believe it."

"Do you believe it this time?" Joe is still sneering, but not quite as much. He senses we're getting to the brassier tacks now, where I take off my realtor's hat and let him know what's right and what's wrong in the larger sphere, which he can then ignore.

"I sense your reluctance pretty plainly, Joe."

"Right," Joe says adamantly. "If you feel like you're tossing your life in the ter-let, why go through with it, right?"

"You'll have plenty more opportunities before you're finished."

"Yup," Joe says. I hazard another look toward Phyllis, whose mushroom head is in motionless silhouette inside my car. The glass has already fogged up from her heavy body exhalations. "These things aren't easy," he says, and tosses his stubby cigarette directly into the toilet he was no doubt referring to.

"If we're not going to do this, we better get Phyllis out of the car before she suffocates in there," I say. "I've got some other things to do today. I'm going away with my son for the holiday."

"I didn't know you had a son," Joe says. He, of course, has never asked me one question about me in four months, which is fine, since it's not his business.

"And a daughter. They live in Connecticut with their mother." I smile a friendly, not-your-business smile.

"Oh yeah."

"Let me get Phyllis," I say. "She'll need a little talking to by you, I think."

"Okay, but let me just ask one thing." Joe crosses his short arms and leans against the doorjamb, feigning even greater casualness. (Now that he's off the hook, he has the luxury of getting back on it of his own free and misunderstood will.)

"Shoot."

"What do you think's going to happen to the realty market?"

"Short term? Long term?" I'm acting ready to go.

"Let's say short."

"Short? More of the same's my guess. Prices are soft. Lenders are pretty retrenched. I expect it to last the summer, then rates'll probably bump up around ten-nine or so after Labor Day. Course, if one high-priced house sells way under market, the whole structure'll adjust overnight and we'll all have a field day. It's pretty much a matter of perception out there."

Joe stares at me, trying to act as though he's mulling this over and fitting his own vital data into some new mosaic. Though if he's smart he's also thinking about the cannibalistic financial forces gnashing and churning the world he's claiming he's about to march back into–instead of buying a house, fixing his costs onto a thirty-year note and situating his small brood behind its solid wall. "I see," he says sagely, nodding his fuzzy little chin. "And what about the long term?"

I take another stagy peek at Phyllis, though I can't see her now. Possibly she's started hitchhiking down Route 1 to Baltimore.

"The long term's less good. For you, that is. Prices'll jump after the first of the year. That's for sure. Rates'll spurt up. Property really doesn't go down in the Haddam area as a whole. All boats pretty much rise on a rising whatever." I smile at him blandly. In realty, all boats most certainly *do* rise on a rising whatever. But it's still being right that makes you rich.

Joe, I'm sure, has been brooding all over again this morning about his whopper miscues–miscues about marriage, divorce, remarriage, letting Dot marry a Hell's Commando, whether he should've quit teaching trig in Aliquippa, whether he should've joined the Marines and right now be getting out with a fat pension and qualifying for a VA loan. All this is a natural part of the aging process, in which you find yourself with less to do and more opportunities to eat your guts out regretting everything you *have* done. But Joe doesn't want to make another whopper, since one more big one might just send him to the bottom.

Except he doesn't know bread from butter beans about which is the fatal miscue and which is the smartest idea he ever had.

"Frank, I've just been standing here thinking," he says, and peers back out the dirty bathroom louvers as if he'd heard someone call his name. Joe may at this moment be close to deciding what he actually thinks. "Maybe I need a new way to look at things."

"Maybe you ought to try looking at things across a flat plain, Joe," I say. "I've always thought that looking at things from above, like you said, forced you to see all things as the same height and made decisions a lot harder. Some things are just bigger than others. Or smaller. And I think another thing too."

"What's that?" Joe's brows give the appearance of knitting together.

He is vigorously trying to fit my "viewpoint" metaphor into his own current predicament of homelessness.

"It really won't hurt you to take a quick run over to this Penns Neck house. You're already down here. Phyllis is in the car, scared to death you're not going to look at it."

"Frank, what do you think about me?" Joe says. At some point of dislocatedness, this is what all clients start longing to know. Though it's almost always insincere and finally meaningless, since once their business is over they go right back to thinking you're either a crook or a moron. Realty is not a friendly business. It only seems to be.

"Joe, I may just queer my whole deal here," I say, "but what I think is you've done your best to find a house, you've stuck to your principles, you've put up with anxiety as long as you know how. You've acted responsibly, in other words. And if this Penns Neck house is anywhere close to what you like, I think you ought to take the plunge. Quit hanging onto the side of the pool."

"Yeah, but you're paid to think that, though," Joe says, sulky again in the bathroom door. "Right?"

But I'm ready for him. "Right. And if I can get you to spend a hundred and fifty on this house, then I can quit working and move to Kitzbühel, and you can thank me by sending me a bottle of good gin at Christmas because you're not freezing your nuts off in a barn while Sonja gets further behind in school and Phyllis files fucking divorce papers on you because you can't make up your mind."

"Point taken," Joe says, moodily.

"I really don't want to go into it any further," I say. There's no place further to go, of course, realty being not a very complex matter. "I'm going to take Phyllis on up to Penns Neck, Joe. And if she likes it we'll come get you and you can make up your mind. If she doesn't I'll bring her back anyway. It's a win-win proposition. In the meantime you can stay here and look at things from above."

Joe stares at me guiltily. "Okay, I'll just come along." He virtually blurts this out, having apparently blundered into the sanction he was looking for: the win-win, the sanction not to be an idiot. "I've come all this fucking way."

With my damp right arm I give a quick thumbs-up wave out to Phyllis, who I hope is still in the car.

Joe begins picking up change off the dresser top, stuffing a fat wallet into the tight waistband of his shorts. "I should let you and Phyllis figure this whole goddamn thing out and follow along like a goddamn pooch."

"You're still looking at things from above." I smile at Joe across the dark room.

"You just see everything from the fucking middle, that's all," Joe says, scratching his bristly, balding head and looking around the room as though he'd forgotten something. I have no idea what he means by this and am fairly sure he couldn't explain it either. "If I died right now, you'd go on about your business."

"What else should I do?" I say. "I'd be sorry I hadn't sold you a house, though. I promise you that. Because you at least could've died at home instead of in the Sleepy Hollow."

"Tell it to my widow out there," Joe Markham says, and stalks by me and out the door, leaving me to pull it shut and to get out to my car before I'm soaked to my toes. All this for the sake of what? A sale.

David Mamet

from *Glengarry Glen Ross*

Always be closing.

Practical Sales Maxim

ACT ONE

Scene One

A booth at a Chinese restaurant, Williamson and Levene are seated at the booth.

LEVENE: John . . . John . . . John. Okay. John. John. Look: *(Pause.)* The Glengarry Highland's leads, you're sending Roma out. Fine. He's a good man. We know what he is. He's fine. All I'm saying, you look at the *board,* he's throwing . . . wait, wait, wait, he's throwing them *away,* he's throwing the leads away. All that I'm saying, that you're wasting leads. I don't want to tell you your *job.* All that I'm saying, things get *set,* I know they do, you get a certain *mindset.* . . . A guy gets a reputation. We know how this . . . all I'm saying, put a *closer* on the job. There's more than one man for the . . . Put a . . . wait a second, put a *proven man out* . . . and you watch, now *wait* a second–and you watch your *dollar* volumes. . . . You start closing them for *fifty* 'stead of *twenty-five* . . . you put a *closer* on the . . .

Williamson: Shelly, you blew the last . . .

Levene: No. John. No. Let's wait, let's back up here, I did . . . will you please? Wait a second. Please. I didn't "blow" them. No. I didn't "blow" them. No. One kicked *out,* one I closed . . .

Williamson: . . . you didn't close . . .

Levene: . . . I, if you'd *listen* to me. Please. I *closed* the cocksucker. His *ex,* John, his *ex, I* didn't know he was married . . . he, the *judge* invalidated the . . .

Williamson: Shelly . . .

Levene: . . . and what is that, John? What? Bad *luck.* That's all it is. I pray in your *life* you will never find it runs in streaks. That's what it does, that's all it's doing. Streaks. I pray it misses you. That's all I want to say.

Williamson *(Pause):* What about the other two?

Levene: What two?

Williamson: Four. You had four leads. One kicked out, one the *judge,* you say . . .

Levene: . . . you want to see the court records? John? Eh? You want to go down . . .

Williamson: . . . no . . .

Levene: . . . do you want to go down*town* . . . ?

Williamson: . . . no . . .

Levene: . . . then . . .

Williamson: . . . I only . . .

Levene: . . . then what is this "you *say*" shit, what is that? *(Pause.)* What is that . . . ?

Williamson: All that I'm saying . . .

Levene: What is this "you *say*"? A deal kicks out . . . I got to *eat. Shit,* Williamson, *shit.* You . . . Moss . . . Roma . . . look at the *sheets* . . . look at the *sheets.* Nineteen *eighty,* eighty-*one* . . . eighty-*two* . . . six months of eighty-two . . . who's there? Who's up there?

WILLIAMSON: Roma.

LEVENE: Under him?

WILLIAMSON: Moss.

LEVENE: Bullshit. John. Bull*shit.* April, September 1981. It's *me.* It isn't *fucking* Moss. Due respect, he's an *order* taker, John. He *talks,* he talks a good game, look at the *board,* and it's *me,* John, it's me . . .

WILLIAMSON: Not lately it isn't.

LEVENE: Lately kiss my ass lately. That isn't how you build an org . . . talk, talk to Murray. Talk to Mitch. When we were on Peterson, who paid for his fucking *car?* You talk to him. The *Seville* . . . *?* He came in, "You bought that for me Shelly." Out of *what?* Cold *calling. Nothing.* Sixty-*five,* when we were there, with Glen *Ross* Farms? You call 'em downtown. What was that? *Luck?* That was "luck"? *Bull*shit, John. You're burning my ass, I can't get a fucking *lead* . . . you think that was luck. My stats for those years? Bull*shit* . . . over that period of time . . . ? Bull*shit.* It wasn't luck. It was *skill.* You want to throw that away, John . . . ? You want to throw that away?

WILLIAMSON: It isn't me . . .

LEVENE: . . . it isn't you . . . ? Who *is* it? Who is this I'm talking to? I need the *leads* . . .

WILLIAMSON: . . . after the thirtieth . . .

LEVENE: Bull*shit* the thirtieth, I don't get on the board the thirtieth, they're going to can my ass. I need the leads. I need them now. Or I'm gone, and you're going to miss me, John, I swear to you.

WILLIAMSON: Murray . . .

LEVENE: . . . you *talk* to Murray . . .

WILLIAMSON: I have. And my job is to marshal those leads . . .

LEVENE: Marshal the leads . . . marshal the leads? What the fuck, what bus did *you* get off of, we're here to fucking *sell. Fuck* marshaling the leads. What the fuck talk is that? What the fuck talk is that? Where did you learn that? In school? *(Pause.)* That's "talk," my friend, that's "talk." Our job is to *sell.* I'm the *man* to sell. I'm getting garbage. *(Pause.)* You're giving it to me, and what I'm saying is it's *fucked.*

WILLIAMSON: You're saying that I'm fucked.

LEVENE: Yes. *(Pause.)* I am. I'm sorry to antagonize you.

WILLIAMSON: Let me . . .

LEVENE: . . . and I'm going to get bounced and you're . . .

WILLIAMSON: . . . let me . . . are you listening to me . . . ?

LEVENE: Yes.

WILLIAMSON: Let me tell you something, Shelly. I do what I'm hired to do. I'm . . . wait a second. I'm *hired* to watch the leads. I'm given . . . hold on, I'm given a *policy. My* job is to *do that.* What I'm *told.* That's it. You, wait a second, *anybody* falls below a certain mark I'm not *permitted* to give them the premium leads.

LEVENE: Then how do they come up above that mark? With *dreck . . . ?* That's *nonsense.* Explain this to me. 'Cause it's a waste, and it's a stupid waste. I want to tell you something . . .

WILLIAMSON: You know what those leads cost?

LEVENE: The premium leads. Yes. I know what they cost. John. Because I, *I* generated the dollar revenue sufficient to *buy* them. Nineteen senny-*nine,* you know what I made? Senny-*nine?* Ninety-six thousand dollars. John? For *Murray . . .* For *Mitch . . .* look at the sheets . . .

WILLIAMSON: Murray said . . .

LEVENE: *Fuck* him. *Fuck* Murray. John? You know? You tell him I said so. What does *he* fucking know? He's going to have a "sales" contest . . . you know what our sales contest used to be? *Money.* A *fortune.* Money lying on the ground. Murray? When was the last time *he* went out on a sit? Sales contest? It's *laughable.* It's cold out there now, John. It's tight. Money is *tight.* This ain't sixty-five. It ain't. It just ain't. See? See? Now, I'm a good *man*—but I need a . . .

WILLIAMSON: Murray said . . .

LEVENE: John. John . . .

WILLIAMSON: Will you please wait a second. Shelly. Please. Murray told me: the hot leads . . .

LEVENE: . . . ah, *fuck* this . . .

WILLIAMSON: The . . . Shelly? *(Pause.)* The hot leads are assigned according to the board. During the contest. *Period.* Anyone who beats fifty per . . .

LEVENE: That's fucked. That's fucked. You don't look at the fucking *percentage.* You look at the *gross.*

WILLIAMSON: Either way. You're out.

LEVENE: I'm out.

WILLIAMSON: Yes.

LEVENE: I'll tell you why I'm out. I'm *out,* you're giving me toilet paper. John. I've *seen* those leads. I saw them when I was at Homestead, we pitched those cocksuckers Rio Rancho nineteen sixty-*nine* they wouldn't buy. They couldn't buy a fucking *toaster.* They're *broke,* John. They're cold. They're deadbeats, you can't judge on that. Even so. Even so. Alright. Fine. Fine. Even so. I go in, FOUR FUCKING LEADS they got their money in a *sock.* They're fucking *Polacks,* John. Four leads. I close two. *Two.* Fifty per . . .

WILLIAMSON: . . . they kicked out.

LEVENE: They *all* kick out. You run in *streaks,* pal. *Streaks.* I'm . . . I'm . . . don't look at the *board,* look at *me.* Shelly Levene. *Anyone. Ask* them on Western. Ask Getz at Homestead. Go ask Jerry Graff. You know who I am . . . I NEED A SHOT. I got to get on the fucking board. Ask them. *Ask* them. Ask them who ever picked up a check I was flush. Moss, Jerry Graff, Mitch himself . . . Those guys *lived* on the business I brought in. They *lived* on it . . . and so did Murray, John. You were here you'd of benefited from it too. And now I'm saying this. Do I want charity? Do I want *pity?* I want *sits.* I want leads don't come right out of a *phone book.* Give me a lead hotter than that, I'll go in and close it. Give me a chance. That's all I want. I'm going to *get* up on that fucking board and all I want is a chance. It's a *streak* and I'm going to turn it around. *(Pause.)* I need your help. *(Pause.)*

WILLIAMSON: I can't do it, Shelly. *(Pause.)*

LEVENE: Why?

WILLIAMSON: The leads are assigned randomly . . .

LEVENE: *Bullshit, bullshit,* you assign them. . . . What are you *telling* me?

WILLIAMSON: . . . apart from the top men on the contest board.

LEVENE: Then put me on the board.

WILLIAMSON: You start closing again, you'll *be* on the board.

LEVENE: I can't close these leads, John. No one can. It's a joke. John, look, just give me a hot lead. Just give me two of the premium leads. As a "test," alright? As a "test" and I promise you . . .

WILLIAMSON: I can't do it, Shel. *(Pause.)*

LEVENE: I'll give you ten percent. *(Pause.)*

WILLIAMSON: Of what?

LEVENE: Of my end what I close.

WILLIAMSON: And what if you don't close.

LEVENE: I *will* close.

WILLIAMSON: What if you *don't* close . . . ?

LEVENE: I *will* close.

WILLIAMSON: What if you *don't?* Then I'm *fucked.* You see . . . ? Then it's *my* job. That's what I'm *telling* you.

LEVENE: I *will* close. John, John, ten percent. I can get hot. You *know* that . . .

WILLIAMSON: Not lately you can't . . .

LEVENE: Fuck that. That's defeatist. Fuck that. Fuck it. . . . Get on my side. *Go* with me. Let's *do* something. You want to run this office, *run* it.

WILLIAMSON: Twenty percent. *(Pause.)*

LEVENE: Alright.

WILLIAMSON: And fifty bucks a lead.

LEVENE: John. *(Pause.)* Listen. I want to talk to you. Permit me to do this a second. I'm older than you. A man acquires a reputation. On the street. What he does when he's *up,* what he does otherwise. . . . I said "ten," you said "no." You said "twenty." I said "fine," I'm not going to fuck with you, how can I beat that, you tell me? . . . Okay. Okay. We'll . . . Okay. Fine. We'll . . . Alright, twenty percent, and fifty bucks a lead. That's fine. For now. That's fine. A month or two we'll talk. A month from now. Next month. After the thirtieth. *(Pause.)* We'll talk.

WILLIAMSON: What are we going to say?

LEVENE: No. You're right. That's for later. We'll talk in a month. What have you got? I want two sits. Tonight.

WILLIAMSON: I'm not sure I have two.

LEVENE: I saw the board. You've got *four* . . .

WILLIAMSON *(Snaps):* I've got *Roma.* Then I've got Moss . . .

LEVENE: *Bullshit.* They ain't been in the office yet. Give 'em some stiff. We have a deal or not? Eh? Two sits. The Des Plaines. Both of 'em, six and ten, you can do it . . . six and ten . . . eight and eleven, I don't give a shit, you set 'em up? Alright? The two sits in Des Plaines.

WILLIAMSON: Alright.

LEVENE: Good. Now we're talking. *(Pause.)*

WILLIAMSON: A hundred bucks. *(Pause.)*

LEVENE: Now? *(Pause.) Now?*

WILLIAMSON: Now. *(Pause.) Yes . . . When?*

LEVENE: Ah, *shit,* John. *(Pause.)*

WILLIAMSON: I wish I could.

LEVENE: You fucking asshole. *(Pause.)* I haven't got it. *(Pause.)* I haven't got it, John. *(Pause.)* I'll pay you tomorrow. *(Pause.)* I'm coming in here with the sales, I'll pay you *tomorrow. (Pause.)* I haven't *got* it, when I pay, the *gas* . . . I get back the hotel, I'll bring it in tomorrow.

WILLIAMSON: Can't do it.

LEVENE: I'll give you thirty on them now, I'll bring the rest tomorrow. I've got it at the hotel. *(Pause.)* John? *(Pause.)* We do that, for chrissake?

WILLIAMSON: No.

LEVENE: I'm asking you. As a favor to me? *(Pause.)* John. *(Long pause.)* John: my *daughter* . . .

WILLIAMSON: I can't do it, Shelly.

LEVENE: Well, I want to tell you something, fella, wasn't long I could pick up the phone, call *Murray* and I'd have your job. You know that? Not too *long* ago. For what? For *nothing.* "Mur, this new kid burns my ass." "Shelly, he's out." You're gone before I'm back from lunch. I bought him a trip to Bermuda once . . .

WILLIAMSON: I have to go . . . *(Gets up.)*

LEVENE: Wait. Alright. Fine. *(Starts going in pocket for money.)* The one. Give me the lead. Give me the one lead. The best one you have.

WILLIAMSON: I can't split them. *(Pause.)*

LEVENE: Why?

WILLIAMSON: Because I say so.

LEVENE *(Pause):* Is that it? Is that *it?* You want to do business that way . . . ?

Williamson *gets up, leaves money on the table.*

LEVENE: You want to do business that way . . . ? Alright. Alright. Alright. Alright. What is there on the other list . . . ?

WILLIAMSON: You want something off the B list?

LEVENE: *Yeah.* Yeah.

WILLIAMSON: Is that what you're saying?

LEVENE: That's what I'm saying. Yeah. *(Pause.)* I'd like something off the other list. Which, very least, that I'm entitled to. If I'm still *working* here, which for the moment I guess that I am. *(Pause.)* What? I'm sorry I spoke harshly to you.

WILLIAMSON: That's alright.

LEVENE: The deal still stands, our other thing.

Williamson *shrugs. Starts out of the booth.*

LEVENE: Good. Mmm. I, you know, I left my wallet back at the hotel.

Ron Hansen

Can I Just Sit Here For a While?

He was called a traveler and that was another thing he loved about the job. If you wanted the hairy truth, Rick Bozack couldn't put his finger on any one thing that made the job such a clincher; it might have been his expense account or the showroom smell of his leased Oldsmobile or the motel rooms: God, the motel rooms, twin double beds and a stainless steel Kleenex dispenser and a bolted-down color TV topped with cellophane-wrapped peppermints which the maid left after she cleaned. He loved the thermos coffee canister the waitress banged down on his table at breakfast, he loved the sweat on his ice-water glass, he loved the spill stains blotting through the turned-over check, and he loved leaving tips of 20 percent even when the girl was slow and sullen and splashed coffee on his newspaper. His sales, his work, his vocation, that was all bonus. The waiting, the handshakes, the lunches, The Close, jeepers, that was just icing.

If you asked Rick Bozack what he did for a living, he wouldn't come out with a song and dance about selling expensive incubators and heart and kidney machines for Doctor's Service Supply Company, Indianapolis. Not off the top of his head he wouldn't. Instead he'd flash on a motel lobby with all the salesmen in their sharp tailored suits, chewing sugarless gum, while the sweet thing behind the counter rammed a roller over a plastic credit card and after-shaves mingled in the air. It was goofy when he thought about it, but walking out through those fingerprinted glass doors, throwing his briefcase onto the red bucket seat, scraping the frost off the windshield, and seeing all those other guys out there in the parking lot with him, grimacing, chipping away at their wipers, blowing on their fingers, sliding their heater controls to Defrost, he felt like a team player again, like he was part of a fighter squadron.

What was this Death of a Salesman crap? he'd say.

What were they feeding everybody about the hard life on the road?

You'd have to be zonkers not to love it.

Then Rick had a real turnaround. A college buddy said something that really clobbered him. Rick and his wife, Jane, had returned to South Bend, his home, for the Notre Dame alumni picnic, and they had collided there with people they hadn't even thought of in years. They sat all night at a green picnic table with baked beans and hot dogs and beer, laughing so much their sides hurt, having a whale of a good time together. They swapped pictures of their kids and Rick drew a diagram of an invention he might get patented, which would rinse out messy diapers for daddies right there in the toilet bowl. He told all comers that he was thirty-four years old and happily married, the father of two girls, and he woke up every morning with a sapsucker grin on his face. Then Mickey Hogan, this terrific buddy in advertising who had just started up his own firm, said you don't know the thrill of business until it's your own, until every sale you make goes directly into your pocket and not to some slob back in the home office.

This guy Hogan wasn't speaking *de profundis* or anything, but Rick was really blown away by what he said. It was one of those fuzzy notions you carry with you for years and then it's suddenly there, it's got shape and bulk and annoying little edges that give you a twinge when you sit down. That's how it was. He and Jane talked about it all the way back to their three-bedroom apartment on Rue Monet in Indianapolis. "How much of what I earn actually makes my wallet any fatter? What do I have besides an income? When am I going to get off my duff and get something going on my own?"

Jane was great about it. She said it was his decision and she loved him and she'd go along with whatever his choice was, but she had watched him waste himself at Doctor's Service Supply Company, Indianapolis. She knew he was a great salesman but he had all the earmarks of a fantastic manager too. She had been hoping he'd come up with something like this but didn't wnat to influence him one way or the other. "I don't want to push," were her words.

Jane's enthusiasm put a fire under Rick and he began checking things out on the sly: inventory costs, car leases and office space rentals, government withholding tax and F.I.C.A. regulations, and though it seemed dopey and juvenile, the couple decided that they'd both stop smoking, watch their caloric intake, avoid between-meal treats, and exercise regularly. Sure they were mainly concerned with hashing out this new business venture, but how far afield was it to take stock of yourself, your physical condition, to discipline yourself and set goals? That was Rick's comment and Jane thought he was "right on the money."

The two of them let a half-gallon of ice cream melt down in the stainless steel sink, got out the scale and measuring tape, bought matching jogging outfits and they took turns with Tracy and Connor at breakfast while one of them jogged around the block.

And Rick was no slouch when on the road. He jogged in strange cities and on gravel country roads and in parking lots of motels. Other salesmen would run at him in sweatbands and heavy T-shirts and Rick would say, "How's it going?"

"How's it going?" they'd reply.

Rick imagined millions of joggers saying the same things to each other. It felt as good as the days of the Latin Mass, when you knew it was just as incomprehensible in Dusseldorf, West Germany, or Ichikawa, Japan.

On one of his business trips to South Bend, he jogged on the cinder track of Notre Dame's football stadium, where who should he see but Walter Herdzina, a terrific friend of his! Rick was flabbergasted. The guy had aged—who hadn't?—but he remembered Rick like it was only yesterday, even recited some wild dorm incidents that Rick had put the blackboard eraser to. The two men ran an eight-minute mile together and leaned on their knees and wiped their faces on their sweatshirts, and after they had discussed pulse rates, refined sugar, and junk foods, his buddy Walter Herdzina said, "You ought to move back to South Bend."

Jane, bless her heart, kept bringing up South Bend too. It was smack in the middle of his territory, and a natural home base, but he had never really thought about South Bend much before the alumni picnic. When Head Office hired Rick they had naturally assumed he'd want a giant metropolis like Indianapolis to settle in so he could have some jam-packed leisure time, and he had never mentioned his strong links further north. And it wasn't unusual for Rick to spend three or four days in South Bend and not give anyone except his mom a call. But now there was a come-as-you-are feeling, some real hometown warmth there, which he hadn't noticed before.

In September he closed a deal with a gynecological clinic that would earn him six thousand dollars, what salesmen called The Cookies. But instead of driving home for a wingding celebration, he decided to make some business phone contacts, thank you's actually, to ride with his hot streak, see what fell in his lap. And he had an inkling maybe some doctors up there considered him somewhat remote.

So he stopped in the lobby of a downtown bank building to use its plush telephone booths. Then, on an impulse, he asked to see someone in the business loan department. A receptionist said a loan vice president could see him and Rick walked into his office and how's this for coincidence? The banker was Walter Herdzina! You could've knocked Rick over with a feather. "Boy, you're really going places," he said. Walter grinned. "They'll probably wise up and kick me downstairs again before I get the chair warm."

Rick spoke off the top of his head. He had been with Doctor's Service Supply Company, Indianapolis, for six years after three years with Johnson & Johnson. He had built up a pretty good trade representing Indiana and southern Michigan and had offers from industries in Minnesota and California to switch over to a district manager's job and a substantial boost in salary. What he wanted to know was, could a banker like Walter with years of experience and an eye for markets and money potential give him a solid reason why he shouldn't go into business for himself? Start his own distributorship?

The buddy in banking glanced at his watch and suggested they go out for lunch.

Rick figured that meant No. "This is pretty off-the-wall," he said. "I really haven't had time to analyze it or work up any kind of prospectus."

Walter put a hand on his shoulder. "Let's talk about it at lunch."

Mostly they talked about rugby. It had been a maiden sport at Notre

Dame when they played it, but now it had taken the school by storm. Why? Because when you got right down to it, men liked seeing what they were made of, what kind of guts they had.

"Lessons like that stick," said Walter. "I get guys coming to me with all kinds of schemes, inventions, brilliant ideas. I can tell right away if they were ever athletes. If they never hurt themselves to win at something, well, I'm a little skeptical."

Walter ordered protein-rich halibut; Rick had the Dieter's Salad.

Rick told the banker traveler stories. He told him anecdotes about sales. He had sold insurance and mutual funds and, for a summer, automobiles, and he had discovered a gimmick, well not that, a *tool,* which hadn't failed him yet. It was called the Benjamin Franklin Close.

"Say you get a couple who're wavering over the purchase of a car. You take them into your office and close the door and say, 'Do you know what Benjamin Franklin would do in situations like this?' That's a toughie for them so you let them off the hook. You take out a tablet and draw a line down the center of the page, top to bottom. 'Benjamin Franklin,' you say, 'would list all the points in favor of buying this car and then he'd list whatever he could against it. Then he'd total things up.' The salesman handles all the benefits. You begin by saying, 'So okay, you've said your old car needs an overhaul. That's point one. You've said you want a station wagon for the kids; that's point two. You've told me that particular shade of brown is your favorite.' And so on. Once you've tabulated your pitches, you flip the tablet around and hand across the pen. 'Okay,' you tell them. 'Now Benjamin Franklin would write down whatever he had *against* buying that car.' And you're silent. As noiseless as you can be. You don't say boo to them. They stare at that blank side of the paper and they get flustered. They weren't expecting this at all. Maybe the wife will say, 'We can't afford it,' and the husband will hurry up and scribble that down. Maybe he'll say, 'It's really more than we need for city driving.' He'll glance at you for approval but you won't even nod your head. You've suddenly turned to stone. Now they're struggling. They see two reasons against and twelve reasons for. You decide to help them. You say, 'Was it the color you didn't like?' Of course not, you dope. You put that down as point three in favor. But the wife will say, 'Oh no, I like that shade of brown a lot.' You sit back in your chair and wait. You wait four or five minutes if you have to, until they're really uncomfortable, until you've got them feeling like bozos. Then you take the tablet from them and make a big show of making the tally. They think you're an idiot anyway; counting out loud won't surprise them. And when you've told them they have twelve points in favor, two points against, you sit back in your chair and let that sink in. You say, 'What do you think Benjamin Franklin would do in this situation?' You've got them cornered and they know it and they can't think of any way out because there's only one way and they never consider it. Pressed against the wall like that the only solution is for the man or woman to say, 'I– Just– Don't– *Feel*– Like– It– Now.' All the salesman can do is recapitulate. If they want to wait, if the vibes don't feel right, if they don't sense it's the appropriate thing to do, they've got him. I just don't feel like it now. There's no way to sell against that."

Walter grinned. He thought Rick might have something. Even in outline the distributorship had real sex appeal.

So that afternoon Rick drove south to Indianapolis with his CB radio turned down so he wouldn't have all the chatter, and he picked up a sitter for his two little roses and took Jane out for dinner that night, claiming he wanted to celebrate the six-thousand-dollar commission. But after they had toasted The Cookies, he sprang the deal on her, explained everything about the lunch and Walter's positive reaction, how it all fit together, fell into place, shot off like a rocket, zoomed. And what it all boiled down to was they could move to South Bend, buy a house, and in two months, three months, a year, maybe he'd have himself a business.

Jane was ecstatic. Jane was a dynamo. While Rick did the dog-and-pony show for his boss and got him to pick up the tab for a move to the heart of Rick's territory, Jane did the real work of selecting their home and supervising the movers. Then Rick walked Tracy and little Connor from house to house down the new block in South Bend, introducing himself and his daughters to their new neighbors. There were five kids the same age on just one side of the street! Rick saw Tracy and Connor as teenagers at a backyard party with hanging lanterns and some of Rick's famous punch, and maybe two thousand four hundred boys trying to get a crack at his girls.

He drank iced tea with a stockbroker who crossed his legs and gazed out the window as Tracy tried to feed earthworms to his spaniel.

"Plenty of playmates," said Rick.

"This place is a population bomb."

"Yeah, but I love kids, don't you? I get home from a week on the road and there's nothing I like better than to roll on the floor a few hours with them."

"But your kids are girls!" the man said. He spit ice cubes back into his glass.

Rick shrugged. "I figure my wife will tell me when I should stop it."

What'd he think? Rick'd be copping feels, pawing them through their training bras? Maybe South Bend had its creepy side after all. Maybe a few of these daddies could bear some scrutiny.

Rick gave a full report to his wife, Jane, as they sat down with beers on the newly carpeted floor of the living room, telling her about all the fascinating people he had met in just a casual swing down the block. She said, "I don't know how you can just go knocking on doors and introducing yourself. I can't think what to converse about when I'm with strangers."

"That's one of the things that comes with being a traveler. You just assume you're welcome until someone tells you otherwise."

But how did that square with the uneasiness Rick Bozack felt with his old chum Mickey Hogan? A year ago Mickey had been an expensive copywriter, but then he had gone out on a limb to take over a smaller house that had been strictly an art and layout jobber and the gamble had paid off in spades. Mickey turned the firm into a real comer in South Bend, what they call in the trade a "hot shop."

But then Mickey had always been a brain. They had been rugby buddies at Notre Dame; they used to shoot snooker together and wear each other's tennis shoes and generally pal around like they were in a rowdy television commercial for some brand of beer. Now Mickey was almost skinny and as handsome as Sergio Franchi; and taking full advantage of it, don't let anybody kid you. They had doubled to the Notre Dame/Army game last season and Mickey brought along a knockout who kept sneaking her hand under Mickey's blue leg-warmer. Rick couldn't keep his eyes off her. Even Jane noticed it. "Boy, I bet she put lead in your pencil," she said.

So Rick was delighted, but amazed, when in February Mickey said he'd make the third for a terrific bunch of seats at the Notre Dame/Marquette basketball game. Mickey was even sitting on the snow-shoveled steps of his condominium, like some company president on the skids, when Rick pulled up along the curb. And now Mickey was smoking a black cigarillo as Rick told him how astonished he was these days to see that everyone he met was about his age; they had all risen to positions of authority and he was finding they could do him some good. You always thought it was just your father who could throw a name around. Now Rick was doing it himself. And getting results! "I'm really enjoying my thirties," Rick said, and then smiled. "I've got twenty credit cards in my wallet and I don't get acne anymore."

Mickey looked at him, bored.

"Okay; maybe not twenty credit cards, but my complexion's all cleared-up." Rick had forgotten how much of a jerk Mickey could be.

Rick kept the engine running and shoved The Captain and Tenille in his tape deck so Mickey could nestle with some good tunes, and he pressed the door chimes to a house the Herdzinas had just built: eighty-thousand smackers minimum. A small girl in pink underpants opened the door.

"Hi," said Rick in his Nice Man voice.

The girl shoved a finger up her nose.

Karen Herdzina hugged him hello. The hugging was a phenomenon that was totally new to South Bend and Rick never felt he handled it well. He lingered a bit too long with women and with men he was on the lookout for a quick takedown and two points on the scoreboard.

"I'll put some hustle into Walt," she said. "Tell him to get it in gear."

Walter came out of the bedroom with a new shirt he was ripping the plastic off of. "Mickey in the car?"

Rick nodded. "But it really belts out the heat."

Walter unpinned the sleeves and the cardboards and shoved the trash into a paper sack that had the cellophane wrappers of record albums in it.

"Look at that," he said. "My wife. She goes out spending my hard-earned money on records. The Carpenters, John Denver. I don't know what gets into her sometimes."

"I kind of enjoy John Denver," said Rick.

Walter leaned into Rick as they walked to the thrumming Oldsmobile, fanning three tickets out like a heart-stopping poker hand. "How about these beauties, Richard?"

"Wow. What do I owe ya?"

He frowned, pushed the tickets in his wallet. *"De nada,"* said Walter. "Buy me a beer."

As Rick drove lickety-split to the game, he and Walter talked about their budding families. You could see it was driving Mickey bananas. Here he was a bachelor, giving up a night when he could've probably had some make-out artist in the sack, and all he was hearing was talk about drooling and potties and cutting new teeth. So as he climbed up onto the beltway, Rick introduced the topic of basketball and Walter straddled the hump in the back seat and scrunched forward to talk about the Marquette scoring threat, particularly a couple of spades who'd make All-American, easy. Mickey introduced the topic of Doctor's Service Supply Company, Indianapolis, and asked Walter if he knew Rick was considering his own distributorship.

The banker said, "Heck, I'm the one who put the gleam in his eye." He returned to the back seat and crossed his kid leather gloves in his lap. "I think that's a tremendous opportunity, Rick. Where've you gone with it lately?"

"He's been testing the waters," said Mickey.

"I've had it on the back burner until Jane and the kids get a better lay of the land," said Rick. "I think it might be a pretty good setup though. Almost no time on the road and very little selling. I'll see what it's like to stay around the house and carry those canvas money bags up to a teller window."

Walter said, "I read somewhere that every person who starts a new business makes at least one horrible mistake. Something really staggering. If you get through that and you don't get kayoed, I guess you got it made."

They were quiet for several minutes, as if in mourning for all those bankrupts who had been walloped in the past. The 8-track clicked from 3 to 4. Mickey tapped one of his black cigarillos on a thumbnail.

"You like those things?" Rick asked.

Mickey lit it with the car lighter. "Yep," Mickey said. "I like them a lot."

Rick turned into the Notre Dame parking lot. "Since I gave up smoking, I notice it all the time. This health kick's really made a difference. I'm down two notches on my belt, my clothes don't fit, and I want to screw all the time now." He switched off the ignition. "How's that for a side benefit?"

Mickey said, "You smile a lot, you know that?"

It was an okay game; nothing spectacular as far as Rick was concerned. In fact, if you conked him on the head he might even have said it was boring. Where was the teamwork? Where was the give and take? A couple of black guys were out there throwing up junk shots, making the white guys look like clods, propelling themselves up toward the basket like they were taking stairs three at a time. It went back and forth like that all night, and except for the spine-tingling Notre Dame fight songs, except for the silver flask of brandy they passed up and down the row, he wished he was in a motel room somewhere eating cheese slices on crackers.

At the final buzzer the three men filed out with the crowd, waving to other old buddies and asking them how tricks were. The Oldsmobile engine turned slowly with cold before it fired. Mickey removed The Captain and Tenille from the tape deck. Mister Sophisticated.

Rick took the crosstown and shoved in a tape of Tony Orlando. Walter was paging through one of the catalogues for Doctor's Service Supply Company, Indianapolis, when he noticed a pizza parlor was still open, how did that sound? Rick admitted it didn't blow the top of his head off but he guessed he could give it a whirl. Mickey just sat there like wax.

Rick swerved in next to a souped-up Ford with big rear wheels that looked like boulders. "Secret Storm" was printed in maroon on the fender. As they walked to the entrance, Rick saw the three of them in the reflecting front windows, in blue shirts and rep ties and two-hundred-dollar topcoats, frowns in their eyes and gray threads in their hair and gruesome mortgages on their houses.

Walter stood with Rick at the counter as he ordered a combination pizza. An overhead blower gave them pompadours. "That was fun," said Rick.

"My wife encourages me to go out with the boys. She thinks it'll keep me from chasing tail."

Rick wished he had been somewhere else when Walter said that. It said everything about the guy.

Mickey had walked to the cigarette machine and pressed every button, then, deep in his private Weltschmerz, he wandered past a sign in the restaurant that said "This Section Closed." Rick backed away from the counter with three beers, sloshing some on his coat, and made his way to the forbidden tables where Mickey was sitting.

Mickey frowned. "How long are we going to dawdle here?"

"You got something you wanted to do?"

"There's *always* something to do, Rick."

A girl in a chef's hat seated an elderly couple in the adjoining area. She had pizza menus that she crushed to her breast as she sidestepped around benches toward the drinking buddies, bumping the sign that said "This Section Closed," schoolmarm disapproval in her eyes. Mickey rocked back in his chair. "Can I just sit here for a while? Would it ruin your day if I just sat here?"

The girl stopped and threw everything she had into the question and then shrugged and walked back to the cash register.

Rick almost smacked his forehead, he was that impressed. Mickey could get away with stuff that would land Rick in jail or in small claims court.

Soon he and Walter tore into a combination pizza, achieving at once a glossy burn on the roofs of their mouths. Mickey must not have wanted any. He seemed to have lost the power of speech. After a while Walter asked the two if they had read a magazine article about a recent psychological study of stress.

Rick asked, "How do you find time to read?"

Walter said, "I can't. My wife gets piles of magazines in the mail, though, and gives me digests of them at dinner."

Mickey looked elsewhere as Walter explained that the theory of this particular study was that whenever a person shifted the furniture of his life in any significant way at all, he or she was increasing the chances of serious illness. Change for the better? Change for the worse? Doesn't matter. If your spouse dies you get a hundred points against you. You get fired, that's fifty. You accomplish something outstanding, really excellent, still you get in the neighborhood of thirty points tacked onto your score. The list went on and on. Mortgages counted, salary bonuses, shifts in eating habits. Walter said, "You collect more than three hundred of these puppies in a year and it's time to consult a shrink."

Neither Walter nor Rick could finish his pizza, so Rick asked the kitchen help for a sack to carry the remains in. Then the three men walked out into the night gripping their collars at their necks, their ears crimped by the cold. It was close to zero. They could hear it in the snow.

There were three boys in the car that was christened "Secret Storm," each dangling cheeze pizza over his mouth.

Rick opened the car door on his side and bumped the trim on the souped-up Ford. He smiled and shrugged his shoulders at the kid on the passenger's side.

The kid called him a son of a bitch.

Mickey immediately walked around the car. "What'd he call you?"

"Nothing, Mickey. He was kidding."

But Mickey was already thumping the kid's car door with his knee. "I want to hear what you called him."

The door bolted open against Mickey's camel's hair coat, soiling it, and a kid bent out unsnapping a Catholic high school letterman's jacket. Before he had the last snap undone, Mickey punched the kid in the neck. The kid grabbed his throat and coughed. Mickey held his fists like cocktail glasses.

Walter stood in the cold with his gloved hands over his ears as Rick tried to pull Mickey away from the fracas. The kid hooked a fist into Rick's ear and knocked him against the car. Mickey tackled the kid and smacked him against the pavement. Dry snow fluffed up and blew. Rick covered his sore ear and Mickey tried to pin the kid's arms with his knees but the other boys were out of the Ford by then and pleading with the kid named Vic to let the guy go. It was at once obvious to Rick that the boys weren't aware they were dealing with three virile males in the prime of their lives, who had once played rugby at Notre Dame in the days when it was just a maiden sport.

Rick and Walter managed to untangle their buddy and haul him inside the car. Rick started the engine and spun his wheels in snow as he gunned the Oldsmobile out of the place. One of the kids kicked his bumper. The others were breathing on their hands.

"I don't believe it," said Rick.

Mickey was huffing; no jogger, he. "You don't believe what?" Mickey said.

"You're thirty-five years old, Mick! You don't go banging high school kids around."

Walter wiped the back window with his glove. "Oh no," he groaned.

Mickey turned around. "Are they following us?"

"Maybe their home's in the same direction," said Rick.

Mickey jerked open the door. Cold air flapped through the catalogues of Doctor's Service Supply Company, Indianapolis. "Let me out," Mickey said.

"Are you kidding?" Rick gave him a look that spoke of his resolute position on the question while communicating his willingness to compromise on issues of lesser gravity.

And yet Mickey repeated, "Let me out."

"What are you going to do?"

"Shut up and let me out of this car."

Walter said, "I think those are *Catholic* kids, Michael."

They were on a potholed residential street of ivied brick homes and one-car garages. There were white globes on eight-foot green streetlamps. Rick made a right-hand turn and so did the other car.

Mickey pushed the door wide open and scraped off the top of a snow pile. He leaned out toward the curb like a sick drunk about to lose it until Rick skidded slantwise on the ice pack and stopped. Then Mickey trotted out and slipped on the ice and sprawled against the right front door of the Ford.

The boy named Vic cracked his noggin on the doorframe trying to get out and he sat back down pretty hard, with tears in his eyes and both hands rubbing his hair.

"All right, you bastard," the driver said, and lurched out, tearing off *his* letterman's jacket. (Rick had worked like hell and never got one. And there weren't any razzle-dazzle black kids around then either.) The third kid got out and put his hand in his jeans pocket. He stripped a stick of gum and folded it in his mouth. Rick walked over to him and the kid's eyes slid. "Bob's going to make mincemeat out of your friend, man."

Mickey and the kid named Bob stepped over a yard hedge and Mickey was now hanging his coat on a clothesline pole. Walter was on the sidewalk stamping snow off his wing tips.

"Can you believe this weather?" Rick asked the kid. "My nose is like an ice cube."

The kid smiled. "Colder than a witch's tit, ain't it?"

The kid was in Rick's pocket. Rick still had the goods, all right.

Mickey and the boy named Bob were closing in the night-blue back yard like boxers about to touch gloves, when Mickey swung his fist into the kid's stomach and the kid folded up like a cardtable chair. "Ow! Oh man, where'd you hit me? Geez, that hurts."

A light went on in an upstairs bathroom.

Vic got out of the car, still holding his head, and the other kid tripped through the snow to help Bob limp to the Ford. "Get me to a hospital quick!"

"Oh, you're okay, Bob," said Vic.

"You don't know, man! I think he might've burst my appendix or something! I think he was wearing a ring!"

Mickey carefully put on his coat and sucked the knuckles of his hand when he sat down inside the car. Rick drove to Mickey's condominium first. Mickey was touching a bump on his forehead, smirking in Rick's direction.

"What made you want to do that, Mick?"

"Are you going to let some punk call you a son of a bitch?"

Rick slapped the steering wheel. "Of course! I do it all the *time.* Is that supposed to destroy you or something?"

Mickey just looked at the floormats or out the window. He jumped out when Rick parked in front of his place, and he didn't say goodbye.

Walter seated himself in the front bucket seat. "Whew! What an evening, huh?"

"I feel like I've run fourteen miles."

Walter crossed his legs and jiggled his shoe until Rick drove onto Walter's driveway whereupon he shook Rick's hand and suggested they do this again sometime and also wished him good luck in getting his business out of the starting gate.

The light was on in the upstairs bedroom of the Bozacks' blue Colonial home. Jane had switched the lights off downstairs. Rick let himself in with the milk box key and hung up his coat. He opened and shut the refrigerator door and then found himself patting his pockets for cigarettes. He went to the dining room breakfront and found an old carton of Salems.

He got a yellow ruled tablet and a pen from the desk and sat down in the living room with a lit cigarette. He printed VENTURE at the top. He drew a line down the center of the paper and numbered the right-hand side from one to twelve. After a few minutes there, Jane came down the stairs in her robe.

"Rick?"

"What?"

"I wanted to know if it was you."

"Who else would it be?"

"Why don't you come up? I'm only reading magazines."

"I think I'd like to just sit here for a while."

"In the *dark?*"

He didn't speak.

"Are you smoking?"

"Yep. I was feeling especially naughty."

She was silent. She stood with both feet on the same step. "You're being awfully mysterious."

"I just want to sit here for a while. Can I do that? Can I just sit here for a while?"

Jane climbed the stairs to their bedroom.

Rick stared at the numbered page. Why quit the team? Why risk the stress? Why give up all those cookies.

If pressed against the wall he'd say, "I just don't feel like it now."

Richard Price

from *Ladies' Man*

I was not in the mood to walk around all day, kissing ass, hawking room spray to shut-ins. And if I wasn't in the mood to do what I had to do I was a goner. My job would turn into a nightmare. One thing I had learned in the last few years was that people picked up where you were coming from immediately, and if you were knocking on doors with a look on your face like who flung it and left it you would have so many slammed doors in your kisser you'd get windburn. And I had a face like a neon sign, too.

The bus left me off by the diner. The minute I swung open the door I got hit with that diner smog and that pain-in-the-ass crackle-hiss soundtrack of frying eggs and home fries. I started down the narrow aisle between the red vinyl booths and counter stools, my sample case, like a bad conscience, smacking into my calf with every step.

"Kenny, you look like shit." Cheeseburger George the grill man looked up from pushing around his cholesterol disasters.

"Thank you, George, have a nice day."

The Bluecastle House boys were sitting at our table in the far corner. Al Fiorita, Jerry Gold and Maurice de la Creep, sitting there in their jackets and ties squinting and wheezing from a combination of cigarette and griddle grease smoke. They hadn't seen me come in. Fat Al was in the middle of a story. Charlene blocked my path taking an order from two ugly Catholic School girls in maroon stadium coats. I could see Charlene's bra and slip outline through her waitress whites. She was emaciated and tall. Sunlight blasted through the wispy ringlets of her teased hair. Charlene always reminded me of mummies–she had high cheekbones, pinched lips and weird middle-aged skin, taut and glossy, as if she preserved it in diaphragm jelly. I touched her back. "Excuse me." I leaned toward the girls. "Do you mind if I borrow your waitress for a few minutes?" I gently squeezed Charlene's shoulder. "I need to have sex with her." Charlene clucked, slapping my arm with her order pad. The girls giggled and snorted into their fists, and I moved on down the line.

"So anyways, I ast this guy if he got a couple of minutes, you know, so, ah, we could talk about this." Al winked up at me and continued. "An' he says to me, 'Bawh? Ah doan hayv tahm to shake mah dick after ah take a pee, an *you* wan a coupla minutes? Hayl no!' " Jerry and Maurice broke up. Al basked in their laughter, sat fat and sassy like a vanilla pimp in his Windsor knot, matching cuff links and tie pin.

"Hey." He raised an arm to me, still glowing, "Death of a salesman!"

"Death of a salesman you." I smirked sliding in next to Jerry. Some joke. I parked my case under the table and poured myself some coffee.

"Hey." Al nudged me. "Maurice got a joke. Maurice, tell him your joke."

Maurice chortled as he scratched furiously at his head, loosening enough dandruff to snow in Buffalo. Poor Maurice. He was the ugliest, grossest dude I'd ever met. Nose hair, face creases, and bad breath. Thirty years a Bluecastle House man. They sent him into neighborhoods with lots of half-blind, senile people. He was a living memo to me to find some other line of work, and fast.

"What's the Greek national anthem?" he gloated.

"How the hell . . ."

"Never leave your buddies' behind!" He almost screamed with glee. Al and Jerry started laughing again, not with Maurice, as the saying goes, but at him.

"Don't fuckin' tell *me,* tell Cheeseburger George." I nodded toward the grill.

"Cheeseburgers." Maurice chuckled. "When I was in Italy, all the whores called the white soldiers Cheeseburgers, the niggers were Hamburgers. They'd say, 'No cheese-a-boorgers joos a ham-a-boorgers.' They loved niggers."

"They only said that when *you* were around, Maurice." Al winked at us.

"No, they had a special name for Maurice." Jerry wiped his lips. "Alpo."

Maurice half-cursed, half-laughed, along with everybody.

"Kenny, guess what?" Jerry lightly slapped my arm. "You know that coconut room spray? I sold six cans yesterday to a synagogue on Essex Street."

"Okay, boys and girls." Al emptied two huge cardboard boxes of ketchup-sized foils onto the table. I stared with disgust at the familiar blue-green wrappers.

"Awright, what's the story here, cream sachet again?" I picked one up and flipped it back into the pile. "That shit don't move, whata they always givin' us cream sachet for?"

"It moves," Al said confidently. Fat Al. He was one of those "successful" salesmen. He even had a magnetized plastic ivory dollar-bill symbol on his dashboard.

"C'mon, Al, I had two hundred a these last week. I think I gave away twenty. Whatever happened to those liberation Afro Pics?"

"Where you gonna go with Afro Pics in the West Village?" Jerry grabbed two enormous fistfuls of sachet and stuffed one in each of his sport jacket pockets. When he stood up he looked like a pack mule. It always amazed me how little people cared about their appearance. Especially in our line of work. It took such little effort to make yourself presentable. If you didn't think enough of yourself to look groomed, how the hell could you expect anybody else to dig you?

I laughed out loud and everybody turned their heads to the window to see what I broke up about. Less than an hour ago I was freaking out because my existence made me feel like a gerbil on an exercise wheel, now I was riffing with equal intensity about good grooming. Life was wild.

"Hey, death of a salesman!" Maurice gave out a horselaugh that would embarrass a horse and flipped a cream sachet foil into my lap.

When I dropped out of college all I had was twenty-five credits to go. I always wound up thinking about that on mornings like this.

"Let's go, head 'em out!" Al got up from the table with an exaggerated groan, lugged his green alligator case from under the table and we all followed him down the aisle like an executive road gang.

"George"—I flipped a cream sachet foil onto the grill—"you look like shit."

When we hit the street I was not in an up-and-at-'em mood. I didn't even think I could sell a blood clot to a hemophiliac but I lucked out on my first shot—scored for a twenty-dollar sale on Bank Street to a kind-faced old German lady in a faded floral housedress. She had sandbag breasts and big red hands. Those hands looked as if they were in raw meat all day. She lived in a long, dimly lit apartment with clunky dark wooden furniture, brocade covers over everything and about six thousand prowling cats. We sat on facing sofas, me with the case and her with those huge meathooks folded calmly in her lap and a ruddy creased smile on her refugee face. She bought everything I showed her—hand lotion, room spray, an ironing board protector. She never said a word, just nodded for "one" when I asked, "Now how many should I put you down for, one or two?" When she bought a Car-Vac, my portable car rug vacuum cleaner in a can, I knew she was just buying all that shit so I would stick around and keep making human noises. That stuff always tore me up. I would always get those lonely older ladies who would buy anything I had to sell just to have my company. If they ordered something, not only would I have to sit there to sell it, but I would have to come back the end of the week and deliver it. And they would always have cats. Millions of cats. I was allergic to cats, too. I hated them. I'd sit there on some overstuffed cat-hair couch running my bullshit, sneezing my brains out, eyes like red stars, and these poor ladies would be holding their own hands nodding nodding nodding, smiling smiling smiling, sometimes silent like the German lady, sometimes gushing out the spew of their sad sad lives, getting up, bustling around with their bookcase behinds, offering me tea, coffee, sponge cake, cheesecake, pound cake, cupcake, kugel, babka—you name it. And half of them couldn't even speak English.

Anyway, after she bought the Car-Vac and introduced me to seven or eight cats—and you have no idea what an absolute schmuck you feel like nodding hello to a cat—I had to split. I felt as if there was a big hairy angora stuffed comfortably inside each lung and I wasn't so much breathing as leaking air. I even started sneezing blood.

But I made her day. Every day on the job I made somebody's day. Made that human connection. There were more lonely people in New York than in entire European countries. And every day I found at least one and pulled her back into the real world for thirty minutes. As much as I bitched about cats and crazies, making that connection hit the spot with me. I got a nice little high every time I scored a lonely. Without getting grandiose about it, it was a side benefit that sometimes made my work tolerable. But there was an element of half-assed compromise in that aspect of my life too. Because, despite the good moments, the bottom line was that I still had to sell them some bullshit ironing board cover or hand cream. And I spent a lot of time knocking on empty apartment doors or spieling to jerk-offs.

The German lady was followed by a half-hour of nothing, then two back-to-back sales on Greenwich Avenue and then I totally lucked out. I caught three housewives kibitzing in the home of a fourth. When I announced through the locked door that I was the Bluecastle Housewares man I heard one broad say, "I don't know about Bluecastle Housewares, but I can sure use a man." They all cracked up, the locks were unlocked and I was home free. I was the absolute master of the soft-core innuendo. I knew how to come on saucy but not smutty, naughty but not filthy. I could read a person's tolerance level for the risqué as fast as it took an expert to pick your watch while shaking your hand. I didn't waste any time with these four. I whipped out my foaming hand lotion and demonstrated it by rubbing it first into my hands, then into their hands. I said, "It's also good for a couple of other things, but I won't go into that," and gave an X-rated wink. I had no idea what the hell that was supposed to mean, but they had a group apoplexy. I walked out of there a half-hour later with a forty-dollar order and my gut sloshing with coffee.

So it was almost noon and I had written close to eighty dollars. That was a decent day right there. Usually I would try to write up seventy-five to a hundred dollars a day, pull a five-day week, take home two-fifty to three hundred, and I was happy. I was no freak for money. I wasn't going to Red China for a vacation or buying a brownstone. I didn't have kids, my place was within my means, La Donna chipped in some, I had nice clothes, so with an eighty-dollar morning I was very happy. If I scored for fifteen, twenty dollars more early in the afternoon I would knock off and go to a movie instead of busting my nates for the extra few bucks I might make over that. And that's the way I was. I didn't have it so bad. The job was okay. Better than most. And if I took a year out of my life and finished college? Then what? What was I supposed to become, a social worker? Would I go to graduate school? Would I become a $60,000-a-year ad exec giving blowjobs to the Cheerios account representative so I could keep writing jingles? Bullshit. And teaching was a nice little pipe dream, but unless I was willing to do the South Bronx, who was hiring? So big deal I read books. So did a housewife. Besides, I had the diction of a neighborhood bookie, and my degree was geared for business administration. So, later for that. I made more money than most college graduates, did more good for people, too. And I didn't feel inferior because I didn't have my degree. I was smart. I was one of the smartest people I knew. I didn't need a piece of paper to tell me that.

So I was feeling good. Feeling more like a person, a talker, I went back to the diner for lunch. I ordered good food. I didn't eat garbage. A nice strip steak, some cottage cheese and Tab. Kept myself good and tight, lots of protein. Fucking Al might have been King Shit when it came to sales, but I'd still be doing a hundred and fifty sit-ups a day when he'd be pushing up daisies. After lunch I sat, I relaxed, I had coffee and read the paper. Maurice came in. He sat down across from me, flipped his order pad on the table and twisted in the booth to flag down Charlene.

"Relax, Maurice." Charlene was wiping the counter and spoke to him with controlled distaste.

Grabbing his pad, I did a quick tally of his day's sales: sixty dollars. I won. One order caught my eye. It was for eight shower caps, paid in full.

"Hey, what's this?" I turned the pad to him.

"Eight shower caps," he chuckled.

"Yeah, I see that. Who the hell buys eight shower caps? Whata you doing, you workin' seniles again?"

"Nah, it was a girl. I showed her all the different colors she could get and she liked them all so she got 'em all." He laughed. "Char-le-ene," he singsonged, tickled with himself.

Anytime I felt low all I had to do was compare myself to Maurice. But sometimes I wondered what he had been like twenty years earlier when he was my age. Or better still, what was *I* going to be in twenty years? Well, shit, at least I wouldn't be like Maurice. But what did that leave, Fat Al? Maybe not that way either. But one thing I would be, if things didn't change, was a fifty-year-old Bluecastle Housewares man. No good. No good at all. The notion nauseated me, wrenched me out of the diner and back to work.

It was pushing three-thirty and I hadn't made one connection since lunch. I was in a rage, in a panic. I got into the nervous habit of squeezing my crotch, like I was applying a tourniquet. That afternoon became a disaster. I blew sales right and left. I was surly, impatient—as if it was *their* fucking fault that *I* had to stomp around in icy February weather selling that bullshit and the least they could goddamn do was *buy* the crap, for Christ's sake.

At a three-story brick building on Eleventh Street I finally decided that this was it, whatever I did in that building was it for the day. There was no elevator and the hallways were somebody's idea of the future. They were wallpapered with what looked like silver foil. There were only twelve apartments. No one was home in the first eight. A real nelly faggot came to the door in the ninth; a short, skinny, limp wrist with a sinus cold that gave him a nose like Rudolph the reindeer. He kept schlepping on his beak while eyeing the contents of my case through the six inches the chain lock allowed. He closed the door on me without saying sorry or no thank you, and I was stuck with all my cans and boxes sprouting around my feet like mushrooms. I muttered "Faggot" louder than I meant to, but I doubt that he heard me, and I had mixed feelings about that fact.

The name on the next door was Gordon. At that point I wasn't expecting anything miraculous. Even though I felt sorry for myself, I was also feeling a little better because after two more doors I could go home.

"Just a minute."

She sounded young and I quickly tucked my shirt into the elastic band of my shorts to flatten my gut. Three chains unlocked, the door swung open, and hey hey there she was, about five-ten, long red hair like Rita Whatever and wearing, no lie, a nightgown. It was two-forty-five in the P.M. and she was wearing a nightgown.

"Yeah?" She was half-smiling as though she had just woke up from a nice dream, and she leaned her head sleepily on the door frame, totally relaxed, totally unparanoid about me.

"Hi! I've got a free gift from Bluecastle for you!" What a schmuck. I raised my sample case slightly and pointed my chin at the apartment door. "Mind if I come in?"

"Oh yeah? What kind of free gift?" She yawned and rubbed the heel of her hand into her eyes. " 'Scuse me."

"We ran out of whips and vibrators." I pulled out one of those shit-ass cream sachet foils from my jacket pocket and held it up casually between two fingers, like an ID.

"Hawaii Five-O, ma'am, mind if we come in and look around?" My best shot.

"That's not much of a gift." Her skin was lightly sprayed with acne scars and a vaguely sour morning mouth smell drifted over to me. Nothing turned me off like bad breath, but I knew morning mouth was unavoidable.

"It's a door opener; I got better stuff in here." I tapped my case. She wasn't that nice-looking. It felt very important to feel that. I kept thinking about morning mouth and how someday we were all going to die no matter what.

She slowly turned from the door and walked unsteadily into the living room. I followed her in. The light from the living room window revealed her legs through her nightgown, and I immediately got one of those boners that start from the heart. For a fast two seconds I rubbed my crotch viciously behind her back, clenching my teeth and looking like a psycho.

She sat down in a flimsy, white, slightly unraveled wicker chair and hunched over, elbows on knees, hands crossed to her shoulders like she was shielding her tits from me. I sat across from her on a burgundy fake velvet sofa and opened my case between my feet. I could tell she lived alone. Two gilt-framed pictures of her parents, lot of plants, tortoise shell window shades, a portable typewriter on a cheap one-piece molded white plastic table, a stack of *New York* and *Ms.* magazines piled on the bottom rack of a TV stand, a small TV with aluminum foil on the antenna—I could tell plenty. And I could see somewhat between her knees if I ducked my head a little.

She nodded toward the case, a smirk on her face as if she had read my mind.

"So let's hear it."

The sleep was gone from her eyes, which were light green. I preferred dark eyes.

"You like coconuts? Everybody likes coconuts, right?" I plucked out a small aerosol can of room spray and shpritzed briefly in front of her. I inhaled with my eyes at half-mast as if I was smelling baked bread. Her eyelids fluttered as she jerked her head back, coughing into her fingers. Her knees parted for a second and I saw thigh.

"What? You don't like that!" I looked stunned. "It smells like Pago Pago in here now!"

She waved her hand in front of her face as if to clear the air. She had intelligent eyes; they had character. I parted my legs a little. I wanted her to know I had a hard-on.

"Do you know who my biggest customer for coconut room spray is? And I'm not lying." I leaned back and squinted. "Take a guess."

"Somebody in your immediate family, I imagine." She pumped a cigarette from a matching unraveling white wicker lamp table next to her.

"Nope, Terence Cardinal Cooke." I narrowed my eyes and pointed a finger. "He *loves* the stuff and has instructed the custodian at Saint Patrick's to snag a dozen cans every time I come by the church. Next time you go in there, smell the air."

"C'mon, what else you hiding in there?" She arched her eyebrows, and I swear to God she stared right at my crotch. I brought my knees together and did a nosedive into my case, fumbled around like I had three hands and whipped out the foam lotion, flipping it up like a baton and one-handing it.

"Here"—I wriggled my fingers—"give me your hand."

I rested the cold, bony back of her hand in my palm, shook up the can and shot a thick jet of cream onto her lifeline.

"Am I getting a light trim around the knuckles?" That eyebrow arch again.

"Very humorous. You're very quick." I smiled while rubbing the foam into her palm and fingers with both of my hands. It began to break down into a jellylike lotion. As I worked my ten fingers through her five, slithering through the taut webs and swirling around the joints my groin started pounding like a marathon runner's heart. I ran my middle fingers up and down her palm. She had make-up on from the night before; a slice of earlobe peeked through her red hair. My knees parted company again and my Adam's apple started doing elevator takes in my throat. "How does that feel?" My voice came out like Andy Devine.

"Mmm." Her eyes were closed.

I couldn't bring myself to spiel. Screw the spiel. She started weaving slightly and let her head hang back so her chin was stabbing up at the ceiling. I grabbed the can and shpritzed more foam on our hands to keep it going. For a split second her fingers massaged mine and I thought my brains would spew out my ears. I started grinding in my seat, staring between her knees. I squeezed myself with a greasy hand. No panties. Oh, my fucking God, she wasn't wearing panties. Suddenly the phone rang, and I jumped like I was snapping out of a nightmare. I think I actually said "Aw!" like a kid. She shook her head and smiled.

"I'll be back!" She got up and went through louvered double doors into the bedroom. I started following her in, hunched over and slobbering like Fred Flintstone on Spanish fly, but pulled myself together and returned to the couch. I gave myself five. This was it. This was fucking it. Finally, after six years of door to door, I was getting some nut. I jumped up and started dancing in front of the mirror. Screw La Donna. She could sleep like the dead from now on. I smoothed down my hair and shot my cuffs. I was bad. I was slick. I looked like fuckin' Marcello. I thanked God my mother was dark; the old man's side looked like anemic bookworms. I pulled down my tie knot, then pushed it back up. It looked better down and down it went. Made me look more laid back. Up for anything. I sat back on the couch and waited, patting my banana like I'd pat a Doberman I was trying to restrain. Twenty minutes went by. Thirty. Maybe she's putting in her diaphragm. I could've done it for her. I put in La Donna's diaphragm all the time. The double doors opened.

"Hi." She smiled. I stood at attention as if someone had just announced, "Gentlemen, the queen."

"Hey look, I'm sorry I'm taking so long."

"No problem," I lied.

"Listen, this is gonna be a real long call. Maybe you could come back some other time? I'm *really* sorry." She whirled her head on "really." I could see the cranberry tips of her nipples through the nightgown. I felt torpedoed.

"Well." I clucked my tongue. "You know I don't come around here that often." I pulled up my goddamn tie knot. "I can wait." It was all over.

"No, that's okay. Why don't you stop by whenever, okay? I'm really sorry."

"Right." I felt so down I thought I was dying.

"You can let yourself out . . . That hand lotion was nice." Another apologetic smile and she was gone, back into the bedroom.

I felt like pissing on her couch. It was three-thirty. I should have split right then, but I felt as if she owed me something and I started stalking the apartment like it was mine by right of rage. I wound up in her bathroom; cutesy big-eyed animal print wallpaper and matching shower curtain. Bright yellow plastic toilet seat. I swept back the shower curtain like I was looking for evidence. The bathtub was filled with stray hairs and a Japanese loofa sponge lay there like the corpse of a sunken ship in a drained ocean. A fat roach waddled across a thin bar of gold translucent soap in a bright yellow soap dish shaped like a seashell on the small sink. The basin had large bright green copper water stains under each faucet. The floor was covered with a cheap cut-it-yourself green rug. She had done a shitty job of laying it down; it was bunched and rolled around the toilet base at one end and didn't reach the edge of the bathtub at the other. Her medicine cabinet contained the usual shit. Nylon floral cosmetic bag, filled with eye shadow, pencil liners and lipsticks. A small jar of Vaseline on a shelf with supermarket-brand aspirin and a hair-caked leg razor. Antidiarrhea pills in an amber prescription bottle. *That* disgusted me. Hairs in the bathtub, the fat roach halfway up the wall, his antenna swishing in slow motion. The place was a pit and she was a slob. A big dark gold towel didn't match anything else in the room. It was damp probably from the evening before because she didn't take the time and trouble to fold it over the bar but just jammed it in the goddamn towel rack like who gives a royal fuck. I couldn't find a diaphragm or birth control pills. I hated that bathroom. It stunk of her privacy and I was up for heavy sabotage, demolition, but I couldn't think of anything to do.

I was staring at a stalactite of hardened green toothpaste frozen from the topless tube to the white enamel of the sink when I got hit with a frightening flash of not knowing where I was. Dizziness. I got scared. I couldn't sense me. I panicked for a second, then snapped out of it. Suddenly I didn't want to get caught in there. She would eat me alive. I got out fast. I felt like an intruder, which I was. Her double doors were still closed and I split.

I did the last apartment.

"Free gift from Bluecastle."

"I can't take it" from inside.

"Good." I clomped down the stairs. "I can't take it either."

Sinclair Lewis

from *Elmer Gantry*

Elmer Gantry was twenty-eight, and for two years he had been a traveling salesman for the Pequot Company.

Harrows and rakes and corn-planters; red plows and gilt-striped green wagons; catalogues and order-lists; offices glassed off from dim warehouses; shirt-sleeved dealers on high stools at high desks; the bar at the corner; stifling small hotels and lunch-rooms; waiting for trains half the night in foul boxes of junction stations, where the brown slatted benches were an agony to his back; trains, trains, trains; trains and time-tables and joyous return to his headquarters in Denver; a drunk, a theater, and service in a big church.

He wore a checked suit, a brown derby, striped socks, the huge ring of gold serpents and an opal which he had bought long ago, flower-decked ties, and what he called "fancy vests"—garments of yellow with red spots, of green with white stripes, of silk or daring chamois.

He had had a series of little loves, but none of them important enough to continue.

He was not unsuccessful. He was a good talker, a magnificent handshaker, his word could often be depended on, and he remembered most of the price-lists and all of the new smutty stories. In the office at Denver he was popular with "the boys." He had one infallible "stunt"—a burlesque sermon. It was known that he had studied to be a preacher but had courageously decided that it was no occupation for a "real two-fisted guy," and that he had "told the profs where they got off." A promising and commendable fellow; conceivably sales-manager some day.

Whatever his dissipations, Elmer continued enough exercise to keep his belly down and his shoulders up. He had been shocked by Deacon Bains' taunt that he was growing soft, and every morning in his hotel room he unhumorously did calisthenics for fifteen minutes; evenings he bowled or boxed in Y. M. C. A. gymnasiums, or, in towns large enough, solemnly swam up and down tanks like a white porpoise. He felt lusty, and as strong as in Terwillinger days.

Yet Elmer was not altogether happy.

He appreciated being free of faculty rules, free of the guilt which in seminary days had followed his sprees at Monarch, free of the incomprehensible debates of Harry Zenz and Frank Shallard, yet he missed leading the old hymns, and the sound of his own voice, the sense of his own power, as he held an audience by his sermon. Always on Sunday evenings (except when he had an engagement with a waitress or a chambermaid) he went to the evangelical church nearest his hotel. He enjoyed criticizing the sermon professionally.

"Golly, I could put it all over that poor boob! The straight gospel is all right, but if he'd only stuck in a couple literary allusions, and lambasted the saloon-keepers more, he'd 've had 'em all het up."

He sang so powerfully that despite a certain tobacco and whisky odor the parsons always shook hands with extra warmth, and said they were glad to see you with us this evening, Brother.

When he encountered really successful churches, his devotion to the business became a definite longing to return to preaching; he ached to step up, push the minister out of his pulpit, and take charge, instead of sitting back there unnoticed and unadmired, as though he were an ordinary layman.

"These chumps would be astonished if they knew what I am!" he reflected.

After such an experience it was vexatious on Monday morning to talk with a droning implement-dealer about discounts on manure-spreaders; it was sickening to wait for train-time in a cuspidor-filled hotel lobby when he might have been in a church office superior with books, giving orders to pretty secretaries and being expansive and helpful to consulting sinners. He was only partly solaced by being able to walk openly into a saloon and shout, "Straight rye, Bill."

* * *

In a religious mood (which fortunately did not prevent his securing some telling credit-information by oiling a bookkeeper with several drinks) he came to Sautersville, Nebraska, an ugly, enterprising, industrial town of 20,000. And in that religious mood he noted the placards of a woman evangelist, one Sharon Falconer, a prophetess of whom he had heard.

The clerk in the hotel, the farmers about the implement warehouse, said that Miss Falconer was holding union meetings in a tent, with the support of most of the Protestant churches in town; they asserted that she was beautiful and eloquent, that she took a number of assistants with her, that she was "the biggest thing that ever hit this burg," that she was comparable to Moody, to Gipsy Smith, to Sam Jones, to J. Wilbur Chapman, to this new baseball evangelist, Billy Sunday.

"That's nonsense. No woman can preach the gospel," declared Elmer, as an expert.

But he went, that evening, to Miss Falconer's meeting.

The tent was enormous; it would seat three thousand people, and another thousand could be packed in standing-room. It was nearly filled when Elmer arrived and elbowed his majestic way forward. At the front of the tent was an extraordinary structure, altogether different from the platform-pulpit-American-flag arrangement of the stock evangelist. It was a pyramidal structure, of white wood with gilded edges, affording three platforms; one for the choir, one higher up for a row of seated local clergy; and at the top a small platform with a pulpit shaped like a shell and painted like a rainbow. Swarming over it all were lilies, roses and vines.

"Great snakes! Regular circus lay-out! Just what you'd expect from a fool woman evangelist!" decided Elmer.

The top platform was still unoccupied; presumably it was to set off the charms of Miss Sharon Falconer.

The mixed choir, with their gowns and mortar-boards, chanted "Shall We Gather at the River?" A young man, slight, too good-looking, too arched of lip, wearing a priest's waistcoat and collar turned round, read from Acts at a stand on the second platform. He was an

Oxonian, and it was almost the first time that Elmer had heard an Englishman read.

"Huh! Willy-boy, that's what he is! This outfit won't get very far. Too much skirts. No punch. No good old-fashioned gospel to draw the customers," scoffed Elmer.

A pause. Every one waited, a little uneasy. Their eyes went to the top platform. Elmer gasped. Coming from some refuge behind the platform, coming slowly, her beautiful arms outstretched to them, appeared a saint. She was young, Sharon Falconer, surely not thirty, stately, slender and tall; and in her long slim face, her black eyes, her splendor of black hair, was rapture or boiling passion. The sleeves of her straight white robe, with its ruby velvet girdle, were slashed, and fell away from her arms as she drew every one to her.

"God!" prayed Elmer Gantry, and that instant his planless life took on plan and resolute purpose. He was going to have Sharon Falconer.

Her voice was warm, a little husky, desperately alive.

"Oh, my dear people, my dear people, I am not going to preach tonight—we are all so weary of nagging sermons about being nice and good! I am not going to tell you that you're sinners, for which of us is not a sinner? I am not going to explain the Scriptures. We are all bored by tired old men explaining the Bible through their noses! No! We are going to find the golden Scriptures written in our own hearts, we are going to sing together, laugh together, rejoice together like a gathering of April brooks, rejoice that in us is living the veritable spirit of the Everlasting and Redeeming Christ Jesus!"

Elmer never knew what the words were, or the sense—if indeed any one knew. It was all caressing music to him, and at the end, when she ran down curving flower-wreathed stairs to the lowest platform and held out her arms, pleading with them to find peace in salvation, he was roused to go forward with the converts, to kneel in the writhing row under the blessing of her extended hands.

But he was lost in no mystical ecstasy. He was the critic, moved by the play but aware that he must get his copy in to the newspaper.

"This is the outfit I've been looking for! Here's where I could go over great! I could beat that English preacher both ways from the ace. And Sharon— Oh, the darling!"

She was coming along the line of converts and near-converts, laying her shining hands on their heads. His shoulders quivered with consciousness of her nearness. When she reached him and invited him, in that thrilling voice, "Brother, won't you find happiness in Jesus?" he did not bow lower, like the others, he did not sob, but looked straight up at her jauntily, seeking to hold her eyes, while he crowed, "It's happiness just to have had your wondrous message, Sister Falconer!"

She glanced at him sharply, she turned blank, and instantly passed on.

He felt slapped. "I'll show her yet!"

He stood aside as the crowd wavered out. He got into talk with the crisp young Englishman who had read the Scripture lesson—Cecil Aylston, Sharon's first assistant.

"Mighty pleased to be here tonight, Brother," bumbled Elmer. "I happen to be a Baptist preacher myself. Bountiful meeting! And you read the lesson most inspiringly."

Cecil Aylston rapidly took in Elmer's checked suit, his fancy vest, and "Oh. Really? Splendid. So good of you, I'm sure. If you will excuse me?" Nor did it increase Elmer's affection to have Aylston leave him for one of the humblest of the adherents, an old woman in a broken and flapping straw hat.

Elmer disposed of Cecil Aylston: "To hell with him! There's a fellow we'll get rid of! A man like me, he gives me the icy mitt, and then he goes to the other extreme and slops all over some old dame that's probably saved already, that you, by golly, couldn't unsave with a carload of gin! That'll do you, my young friend! And you don't like my check suit, either. Well, I certainly do buy my clothes just to please you, all right!"

He waited, hoping for a chance at Sharon Falconer. And others were waiting. She waved her hand at all of them, waved her flaunting smile, rubbed her eyes, and begged, "Will you forgive me? I'm blind-tired. I must rest." She vanished into the mysteries behind the gaudy gold-and-white pyramid.

Even in her staggering weariness, her voice was not drab; it was filled with that twilight passion which had captured Elmer more than her beauty. . . . "Never did see a lady just like her," he reflected, as he plowed back to his hotel. "Face kinda thin. Usually I like 'em plumper. And yet—golly! I could fall for her as I never have for anybody in my life. . . . So this darn' Englishman didn't like my clothes! Looked as if he thought they were too sporty. Well, he can stick 'em in his ear! Anybody got any objection to my clothes?"

The slumbering universe did not answer, and he was almost content. And at eight next morning—Sautersville had an excellent clothing shop, conducted by Messrs. Erbsen and Goldfarb—and at eight Elmer was there, purchasing a chaste double-breasted brown suit and three rich but sober ties. By hounding Mr. Goldfarb he had the alterations done by half-past nine, and at ten he was grandly snooping about the revival tent. . . . He should have gone on to the next town this morning.

Sharon did not appear till eleven, to lecture the personal workers, but meanwhile Elmer had thrust himself into acquaintanceship with Art Nichols, a gaunt Yankee, once a barber, who played the cornet and the French horn in the three-piece orchestra which Sharon carried with her.

"Yes, pretty good game, this is," droned Nichols. "Better'n barberin' and better'n one-night stands—oh, I'm a real trouper, too; play characters in tent-shows—I was out three seasons with Tom shows. This is easier. No street parades, and I guess prob'ly we do a lot of good, saving souls and so on. Only these religious folks do seem to scrap amongst themselves more'n the professionals."

"Where do you go from here?"

"We close in five days, then we grab the collection and pull out of here and make a jump to Lincoln, Nebraska; open there in three days. Regular troupers' jump, too—don't even get a Pullman—leave here on the day coach at eleven P.M. and get into Lincoln at one."

"Sunday night you leave, eh? That's funny. I'll be on that train. Going to Lincoln myself."

"Well, you can come hear us there. I always do 'Jerusalem the Golden' on the cornet, first meeting. Knocks 'em cold. They say it's all this gab that gets 'em going and drags in the sinners, but don't you believe it—it's the music. Say, I can get more damn' sinners weeping on an E-flat cornet than nine gospel-artists all shooting off their faces at once!"

"I'll bet you can, Art. Say, Art— Of course I'm a preacher myself, just in business temporarily, making arrangements for a new appointment." Art looked like one who was about to not lend money. "But I don't believe all this bull about never having a good time; and of course Paul said to 'take a little wine for your stomach's sake' and this town is dry, but I'm going to a wet one between now and Saturday, and if I were to have a pint of rye in my jeans—heh?"

"Well, I'm awful' fond of my stomach—like to do something for its sake!"

"What kind of a fellow is this Englishman? Seems to be Miss Falconer's right-hand man."

"Oh, he's a pretty bright fellow, but he don't seem to get along with us boys."

"She like him? Wha' does he call himself?"

"Cecil Aylston, his name is. Oh, Sharon liked him first-rate for a while, but wouldn't wonder if she was tired of his highbrow stuff now, and the way he never gets chummy."

"Well, I got to go speak to Miss Falconer a second. Glad met you, Art. See you on the train Sunday evening."

They had been talking at one of the dozen entrances of the gospel tent. Elmer had been watching Sharon Falconer as she came briskly into the tent. She was no high priestess now in Grecian robe, but a business-woman, in straw hat, gray suit, white shirt-waist, linen cuffs and collar. Only her blue bow and the jeweled cross on her watch-fob distinguished her from the women in offices. But Elmer, collecting every detail of her as a miner scoops up nuggets, knew now that she was not flat-breasted, as in the loose robe she might have been.

She spoke to the "personal workers," the young women who volunteered to hold cottage prayer-meetings and to go from house to house stirring up spiritual prospects:

"My dear friends, I'm very glad you're all praying, but there comes a time when you've got to add a little shoe-leather. While you're longing for the Kingdom—the devil does his longing nights, and daytimes he hustles around *seeing* people, *talking* to 'em! Are you ashamed to go right in and ask folks to come to Christ—to come to our meetings, anyway? I'm not at all pleased. Not at all, my dear young friends. My charts show that in the Southeast district only one house in three has been visited. This won't do! You've got to get over the idea that the service of the Lord is a nice game, like putting Easter lilies on the altar. Here there's only five days left, and you haven't yet waked up and got busy. And let's not have any silly nonsense about hesitating to hit people for money-pledges, and hitting 'em hard! We can't pay rent for this lot, and pay for lights and transportation and the wages of all this big crew I carry, on hot air! Now you—you pretty girl there with the red hair—my! I wish I had such hair!—what have you done, sure-enough *done*, this past week?"

In ten minutes she had them all crying, all aching to dash out and bring in souls and dollars.

She was leaving the tent when Elmer pounced on her, swaggering, his hand out.

"Sister Falconer, I want to congratulate you on your wonderful meetings. I'm a Baptist preacher—the Reverend Gantry."

"Yes?" sharply. "Where is your church?"

"Why, uh, just at present I haven't exactly got a church."

She inspected his ruddiness, his glossiness, the odor of tobacco; her brilliant eyes had played all over him, and she demanded:

"What's the trouble this time? Booze or women?"

"Why, that's absolutely untrue! I'm surprised you should speak like that, Sister Falconer! I'm in perfectly good standing! It's just— I'm taking a little time off to engage in business, in order to understand the workings of the lay mind, before going on with my ministry."

"Um. That's splendid. Well, you have my blessing, Brother! Now if you will excuse me? I must go and meet the committee."

She tossed him an unsmiling smile and raced away. He felt soggy, lumbering, unspeakably stupid, but he swore, "Damn you, I'll catch you when you aren't all wrapped up in business and your own darn-fool self-importance, and then I'll make you wake up, my girl!"

* * *

He had to do nine days' work, to visit nine towns, in five days, but he was back in Sautersville on Sunday evening and he was on the eleven-o'clock train for Lincoln—in the new brown suit.

His fancy for Sharon Falconer had grown into a trembling passion, the first authentic passion of his life.

It was too late in the evening for a great farewell, but at least a hundred of the brethren and sisters were at the station, singing "God Be with You Till We Meet Again" and shaking hands with Sharon Falconer. Elmer saw his cornet-wielding Yankee friend, Art Nichols, with the rest of the evangelistic crew—the aide, Cecil Aylston, the fat and sentimental tenor soloist, the girl pianist, the violinist, the children's evangelist, the director of personal work. (That important assistant, the press agent, was in Lincoln making ready for the coming of the Lord.) They looked like a sleepy theatrical troupe as they sat on their suit-cases waiting for the train to come in, and like troupers, they were dismayingly different from their stage rôles. The anemically pretty pianist, who for public uses dressed in seraphic silver robes, was now merely a small-town girl in wrinkled blue serge; the director of personal work, who had been nun-like in linen, was bold in black-trimmed red, and more attentive to the amorous looks of the German violinist than to the farewell hymns. The Reverend Cecil Aylston gave orders to the hotel baggageman regarding their trunks more like a quartermaster sergeant than like an Oxonian mystic.

Sharon herself was imperial in white, and the magnet for all of them. A fat Presbyterian pastor, with whiskers, buzzed about her, holding her arm with more than pious zeal. She smiled on him (to Elmer's rage), she smiled equally on the long thin Disciples-of-Christ preacher, she shook hands fervently, and she was tender to each shout of "Praise God, Sister!" But her eyes were weary, and Elmer saw that when she turned from her worshippers, her mouth drooped. Young she seemed then, tired and defenseless.

"Poor kid!" thought Elmer.

The train flared and shrieked its way in, and the troupe bustled with suit-cases. "Good-by–God bless you–God speed the work!" shouted every one . . . every one save the Congregational minister, who stood sulkily at the edge of the crowd explaining to a parishioner, "And so she goes away with enough cash for herself, after six weeks' work, to have run our whole church for two years!"

Elmer ranged up beside his musical friend, Art Nichols, and as they humped up the steps of a day-coach he muttered, "Art! Art! Got your stomach-medicine here!"

"Great!"

"Say. Look. Fix it so you sit with Sharon. Then pretty soon go out for a smoke–"

"She don't like smoking."

"You don't need to tell her what for! Go out so I can sit down and talk to her for a while. Important business. About–a dandy new town for her evangelistic labors. Here: stick this in your pocket. And I'll dig up s'more for you at Lincoln. Now hustle and get in with her."

"Well, I'll try."

So, in the dark malodorous car, hot with late spring, filled with women whose corsets creaked to their doleful breathing, with farmers who snored in shirt-sleeves, Elmer stood behind the seat in which a blur marked the shoulders of Art Nichols and a radiance showed the white presence of Sharon Falconer. To Elmer she seemed to kindle the universe. She was so precious, every inch of her; he had not known that a human being could be precious like this and magical. To be near her was ecstasy enough . . . almost enough.

She was silent. He heard only Art Nichols' twanging, "What do you think about us using some of these nigger songs—hand 'em a jolt?" and her drowsy, "Oh, let's not talk about it tonight." Presently, from Art, "Guess I'll skip out on the platform and get a breath of air," and the sacred haunt beside her was free to the exalted Elmer.

He slipped in, very nervous.

She was slumped low in the seat, but she sat up, peered at him in the dimness, and said, with a grave courtesy which shut him out more than any rudeness, "I'm so sorry, but this place is taken."

"Yes, I know, Sister Falconer. But the car's crowded, and I'll just sit down and rest myself while Brother Nichols is away—that is, if you'll let me. Don't know if you remember me. I'm—I met you at the tent in Sautersville. Reverend Gantry."

"Oh," indifferently. Then, quickly: "Oh, yes, you're the Presbyterian preacher who was fired for drinking."

"That's absolutely—!" He saw that she was watching him, and he realized that she was not being her saintly self nor her efficient self but a quite new, private, mocking self. Delightedly he went on, "—absolutely incorrect. I'm the Christian Scientist that was fired for kissing the choir-leader on Saturday."

"Oh, that was careless of you!"

"So you're really human?"

"Me? Good Heavens, yes! Too human."

"And you get tired of it?"

"Of what?"

"Of being the great Miss Falconer, of not being able to go into a drug-store to buy a tooth-brush without having the clerk holler, 'Praise God, we have some dandy two-bit brushes, hallelujah!' "

Sharon giggled.

"Tired," and his voice was lulling now, "of never daring to be tired, which same is what you are tonight, and of never having anybody to lean on!"

"I suppose, my dear reverend Brother, that this is a generous offer to let me lean on you!"

"No. I wouldn't have the nerve! I'm scared to death of you. You haven't only got your beauty—no! please let me tell you how a fellow preacher looks at you—and your wonderful platform-presence, but I kind of guess you've got brains."

"No, I haven't. Not a brain. All emotion. That's the trouble with me." She sounded awake now, and friendly.

"But think of all the souls you've brought to repentance. That makes up for everything, doesn't it?"

"Oh, yes, I suppose it— Oh, of course it does. It's the only thing that counts. Only— Tell me: What really did happen to you? Why did you get out of the church?"

Gravely, "I was a senior in Mizpah Theological Seminary, but I had a church of my own. I fell for a girl. I won't say she lured me on. After all, a man ought to face the consequences of his own foolishness. But she certainly did— Oh, it amused her to see a young preacher go mad over her. And she was so lovely! Quite a lot like you, only not so beautiful, not near, and she let on like she was mad about church work—that's what fooled me. Well! Make a long story short: We were engaged to be married, and I thought of nothing but her and our life together, doing the work of the Lord, when one evening I walked in and there she was in the arms of another fellow! It broke me up so that I— Oh, I tried, but I simply couldn't go on preaching, so I quit for a while. And I've done well in business. But now I'm ready to go back to the one job I've ever cared about. That's why I wanted to talk to you there at the tent. I needed your woman's sympathy as well as your experience—and you turned me down!"

"Oh, I am so, so sorry!" Her hand caressed his arm.

Cecil Aylston came up and looked at them with a lack of sanctity.

When they reached Lincoln, he was holding her hand and saying, "You poor, dear, tired child!" and, "Will you have breakfast with me? Where are you staying in Lincoln?"

"Now see here, Brother Gantry—"

"Elmer!"

"Oh, don't be ridiculous! Just because I'm so fagged out that it's nice to play at being a human being, don't try to take advantage—"

"Sharon Falconer, will you quit being a chump? I admire your genius, your wonderful work for God, but it's because you're too big to just be a professional gospel-shouter every minute that I most admire you. You know mighty good and well that you like to be simple and even slangy for a while. And you're too sleepy just now to know whether you like me or not. That's why I want us to meet at breakfast, when the sleepiness is out of the wonderful eyes—"

"Um. It all sounds pretty honest except that last stuff—you've certainly used that before. Do you know, I like you! You're so completely brazen, so completely unscrupulous, and so beatifically ignorant! I've been with sanctimonious folks too much lately. And it's interesting to see that you honestly think you can captivate me. You funny thing! I'm staying at the Antlers Hotel in Lincoln—no use, by the way, your trying to get a room near my suite, because I have practically the whole floor engaged—and I'll meet you at breakfast there at nine-thirty."

* * *

Though he did not sleep well, he was up early and at his toilet; he shaved, he touched up his bluff handsomeness with lilac water and talcum, he did his nails, sitting in athletic underwear, awaiting his new suit, sent down for pressing. The new purpose in a life recently so dispirited gave vitality to his bold eyes and spring to his thick muscles as he strode through the gold-and-marble lobby of the Antlers Hotel and awaited Sharon at the restaurant door. She came down fresh in white crash bordered with blue. As they met they laughed, admitting comradeship in folly. He took her arm gaily, led her through a flutter of waitresses excited over the coming of the celebrated lady of God, and ordered competently.

"I've got a great idea," said he. "I've got to beat it this afternoon, but I'll be back in Lincoln on Friday, and how'd it be if you billed me to address your meeting as a saved business-man, and I talked for half an hour or so on Friday evening about the good, hard, practical, dollars-and-cents value of Christ in Commerce?"

"Are you a good talker?"

"A knock-out."

"Well, it might be a good idea. Yes, we'll do it. By the way, what is your business? Hold-ups?"

"I'm the crack salesman of the Pequot Farm Implement Company, Sharon, and if you don't believe it–"

"Oh, I do. [She shouldn't have.] I'm sure you tell the truth–often. Of course we won't need to mention the fact that you're a preacher, unless somebody insists on asking. How would this be as a topic–'Getting the Goods with a Gideon Bible'?"

"Say, that would be elegant! How I was in some hick town, horrible weather, slush and rain and everything–dark skies, seemed like sun never would shine again–feet all soaked from tramping the streets–no sales, plumb discouraged–sat in my room, forgotten to buy one of the worldly magazines I'd been accustomed to read–idly picked up a Gideon Bible and read the parable of the talents–found that same day *you* were in town–went and got converted–saw now it wasn't just for money but for the Kingdom of Christ, to heighten my influence as a Christian business-man, that I had to increase sales. That bucked up my self-confidence so that I increased sales to beat the band! And how I owe everything to your inspired powers, so it's a privilege to be able to testify. And about how it isn't the weak skinny failure that's the fellow to get saved, but takes a really strong man to not be ashamed to surrender all for Jesus."

"Why, I think that's fine, Brother Elmer, I really do. And dwell a lot on being in your hotel room there–you took off your shoes and threw yourself down on the bed, feeling completely beaten, but you were so restless you got up and poked around the room and picked up the Gideon Bible. I'll feature it big. And you'll make it strong, Elmer? You won't let me down? Because I really will headline it in my announcements. I've persuaded you to come clear from Omaha–no, that's not far–clear from Denver for it. And if you do throw yourself into it and tear loose, it'll add greatly to the glory of God, and the success of the meeting in winning souls. You will?"

"Dear, I'll slam into 'em so hard you'll want me in every town you go to. You bet."

"Um, that's as may be, Elmer. Here comes Cecil Aylston–you know my assistant? He looks so cross. He is a dear, but he's so terribly highbrow and refined and everything and he's always trying to nag me into being refined. But you'll love him."

"I will not! Anyway, I'll struggle against it!"

They laughed.

The Rev. Cecil Aylston, of the flaxen hair and the superior British complexion, glided to their table, looked at Elmer with a blankness more infuriating than a scowl, and sat down, observing:

"I don't want to intrude, Miss Falconer, but you know the committee of clergy are awaiting you in the parlor."

"Oh, dear," sighed Sharon. "Are they as terrible as usual here? Can't you go up and get the kneeling and praying done while I finish my scrambled eggs? Have you told them they've got to double the amount of the pledges before this week is over or the souls in Lincoln can go right on being damned?" Cecil was indicating Elmer with an alarmed jerk of his head. "Oh, don't worry about Elmer. He's one of us—going to speak for us Friday—used to be a terribly famous preacher, but he's found a wider field in business—Reverend Aylston, Reverend Gantry. Now run along, Cecil, and keep 'em pious and busy. Any nice-looking young preachers in the committee, or are they all old stiffs?"

Aylston answered with a tight-lipped glare, and flowed away.

"Dear Cecil, he is so useful to me—he's actually made me take to reading poetry and everything. If he just wouldn't be polite at breakfast-time! I wouldn't mind facing the wild beasts of Ephesus, but I can't stand starch with my eggs. Now I must go up and join him."

"You'll have lunch with me?"

"I will not! My dear young man, this endeth my being silly for this week. From this moment on I'll be one of the anointed, and if you want me to like you— God help you if you come around looking pussy-catty while I'm manhandling these stiff-necked brethren in Christ! I'll see you Friday—I'll have dinner with you, here, before the meeting. And I can depend on you? Good!"

Phillip Lopate

from *The Rug Merchant*

Holiday Season

A week had passed since he'd received his landlord's letter; the store had suddenly gotten busy with Christmas Day drawing near. Sales were taking a healthy upturn. Occupied with customers all day, Cyrus put off thinking about his long-range rent problems. Irrational as he knew it to be, he hoped that the volume of business would triple and stay at that level, making it unnecessary for him to act further.

He was trying to steal a few moments with the crossword puzzle when the doorbell tinkled, as it had been doing all morning.

A shy young couple entered the store, staying put a few feet from the threshold. They looked Puerto Rican or Italian; newlyweds, Cyrus imagined. He liked them. With all his new customers, he had immediate intuitive flashes of like and dislike.

"Can I help you with anything?"

"We're not sure. . . ." The young bride looked at her husband for help.

"Fine. Take your time and look around. It might help to know what size rug you were interested in."

"It's for under a dining room table," the muscular young man said softly.

"Well, that tells me something. What colors did you have in mind?"

"I guess earth tones?" the dark-haired young woman said apologetically. "Like orange or beige. Not so much red–right?" she appealed to her husband.

"Fine. That should be no problem," said Cyrus. "And did you have a certain style or design preference?" Cyrus was going down his usual checklist, zeroing in like a medical diagnosis. Next he would ask about price.

"We don't really know much about Oriental rugs," said the young man.

"Why don't you step over here. Let's see . . . ," said Cyrus, gazing at his stacks. "It's a little hard to get away from red in the traditional Persians. But there are rugs with some red in them, and then there are *red* rugs. May I know what sort of amount you were planning to spend on this?"

The woman looked panicked. He realized he had asked the question too soon with them; it was all a matter of tact, he should have sensed it. "Well, we can just pull out a few rugs and you will see what you like anyway."

He had shown them five, and was in the midst of unrolling several other possibilities, when another couple walked in with an air of expecting immediate service. Cyrus wound up the conversation and left the newlyweds to ponder the choices alone, going over to this older pair. The woman was thin, pinched, with glasses and a mistrustful expression, as though she smelled something a little "off"; and the man was stooped, balding, also bespectacled, with a mournfully tweedy, academic appearance. They were both very educated Upper West Side. Cyrus was not sure he liked this particular example of the species.

"We're just at the beginning of the shopping pwocess. We'd like to see something with an ivowy gwound," said the man, in a professorial English accent which turned *r*s into *w*s.

"We want to stay away from a central focus. No medallions in the middle," the woman said scornfully.

"We're not interested in a pwain open field with a medallion," her husband explained. "You see, we have a firepwace that's the center of attention. So we don't want too dwamatic a wug, with too centwal a focus. We'd pwefer something that will—in a manner of speaking—fade into the backgwound, yet not be too innocuous."

"And what sort of design or style, may I ask?"

"Geometric. Angled, not floral," the woman said sourly, as if he were trying to sell her yesterday's fish.

"You see, we have wather modern furniture."

"About how big is your room, please?"

"I don't think we can get much wider than ten feet because we start wunning into the firepwace."

"And it would help if I knew the approximate price range before we start. . . ."

"Oh—anywhere from five hundred to five thousand. To add to our awea of indecision, we could either go to a high quality Persian or—an imitation."

Cyrus began showing them some of his better rugs. The woman kept saying, "I'm not crazy about that green" or, "I'm not wild about that rusty red," in a hard, carping voice, while the man asked him questions. Usually Cyrus enjoyed playing the pedagogue—it was a role required of any rug dealer in America—but in this particular case, he sensed the man was picking his brains so that they could go armed with knowledge afterward to the rug district on lower Fifth Avenue. They had no intention of buying anything from him. "Excuse me for a moment, I must attend to my other customers."

The young couple had narrowed their choices to three. Now they asked the prices, and were pleasantly surprised that the rugs seemed to be within their budget—or, at any event, not far beyond. Cyrus helped them to settle on a favorite, and the young man wrote out a check. Why could not merchandising always be this way?

"Thank you so much. If you have any problems, just bring it back and exchange it for something else."

"Oh, no, we love it."

"I am glad. I only say that because sometimes the colors appear different when you get it home than in the store. I also recommend that you put a pad under it. That can double the life of the rug."

After Cyrus had tied up the rug and sold them a pad and bade them a happy good-bye, he went back to the critical couple.

"Would you consider a Heriz?" he asked, fully aware by now that all their knowledge of Orientals was a bluff.

"Only if it's very pale," said the woman.

Cyrus unrolled a superb one, among the best in the store, just to see how far their captiousness would extend. "This has your ivory background. It also has this wonderful gray which, depending upon the way the light is that day, can go toward blue or green. It's a very subtle design, very clever. Almost reminds me of a Paul Klee," said Cyrus.

"Are all the Herizes coarse like this?" she asked.

"Excuse me?"

She rubbed her hand against the wool, making a face. "It feels so scratchy."

"I'm sorry, but you are rubbing it against the grain. See what happens when you do it the other way. Believe me, this is good old wool, the burrs are still in it after years and years, which is a sign that it is hand-spun, not chemically processed wool. And this is all hand-knotted, not just 'hand-tufted.' Last week I saw in the paper, a big department store—which shall go nameless—had run an ad that said 'hand-knotted fringe.' Certainly," he smiled. "But the rug itself was machine-made. So you have to be careful."

"Why is it so thin for this price? Are all the Herizes this thin?"

"First of all, thickness is no indicator of quality—or longevity. Second of all, the more detail in the design, the thinner it has to be sheared to give it that clarity. All the thick-sheared rugs today have blurrier designs." Cyrus noted the woman's disbelieving expression; he was beginning to lose patience. "Let me explain something to you. The reason Oriental rugs are having such thick piles today is that they are geared for the American housewife, who is so used to broadloom that she equates thickness with quality."

"That sounds sexist."

"I don't mean it to be, I am simply stating a fact. Perhaps I should have said, 'the American customer,' regardless of gender."

"Yes, I'd like that better."

"What was the name of that wug we saw at John and Fwedewika's? That was spectacularly beautiful. An Isfahan—wasn't it? I think we'd rather fancy an Isfahan. You don't have any in stock, I suppose?"

"Yes, I do." Cyrus was thinking to himself: First they ask for something geometric, then they want to see an Isfahan, which is completely floral, the opposite! "Does it need to have an ivory background, or—"

"It doesn't matter. Whatever."

"And we also wanted to see Chinese art decos," the woman called after him querulously.

Cyrus stopped in his tracks. "I have a good adaptation of a Chinese art deco rug from the thirties, which they are manufacturing now in India. It is very similar in appearance, and of course a good deal cheaper than the antique. Shall I show it to you?"

"Yes. And the Isfahans, don't forget," the man said, pointing his pipe.

Meanwhile, other customers entered the store; Cyrus gave less of his attention to the middle-aged couple as the afternoon wore on. When they left—empty-handed, of course, after seeing practically his entire stock—he was deeply relieved; but it surprised him that, even after all these years, such people still had the power to upset him.

Broken City

Every other Sunday Aberjinnian conducted a short-notice auction in one of the hotels in the metropolitan area. He would rent a public room, and place an ad in the newspaper saying something like: a shipment of Oriental carpets had been refused by an importer who had over-ordered, with the result that twenty-five bales of carpets were to be auctioned off piece by piece at bargain prices. The truth was, the auctioneer owned the rugs and had no intention of selling them at a sacrifice. Aberjinnian's auctions were not intended for the *cognoscenti,* but for Sunday strollers out for a little excitement.

At the Sheraton Center, Cyrus took the escalator to the second floor and wandered around the corridors until he found the Imperial Room. Already a small crowd of people were bending their heads like penguins over the carpets, which had been laid atop the red hotel broadloom. Zack, Aberjinnian's assistant, a burly Israeli with mustache and muscular arms, moved through the crowd asking if anyone would like a particular rug to be brought up front. This was a way of baiting customers into bidding later, since in the end all the rugs, regardless of expressed interest, were carted to the front for auctioning.

Cyrus could have arrived at the end of the auction to discuss his business proposal, but he had never seen Aberjinnian "perform." He had first met the Armenian in the showrooms of lower Fifth Avenue, as a middleman, not an auctioneer meeting the general public. "Please be seated everyone. Please take a seat. The auction is about to begin," Zack announced, circulating. Eventually the audience was seated in folding chairs and waiting. A low murmur went through the crowd: Where is he? Where's the auctioneer?

A side door suddenly opened, and Aberjinnian shambled on, positioning himself between two clamp floodlights. As always he wore brown, a color that took dirt well. His polyester suit shone with cocoa embossed squares, and he wore a mud-colored sweater over a tan shirt and wide brown tie. He squinted with his hand shadowing his brow, seeming to be bothered by the floodlights.

"I am not used to having the audience so spread out. If you will please move from the sides to the middle more, and come closer up, you will all see better and I can save my voice." Only two people obliged. "Suit yourself." He cleared his throat tentatively. "I am going to say first a little about Oriental rugs, though I am sure you do not need to be told about them. In fact you probably know more than I do!" A few chuckles. "But just in case there are some out there who are not experts in the field, I will explain that these carpets are all handmade. Their value is going always up and up, because you cannot get handwoven goods like these any more, they are all becoming machine-made. Smart investors know that they are one of the wisest investments you can make. You can pass them on from generation to generation as heirlooms; you can even sell them to the museum. Any questions so far? Yes?"

"Where do they come from?" asked an elderly man with beautiful white hair.

"Most of them come from—a country in the Middle East I cannot tell you the name of, because I would get into trouble. This much I can say: they come from a country where labor is still very cheap. But it is rapidly becoming industrialized, so in the very near future these rugs will be a thing of the past. Are there any further questions? Please, don't be afraid to ask."

"Are they used?"

He winced, as though insulted. "They are all new carpets. These are not secondhand goods, believe me, you can take my word for it. These are the antiques of the future." He paused, pleased with his verbal formulation. "No further questions? I must tell you that I went recently to Iran and I came back empty-handed. Because they are asking such high prices that it is impossible to pay. Here is a commodity where you know the value can only increase. And they don't need elaborate care. If you want to clean them, just use ordinary soap and water. Any last questions?"

"What kinds of dyes are used?"

"The dyes are all natural. You people ask such suspicious questions, you are very tough. I feel like I am in a roomful of police inspectors! We could go on with this delightful conversation for hours, but some of you would like the auction to begin. Please, what do you say? Let's start. Zack, will you hold up the first item?"

The initial bids were cautious and low, invoking the auctioneer's disgust. "I thought this was New York City. This is not very fast. Is this New York City, Zack?"

"It looks that way outside."

"I have my doubts. Continue."

A few rugs later, Aberjinnian broke off the bidding again to demand of his assistant: "Why did you drag me all the way here for this? I am never coming back to this town. This is—this is a broken city. Excuse me, but you will read about this auction in the paper tomorrow. I had heard that New York City was in trouble, but not this much! Have we no more bids? Do I hear two hundred? Excuse me, does anyone here even have two hundred dollars?" A few nervous titters. One man slowly raised his hand. "Finally! Two hundred, two hundred twenty-five? . . . Ladies and gentlemen, you want bargains, all right. I can understand that. But this way you will drive me bankrupt! This is not fair, that is not the American way. I am entitled to make a living too. Do I hear two hundred *ten* dollars? You want me to lose my shirt, I understand. I am waiting. . . . All right, I see a hand, now how about two hundred fifty? No one. Two hundred ten once, twice—take it away, Zack, they can have it. It breaks my heart, but what can I do? . . . This hunting rug is one of the handsomest in the show. We must have a minimum reserve of six hundred dollars and at least two bids."

"Three hundred!" yelled out a man.

"No, this is not a Chinese auction, this is an American auction, the price goes *up*. Maybe the gentleman does not understand the meaning of the word *minimum.* The lowest bid we can accept is six hundred dollars. This is a Shah Abbas carpet, the only carpet to be named after an individual."

"Three hundred fifty!"

"The man is a comedian. Three hundred *fifty?* You see this design of the hunting scene? You would pay three hundred fifty if an artist gave you that on cardboard! Here you would be getting it handwoven. It took two people one and a half *years* to make this. And no vacations. No Christmas, no Labor Day. Show them the back. You can tell the quality of a rug by how tight the weave is. Feel it." He instructed Zack to take it over to the audience; some leaned over to feel, but most were reluctant to touch the wool. "You don't have to buy, just feel it! That way you can go home and at least you will have learned something."

"Five hundred dollars."

"I am glad to see someone appreciates quality. That is still very low. Six hundred, six hundred and fifty? Yes? . . . That is too low. Put it away, Zack. Tonight you people will dream about this hunting scene, and for the rest of your life you will kick yourself for not buying it. I feel sad for you. Take it down." His assistant started to fold the rug away. "No, wait," the auctioneer detained him. "One moment, I just want to ascertain something for myself." Aberjinnian faced the audience with hands on his hips, like a cross teacher scolding a classroom of children. "Why are you people here? What *do* you like? Do you prefer Chinese rugs? Indian? Moroccan? Russian? We have a carpet for every taste. I want each of you to leave with something of your own today. This beautiful young lady, why didn't you bid? Don't you want to go home with anything? I know. You are waiting for the door prize! We have no door prizes here. Show them the next rug.

"Does anybody like this rug? . . . I am *sure* that no one likes this rug at all, that's why you are not speaking up! Look—you don't have to bid if you say you like it. I want to know just for my own information. How many people think this is a nice rug?" Over a third of the audience raised their hands. "Well, then bid! Why are you here? Are you all relatives of each other? You are ganging up on me! You are all in league, I can feel it. I want to hear a bid of five hundred dollars for this rug. There's one! Five hundred from the woman with the feather hat—how about five hundred fifty? . . . No? You are purposely tormenting me. All right, miss, the rug is yours, I give up, you can pick it up afterward.

Highway robbery. *Next!* All right. This time I am not setting a minimum. We will all play a little game. You like games, don't you? I want to find out what you in New York *think* this rug is worth."

"One hundred fifty!"

"One hundred fifty *dollars* or pounds sterling? You are insulting me now. If this is all you think such a fine rug is worth, what will you say when I show you the magnificent silk Kashan I have in store? . . . Fine, we will take a two-minute break so people can come up to the front and request individual rugs. I'm not going to auction off rugs that no one is interested in! Please, people, this is taking up my time, it is taking up your time. It will go much faster if you participate."

At intermission, the crowd milled around, smoking cigarettes and chatting. Some went up guiltily to the front to do their homework. When the second half began, the auctioneer continued flogging the audience and expressing astonished disenchantment, though from Cyrus's viewpoint he was getting quite good prices for the merchandise. Aberjinnian had structured his auction in such a way that, toward the very end, when he introduced the large Indo-Kashan he had been promising all along, this fairly undistinguished rug sold for an inflated three thousand dollars.

Cyrus waited until the crowd placing orders at the front table had thinned out, before approaching his friend.

"You are a master. I stand in awe."

"Junk, all junk," Aberjinnian said in an undertone. "Imagine if I had had quality stuff. Why didn't you bid, Irani? I saw you out there."

"I was tempted. The adrenaline starts flowing in an auction—you have the itch to raise your hand, even when you know better."

"Come, we'll sit in the corner and talk. I would buy you a drink downstairs but I have to stay and keep an eye on things here. . . . Shall I send out for tea?"

"No, please don't bother."

"All right. Zack, I'll be in the corner talking with this gentleman. Please finish wrapping up here." He led Cyrus to the end of the long ballroom, where two folding chairs waited for them.

"So. I am surprised to see you. After you did not attend the last time I invited you—to the good auction—I thought you might be angry at me."

"Not at all. I was just very busy."

"I understand. Still, it's a pity you did not make the last one because I had some really decent pieces there to sell."

"Unfortunately, I already have too much stock. I need to get rid of what I have first."

"The way to make money in rugs is at the buying end, not the selling end. I'd have given you a much better price than these fools paid today. But that's your affair. You have your own suppliers."

"I am glad I finally saw you in action. It was a fascinating performance," said Cyrus.

"All psychology. I manipulate their hostility, because they are all essentially racists who hate people from our part of the world. I get them to think they are putting me through an auctioneer's nightmare. They want me to suffer, so I suffer in front of them—but not too much, because they are also essentially good kind Americans."

"Amazing. But why did you tell them the dyes in the rugs were vegetable when they are chemical?"

"Tell them anything, so long as they buy. Besides, I told them the dyes were *natural.* One man's natural is another man's artificial. In the Middle East there is nothing more natural at present than using aniline dyes. I know, you think that makes me a con artist. I am—but a con artist with substance. I like that," he grinned. "Maybe I will have cards printed up: 'Aberjinnian, Con Artist with Substance.' "

WILLIAM PRICE FOX

200,000 Dozen Pairs of Socks

Doug Crawford was the New Jersey salesman for the Triple A Folding Box Company, but his heart was never in it. Doug's heart belonged to golf. He had won the club championship at Twelve Oaks seven times, the county championship four and the state twice. Three times he had qualified for the National Open. Every fall when the northern courses began to freeze and the birds and the pros headed south he would try to decide between staying with his $17,000, expenses-paid-plus-Christmas-bonus job and playing professionally on the winter tour. Every year for the past eight he'd come up with the same decision. His game wasn't quite ready; he would stay with Triple A one more year.

It was warm for late September, and the air conditioning was on in the club bar. The bartender had gone to the stock room, leaving Doug sitting alone cracking and eating pistachio nuts and waiting for his two guests, Hilton Wren, the sales manager for Loomis Socks, and Leo Maddox, the chief buyer for the Butler Brothers chain stores.

As the company golfer for Triple A Folding Box, Doug had played with most of the purchasing agents in the New England territory. He had played with men so wild and strong they would hit a full foot behind the ball, plough up the turf and finish the swing with the heavy earth dripping from the quivering wood. He played with men so slow they would have to let foursomes of women go through. One client, who bought toilet-tissue boxes, would, when the club hit the ball, stop the swing, drop the club, grab his hair and scream "Oh, no, Oh, no." The caddies had called him "Oh-no Burnside." Another guest of the company had been a purchasing agent who had arrived at the first tee with the leather handles of his clubs sticking out of the top of his bag and announced that this was his first game of golf. He had hit his first tee shot off the neck of the driver. The ball came straight back and struck him on the ankle, fracturing it. Doug and the caddies had to carry him to his car and drive him to the hospital. Later, Triple A lost the account. Doug was bitter after this and every time he played with a new purchasing agent he was afraid something would go wrong.

As the clock at the end of the bar chimed ten-fifteen, Hilton and Leo entered the room. Hilton was always on time. Leo shook Doug's hand limply and looked around the wood-paneled room. "So this is Twelve Oaks? Heard a lot about this palce. Pretty fancy." Leo was a short, heavy-set man with long black hair on the back of his hands and a thick pelt on his head combed straight back. He was perspiring. He looked from Hilton to Doug. "I could use an eye-opener. Can we get a drink around here?" The bartender came over, and Leo ordered a dry Gibson. Hilton joined him; Doug ordered a sherry on the rocks. Leo drank rapidly and ordered another.

On the second drink Hilton's eyes began to water. He was telling Leo about his promotional idea called Sockorama-Unisphere. Socks from all of the nations of the world would be hung from a big plastic copy of the World's Fair Unisphere with Loomis Socks blanketing the entire United States and part of Canada. If Leo bought the idea it would mean a floor model in each of his 660 stores and an order for 200,000 dozen pairs of socks. It would also mean an order for over 2 1/2 million folding boxes for Doug. Hilton said, "I checked the Fair publicity boys and they said okay on the Unisphere. They figure it will be great publicity for everybody." Hilton had a thin nervous face. He sipped at his Gibson and kept watching Leo. "Wait till you see it, Leo. Just wait. I figure it will pay for itself in a week. And we'll be getting all that overflow advertising from the Fair. I tell you, it's got to work."

The two Gibsons hadn't fazed Leo. "Let me think about it, Hilt. You know how crowded my aisles get. Main problem is space."

"I already worked that out, Leo. You've got to see the model. I got the space problem all licked."

Leo finished his drink. He looked at the bottom of his glass and decided he didn't want another. "I'll give it some thought, Hilt." He turned to Doug. "Let's see your course."

Doug had always been a careful dresser. If he appeared on the first tee wearing white slacks, he also had on white shoes. If black slacks, black shoes. His golf glove always matched his hat, and his Izod socks and shirts seemed to be cut from the same bolt of cloth. Today Doug wore all white.

Leo wore grey-and-red-checked pleated Bermuda shorts. They were too long at the knee and too tight across the back. He didn't wear a belt. He had on a beige fishnet shirt, without an undershirt. Tufts of heavy black hair stuck through the big openings in the net, as did one dark nipple. He wore short elastic-topped black socks with a red clockwork pattern down the side and light tan ripple-soled golf shoes. He stuffed three golf balls into each of his tight back pockets and said, "Okay, I'm ready, let's go."

On the first tee Doug carefully put on and smoothed out the fingers of his white golf glove and looked down the fairway. The wind was riffling the leaves in the tall oaks at the side of the tee and the bright sun dappled the high spots on the fairway. It was a perfect day. Leo pulled out all four woods and gripping them all together began swinging them back and forth, loosening up the deep muscles in his back. He grunted as he swung. Leo was a powerful man with big forearms and enormous legs. He began swinging the four clubs in a circle, as if winding up to throw a hammer.

Doug nudged Hilton at the ball washer. "What's he shoot?"

"You mean his handicap?"

Doug nodded. Hilton was stretching his golf glove on. He was wearing bright red slacks and a blue-green long-sleeved shirt. "Says thirty-five. I've never played with him before."

Doug tried not to flinch. Hilton smacked his right hand into his left and wiggled his gloved fingers. He lowered his voice. "And for every stroke of that thirty-five, he's got over twenty retail outlets. You just keep thinking about that."

Leo handed the four woods to the caddy and pulled out his putter.

He placed the club across the small of his back, locked it on the inside of his elbows, and began swaying back and forth.

Hilton lit a cigarette. "Two hundred thousand dozen pairs of socks. That's a lot of boxes, Doug."

"We could use the business. It's been a bad quarter."

They joined Leo by the tee markers. Hilton said, "Okay, Doug, it's your club. Show us the way."

Doug teed his ball and pulled a few blades of grass up and tossed them in the air. The wind was crossing from the right. He swung easily and finished the shot high. Out beyond the 200-yard marker the ball rose and curled into a high rising fade and came to rest within ten yards of the 250-yard marker.

Hilton said, "Nice shot. Okay, Leo."

Leo squatted down and pressed a tee in with his thumb.

Hilton said, "Like this, Leo." He held up a ball and a tee together. "Make the ball do the work."

"I forgot. I'm used to the automatics at the driving range." Leo gripped the driver and took four more lunging practice swings; his neck, arms, and leg veins turned a deep blue and bulged out. Then he stopped and backed up, wheezing. His hands were wet from the practice swings. Hilton started to give him a towel, but before he could get to him, Leo had dried his hands on the back of his pants and was ready to hit. He swung viciously, missing the ball completely. The heavy swing jerked him forward and he took a quick step to keep from falling down.

Hilton said quickly, "Here, Leo, dry your hands. Take a Mulligan. It's okay on the first."

Leo tossed the towel back and lined himself up. He swung again. The club whipped back in a blinding backswing and whistling through grazed the top of the ball, trickling it out ten yards beyond the tee markers. Leo whirled around and slammed the driver into the ground. "Can't understand it. Can't. Hit 'em a goddamn mile at the driving range."

Hilton said, "Don't worry, Leo. You got it out of your system. You'll be okay now." Hilton drove 180 yards down the right side of the fairway.

Leo addressed the ball again, this time at the front of the long tee for his third shot.

Suddenly the public address system from the pro shop crackled and a voice announced: "Will someone in the threesome on the first tee tell the party about to drive that he must tee off from between the markers."

Leo was furious. He glared toward the pro shop.

Hilton looked at Doug. "What's going on?"

Doug shook his head. "Must be some mistake."

Hilton said, "Don't let it bother you, Leo. Go ahead."

Leo spat on the ground and went back to the ball. The announcer spoke again. "Will someone in that threesome *please* tell the party about to drive that he must tee off from between the markers."

Leo stepped back from the ball and cupping his hands shouted, "You stupid son-of-a-bitch, I'm shooting three."

Hilton laughed quickly, trying to turn the incident into a joke, but seeing that Leo was still mad, he covered his mouth with the corner of his towel and pretended he was coughing. The coughing rattled him and he felt a headache rising and beginning to pound behind his eyes.

Leo finally hit. The ball hooked sharply toward the hurricane fence beyond the narrow rough, hit the fence, and bounded back onto the fairway.

Hilton said, "Okay, Leo, it'll play." They started off.

On the first hole Doug sank a six-foot putt for a three. Hilton had a six, Leo an eleven.

On the second hole Leo's swing was even faster than on the first tee. The ball hooked quickly into the tall grass and pine trees. Hilton watched it disappear. His headache was getting worse and he could taste the Gibson at the back of his throat. Pinching his nose and eyes with his thumb and forefinger, he decided he'd better stay with Leo as much as possible to discuss Sockorama. Hilton's game had once been a sound ten handicap but since he had been playing with customers so long and so regularly, it had gone to a seventeen. It had changed from a long, bold game to a timid, chameleon-like affair that adapted itself to any purchasing agent. If the purchasing agent sliced, Hilton sliced. If the purchasing agent hooked, Hilton hooked. Hilton looked toward the woods where Leo's ball had gone. He groaned, without making any noise, turned his right hand back, swung and followed Leo into the trees.

On the fourth hole Doug drove almost 280 yards. No one spoke.

Leo hit. The ball hugged the ground and bounced out 170 yards into the middle of the fairway.

Hilton said, "Okay, Leo, right where you want to be. I'll take those all day, any day. Right, Doug?"

Doug smiled, "That's the place to be."

As they left the tee Hilton put his arm on Leo's shoulder, hoping to ask about Sockorama. Leo pushed his hand off. "Cut it out, will you? I'm sweating too much already."

Hilton joined Doug in the middle of the fairway. "I shouldn't have had those Gibsons. It's crazy to try and drink with Leo. He's got a cast-iron stomach." He watched Leo flog at the ball, sending it scuttling into the trees again. "Christ, if he'd only hit a few good shots."

Doug shook his head. "He swings too fast."

Hilton went on, "I know him, I know his type. If he gets off a few good shots he's a different man. I bet you a hundred dollars the minute he starts playing better he'll feel better about buying."

On the sixth hole Leo hit a solid spoon shot almost 200 yards to the back of the green. Hilton moved in quickly and shouted, "Beautiful, Leo! Really beautiful! Quail-high, all the way. That's what I call a golf shot. You see how she sat down?"

Leo smiled and lit a cigar. Hilton was afraid the shot would be Leo's only good one of the day. "Leo, I wish you'd fill me in on the Sockorama decision. I got the artist's sketches all together and the models practically built."

Leo's smile vanished. He kept his cigar in his mouth and spoke around it. "As of right now Sockorama is dead. Now leave me alone. Let me play my game. I'm just beginning to loosen up."

"But Leo, I got the sketches and the model is. . . ."

Leo walked off and joined Doug. "I can't concentrate. That bastard won't get off my back. He never stops selling."

Doug didn't answer. He was four under par and every shot he'd hit had gone exactly where he wanted. He watched a low wedge of Canadian geese sweep before them and settle behind the trees in the lake on the twelfth hole. His feet felt light on the springy fairway, and as he inhaled the heavy smell of the fresh-cut grass, he thought of his father and recalled the day they had seen the men's tennis finals at Forest Hills. When it was over, and after the applause had stopped and the crowd was leaving, his father had turned to him and solemnly said, "Son, it's a nice game but there's just no game like golf."

Leo touched Doug's elbow and spoke again. "You know something?"

"What?"

"I like you. You know why I like you? I like you because you ignore me. I like that. I come out for a little fun and a little relaxation and what do I get? Hell, I might as well be in the office. I tell you, I work harder out here fighting off Hilton than I do in town. At least there, I can tell the girl to get rid of him. Out here I'm trapped."

He pulled out his handkerchief and wiped his face. "It's like when I go to the golf outings. Every time I look around or go to the toilet there's a salesman grinning at me, wanting to do me a favor, or buy me a drink or ask about how my wife and kids are. They treat me like some kind of prince. Ha, that's a laugh. Leo Maddox, the prince of Butler Brothers. I tell you, Doug, it's relaxing being around you. You're different."

Hilton came over. He put one hand on Doug's shoulder and one on Leo's. "How you two getting along?"

Leo said, "We're in love. That good enough?"

Hilton barked a short laugh and crossed over to his ball. He lit a cigarette with the butt of the one he was finishing. He was afraid Doug's smooth game might be upsetting Leo. Still, they were walking together and Leo was talking, even joking. Maybe Doug had given Leo a lesson. If Leo would only change his mind and buy the Sockorama! Two hundred thousand dozen first-line socks. Maybe that would convince Loomis he was needed on the inside of the company. Twenty-four years in sales; he'd been out in the field too long. His nerves were beginning to show through. A man can sell only so many years. Maybe some day he would be vice president in charge of sales; then he could use his experience with the younger men. Go out in the field with them, show them the tricks of the trade. How to look the buyer in the eye. How to amuse him and then switch over into straight business. He could tell the younger salesmen how not to smoke unless the buyer does, and then to be careful where the smoke drifts. How to watch for nervous mannerisms, toe-tappers, finger-snappers, facial tics. How to apply sales psychology. How to find out if the buyer is Catholic, Jewish, Mason. How to feel them out about jokes, religion, women, maybe kickbacks. Hilton looked out across the fairway. He would be firm to the younger men and keep their respect. Check everything on expense reports. Great idea: put phones in the salesmen's cars. Like a taxi fleet. That way he could always find them. It would keep them on their toes and out of the movies and the whorehouses. All he needed was the Sockorama job. With that he would be on top of the world. Maybe he could get the publicity boys at *Men's Hosiery Review* to have a page showing him and Leo and the Sockorama promotion. He would put the Unisphere in between them and have Leo and him shaking hands across it. Leo would love to have his picture in *Men's Hosiery.* He would need a slogan to go under the picture. "Hands Across the World." No, he would have to do better than that. He would think about it later.

They were on the eighth tee in the shade of a big oak tree. The wind was stronger. Doug teed his ball low and hit his longest drive.

Hilton said, "Nice shot, Doug. Okay, Leo, you can let out here."

Leo's dark eyes narrowed as if he were going to try to drive the green 520 yards away. He shifted his hands to the very end of the club handle for a fuller swing and crouched over so he could generate more power. It was the fastest backswing Doug had ever seen. Leo missed the ball completely. The flying club shot out of his hands. It whistled up into the oak tree and wrapped around a big limb above them. When it stopped vibrating the leather handle hung down on one side and the driver head hung down the other. No one spoke. Leo's face was white with red splotches. Hilton was dead white. One of the caddies vanished into the bushes cramming a towel into his mouth to keep from exploding, while Doug and Leo looked up at the club above them draped over the limb like a weary cobra.

Doug stepped forward and pulled out a brand new Titlist ball, teed it up, and handed Leo his own driver. "Forget it, Leo. This time I want you to lock your head down and take the club back nice and slow. Keep your head down, now; I'll watch the ball for you."

Leo hit the drive down the middle, 210 yards. Doug walked along with him.

Leo handed Doug his club. "It's that lousy Hilton. He got me all upset with that Sockorama idea."

Doug didn't hear Leo. He was planning his second shot. He felt enormous power and leverage in his legs and wrists and a fine sensitive control in his fingers. Every shot he had hit had been perfect. His game was finally right; it would never be better. He made up his mind. If he tied or beat the course record for eighteen holes he would quit Triple A and take his chances with the professionals. He could pick up the tour in Louisiana. Yes, it would work. If he could keep his game around 70 he could do it. Maybe not the big money at first, but he would be learning the ropes and the courses. And if he got hot? Maybe he could get on "All Star Golf" on television. Each appearance meant $3000. A couple of those and he would be all right. He wondered if he could still try it. He was only thirty-four. How old was Boros? Snead? How old was Hogan? A gloomy thought rose behind his eyes. He could always go back to selling boxes if his game went sour. He shook it away.

Leo hit again. Again it was straight and down the middle. Hilton called out from the deep rough. "Nice shot, Leo. Nice."

Leo looked at Doug. He laughed. "You hit a ball three hundred yards and Hilton doesn't say a word. I hit one a hundred and fifty and he says 'Tremendous.' I ask you, what kind of salesman is that?"

Leo walked close to Doug. "You play a lot, don't you?"

"Quite a bit."

"You know, I can't see why this game's so tough. Chances are if I took it up seriously, you know, went out to the driving range a little more, maybe took a few lessons, I might get so I was pretty good. I like to bowl a lot. Now there's a game you'd like, Doug. There's a man's game. I bet you'd be pretty good at it. I'll tell you something, it's got a lot of advantages when you stop and analyze it." He relit his cigar. He was sweating, and the black hair on his chest and back glistened. "There's never any trouble about the weather, that's number one. Number two, if you're in the right crowd there's always a few laughs. Then if you get hungry or want a drink, that's right there too. And once in a while there's a broad in the next alley throwing pretty hard and you get a chance to see a little leg. These things add up. Yeah, you'd like bowling, Doug. You ought to look into it."

They were at Doug's ball. The green was over 250 yards away.

Leo said, "Tell you what, you teach me golf, I'll teach you bowling."

"This is an important shot, Leo."

"Okay, so hit it. There's no one on the green."

Doug hit a full brassie shot. He knew it was good. It traveled low all the way and settled on the right side of the green about twenty-five feet from the pin.

Leo said, "Okay, what do you think of my offer? Me teach you bowling, you teach me golfing?"

Doug didn't hear Leo. He was thinking about his score. If he could two-putt for a four and then par the ninth he would have a 30. No one had ever shot below a 31 on the first nine. He began walking fast. He wanted to get away from Leo so he could think and plan the next shot carefully. He couldn't let anything upset him; there was too much at stake.

Hilton joined him. "Listen, Leo says no on Sockorama and I can't tell if he means it or not. We got to have the business. We were shut down fourteen days last month."

Doug was planning his long putt.

Hilton said, "Maybe you can help out. I think he likes you. Maybe you can give him a few more pointers." Hilton dubbed a nine iron. He stabbed the club at the ground and looked at Doug. "You know my game, Doug. You know I play better than this. It's this pressure. It's having Leo along and that Sockorama hanging over my head that's making me press like this."

"You're too tense, Hilton."

"I know. I know. Listen, if Sockorama is dead my forecast for the year is shot. Maybe me too. You might as well know it, things haven't been going too great for me this year. Those Japanese socks are murdering us on price and I don't know where the orders are going to come from. Besides that, my best purchasing agent over at Long and Vogel's up and died on me and the new man they put in won't see me." He shook his head. "Two hundred thousand dozen pairs of first-line. That's a month's production. You any idea what kind of profit that means?" He gritted his teeth. "No man should have that kind of power. They become dictators."

Doug lined up his long twenty-five foot putt and without giving himself a chance to think about it, hit. The ball held the line for half the distance and then slowly curved in. As they left the green the caddies began whispering about the course record.

Leo stood near the apron taking a practice swing. "Hey, Doug, what else am I doing wrong? I got the head and the backswing all set. Give me something else to work on."

Doug walked over. "That's all for now, Leo. Just stay with that. I'll show you some more later."

Leo grinned. "You're the boss."

On the ninth tee Leo hit his finest shot. It carried over 200 yards and rolled out another twenty-five. He hit his second shot to the edge of the green. As Leo and Doug came up to the apron Leo said, "It's really great; I think I got it. I really think I got it. Just keep the head locked down and swing easy. Wonder why nobody ever told me that before?"

Doug was thinking about the southern courses and how much money he would need to break even for the rest of the year. He decided he could do it with $4000.

Leo said, "If I give Loomis this Sockorama, you get the box business, is that right?"

Doug barely heard him. "Yeah, Leo, I get the boxes."

Leo slapped him on the back. "Okay, I'll give it to them. I don't like it. I don't like it at all. Matter of fact it stinks, but maybe it will move socks. American public is crazy anyhow, they might buy anything."

Doug smiled. "Thanks, Leo."

Leo said, "Don't say anything about it to Wren. I want him to sweat a little more."

Leo lagged his putt up six inches short of the hole and tapped in his first par of the day. Doug was thirty feet from the hole. He putted quickly. The ball was in all the way. He had a 29, two strokes below the record 31 for nine holes. He handed the caddy the putter and took the driver. All he needed now was a 36 on the back nine to break the course record. He started for the tenth tee. He was sure now, he would definitely go on the tour. Leo spoke. Doug didn't want to talk or listen to anyone. He wanted to be alone for a minute. He had to make plans. He had to play the back nine carefully, not take any chances. Maybe he would use his spoon from the trees and play it safe.

Leo called out again, but Doug kept walking.

Hilton shouted, "Come on, Doug."

Doug stopped. They were standing on the far side of the green. Hilton said, "Come on, Doug. We're having one for the road."

Doug wanted to pretend he hadn't heard. If he stopped now he would never be able to keep the fine putting touch and the perfect game he had going. He couldn't stop now. Even a few minutes' interruption would break the spell. Hilton had removed his golf glove. Leo was peeling his off and grinning.

"Come on, Doug. Just one, that's all."

Doug handed the caddy his driver and slowly followed the two men toward the club house and the bar. He couldn't believe what was happening.

Leo said, "You see how that five iron sat down?"

Doug nodded. He was afraid to speak.

Inside Leo ordered three Gibsons. As the seconds passed Doug felt the fine putting touch oozing out of the tips of his fingers. He shoved his fists deep into his pockets hoping to stop the leak.

Leo proposed a toast. "To Doug Crawford, a great golfer, a great teacher."

They drank.

Leo continued, "You know, I learned more about golf today than I have in my whole life?" He smiled and laid his hand on Doug's arm. "Okay, Doug, you propose the next toast. Tell Hilton here what I told you."

Doug looked down at Leo's fingernails. They seemed to be as thick as oyster shells. He raised his glass. "To Leo and Sockorama." He looked at Hilton. "Leo's giving us the Sockorama job."

Everyone shook hands. Hilton beamed. His arm shot up signaling the waiter for another round.

The Gibson hit Doug like an axe. He stood up. "I've got to play the next nine. I can break the course record." There was no conviction in his voice and Leo pulled him back into his seat.

"Come on, drink up. You can always break the record. Come back and do it tomorrow." He took a big drink, spread some cheese on a cracker and laughed at Doug. "How many days in your life do you see a dog like Sockorama-Unisphere sold? Jesus, what a lousy name."

Hilton said, "Maybe we could change the name."

"Naw, leave it. Probably sell socks like crazy."

Doug said slowly, "All I need is a thirty-six and I got the record. No one's ever had a twenty-nine on the first nine."

Leo slapped him on the back. "You still talking about records? Come on, drink up there, lad. We're lapping you."

Doug's hands were cold. The putting touch was gone. He gripped the stem of his Gibson glass and raised it to his lips. Maybe next year was the right year for the tour. He looked at the Gibson. It seemed greasy on the surface. Two and a half million four-color rotogravure boxes with no chiseling on price; it would be the largest piece of new business of the year. He could stay with Triple A through Christmas to pick up his holiday bonus and then join the tour in Florida. Maybe he could play until then. The courses might not freeze so early this year, the winters seemed to be getting milder. Doug finished his drink and swallowed the onion.

Hilton made him a double-decker cheese-and-cracker sandwich. "Here you go, Doug boy. We've got to keep you in good shape." He slapped Doug on the back and grinned at Leo. "Didn't I tell you he was the greatest golf teacher in the world?"

Leo ordered another round and bit off the end of a fresh cigar. Doug finally removed his golf glove and watched Leo blow his first puff of smoke toward the ceiling. After the third round of Gibsons had been served, Hilton pushed the cheese-and-cracker tray to the far side of the table and, clicking his ball point pen down, he began sketching the Sockorama-Unisphere model on the tablecloth.

JACK MATTHEWS

The Story Mac Told

Mac McIlhenny crossed over from Davenport into Moline at sundown on April 2, and pointed his new Thunderbird upriver toward the Sandman Motel on the highway north of town.

"This is Biddle's territory, sure as hell," he thought, flipping his radio tuner in an attempt to pick up some music as a relief from the evening news.

"Or *was,*" he whispered, trying out the sound of it, and experiencing a slight cold thrill at the thought of how impermanent positions and friendships can prove. "Unless I can talk him out of it," he said, veering his T-Bird to the right, and staying in the main flow of traffic. It had been almost ten years since he'd been in Moline, and he was only vaguely confident of the motel's location.

"Right on the river, though," he said. Like most salesmen, he talked to himself, spending thirty or forty hours a week alone on the road.

"Sometimes *fifty* hours," he said.

When the lighted motel sign appeared to the left of the highway, Mac edged his car into the center lane, and said, "Biddle, you bibulous bastard, your time has come. You can't quit now. The big Mac has arriven."

He nosed the T-Bird into the first slot, and then paused briefly, holding the door before opening it, because a man was asleep in the car beside him. Asleep in a motel parking lot? Maybe drunk. All he could see was the top of the man's head, but that top seemed familiar, somehow, like the head of an army buddy. For an instant, he thought it might be Biddle; but then he knew it couldn't be. If you live long enough, Mac told himself darkly, *everything* begins to look like something you've seen before, even if you can't remember what it was. Or someone.

Mac sighed and punched the door all the way open, banging it dully but solidly against the door where the man's head rested; but the head didn't move. Mac pulled his suitcase out.

"Maybe dead," he mumbled, shrugging his shoulders into his old-fashioned-style trench coat, which he'd had to order special from a store in Montreal.

Axiom: Never walk into a motel without wearing a coat and hat, and having your tie straight. "That is what those of us who know an aspirin from a dishrag call character," Mac said.

He straightened both his hat and tie with quick movements of his right hand, carrying his suitcase with the other. A man's pride is still in his dress. Even in *this* day and age. Even when most people don't know what in the hell is what. Yes, sir! Abso-damn-lutely!

The lobby of the motel was empty, but it had the look of a busy place, as if fifteen convention types had just this minute left in a hurry. Herded out by a little border collie of a woman with an orange bouffant hairdo.

A thin haze of cigarette smoke hung in the air, like the aftermath of an explosion.

However, the appearance of a well-built middle-aged woman with a cigarette hanging from the corner of her mouth explained that. Her thick chocolate-colored hair was fashionably molded about her head, and she was busily shuffling papers in her hands. One of her eyes was closed wisely against the cigarette smoke that curled in a thin white line up the side of her face. It gave her a cynical, knowing look. Mac hadn't seen her when he'd first entered, because of a tall rotatable metal postcard holder, showing scenes of Moline, bends in the Mississippi, and the Sandman Hotel.

"Honey," Mac said, dropping his heavy suitcase on the floor and sliding the palms of his big hands onto the counter, "my name is Mac McIlhenny, and I just know you've been waiting for me."

"Yes, Mr. McIlhenny," the woman said in a hoarse voice, shoving one of the papers forward. "Just sign here." She didn't even unwink her eye, and her promptness surprised him a little. Somehow, she could have been older than he was. He coughed a deep bass laugh in the direction of the post-cards. But when she didn't look up, he signed the card and picked up his key.

"How about my friend, then," Mac said. "Bet you don't know who *he* is!"

"Would that be Mr. Biddle?" she asked, pulling her cigarette out and raising both eyebrows politely.

"Damn!" Mac said. "You're clairvoyant, that's what you are. At least that's your first name, isn't it?"

"What is?"

"Your first name *is* Claire, isn't it?"

She didn't seem to get the joke, not that it was much.

"Hardly. He just asked for you a little while back. He only got in about an hour ago, and he asked for you before he went into the bar."

"Into the bar," Mac echoed, trying his W. C. Fields voice on her. "That's our bibulous old bastard of a Biddle! Am I right, or am I right, Claire?"

The woman smiled tiredly with half of her mouth, pressed her cigarette out in an ashtray, and nodded. As if she knew all about both of them.

But Mac didn't go straight to the bar. He took his things to Room 214 overlooking the parking lot and swimming pool, thinking of arguments to use with Biddle. It was like developing a close, which means you have to know the man you're talking to. In some ways, better than he knows himself. Only success in this case wouldn't put even a twenty-dollar bill in Mac's pocket; no, the profit lay somewhere else. Sentiment.

"Biddle," he said, filling his wash basin with hot water, "goddamnit, man, you can't quit now! I mean, old Mac McIlhenny isn't going to *let* you quit. So let's get that shit straight right away. Listen, we've had adjoining territories for too many years. Am I right or am I right? Right?"

Mac sank his face into a hot wet washcloth and slowly inhaled the warmth; then he exhaled. "Biddle, are you drunk? How's come you're drinking so much, fella?"

There was no more answer in Mac's mind than there was in the motel-smelling room (he thought of his old joke; a woman wearing perfume that smelled like a motel room). For an instant, after drying his face, Biddle's image evaporated, and Mac just stood there, thinking.

When he put on a clean shirt, he said, "What has four wheels, hemorrhoids, and a dream?" He thought about that old rhetorical question (one of his corny favorites) for an instant, staring out the window at the empty swimming pool and winding his watch out of habit.

Then he tied his tie and took some "Eternal Rest" brochures from the breast pocket of his coat. "I won't need these, I guess," he mumbled, throwing them on the neatly made bed. The spread and drapes were both a chocolate color, and there were pastel reproductions of cute mountain landscapes in wide aluminum frames lined along the back wall.

A conversation jumped suddenly into Mac's head. He had been talking with another salesman in Rapid City, telling him about one of his hobbies, which was creating epitaphs. "It's sort of a fringe benefit I've developed for myself," he'd said. "A little extra. Hell, nobody'd ever *buy* the goddamn things. Nobody cares about epitaphs these days, anyway, so–you know–I can sort of joke about them. 'Get rid of 'em fast.' That's their motto today. And I'm not saying they're wrong. People used to be too morbid and sentimental about death, for Christ's sake. But today, nobody cares about words on the marble; nobody'd ever bother to read them, except maybe some nut like yours truly. No, these days, they just dump 'em in the ground, put up the dates, and tell who they were the wife or husband of . . ."

"How long you been selling gravestones?" the other salesman interrupted.

"Huh-uh!" Mac said, holding up his big meaty hand in a stop gesture. *"Memorial* plaques."

"Well, how long have you been selling memorial plaques then?"

"Thirty-two meaningful goddamn years," Mac answered. "Oh, for a while I sold commercial cement like a damned lunatic, and really made some thick cash in those days, but basically I've remained faithful to my lawfully wedded wife, in a manner of speaking, which is memorial plaques."

"What are some of those epitaphs you've made up?" the man asked.

Then it was a strange thing happened: Mac couldn't remember a single one of the hundreds of epitaphs he'd made up and written down in notebooks over the years. As he sat there trying to think of one, he was gradually aware of the look the other salesman was giving him; and then suddenly, there was this *little* breakthrough, at least, and he thought of two of them:

I ALWAYS WAS EARTHY

and

DUST TO BUST AND BUST TO DUST

But the best ones (there were a hundred better than those) had simply flown away. Flown a-fucking-way. Like so much in this vale of tatters. Maybe it was because he hadn't had anybody show this much interest in hearing them for a long time and he wasn't used to recalling them. Maybe a little too much sauce.

"Some people think they're kind of sick," Mac said meditatively, three beats too late, "but hell, if you can't laugh at a few things in this world, I always say, what use is there?"

"I don't know," the other salesman answered.

Mac tried to remember what it was the other fellow sold; then it came to him; he sold electronic equipment. And his name was Chalmers or Chambers or something like that. And he was nothing but a goddamn kid. A wonder he didn't start sucking his thumb while Mac was talking and hefting another double.

"Most people float in life," Mac said, agitating the Cutty Sark in his glass. Biddle was sitting in the booth opposite, looking vaguely drunk and all-used-up. In fact, he was in pretty bad shape and looked like a man sitting perfectly erect, but asleep in his clothes.

"Surfaces," Mac said, leveling his hand laterally through the dark air of the Captain's Bar. (Nautically appointed, it might have given the secret prod to the metaphor.)

Biddle ate from the nut bowl, dozing.

"They don't dive down," Mac said, completing his thought and gazing soberly into his glass, as if contemplating those very depths that numb-asses should reach.

"They don't sink, you mean," Biddle said. His voice was a strained nasal tenor, and it didn't carry over five or six feet. It's a wonder he could sell a damned thing. Mac's voice, on the other hand, could rattle the sashes and make the china dance when he laughed or got wound up on a pitch.

"You shouldn't be so negative," Mac said. "Just what are you going to *do* after you quit? Let me ask you that. Do you have another position, for Christ's sake?"

"I shouldn't have agreed to meet with you, Mac," Biddle said. "I might have known you'd try to change my mind." Then he got a drunkenly troubled look on his face. "Incidentally, why *do* you? I mean, what's it to you, *really,* if I decide to quit? What's your stake in it?"

"Enough things in this world are unstable, uncertain," Mac said tentatively. But then, as if he didn't like the sound of what he was saying, he gestured with his hand and said, "No use adding to them, in my view."

"Sometimes you can't help it," Biddle said. He was a little odd-looking, in his way. From a distance, you thought he was fairly good-looking, fairly standard in appearance; but then upon approaching him, you saw that the good height was too angular . . . and the nose was really blunt and snubbed–too wide for such a narrow face; and the wide sweep of gray hair at the sides of his head was a little wild, like the hair of a mad scientist in an old movie. And his complexion was sallow, and he had little dark triangles under his eyes. Next to Mac's steaming ruddiness, he looked like a sure-as-hell quitter, a naysayer.

"When I work my territory," Mac said in a slow solemn voice, "do you know what I like to think?"

Biddle frowned at nothing and then shook his head.

"I like to think of old Biddle doing his part across the river. I like to think of him there, doing his bit, taking care of his territory the way I know it should be taken care of. Just like I like to think of old Stegmaier doing his part in the Northwest states, and Lannigan back East. Not to mention Carnap and Kline."

"Christ," Biddle said, "you make it sound like a football game! Zone defense, for God's sake!"

"That's not entirely incorrect," Mac said with dignity. "Not entirely incorrect *at all!* It happens to be a connection I've often made. Teamwork, Biddle. *That's* what it is!"

For a moment, Biddle just stared at him, as if he couldn't quite focus him right. And then he said, "Well, I'll tell you something: I've heard the referee blow his whistle for the two-minute warning."

Mac shook his head sadly. Things were not going right; they were not going right at all. "Biddle," he said, "this isn't *like* you. What the hell's happened?"

"I just told you," Biddle said. And then, to Mac's utter astonishment (because people might laugh at him now and then, but they didn't really brush off Mac's arguments), Biddle got up, fingered two tens out on the table for their drinks, and, without another word, walked out of the lounge.

"Well, I'll be a constipated turkey," Mac said, briefly agitating the Cutty Sark in his glass, and then drinking it down.

When he finished it, he held his glass (nothing but crushed ice in it, now) and sat gazing through the window. Beyond the lighted walks by the empty swimming pool the sky was darkening. Before long, it would be as murky as the interior of the Captain's Bar. Around the pool there still seemed to be a faint, pathetic echo of something festive, warm, and human.

When the woman brought his refill, Mac gave her a long look and said, "Thank you, bartendress."

She smiled perfunctorily, and said, "That'll be two seventy-five, sir."

"Just let 'em add up," Mac said to her knees. She was wearing a frilly white blouse, short puffed-out skirt, and silver-gray hose. Her legs were good, but the expression on her face was that of a woman who's just smelled something really foul. "She is exactly the kind of bartendress you should never refer to as a bartendress," Mac said to himself as she strode away. And then it occurred to him that there were fewer and fewer of that kind of bartendress around every year. "Your old jokes, McIlhenny, no longer amuse as they once did. Or as you thought they did. Or as you *think* you once thought they did."

The fact was, he was almost alone in the bar. Two mod chaps, wearing soft pale turtlenecks and coiffured hair, were sitting at the bar, leaning with their elbows on its heavy vinyl-padded dashboard. They were talking chummily about something, and the goddamn snotty bartendress (who just might conceivably have been a younger sister of the woman at the desk in the lobby) looked at them respectfully every time she walked past. Also, there was a single dude sitting at another table by the window. He was pale, bald, and almost as old as Mac. His tie was sticking outside his coat like an idiotic tongue. Just then, two middle-aged women, wearing pants suits and laughing heartily, entered, and sat at a table against the wall. They didn't even look his way when they went by. To hell with all of them, Mac said, just barely moving his lips.

And by the time he had finished this Cutty Sark he was feeling the fumes a little (as he liked to put it) and thinking of phoning old Biddle in his room. "That son of a bitch can't get away from me *that* easily!" Because there was just one hell of a lot old Biddle had to be told.

So he paid the bartendress (entertaining a brief fantasy of stuffing the bills up her nostrils) and walked out into the lobby. It was comfortably empty; however, Claire, the voyant, was still there at the desk, smoking another cigarette and clipping something from a newspaper with scissors. The carpet seemed to have grown thicker.

"Honey," Mac said as he walked past, "don't be discouraged, because I haven't left yet."

The eyes she lifted to gaze upon him were not quite a thousand years old. Mac could tell she didn't really mind the way he acted, but then she wasn't amused either. Which sort of added up to a Special Extravaganza of Nothing.

He went outside and was surprised by the cold wind that whipped his coat open and ruffled what was left of his hair. "That's a river wind," he said. "I can smell it all the way from Minneapolis." The rope on the flagpole had come loose, and it was rattling and banging at the pole, sounding like the hammer of a lunatic smithy at the forge. A car glided behind him, its headlights projecting his shadow in a long, slowly turning glide on the asphalt before him.

When he got to his T-Bird and unlocked it, Mac reached in the glove compartment and got out some prescription antacid medicine, and put it in the pocket of his trench coat.

Then he started back to the motel, in one of whose rooms Biddle was probably at this very instant lying drunk on his back, with one arm thrown over his face. Suddenly, in the cold wind that beat upon him, Mac got a faint whiff of good cooking odors from the kitchen.

"By God," he said, "we're going to have to do something about that!"

After a little freshening up, Mac picked up the phone in his room and said, "Claire?"

The woman's voice paused an instant, and then said, "What can I do for you, Mr. McIlhenny?"

"Honey, I want to talk to Biddle. Be a good girl and ring him for me, will you?"

"That's room number 137. I'll ring it for you."

The phone rang too many times. Most people would have hung up, but Mac just sat there, a little drunk and a little just-plain dazed, until unexpectedly, the receiver was lifted, and Biddle's nerdy little voice said hello.

"I think you've slept long enough, sonny," Mac said. "I think you and I have a score to settle."

"Hello, Mac. I figured you'd call."

"Listen, I've got to have a word with you. If you think I said all I have to say down there in the bar, you don't know your old Mac."

"I didn't think for a minute you were through," Biddle said prissily. His voice was suddenly far away, as if somebody on a connected line had lifted the receiver, draining off the pressure of sound. Long distance, right here in the Sandman Motel. "Distance is more than space," Mac said to himself.

"Let's go back to where we were," Mac said out loud, "and start over. I refer to the bar."

"No, I've had enough, Mac."

"Enough what? To drink?"

"That, too. Leave it alone, will you?"

"What do you mean, 'that too'?"

"I've had enough of selling, Mac; enough of the territory; enough of the pitch; enough of . . . well, shit, I might as well say it: enough of *you.*" (So Biddle *could* say it: shit!)

"You don't know what you're saying, Biddle!"

"Look, I think what I really need is some shut-eye. Okay?"

"I'll come to your room, then. Or you can come here. It makes no difference."

"No, it doesn't make any difference, and that's something I wish you would for God's sake get straight. I've made up my mind, and that's final. What I can't figure out is why *you* should be so concerned . . . why you should have come over here in the first place, when . . . well, Mac, let's face it: you and I have never been all that chummy before, so why in the hell should you take it upon yourself to come here and try to talk me out of a perfectly natural decision, which is to *retire,* for God's sake! I'm telling you, man, I've *had* it! I've got four grandchildren, and I've already had a coronary. I assume you knew that, didn't you? Well, whether you did or not, it's true. So what the hell difference does it make to *you,* whether or not I decided to do what is after all, the perfectly *natural* thing, for Christ's sake, and. . . ."

Biddle stopped talking, and, for an instant, Mac was quiet, too, listening to his own breath in the receiver; and then–before he could rally an argument and say anything–Biddle quietly said good-bye and hung up.

"All I wanted to do was tell him a story," Mac said. "Just one little story. A man's in pretty bad shape, when he doesn't even want to hear one story!"

He went over to his suitcase, then, and got out his stainless-steel flask filled with Cutty Sark and unscrewed the cap. He referred to this as his "Emergency Ration Kit," and his wife liked the phrase and always laughed. He shook his head and went out of his room and down the hall to the ice machine, growling like a science fiction monster in a warm tiny alcove. He shoveled a pint of cubes into his plastic pitcher and returned to his room, stepping to the side on the way to let two little girls, about three or four years old, run past, laughing and trailing their hands along the wall.

"Just the age of the old Mac's grandchildren," he whispered, as he let himself into the room.

And thinking of them, he decided to phone his wife, which he did, and found that she was feeling better and might even decide to play golf with Norma tomorrow.

"It's cold as a titches wit, here," Mac told her. "Even spitting a little snow. Too cold to think of golf."

"Well, be careful driving," she said. "Take it easy on the curves, and that goes for highways as well as women."

Mac rumbled a brief laugh at the old joke between them, and then, after another minute or so of casual talk, he hung up. He went over and picked up the faithful old Cutty Sark, sipped it, and then went over to his travel case on the dresser, and sat down.

Sighing, he began to look over some accounts that he would have to take care of back in his own territory, within the week. He added up the mileage in his mind and then shook his head. "It's going to be a bitch of a week," he grumbled, "and here I have to wet-nurse Biddle like he was some college kid who's just discovered existentialism! Who would have thunk it!"

The thought of this shook him a little, and he finished his drink.

"Maybe I can tell him the story tomorrow at breakfast," he said, standing up and checking the room key in his pocket, before leaving once again for the lobby.

When he went down the heavily carpeted stairs at the end of the hallway, he whispered, "Let me tell you something, though: it won't be exactly the same with Biddle gone!"

But the story wouldn't wait. It had to be told, whether Mac would tell it to Biddle or not.

And when he came into the lobby, and saw Claire sitting there all alone at the desk, reading a copy of *Better Homes and Gardens,* he said to himself, "What the hell, she's got a nice look about her."

This was true: it wasn't just the drink, even though he was getting along toward being pretty well smashed, or somewhat semi-pounded, by this time. He went over to her and leaned on the counter. "Honey," he said, "I remember one time in Milwaukee that something happened to me that you wouldn't believe it if your mother told you."

There was no doubt about it, Mac said, the best thing about Claire was the way she moved her eyes. Now, she raised them like they weighed about five pounds each and fixed them on old Mac. She had a big face, but it was pretty and womanly (even though, when you got up close, she was about fifty, maybe fifty-five), and she had a lot of little wrinkles about her eyes, which indicated that she must have done a lot of laughing in her life, even though Mac himself had yet to witness anything approaching what you would really call a smile.

Now, when she neither encouraged him nor protested, he went ahead: "You see, I had a sideline back then, which was selling commercial cement. In fact, for a couple of years there, it was touch and go, whether I was selling memorial plaques, my present business, with commercial cement as a sideline, or vice damn versa. It was a big thing, for a while, and the biggest sale I suppose I've ever pulled off—I'm speaking *gross,* now, and *immediate commission* . . . not increments, or anything like that . . . well, anyway, the biggest sale was probably right back there in Milwaukee. The one I am going to tell you about right now."

The woman at the desk had still not spoken or responded in any way, but now a vague look of what might have been incipient fascination came over her face. It was almost as if something in the bureaucracy of her brain had decided upon an issue all by itself, independently of anything the rest of her wanted to think.

Mac took note instinctively of this alteration, and went on. "You see, there were three or four of us up there in one of the suburb motels—I forget the name of the suburb, it's been so long ago—and all of us were after this really, what you'd call fantastic, tremendous account with the D. L. Factor Company, which was about to put up a cluster of shopping centers there. Let me tell you, honey, it was one hell of a sum of money involved, which if I told you, you'd likely faint right there, and fall off your chair, so I'd have to jump back there and catch you.

"So I come breezing into this motel, you know—it was a real nice place, a little like this one—and I ask to see the guest register, because I wanted to know who the opposition was. I mean to tell you, I was already determined to get that account if it killed me.

"Well, it took a little bribe, a quick little hustle, if you know what I mean, but finally the clerkess let me look at the register, and I went down the names of the people I was going to compete against, and by God I came across the name of Wayne Raebeck.

"Now I know that doesn't mean clam chowder to you, honey, but I'll tell you something: it made my blood freeze. You know why?"

Mac paused and stared hard at the woman across from him, until she slowly, almost against her will, shook her head no.

He winked and went on.

"Well, I'll just tell you why: Wayne Raebeck was probably the best salesman of anything you can name who's ever put his feet in one or two-toned shoes. You think *I'm* a salesman? Let me tell you something. Wayne Raebeck made me look tired, ruptured, and tongue-tied. That son of a bitch was a legend in his own time. He had a reputation that you could cut with a steak knife. I want to tell you, that fellow could talk a cat out of a sardine factory!

"So there I was, faced with the near impossible. It was like playing football against God and ten angels from heaven. What should I do? Well, what would anybody with good sense do? What he would do is by God *study the opposition,* because every man born of woman has a weakness. Know your enemy. That used to be a slogan in ancient times. At least it should have been. Anyway, understand the Opposition better than he understands himself.

"So I got my ass . . . pardon my French, Claire: I got myself up to my room, and I phoned an old Turk named Jim C. Williams, in Kansas City, who was the smartest man I have ever known in my life. That's 'Jim C.,' not 'James'—no, not ever! Anyway, I phoned Jim C., and I said to him, 'Jim, how can a fellow beat Wayne Raebeck, face to face?' And Jim C., he just paused and said, 'Well, Mac, there is *no* way to do a thing like that. You just can't reasonably expect to beat that fellow.'

"And do you know what I said? I said, 'Jim, any man born of woman can be beat in some way, and you know it. Every man has his Achilles heel, I don't care how smart or how lucky or how determined he is.'

"Well, Jim C. paused a minute, which was all I needed. I went on ahead, giving him a lot of suggestions about what might be useful to me in bringing off this contract against the mighty Wayne Raebeck. One way to solve a problem is to listen to yourself talk about it. After a bit, Jim C. said, well, maybe I was right. And I said, 'I know I am, Jim.' Already, he was kind of interested in the problem, even though he knew it wouldn't mean any dollars in *his* pocket . . . still, Jim C. was an old trooper, and he couldn't resist the sound of the bugle. Also, right along about here, the sun was beginning to shine in the head of the man who stands before you.

"So the two of us talked, and then we talked some more. My phone bill that night was over twenty dollars, and that was way back when you could buy a registered hound dog for that kind of money. Old Jim C. probably knew Wayne Raebeck as well as anybody ever did, because, like a lot of superb winners, Wayne Raebeck was sort of a loner, sort of a mystic, when he wasn't doing the one thing he was cut out for. I just kept on questioning Jim C., and then questioning him some more, until I could tell the old fellow was beginning to wish maybe I'd just go straight to hell and leave him in peace . . . but I hung in there like a bulldog, until . . . until finally, along about midnight, Jim C. said something (I was questioning him about Wayne Raebeck's personal habits, along about this time, on to something in my own thinking) . . . Jim C. made an observation that rang a bell in my head.

"I didn't say anything to Jim C., but just sort of acted like I was discouraged, too, and tired, and ready to call it a night. But inside, a little voice was saying to me, 'Mac, this is it; this is all you need.' And that voice wasn't excited or anything, because it was all there, and I knew from the beginning that I couldn't miss with it. Claire, do you know what that little fact was?"

The woman slowly moved her head back and forth sideways, not taking her gaze from Mac's face.

"Well," Mac went on, poking his index finger into the palm of his left hand, "one thing you have to know is that there was a deadline. And that deadline was ten o'clock the next morning, because the Factor people had made it clear to everybody that they had to finalize the cement contract by then so they could take up options with two subcontracting firms by noon. The Factor people had seen all our materials, and what they were waiting for the next morning was the closing speech, and a few quick answers to questions, by the representatives of the bidding firms (with the two front runners being Wayne Raebeck and dumb old Mac McIlhenny, the man who is reciting this epic poem for you right at this very moment).

"So anyway, what I found out from old Jim C. was that, while it was true that Wayne Raebeck didn't seem to have any known vices or weaknesses—you couldn't get him drunk, because he was never known to drink over one whiskey sour an evening; and you couldn't sic a whore on him—excuse my French, Claire—because he had the kind of self-control every wife dreams of in a husband . . . but he did have one tragic flaw: he was what you'd call a *sleeper*. I mean to say, *he couldn't wake up in the morning without some help.* He couldn't wake up unassisted. I found this out almost by accident, the way you find out a lot of important things. And this was all I needed—I took the ball and ran like hell."

"What did you do?" the woman asked.

"I just knew you'd ask. What I did was to get Wayne Raebeck's room number, and then phone the desk after I knew he was in bed asleep and ask the clerkess who answered what time he'd asked to be awakened the next morning, because I planned to join him for breakfast, but didn't want to bother him this late. She said, well, eight-fifteen, so I said thanks and hung up. And then do you know what I did? I phoned the desk at eight the next morning, said I was Wayne Raebeck in room number such and such, whatever it was, and I was wide awake and they could cancel my call for eight-fifteen."

"And did it work?" the woman asked.

"You bet your best pair of pink bloomers it worked, honey! I closed that contract like it was on an eight-pound latch. I mean, you could hear it click when it closed. Only Wayne Raebeck didn't hear it: he didn't hear a thing, because he was sleeping the morning away. Hell, he didn't know what hit him. I saw him checking out right after noon, and I said, 'Where you been, Wayne? Missed you this morning. Sleep in, or something?" He just gave me a long hard look, like he suspected, but knew damned well he couldn't prove a thing."

"I think that's terrible," Claire said.

Well, this was the story Mac McIlhenny did not have a chance to tell Biddle, because, when Mac came down to the lobby the next morning, he found that Biddle had already gone.

"The son of a bitch checked out early," Mac whispered, leaning with both hands on the counter and staring about ten inches above the clerk's head. He swallowed and then said, "Well, hell, you can't win them all, as my virgin mother used to say. He probably wouldn't have understood anyway!"

All Biddle's life had been headed for this moment. Mac could see it all clearly.

After breakfast, he himself checked out, stopping at the desk once again, where he made a big thing out of asking the clerk there—a plump young man with a black widow's peak and three expensive rings on his fingers—to tell Claire that Mac McIlhenny said good-bye.

"Who?" the clerk asked.

"Mac McIlhenny."

"No, I mean, who should I tell it to?"

"Claire," Mac said. "The clerkess who checked me in last night. A cute little trixie, maybe near my age, but with dimples and a certain look in her eye."

"That's not her name," the clerk said fastidiously, half-closing his eyes in an expression of distrustful disdain. "Her name's Florence."

"What do I care?" Mac said. "Tell her anyway."

At that moment, he could tell the clerk was on the verge of saying something smart, or at least shaking his head in wonder and exasperation; but he caught himself in time. After all, Mac was a paying customer, and both of them fucking well knew it.

So Mac just nodded, as if to let the young fellow know how near he'd come to something or other, and then he picked up his bag and went out the glass doors to his T-Bird and headed back to his own territory, waiting there for him, somewhere on the other side of the river.

Arthur Miller

from *Death of a Salesman*

from ACT TWO

Willy Loman, the salesman, is meeting with his boss, Howard Wagner.

HOWARD: Say, aren't you supposed to be in Boston?

WILLY: That's what I want to talk to you about, Howard. You got a minute? *He draws a chair in from the wing.*

HOWARD: What happened? What're you doing here?

WILLY: Well . . .

HOWARD: You didn't crack up again, did you?

WILLY: Oh, no. No . . .

HOWARD: Geez, you had me worried there for a minute. What's the trouble?

WILLY: Well, tell you the truth, Howard. I've come to the decision that I'd rather not travel any more.

HOWARD: Not travel! Well, what'll you do?

WILLY: Remember, Christmas time, when you had the party here? You said you'd try to think of some spot for me here in town.

HOWARD: With us?

WILLY: Well, sure.

HOWARD: Oh, yeah, yeah. I remember. Well, I couldn't think of anything for you, Willy.

WILLY: I tell ya, Howard. The kids are all grown up, y'know. I don't need much any more. If I could take home—well, sixty-five dollars a week, I could swing it.

HOWARD: Yeah, but Willy, see I—

WILLY: I tell ya why, Howard. Speaking frankly and between the two of us, y'know—I'm just a little tired.

HOWARD: Oh, I could understand that, Willy. But you're a road man, Willy, and we do a road business. We've only got a half-dozen salesmen on the floor here.

WILLY: God knows, Howard, I never asked a favor of any man. But I was with the firm when your father used to carry you in here in his arms.

HOWARD: I know that, Willy, but—

WILLY: Your father came to me the day you were born and asked me what I thought of the name of Howard, may he rest in peace.

HOWARD: I appreciate that, Willy, but there just is no spot here for you. If I had a spot I'd slam you right in, but I just don't have a single solitary spot.

He looks for his lighter. Willy has picked it up and gives it to him. Pause.

WILLY, *with increasing anger:* Howard, all I need to set my table is fifty dollars a week.

HOWARD: But where am I going to put you, kid?

WILLY: Look, it isn't a question of whether I can sell merchandise, is it?

HOWARD: No, but it's a business, kid, and everybody's gotta pull his own weight.

WILLY, *desperately:* Just let me tell you a story, Howard–

HOWARD: 'Cause you gotta admit, business is business.

WILLY, *angrily:* Business is definitely business, but just listen for a minute. You don't understand this. When I was a boy–eighteen, nineteen–I was already on the road. And there was a question in my mind as to whether selling had a future for me. Because in those days I had a yearning to go to Alaska. See, there were three gold strikes in one month in Alaska, and I felt like going out. Just for the ride, you might say.

HOWARD, *barely interested:* Don't say.

WILLY: Oh, yeah, my father lived many years in Alaska. He was an adventurous man. We've got quite a little streak of self-reliance in our family. I thought I'd go out with my older brother and try to locate him, and maybe settle in the North with the old man. And I was almost decided to go, when I met a salesman in the Parker House. His name was Dave Singleman. And he was eighty-four years old, and he'd drummed merchandise in thirty-one states. And old Dave, he'd go up to his room, y'understand, put on his green velvet slippers–I'll never forget–and pick up his phone and call the buyers, and without ever leaving his room, at the age of eighty-four, he made his living. And when I saw that, I realized that selling was the greatest career a man could want. 'Cause what could be more satisfying than to be able to go, at the age of eighty-four, into twenty or thirty different cities, and pick up a phone, and be remembered and loved and helped by so many different people? Do you know? when he died–and by the way he died the death of a salesman, in his green velvet slippers in the smoker of the New York, New Haven and Hartford, going into Boston–when he died, hundreds of salesmen and buyers were at his funeral. Things were sad on a lotta trains for months after that. *He stands up. Howard has not looked at him.* In those days there was personality in it, Howard. There was respect, and comradeship, and gratitude in it. Today, it's all cut and dried, and there's no chance for bringing friendship to bear–or personality. You see what I mean? They don't know me any more.

HOWARD, *moving away, to the right:* That's just the thing, Willy.

WILLY: If I had forty dollars a week–that's all I'd need. Forty dollars, Howard.

HOWARD: Kid, I can't take blood from a stone, I–

WILLY, *desperation is on him now:* Howard, the year Al Smith was nominated, your father came to me and–

HOWARD, *starting to go off:* I've got to see some people, kid.

WILLY, *stopping him:* I'm talking about your father! There were promises made across this desk! You mustn't tell me you've got people to see–I put thirty-four years into this firm, Howard, and now I can't pay my insurance! You can't eat the orange and throw the peel away–a man is not a piece of fruit! *After a pause:* Now pay attention. Your father–in 1928 I had a big year. I averaged a hundred and seventy dollars a week in commissions.

HOWARD, *impatiently:* Now, Willy, you never averaged–

WILLY, *banging his hand on the desk:* I averaged a hundred and seventy dollars a week in the year of 1928! And your father came to me–or rather, I was in the office here–it was right over this desk–and he put his hand on my shoulder–

HOWARD, *getting up:* You'll have to excuse me, Willy, I gotta see some people. Pull yourself together. *Going out:* I'll be back in a little while.

On Howard's exit, the light on his chair grows very bright and strange.

WILLY: Pull myself together! What the hell did I say to him? My God, I was yelling at him! How could I! *Willy breaks off, staring at the light, which occupies the chair, animating it. He approaches this chair, standing across the desk from it.* Frank, Frank, don't you remember what you told me that time? How you put your hand on my shoulder, and Frank . . . *He leans on the desk and as he speaks the dead man's name he accidentally switches on the recorder, and instantly*

HOWARD'S SON: ". . . of New York is Albany. The capital of Ohio is Cincinnati, the capital of Rhode Island is . . ." *The recitation continues.*

WILLY, *leaping away with fright, shouting:* Ha! Howard! Howard! Howard!

HOWARD, *rushing in:* What happened?

WILLY, *pointing at the machine, which continues nasally, childishly, with the capital cities:* Shut it off! Shut it off!

HOWARD, *pulling the plug out:* Look, Willy . . .

WILLY, *pressing his hands to his eyes:* I gotta get myself some coffee. I'll get some coffee . . .

Willy starts to walk out. Howard stops him.

HOWARD, *rolling up the cord:* Willy, look . . .

WILLY: I'll go to Boston.

HOWARD: Willy, you can't go to Boston for us.

WILLY: Why can't I go?

HOWARD: I don't want you to represent us. I've been meaning to tell you for a long time now.

WILLY: Howard, are you firing me?

HOWARD: I think you need a good long rest, Willy.

WILLY: Howard–

HOWARD: And when you feel better, come back, and we'll see if we can work something out.

WILLY: But I gotta earn money, Howard. I'm in no position to–

HOWARD: Where are your sons? Why don't your sons give you a hand?

WILLY: They're working on a very big deal.

HOWARD: This is no time for false pride, Willy. You go to your sons and you tell them that you're tired. You've got two great boys, haven't you?

WILLY: Oh, no question, no question, but in the meantime . . .

HOWARD: Then that's that, heh?

WILLY: All right, I'll go to Boston tomorrow.

HOWARD: No, no.

WILLY: I can't throw myself on my sons. I'm not a cripple!

HOWARD: Look, kid, I'm busy this morning.

WILLY, *grasping Howard's arm:* Howard, you've got to let me go to Boston!

HOWARD, *hard, keeping himself under control:* I've got a line of people to see this morning. Sit down, take five minutes, and pull yourself together, and then go home, will ya? I need the office, Willy. *He starts to go; turns, remembering the recorder, starts to push off the table holding the recorder.* Oh, yeah. Whenever you can this week, stop by and drop off the samples. You'll feel better, Willy, and then come back and we'll talk. Pull yourself together, kid, there's people outside.

Lucia Nevai

Likely Houses

Alice and Willie owned a saltbox shack on the edge of an onion field in upstate New York. They had bought it for next to nothing with every intention of fixing it up. Once in a while, Willie would measure a broken window for glass or drive into Gardnerville for a floorboard, but mostly the task of making the shack into a home like Alice claimed she was used to overwhelmed him and he ignored it.

Alice resigned herself to the debris more successfully as a young wife than as a young mother. Cooped up all day, nursing and changing William, she found that she could vent her fury at her plain surroundings only by imagining things that weren't true. One of the things she would imagine as she sat in her Leatherette kitchen chair—looking out the west window at the wooded hill half a mile across the onion field—was that she lived in the little red house at the top of the hill. It seemed to sit there, the house, in a circle of green and Alice wanted some green around her. She wanted more than furrows and onion tops. She wanted a lawn.

There was a plain dirt plot out the west window littered with Willie's junk. It could have become a lawn, but circumstances had combined to make the transformation impossible that spring. First, Alice found out she was pregnant again. That meant she would be too tired to seed the plot all by herself. Second, Willie got laid off at the garage. That meant there would be no money. Alice found this hard to accept. Frustration rose in her passive gray eyes and molded her usually mild, indefinite features into a forward-moving face, like the front of a well-designed car.

One April day when the sky was steadily sifting rain, Alice stood at her post by the front door watching for Ray to bring the mail. William was in the process of learning how to open the cabinet under the sink, take out all the pots and pans, and bang the lids together like cymbals. "Cripes," muttered Alice, putting her hands over her ears to block out the noise.

"Shut that kid up!" Willie shouted from his chair where he was watching TV commercials. "I can't hear nothing."

"You shut him up!" Alice shouted back. "I'm waiting for the mailman."

"That's not doing nothing," Willie argued.

"If you'd fix the goddamn mailbox so's it wouldn't let the rain ruin the newspaper, maybe you'd have some peace and quiet." He answered her by turning the TV all the way up. When Ray's mail truck pulled up in front, she ran out into the rain, slamming the front door as hard as she could.

"Wet enough for you?" Ray smiled.

"It may be wet, but it don't talk back," Alice huffed. He laughed and drove off. There was nothing to speak of in the mail besides the newspaper. Alice sat in her Leatherette chair and read the want ads with a vengeance until the noise level made her cry. She took the lids away from William and put him in his playpen. He screamed bloody murder. She stuck him in the high chair and put a stack of saltines in front of him. "Always getting your way, aren't you?" she said wearily. While he ate, she turned her back and gazed out the window at the plot.

It would be all picked up, all cleaned up, no car parts, no tools, no toys, no broken rocker, no inner tube. It would be lush and uniform with sweet, bright green grass drinking up the April rain. There would be marigolds in a corner bed and pansies in front and gladiolas in back. There would be a white birdbath on a fluted pedestal and one new white lawn chair—her chair. It would be her room. A place she could go.

As she gazed, the baby kicked inside her belly. "Ow!" she laughed. "Well, there you are, aren't you? It's about time!" She pressed the place on her belly where the kick had come and smiled. "Willie!" she called. "The baby kicked!" She ran in to tell him since he couldn't hear. It was the kind of thing he wanted to know.

"That's my punter!" Willie grinned. "I got a linebacker, now I want a punter! And then we'll just keep right on making them until we got us a whole team. Best team in the world!" He leaned back in his lounge chair and beamed at her proudly. Alice beamed back. She did not remind him that it was her turn to have a girl. There were fewer and fewer moments when Willie was proud. Pride made his baby face cute again, like it was in high school.

"Willie," she said suddenly, "should I get a job?"

He turned the TV down. "Alice," he said, "we've been over this before. Number 1, you can't do nothing but clean house, and I won't have you doing that in your condition. Number 2, all we got is the tow truck. If you did work, how would you get there? You can't drive my tow truck. I might get a call and then I'm making money. Number 3, name one outfit in this country which hires a woman who they know from the outset will quit in three, four months and never come back." He bent forward and increased the volume.

"There is one ad," Alice raised her voice, "for a part-time representative." She found it hard to take a stand against him.

"Part-time representative," she quoted from the paper, "demonstrate educational materials. No experience necessary. Guaranteed $$ per week."

Willie guffawed. "You are so naive! You don't know what that is?"

"What is it?"

"Encyclopedia salesman."

"Oh, no," Alice whimpered. Her face fell. Willie was so knowledgeable. "Why do they call it by another name?"

He laughed again. "Call the number, go ahead. See if I'm right."

"You hold William then," she said, "so I can hear myself think." She wiped the cracker mess from the creases of William's fat hands and plopped him down in Willie's lap. She took the phone into the kitchen as far as the cord would allow. When she returned in fifteen minutes, Willie had forgotten all about their discussion. "I'm doing it!" she announced confidently.

He scowled at her for a moment, alarmed by her unusually triumphant manner. When he realized what she was talking about he grumbled, "Over my dead body!"

"I've met all your criteria," Alice said, using the lady on the phone's phrase.

"Already she's talking funny," Willie said to William. They both looked up at her with sweet, demanding expressions.

"Number 1, they train you," Alice said, pressing her index fingers together chest-high in a list-making gesture. She talked rapidly and her usual lack of logic was not in evidence. "Number 2, for the first four weeks someone will be able to pick me up and take me home. After that, I'm on my own and I can go out as little as once a week. You can give me that tow truck once a week, Willie, *one morning.* Number 3, I can quit anytime to have the baby and come back to work when I feel ready."

Willie looked hurt. His eyes retreated and his jaw set the way it did when his mother was coming over. "Who is *they?*" he asked. "It better not be a *he.*"

"*They* is Barbara Canter, the regional director of Universal Knowledge." Willie shook his head. "Well?" Alice asked after a long pause.

"Well, what?" Willie said. His voice sounded tired.

"Well, can I? She's on the phone."

"Got to be fancy, don't you?" he chided, drawing it out. "Got to be like Carol June and get a job. Well, I'm telling you, Alice, you ain't no Carol June. Carol June's got no family and Carol June's got no heart. You got both. You can't make it out there. You start exposing yourself to those elements and they'll eat you up. You won't even know what hit you. People will walk all over you, Alice Ann."

"Well, then you'd have some company, wouldn't you?" Alice hissed. "Look, Willie, I want a lawn." She put her hands on her hips and bent forward a little to make her point. "I want myself a real grass lawn. I want to sit on it *this* summer with my new baby. You ain't working and you can't give it to me. I don't hold it against you. But don't you hold it against me that I want it."

"Alice Ann, if you get one scratch on that tow truck," Willie pointed his index finger right at her heart, "and I mean a *scratch,* you'll never drive it again. You'll never even sit in it. You'll *walk* to the frigging hospital."

"It's a deal!" Alice snapped. She picked up the phone and said with a quaver in her voice, "Barbara? What time tonight?"

Barbara's home was color-coordinated. It was the only Tudor home in Gardnerville. It had framed pictures from Italy and a grand piano. Barbara's husband, Alberto, traveled to New York City to sing in the opera. Everyone was lucky to be in her home, since this was Barbara's last class. She was being promoted and would be leaving the area with Alberto in a few months. Alice sat on the white sofa with a glass coffee cup and saucer in her lap, feeling awkward and out of place.

"It's a lovely, lovely color," someone named Millie was saying ingratiatingly to Barbara about the french blue carpeting. "What kind of backing does it have?"

"Jute!" Barbara enunciated enthusiastically. She stood before her class, statuesque and energetic in her pastel double-knit suit. She started all her sentences by raising her eyebrows dramatically and widening her eyes. Her manner dispelled any urge to gossip among the five trainees. The gave her their undivided attention as she led them through the Six Steps to a Super Sale. At the end, she held up an order blank. "Every time you get one of these signed, you're closing a deal: it's thirty-five dollars in your pocket. Beginners close one out of every five presentations. And that's not just a statistic–it's history!" People's backs straightened. They had a hell of a company behind them. "Watch closely now," Barbara said, "at this special training film. Lights!" Trainees at either end of the white sofa reached for the table lamp switches.

Alice, who felt exaggeratedly empowered by Barbara's speaking voice, almost immediately went into a daze as the staticky music of the sound track began to waver in the darkened living room. She spent the whole twenty minutes wondering what jute was, where Barbara's husband hid during the training sessions, what a black projector would look like in her own living room, and other things that she really couldn't ask at the question-and-answer period which followed the film.

Suddenly everyone was standing up and saying good night. "Practice the Six Steps to a Super Sale at home this week on your husbands," Barbara said in closing. "They'll tease you at first, but that's men."

* * *

Gardnerville was a humdrum, economically depressed burg in which five of the six main county roads uneventfully converged. It had functioned for Alice as a stern, reproving municipality which withheld things from her family—jobs, food, shoes, clothing, Congoleum, dishwashers, roofing shingles, patio tiles, and driveway shale. Now it became demystified: it was a territory. Alice and Barbara would cruise around side streets and back roads in Barbara's bronze Oldsmobile, looking for likely houses. A likely house had swing sets in back and bikes or trikes in front. Aboveground pools or cars in the driveway were also good signs.

They would call on likely houses until Barbara could demonstrate a complete presentation for Alice, sniffing out and avoiding the deadly stallers ("They'll yes you through the whole Six Steps before admitting they can't sign anything without their husbands"). Three out of five times, Barbara would close a sale. There was a great feeling of exhilaration at a closing. If there was no closing, Alice and Barbara would pad politely back to the Oldsmobile, giggling at the way the wife ate a Cheerio off the kitchen floor or the husband's toupee kept slipping forward.

Alice began to resent going home to her own unlikely house. Instead of being proud, Willie was jealous. His complaints would come hurling at her the minute she stepped in the door. "You're late! What's for dinner? Your kid never shut up this morning. He crapped all over the hall. Where'd you put my socks? Didn't you do a laundry yet? Take this brat off my hands—I want a nap."

Alice would stomp around fuming, cramming laundry into the machine, slamming dishes, feeding snotty William, vacuuming up Willie's inconsiderate mud. She never had time to sit in her Leatherette chair and imagine things. She began to want a husband who was more like Barbara.

The day before Alice was to go out on her own in the tow truck for the first time, Willie got especially pigheaded. He blasted her with his "you can't do nothing but clean house" speech, but he couldn't make her cry. She didn't believe him anymore. She drifted upstairs and lay naked on the white sheets, her arms around her unborn baby, until the fragile May dusk gathered in the uncurtained window.

Stirred to remorse by a made-for-TV movie, Willie climbed the stairs at ten o'clock and stood in the doorway. "Why am I the dumb one?"

he whispered. "You got it all. You got the smarts and you get to have the babies too. What do I get?" Alice crumbled into tiny tears like dew.

It was a delirious May morning. The clouds were voluptuous. Lilac smell—so strong it seemed cheap—wafted over from the house next door. Alice crossed herself for good luck—something she hadn't done since high school. She forced herself up into the cab of the tow truck with her UK briefcase. In order to reach the pedals with her feet, she had to push her belly up against the steering wheel.

Alice drove straight to Heritage Hills, a new subdivision of split-level homes on the north side of Gardnerville. There she called on a Mr. LeVore, a widower working nights for the telephone company. He was just about to go to sleep. His living room floor was covered with asphalt linoleum because he had five sons. Mr. LeVore wanted Universal Knowledge for his sons, but his property taxes were going up in June and he wanted to see the bill before he bought anything new. He suggested Mrs. Riker across the street, who was Miss Poland in 1957 before she came to this country and married a Riker. Mrs. Riker was waxing her kitchen floor and asked Alice to come back in half an hour.

Alice called on a bright, talkative, chain-smoking lady named Benita who was too smart for her own good and figured out at Step Five of the Six Steps exactly how much Universal Knowledge would really cost her on the installment plan, including interest. Benita then tried to get Alice to take her commission off the selling price in exchange for three months of Nutrilife Vitamins, for which Benita was the county distributor. Fortunately, Alice left without ever knowing what Benita was talking about.

Down the street at a very likely house—new avocado appliances and a redwood deck—Alice almost made a double sale to two neighbors, Jean and Jenine. With identical hairdos, they sat together at the dining room table drooling over the offer Alice unfolded with her four-color poster. They were even planning to order the dictionary, the atlas, and the yearbooks when the phone rang. Alice listened, stunned, while Jean's mother talked her out of Universal Knowledge. "Mom's going to give me her old Britannica," Jean told Alice with a shrug.

"Then we can use it too!" Jenine said.

Alice was furious. She left Heritage Hills without going back to old Miss Poland and drove the fifteen miles back to her own neighborhood at sixty-five miles an hour. She needed one more complete presentation to make her quota of five. It was then that she thought of the red house on the hill. She swerved onto the access road and drove across the onion field. As the tow truck climbed the wooded hill, winding to the left and then to the right, every bump and stone in the road slammed the baby against Alice's bladder. Alice was terrified that she would pee in her pants. She tried all the old tricks, singing "Onward, Christian Soldiers," holding herself with one hand, picturing a toilet with the lid up waiting for her somewhere in the near future.

"This is not a likely house!" Alice announced, feeling deceived as she entered the grassy clearing at the top. All of her hopes fell at once. Only the front of the house was painted red and it was a bad red—somebody's leftover deck enamel. The whole clearing was deserted, except for an old woman sitting in a white rocker on the concrete stoop.

Alice waddled through the tickly meadow grass to the stoop. She said hello to the old lady and knocked on the door.

"Come in," the old lady said.

"Oh!" Alice said, turning to her again. "Do they have a bathroom I might use? I live down the hill, but I've been out making sales calls. Now I can't tell you how bad I have to go."

"Don't apologize," the old lady said. "Go on inside. It's on the left. Toilet don't flush, so take the pail and fill it with tap water and pour it down the stool after yourself."

Sun filled the bare bungalow, illuminating every inadequacy of style and comfort. Alice sat on the toilet feeling sorry for the old lady, who obviously lived completely alone. She looked out the bathroom window and saw the roof of her own house at the edge of the onion field. It looked fixed up from here. This enraged Alice because it wasn't fixed up. It wasn't fixed up at all.

"You come down and visit me someday," Alice said to the old lady on her way out.

"Oh, I'm not lonely!" She smiled. "I'm as busy as I could be!" Her face crinkled into a vibrant mask of joy. She gave the impression of perfect freedom, sailing serenely there in her white chair with no obstacles to her enjoyment. "I just rock and think, rock and think!"

"Well, if you ever *do* get lonely, you just come right on down," Alice repeated.

"Good luck with your sales." The old lady smiled.

"Well, you know, it takes two incomes these days," Alice complained, "to get things done around the house and keep the family in shoes and whatnot."

"Don't worry about it," the old lady instructed. "It don't come to nothing anyway. All your wishing and wanting–it don't end up making any difference. Your hubby will die on you and your children will move to California like mine and all that will be left of your life is how much love you actually gave them."

Alice's features filled with hate. She smiled politely and left. Her teeth were gritting as she lunged back down the disappointing hill, and she took the final turn onto the access road at a defiant forty-five miles an hour. A huge green tiller clambered slowly out of the onion field into her path. She could scrape by if she kept going, but she would crease the whole right side of the tow truck. Willie would kill her. Summoning all of her being into a single column of prayer, she begged, "Please, God, not a scratch!" and slammed on the brakes. Her belly flew into the steering wheel. The horizon spun insanely in the windshield and when it stopped, it lay at a tilt. Alice opened her eyes. The front end of the truck was nose to nose with the tiller. The back wheel hung precariously over the drainage ditch.

The tiller's driver climbed out of his seat and stood looking at Alice. His mouth was a line that lay noncommittally in his face. He had the look of someone whose will had bent to the will of the sky again and again without breaking. He looked at Alice with admiration. It had been his assumption that the collision had been averted by a man, a better man than he, for his reflexes were slow and he knew it.

"My fault," he called, "can I do anything?"

In a loud, frustrated voice that echoed over the onion field, Alice cried, "Would you *please* buy a set of goddamn encyclopedias?"

He thought for a moment. His brother-in-law had just bought a set. His wife had been on him to get one. "Yes," he called back, "yes, I would."

Flannery O'Connor

Good Country People

Besides the neutral expression that she wore when she was alone, Mrs. Freeman had two others, forward and reverse, that she used for all her human dealings. Her forward expression was steady and driving like the advance of a heavy truck. Her eyes never swerved to left or right but turned as the story turned as if they followed a yellow line down the center of it. She seldom used the other expression because it was not often necessary for her to retract a statement, but when she did, her face came to a complete stop, there was an almost imperceptible movement of her black eyes, during which they seemed to be receding, and then the observer would see that Mrs. Freeman, though she might stand there as real as several grain sacks thrown on top of each other, was no longer there in spirit. As for getting anything across to her when this was the case, Mrs. Hopewell had given it up. She might talk her head off. Mrs. Freeman could never be brought to admit herself wrong on any point. She would stand there and if she could be brought to say anything, it was something like, "Well, I wouldn't of said it was and I wouldn't of said it wasn't," or letting her gaze range over the top kitchen shelf where there was an assortment of dusty bottles, she might remark, "I see you ain't ate many of them figs you put up last summer."

They carried on their most important business in the kitchen at breakfast. Every morning Mrs. Hopewell got up at seven o'clock and lit her gas heater and Joy's. Joy was her daughter, a large blonde girl who had an artificial leg. Mrs. Hopewell thought of her as a child though she was thirty-two years old and highly educated. Joy would get up while her mother was eating and lumber into the bathroom and slam the door, and before long, Mrs. Freeman would arrive at the back door. Joy would hear her mother call, "Come on in," and then they would talk for a while in low voices that were indistinguishable in the bathroom. By the time Joy came in, they had usually finished the weather report and were on one or the other of Mrs. Freeman's daughters, Glynese or Carramae. Joy called them Glycerin and Caramel. Glynese, a redhead, was eighteen and had many admirers; Carramae, a blonde, was only fifteen but already married and pregnant. She could not keep anything on her stomach. Every morning Mrs. Freeman told Mrs. Hopewell how many times she had vomited since the last report.

Mrs. Hopewell liked to tell people that Glynese and Carramae were two of the finest girls she knew and that Mrs. Freeman was a *lady* and that she was never ashamed to take her anywhere or introduce her to anybody they might meet. Then she would tell how she had happened to hire the Freemans in the first place and how they were a godsend to her and how she had had them four years. The reason for her keeping them so long was that they were not trash. They were good country people. She had telephoned the man whose name they had given as a reference and he had told her that Mr. Freeman was a good farmer but that his wife was the nosiest woman ever to walk the earth. "She's got to be into everything," the man said. "If she don't get there before the dust settles, you can bet she's dead, that's all. She'll want to know all your business. I can stand him real good," he had said, "but me nor my wife neither could have stood that woman one more minute on this place." That had put Mrs. Hopewell off for a few days.

She had hired them in the end because there were no other applicants but she had made up her mind beforehand exactly how she would handle the woman. Since she was the type who had to be into everything, then, Mrs. Hopewell had decided, she would not only let her be into everything, she would *see to it* that she was into everything—she would give her the responsibility of everything, she would put her in charge. Mrs. Hopewell had no bad qualities of her own but she was able to use other people's in such a constructive way that she never felt the lack. She had hired the Freemans and she had kept them four years.

Nothing is perfect. This was one of Mrs. Hopewell's favorite sayings. Another was: that is life! And still another, the most important, was: well, other people have their opinions too. She would make these statements, usually at the table, in a tone of gentle insistence as if no one held them but her, and the large hulking Joy, whose constant outrage had obliterated every expression from her face, would stare just a little to the side of her, her eyes icy blue, with the look of someone who has achieved blindness by an act of will and means to keep it.

When Mrs. Hopewell said to Mrs. Freeman that life was like that, Mrs. Freeman would say, "I always said so myself." Nothing had been arrived at by anyone that had not first been arrived at by her. She was quicker than Mr. Freeman. When Mrs. Hopewell said to her after they had been on the place a while, "You know, you're the wheel behind the wheel," and winked, Mrs. Freeman had said, "I know it. I've always been quick. It's some that are quicker than others."

"Everybody is different," Mrs. Hopewell said.

"Yes, most people is," Mrs. Freeman said.

"It takes all kinds to make the world."

"I always said it did myself."

The girl was used to this kind of dialogue for breakfast and more of it for dinner; sometimes they had it for supper too. When they had no guest they ate in the kitchen because that was easier. Mrs. Freeman always managed to arise at some point during the meal and to watch them finish it. She would stand in the doorway if it were summer but in the winter she would stand with one elbow on top of the refrigerator and look down on them, or she would stand by the gas heater, lifting the back of her skirt slightly. Occasionally she would stand against the wall and roll her head from side to side. At no time was she in any hurry to leave. All this was very trying on Mrs. Hopewell but she was a woman of great patience. She realized that nothing is perfect and that in the Freemans she had good country people and that if, in this day and age, you get good country people, you had better hang onto them.

She had had plenty of experience with trash. Before the Freemans she had averaged one tenant family a year. The wives of these farmers were not the kind you would want to be around you for very long. Mrs. Hopewell, who had divorced her husband long ago, needed someone to walk over the fields with her; and when Joy had to be impressed for these services, her remarks were usually so ugly and her face so glum that Mrs. Hopewell would say, "If you can't come pleasantly, I don't want you at all," to which the girl, standing square and rigid-shouldered with her neck thrust slightly forward, would reply, "If you want me, here I am—LIKE I AM."

Mrs. Hopewell excused this attitude because of the leg (which had been shot off in a hunting accident when Joy was ten). It was hard for Mrs. Hopewell to realize that her child was thirty-two now and that for more than twenty years she had had only one leg. She thought of her still as a child because it tore her heart to think instead of the poor stout girl in her thirties who had never danced a step or had any *normal* good times. Her name was really Joy but as soon as she was twenty-one and away from home, she had had it legally changed. Mrs. Hopewell was certain that she had thought and thought until she had hit upon the ugliest name in any language. Then she had gone and had the beautiful name, Joy, changed without telling her mother until after she had done it. Her legal name was Hulga.

When Mrs. Hopewell thought the name, Hulga, she thought of the broad blank hull of a battleship. She would not use it. She continued to call her Joy to which the girl responded but in a purely mechanical way.

Hulga had learned to tolerate Mrs. Freeman who saved her from taking walks with her mother. Even Glynese and Carramae were useful when they occupied attention that might otherwise have been directed at her. At first she had thought she could not stand Mrs. Freeman for she had found that it was not possible to be rude to her. Mrs. Freeman would take on strange resentments and for days together she would be sullen but the source of her displeasure was always obscure; a direct attack, a positive leer, blatant ugliness to her face—these never touched her. And without warning one day, she began calling her Hulga.

She did not call her that in front of Mrs. Hopewell who would have been incensed but when she and the girl happened to be out of the house together, she would say something and add the name Hulga to the end of it, and the big spectacled Joy-Hulga would scowl and redden as if her privacy had been intruded upon. She considered the name her personal affair. She had arrived at it first purely on the basis of its ugly sound and then the full genius of its fitness had struck her. She had a vision of the name working like the ugly sweating Vulcan who stayed in the furnace and to whom, presumably, the goddess had to come when called. She saw it as the name of her highest creative act. One of her major triumphs was that her mother had not been able to turn her dust into Joy, but the greater one was that she had been able to turn it herself into Hulga. However, Mrs. Freeman's relish for using the name only irritated her. It was as if Mrs. Freeman's beady steel-pointed eyes had penetrated far enough behind her face to reach some secret fact. Something about her seemed to fascinate Mrs. Freeman and then one day Hulga realized that it was the artificial leg. Mrs. Freeman had a special fondness for the details of secret infections, hidden deformities, assaults upon children. Of diseases, she preferred the lingering or incurable. Hulga had heard Mrs. Hopewell give her the details of the hunting accident, how the leg had been literally blasted off, how she had never lost consciousness. Mrs. Freeman could listen to it any time as if it had happened an hour ago.

When Hulga stumped into the kitchen in the morning (she could walk without making the awful noise but she made it—Mrs. Hopewell was certain—because it was ugly-sounding), she glanced at them and did not speak. Mrs. Hopewell would be in her red kimono with her hair tied around her head in rags. She would be sitting at the table, finishing her breakfast and Mrs. Freeman would be hanging by her elbow outward from the refrigerator, looking down at the table. Hulga always put her eggs on the stove to boil and then stood over them with her arms folded, and Mrs. Hopewell would look at her—a kind of indirect gaze divided between her and Mrs. Freeman—and would think that if she would only keep herself up a little, she wouldn't be so bad looking. There was nothing wrong with her face that a pleasant expression wouldn't help. Mrs. Hopewell said that people who looked on the bright side of things would be beautiful even if they were not.

Whenever she looked at Joy this way, she could not help but feel that it would have been better if the child had not taken the Ph.D. It had certainly not brought her out any and now that she had it, there was no more excuse for her to go to school again. Mrs. Hopewell thought it was nice for girls to go to school to have a good time but Joy had "gone through." Anyhow, she would not have been strong enough to go again. The doctors had told Mrs. Hopewell that with the best of care, Joy might see forty-five. She had a weak heart. Joy had made it plain that if it had not been for this condition, she would be far from these red hills and good country people. She would be in a university lecturing to people who knew what she was talking about. And Mrs. Hopewell could very well picture her there, looking like a scarecrow and lecturing to more of the same. Here she went about all day in a six-year-old skirt and a yellow sweat shirt with a faded cowboy on a horse embossed on it. She thought this was funny; Mrs. Hopewell thought it was idiotic and showed simply that she was still a child. She was brilliant but she didn't have a grain of sense. It seemed to Mrs. Hopewell that every year she grew less like other people and more like herself—bloated, rude, and squint-eyed. And she said such strange things! To her own mother she had said—without warning, without excuse, standing up in the middle of a meal with her face purple and her mouth half full—"Woman! do you ever look inside? Do you ever look inside and see what you are *not?* God!" she had cried sinking down again and staring at her plate, "Malebranche was right: we are not our own light. We are not our own light!" Mrs. Hopewell had no idea to this day what brought that on. She had only made the remark, hoping Joy would take it in, that a smile never hurt anyone.

The girl had taken the Ph.D. in philosophy and this left Mrs. Hopewell at a complete loss. You could say, "My daughter is a nurse," or "My daughter is a school teacher," or even, "My daughter is a chemical engineer." You could not say, "My daughter is a philosopher." That was something that had ended with the Greeks and Romans. All day Joy sat on her neck in a deep chair, reading. Sometimes she went for walks but she didn't like dogs or cats or birds or flowers or nature or nice young men. She looked at nice young men as if she could smell their stupidity.

One day Mrs. Hopewell had picked up one of the books the girl had just put down and opening it at random, she read, "Science, on the other hand, has to assert its soberness and seriousness afresh and declare that it is concerned solely with what-is. Nothing—how can it be for science anything but a horror and a phantasm? If science is right, then one thing stands firm: science wishes to know nothing of nothing. Such is after all the strictly scientific approach to Nothing. We know it by wishing to know nothing of Nothing." These words had been underlined with a blue pencil and they worked on Mrs. Hopewell like some evil incantation in gibberish. She shut the book quickly and went out of the room as if she were having a chill.

This morning when the girl came in, Mrs. Freeman was on Carramae. "She thrown up four times after supper," she said, "and was up twict in the night after three o'clock. Yesterday she didn't do nothing but ramble in the bureau drawer. All she did. Stand up there and see what she could run up on."

"She's got to eat," Mrs. Hopewell muttered, sipping her coffee, while she watched Joy's back at the stove. She was wondering what the child had said to the Bible salesman. She could not imagine what kind of a conversation she could possibly have had with him.

He was a tall gaunt hatless youth who had called yesterday to sell them a Bible. He had appeared at the door, carrying a large black suitcase that weighted him so heavily on one side that he had to brace himself against the door facing. He seemed on the point of collapse but he said in a cheerful voice, "Good morning, Mrs. Cedars!" and set the suitcase down on the mat. He was not a bad-looking young man though he had on a bright blue suit and yellow socks that were not pulled up far enough. He had prominent face bones and a streak of sticky-looking brown hair falling across his forehead.

"I'm Mrs. Hopewell," she said.

"Oh!" he said, pretending to look puzzled but with his eyes sparkling, "I saw it said 'The Cedars,' on the mailbox so I thought you was Mrs. Cedars!" and he burst out in a pleasant laugh. He picked up the satchel and under cover of a pant, he fell forward into her hall. It was rather as if the suitcase had moved first, jerking him after it. "Mrs. Hopewell!" he said and grabbed her hand. "I hope you are well!" and he laughed again and then all at once his face sobered completely. He paused and gave her a straight earnest look and said, "Lady, I've come to speak of serious things."

"Well, come in," she muttered, none too pleased because her dinner was almost ready. He came into the parlor and sat down on the edge of a straight chair and put the suitcase between his feet and glanced around the room as if he were sizing her up by it. Her silver gleamed on the two sideboards; she decided he had never been in a room as elegant as this.

"Mrs. Hopewell," he began, using her name in a way that sounded almost intimate, "I know you believe in Chrustian service."

"Well yes," she murmured.

"I know," he said and paused, looking very wise with his head cocked on one side, "that you're a good woman. Friends have told me."

Mrs. Hopewell never liked to be taken for a fool. "What are you selling?" she asked.

"Bibles," the young man said and his eyes raced around the room before he added, "I see you have no family Bible in your parlor, I see that is the one lack you got!"

Mrs. Hopewell could not say, "My daughter is an atheist and won't let me keep the Bible in the parlor." She said, stiffening slightly, "I keep my Bible by my bedside." This was not the truth. It was in the attic somewhere.

"Lady," he said, "the word of God ought to be in the parlor."

"Well, I think that's a matter of taste," she began. "I think . . ."

"Lady," he said, "for a Chrustian, the word of God ought to be in every room in the house besides in his heart. I know you're a Chrustian because I can see it in every line of your face."

She stood up and said, "Well, young man, I don't want to buy a Bible and I smell my dinner burning."

He didn't get up. He began to twist his hands and looking down at them, he said softly, "Well lady, I'll tell you the truth—not many people want to buy one nowadays and besides, I know I'm real simple. I don't know how to say a thing but to say it. I'm just a country boy." He glanced up into her unfriendly face. "People like you don't like to fool with country people like me!"

"Why!" she cried, "good country people are the salt of the earth! Besides, we all have different ways of doing, it takes all kinds to make the world go 'round. That's life!"

"You said a mouthful," he said.

"Why, I think there aren't enough good country people in the world!" she said, stirred. "I think that's what's wrong with it!"

His face had brightened. "I didn't inraduce myself," he said. "I'm Manley Pointer from out in the country around Willohobie, not even from a place, just from near a place."

"You wait a minute," she said. "I have to see about my dinner." She went out to the kitchen and found Joy standing near the door where she had been listening.

"Get rid of the salt of the earth," she said, "and let's eat."

Mrs. Hopewell gave her a pained look and turned the heat down under the vegetables. "*I* can't be rude to anybody," she murmured and went back into the parlor.

He had opened the suitcase and was sitting with a Bible on each knee.

"You might as well put those up," she told him. "I don't want one."

"I appreciate your honesty," he said. "You don't see any more real honest people unless you go way out in the country."

"I know," she said, "real genuine folks!" Through the crack in the door she heard a groan.

"I guess a lot of boys come telling you they're working their way through college," he said, "but I'm not going to tell you that. Somehow," he said, "I don't want to go to college. I want to devote my life to Chrustian service. See," he said, lowering his voice, "I got this heart condition. I may not live long. When you know it's something wrong with you and you may not live long, well then, lady . . ." He paused, with his mouth open, and stared at her.

He and Joy had the same condition! She knew that her eyes were filling with tears but she collected herself quickly and murmured, "Won't you stay for dinner? We'd love to have you!" and was sorry the instant she heard herself say it.

"Yes mam," he said in an abashed voice, "I would sher love to do that!"

Joy had given him one look on being introduced to him and then throughout the meal had not glanced at him again. He had addressed several remarks to her, which she had pretended not to hear. Mrs. Hopewell could not understand deliberate rudeness, although she lived with it, and she felt she had always to overflow with hospitality to make up for Joy's lack of courtesy. She urged him to talk about himself and he did. He said he was the seventh child of twelve and that his father had been crushed under a tree when he himself was eight year old. He had been crushed very badly, in fact, almost cut in two and was practically not recognizable. His mother had got along the best she could by hard working and she had always seen that her children went to Sunday School and that they read the Bible every evening. He was now nineteen year old and he had been selling Bibles for four months. In that time he had sold seventy-seven Bibles and had the promise of two more sales. He wanted to become a missionary because he thought that was the way you could do most for people. "He who losest his life shall find it," he said simply and he was so sincere, so genuine and earnest that Mrs. Hopewell would not for the world have smiled. He prevented his peas from sliding onto the table by blocking them with a piece of bread which he later cleaned his plate with. She could see Joy observing sidewise how he handled his knife and fork and she saw too that every few minutes, the boy would dart a keen appraising glance at the girl as if he were trying to attract her attention.

After dinner Joy cleared the dishes off the table and disappeared and Mrs. Hopewell was left to talk with him. He told her again about his childhood and his father's accident and about various things that had happened to him. Every five minutes or so she would stifle a yawn. He sat for two hours until finally she told him she must go because she had an appointment in town. He packed his Bibles and thanked her and prepared to leave, but in the doorway he stopped and wrung her hand and said that not on any of his trips had he met a lady as nice as her and he asked if he could come again. She had said she would always be happy to see him.

Joy had been standing in the road, apparently looking at something in the distance, when he came down the steps toward her, bent to the side with his heavy valise. He stopped where she was standing and confronted her directly. Mrs. Hopewell could not hear what he said but she trembled to think what Joy would say to him. She could see that after a minute Joy said something and that then the boy began to speak again, making an excited gesture with his free hand. After a minute Joy said something else at which the boy began to speak once more. Then to her amazement, Mrs. Hopewell saw the two of them walk off together, toward the gate. Joy had walked all the way to the gate with him and Mrs. Hopewell could not imagine what they had said to each other, and she had not yet dared to ask.

Mrs. Freeman was insisting upon her attention. She had moved from the refrigerator to the heater so that Mrs. Hopewell had to turn and face her in order to seem to be listening. "Glynese gone out with Harvey Hill again last night," she said. "She had this sty."

"Hill," Mrs. Hopewell said absently, "is that the one who works in the garage?"

"Nome, he's the one that goes to chiropracter school," Mrs. Freeman said. "She had this sty. Been had it two days. So she says when he brought her in the other night he says, 'Lemme get rid of that sty for you,' and she says, 'How?' and he says, 'You just lay yourself down acrost the seat of that car and I'll show you.' So she done it and he popped her neck. Kept on a-popping it several times until she made him quit. This morning," Mrs. Freeman said, "she ain't got no sty. She ain't got no traces of a sty."

"I never heard of that before," Mrs. Hopewell said.

"He ast her to marry him before the Ordinary," Mrs. Freeman went on, "and she told him she wasn't going to be married in no *office.*"

"Well, Glynese is a fine girl," Mrs. Hopewell said. "Glynese and Carramae are both fine girls."

"Carramae said when her and Lyman was married Lyman said it sure felt sacred to him. She said he said he wouldn't take five hundred dollars for being married by a preacher."

"How much would he take?" the girl asked from the stove.

"He said he wouldn't take five hundred dollars," Mrs. Freeman repeated.

"Well we all have work to do," Mrs. Hopewell said.

"Lyman said it just felt more sacred to him," Mrs. Freeman said. "The doctor wants Carramae to eat prunes. Says instead of medicine. Says them cramps is coming from pressure. You know where I think it is?"

"She'll be better in a few weeks," Mrs. Hopewell said.

"In the tube," Mrs. Freeman said. "Else she wouldn't be as sick as she is."

Hulga had cracked her two eggs into a saucer and was bringing them to the table along with a cup of coffee that she had filled too full. She sat down carefully and began to eat, meaning to keep Mrs. Freeman there by questions if for any reason she showed an inclination to leave. She could perceive her mother's eye on her. The first roundabout question would be about the Bible salesman and she did not wish to bring it on. "How did he pop her neck?" she asked.

Mrs. Freeman went into a description of how he had popped her neck. She said he owned a '55 Mercury but that Glynese said she would rather marry a man with only a '36 Plymouth who would be married by a preacher. The girl asked what if he had a '32 Plymouth and Mrs. Freeman said what Glynese had said was a '36 Plymouth.

Mrs. Hopewell said there were not many girls with Glynese's common sense. She said what she admired in those girls was their common sense. She said that reminded her that they had had a nice visitor yesterday, a young man selling Bibles. "Lord," she said, "he bored me to death but he was so sincere and genuine I couldn't be rude to him. He was just good country people, you know," she said, "—just the salt of the earth."

"I seen him walk up," Mrs. Freeman said, "and then later—I seen him walk off," and Hulga could feel the slight shift in her voice, the slight insinuation, that he had not walked off alone, had he? Her face remained expressionless but the color rose into her neck and she seemed to swallow it down with the next spoonful of egg. Mrs. Freeman was looking at her as if they had a secret together.

"Well, it takes all kinds of people to make the world go 'round," Mrs. Hopewell said. "It's very good we aren't all alike."

"Some people are more alike than others," Mrs. Freeman said.

Hulga got up and stumped, with about twice the noise that was necessary, into her room and locked the door. She was to meet the Bible salesman at ten o'clock at the gate. She had thought about it half the night. She had started thinking of it as a great joke and then she had begun to see profound implications in it. She had lain in bed imagining dialogues for them that were insane on the surface but that reached below to depths that no Bible salesman would be aware of. Their conversation yesterday had been of this kind.

He had stopped in front of her and had simply stood there. His face was bony and sweaty and bright, with a little pointed nose in the center of it, and his look was different from what it had been at the dinner table. He was gazing at her with open curiosity, with fascination, like a child watching a new fantastic animal at the zoo, and he was breathing as if he had run a great distance to reach her. His gaze seemed somehow familiar but she could not think where she had been regarded with it before. For almost a minute he didn't say anything. Then on what seemed an insuck of breath, he whispered, "You ever ate a chicken that was two days old?"

The girl looked at him stonily. He might have just put this question up for consideration at the meeting of a philosophical association. "Yes," she presently replied as if she had considered it from all angles.

"It must have been mighty small!" he said triumphantly and shook all over with little nervous giggles, getting very red in the face, and subsiding finally into his gaze of complete admiration, while the girl's expression remained exactly the same.

"How old are you?" he asked softly.

She waited some time before she answered. Then in a flat voice she said, "Seventeen."

His smiles came in succession like waves breaking on the surface of a little lake. "I see you got a wooden leg," he said. "I think you're real brave. I think you're real sweet."

The girl stood blank and solid and silent.

"Walk to the gate with me," he said. "You're a brave sweet little thing and I liked you the minute I seen you walk in the door."

Hulga began to move forward.

"What's your name?" he asked, smiling down on the top of her head.

"Hulga," she said.

"Hulga," he murmured, "Hulga. Hulga. I never heard of anybody name Hulga before. You're shy, aren't you, Hulga?" he asked.

She nodded, watching his large red hand on the handle of the giant valise.

"I like girls that wear glasses," he said. "I think a lot. I'm not like these people that a serious thought don't ever enter their heads. It's because I may die."

"I may die too," she said suddenly and looked up at him. His eyes were very small and brown, glittering feverishly.

"Listen," he said, "don't you think some people was meant to meet on account of what all they got in common and all? Like they both think serious thoughts and all?" He shifted the valise to his other hand so that the hand nearest her was free. He caught hold of her elbow and shook it a little. "I don't work on Saturday," he said. "I like to walk in the woods and see what Mother Nature is wearing. O'er the hills and far away. Pic-nics and things. Couldn't we go on a pic-nic tomorrow? Say yes, Hulga," he said and gave her a dying look as if he felt his insides about to drop out of him. He had even seemed to sway slightly toward her.

During the night she had imagined that she seduced him. She imagined that the two of them walked on the place until they came to the storage barn beyond the two back fields and there, she imagined, that things came to such a pass that she very easily seduced him and that then, of course, she had to reckon with his remorse. True genius can get an idea across even to an inferior mind. She imagined that she took his remorse in hand and changed it into a deeper understanding of life. She took all his shame away and turned it into something useful.

She set off for the gate at exactly ten o'clock, escaping without drawing Mrs. Hopewell's attention. She didn't take anything to eat, forgetting that food is usually taken on a picnic. She wore a pair of slacks and a dirty white shirt, and as an afterthought, she had put some Vapex on the collar of it since she did not own any perfume. When she reached the gate no one was there.

She looked up and down the empty highway and had the furious feeling that she had been tricked, that he had only meant to make her walk to the gate after the idea of him. Then suddenly he stood up, very tall, from behind a bush on the opposite embankment. Smiling, he lifted his hat which was new and wide-brimmed. He had not worn it yesterday and she wondered if he had bought it for the occasion. It was toast-colored with a red and white band around it and was slightly too large for him. He stepped from behind the bush still carrying the black valise. He had on the same suit and the same yellow socks sucked down in his shoes from walking. He crossed the highway and said, "I knew you'd come!"

The girl wondered acidly how he had known this. She pointed to the valise and asked, "Why did you bring your Bibles?"

He took her elbow, smiling down on her as if he could not stop. "You can never tell when you'll need the word of God, Hulga," he said. She had a moment in which she doubted that this was actually happening and then they began to climb the embankment. They went down into the pasture toward the woods. The boy walked lightly by her side, bouncing on his toes. The valise did not seem to be heavy today; he even swung it. They crossed half the pasture without saying anything and then, putting his hand easily on the small of her back, he asked softly, "Where does your wooden leg join on?"

She turned an ugly red and glared at him and for an instant the boy looked abashed. "I didn't mean you no harm," he said. "I only meant you're so brave and all. I guess God takes care of you."

"No," she said, looking forward and walking fast, "I don't even believe in God."

At this he stopped and whistled. "No!" he exclaimed as if he were too astonished to say anything else.

She walked on and in a second he was bouncing at her side, fanning with his hat. "That's very unusual for a girl," he remarked, watching her out of the corner of his eye. When they reached the edge of the wood, he put his hand on her back again and drew her against him without a word and kissed her heavily.

The kiss, which had more pressure than feeling behind it, produced that extra surge of adrenalin in the girl that enables one to carry a packed trunk out of a burning house, but in her, the power went at once to the brain. Even before he released her, her mind, clear and detached and ironic anyway, was regarding him from a great distance, with amusement but with pity. She had never been kissed before and she was pleased to discover that it was an unexceptional experience and all a matter of the mind's control. Some people might enjoy drain water if they were told it was vodka. When the boy, looking expectant but uncertain, pushed her gently away, she turned and walked on, saying nothing as if such business, for her, were common enough.

He came along panting at her side, trying to help her when he saw a root that she might trip over. He caught and held back the long swaying blades of thorn vine until she had passed beyond them. She led the way and he came breathing heavily behind her. Then they came out on a sunlit hillside, sloping softly into another one a little smaller. Beyond, they could see the rusted top of the old barn where the extra hay was stored.

The hill was sprinkled with small pink weeds. "Then you ain't saved?" he asked suddenly, stopping.

The girl smiled. It was the first time she had smiled at him at all. "In my economy," she said, "I'm saved and you are damned but I told you I didn't believe in God."

Nothing seemed to destroy the boy's look of admiration. He gazed at her now as if the fantastic animal at the zoo had put its paw through the bars and given him a loving poke. She thought he looked as if he wanted to kiss her again and she walked on before he had the chance.

"Ain't there somewheres we can sit down sometime?" he murmured, his voice softening toward the end of the sentence.

"In that barn," she said.

They made for it rapidly as if it might slide away like a train. It was a large two-story barn, cool and dark inside. The boy pointed up the ladder that led into the loft and said, "It's too bad we can't go up there."

"Why can't we?" she asked.

"Yer leg," he said reverently.

The girl gave him a contemptuous look and putting both hands on the ladder, she climbed it while he stood below, apparently awestruck. She pulled herself expertly through the opening and then looked down at him and said, "Well, come on if you're coming," and he began to climb the ladder, awkwardly bringing the suitcase with him.

"We won't need the Bible," she observed.

"You never can tell," he said, panting. After he had got into the loft, he was a few seconds catching his breath. She had sat down in a pile of straw. A wide sheath of sunlight, filled with dust particles, slanted over her. She lay back against a bale, her face turned away, looking out the front opening of the barn where hay was thrown from a wagon into the loft. The two pink-speckled hillsides lay back against a dark ridge of woods. The sky was cloudless and cold blue. The boy dropped down by her side and put one arm under her and the other over her and began methodically kissing her face, making little noises like a fish. He did not remove his hat but it was pushed far enough back not to interfere. When her glasses got in his way, he took them off of her and slipped them into his pocket.

The girl at first did not return any of the kisses but presently she began to and after she had put several on his cheek, she reached his lips and remained there, kissing him again and again as if she were trying to draw all the breath out of him. His breath was clear and sweet like a child's and the kisses were sticky like a child's. He mumbled about loving her and about knowing when he first seen her that he loved her, but the mumbling was like the sleepy fretting of a child being put to sleep by his mother. Her mind, throughout this, never stopped or lost itself for a second to her feelings. "You ain't said you loved me none," he whispered finally, pulling back from her. "You got to say that."

She looked away from him off into the hollow sky and then down at a black ridge and then down farther into what appeared to be two green swelling lakes. She didn't realize he had taken her glasses but this landscape could not seem exceptional to her for she seldom paid any close attention to her surroundings.

"You got to say it," he repeated. "You got to say you love me."

She was always careful how she committed herself. "In a sense," she began, "if you use the word loosely, you might say that. But it's not a word I use. I don't have illusions. I'm one of those people who see *through* to nothing."

The boy was frowning. "You got to say it. I said it and you got to say it," he said.

The girl looked at him almost tenderly. "You poor baby," she murmured. "It's just as well you don't understand," and she pulled him by the neck, face-down, against her. "We are all damned," she said, "but some of us have taken off our blindfolds and see that there's nothing to see. It's a kind of salvation."

The boy's astonished eyes looked blankly through the ends of her hair. "Okay," he almost whined, "but do you love me or don'tcher?"

"Yes," she said and added, "in a sense. But I must tell you something. There mustn't be anything dishonest between us." She lifted his head and looked him in the eye. "I am thirty years old," she said. "I have a number of degrees."

The boy's look was irritated but dogged. "I don't care," he said. "I don't care a thing about what all you done. I just want to know if you love me or don'tcher?" and he caught her to him and wildly planted her face with kisses until she said, "Yes, yes."

"Okay then," he said, letting her go. "Prove it."

She smiled, looking dreamily out on the shifty landscape. She had seduced him without even making up her mind to try. "How?" she asked, feeling that he should be delayed a little.

He leaned over and put his lips to her ear. "Show me where your wooden leg joins on," he whispered.

The girl uttered a sharp little cry and her face instantly drained of color. The obscenity of the suggestion was not what shocked her. As a child she had sometimes been subject to feelings of shame but education had removed the last traces of that as a good surgeon scrapes for cancer; she would no more have felt it over what he was asking than she would have believed in his Bible. But she was as sensitive about the artificial leg as a peacock about his tail. No one ever touched it but her.

She took care of it as someone else would his soul, in private and almost with her own eyes turned away. "No," she said.

"I known it," he muttered, sitting up. "You're just playing me for a sucker."

"Oh no no!" she cried. "It joins on at the knee. Only at the knee. Why do you want to see it?"

The boy gave her a long penetrating look. "Because," he said, "it's what makes you different. You ain't like anybody else."

She sat staring at him. There was nothing about her face or her round freezing-blue eyes to indicate that this had moved her; but she felt as if her heart had stopped and left her mind to pump her blood. She decided that for the first time in her life she was face to face with real innocence. This boy, with an instinct that came from beyond wisdom, had touched the truth about her. When, after a minute, she said in a hoarse high voice, "All right," it was like surrendering to him completely. It was like losing her own life and finding it again, miraculously, in his.

Very gently he began to roll the slack leg up. The artificial limb, in a white sock and brown flat shoe, was bound in a heavy material like canvas and ended in an ugly jointure where it was attached to the stump. The boy's face and his voice were entirely reverent as he uncovered it and said, "Now show me how to take it off and on."

She took it off for him and put it back on again and then he took it off himself, handling it as tenderly as if it were a real one. "See!" he said with a delighted child's face. "Now I can do it myself!"

"Put it back on," she said. She was thinking that she would run away with him and that every night he would take the leg off and every morning put it back on again. "Put it back on," she said.

"Not yet," he murmured, setting it on its foot out of her reach. "Leave it off for a while. You got me instead."

She gave a little cry of alarm but he pushed her down and began to kiss her again. Without the leg she felt entirely dependent on him. Her brain seemed to have stopped thinking altogether and to be about some other function that it was not very good at. Different expressions raced back and forth over her face. Every now and then the boy, his eyes like two steel spikes, would glance behind him where the leg stood. Finally she pushed him off and said, "Put it back on me now."

"Wait," he said. He leaned the other way and pulled the valise toward him and opened it. It had a pale blue spotted lining and there were only two Bibles in it. He took one of these out and opened the cover of it. It was hollow and contained a pocket flask of whiskey, a pack of cards, and a small blue box with printing on it. He laid these out in front of her one at a time in an evenly-spaced row, like one presenting offerings at the shrine of a goddess. He put the blue box in her hand. THIS PRODUCT TO BE USED ONLY FOR THE PREVENTION OF DISEASE, she read, and dropped it. The boy was unscrewing the top of the flask. He stopped and pointed, with a smile, to the deck of cards. It was not an ordinary deck but one with an obscene picture on the back of each card. "Take a swig," he said, offering her the bottle first. He held it in front of her, but like one mesmerized, she did not move.

Her voice when she spoke had an almost pleading sound. "Aren't you," she murmured, "aren't you just good country people?"

The boy cocked his head. He looked as if he were just beginning to understand that she might be trying to insult him. "Yeah," he said, curling his lip slightly, "but it ain't held me back none. I'm as good as you any day in the week."

"Give me my leg," she said.

He pushed it farther away with his foot. "Come on now, let's begin to have us a good time," he said coaxingly. "We ain't got to know one another good yet."

"Give me my leg!" she screamed and tried to lunge for it but he pushed her down easily.

"What's the matter with you all of a sudden?" he asked, frowning as he screwed the top on the flask and put it quickly back inside the Bible. "You just a while ago said you didn't believe in nothing. I thought you was some girl!"

Her face was almost purple. "You're a Christian!" she hissed. "You're a fine Christian! You're just like them all—say one thing and do another. You're a perfect Christian, you're . . ."

The boy's mouth was set angrily. "I hope you don't think," he said in a lofty indignant tone, "that I believe in that crap! I may sell Bibles but I know which end is up and I wasn't born yesterday and I know where I'm going!"

"Give me my leg!" she screeched. He jumped up so quickly that she barely saw him sweep the cards and the blue box back into the Bible and throw the Bible into the valise. She saw him grab the leg and then she saw it for an instant slanted forlornly across the inside of the suitcase with a Bible at either side of its opposite ends. He slammed the lid shut and snatched up the valise and swung it down the hole and then stepped through himself.

When all of him had passed but his head, he turned and regarded her with a look that no longer had any admiration in it. "I've gotten a lot of interesting things," he said. "One time I got a woman's glass eye this way. And you needn't to think you'll catch me because Pointer ain't really my name. I use a different name at every house I call at and don't stay nowhere long. And I'll tell you another thing, Hulga," he said, using the name as if he didn't think much of it, "you ain't so smart. I been believing in nothing ever since I was born!" and then the toast-colored hat disappeared down the hole and the girl was left, sitting on the straw in the dusty sunlight. When she turned her churning face toward the opening, she saw his blue figure struggling successfully over the green speckled lake.

Mrs. Hopewell and Mrs. Freeman, who were in the back pasture, digging up onions, saw him emerge a little later from the woods and head across the meadow toward the highway. "Why, that looks like that nice dull young man that tried to sell me a Bible yesterday," Mrs. Hopewell said, squinting. "He must have been selling them to the Negroes back in there. He was so simple," she said, "but I guess the world would be better off if we were all that simple."

Mrs. Freeman's gaze drove forward and just touched him before he disappeared under the hill. Then she returned her attention to the evil-smelling onion shoot she was lifting from the ground. "Some can't be that simple," she said. "I know I never could."

John O'Hara

How Can I Tell You?

A T-Bird and two Galaxies was very good for one day, especially as the T-Bird did not involve a trade-in. The woman who bought it, Mrs. Preston, had come in and asked for Mark McGranville and shown him a magazine ad. "Do you have one of these in stock, in red?" she said.

"Not on the floor, Mrs. Preston," he said. "But I can have one for you inside of two hours."

"You can? Brand-new?"

"Brand-new," he said.

"Red, like this?"

"The exact same color, the same body job, white walls, radio and heater. I could have it in front of your house inside of two hours. And if you were thinking of getting rid of your ranch wagon, I can allow you—well, let's see what the book says."

"Did I say I wanted to trade in my ranch wagon? I love it. I wouldn't think of getting rid of it. I want the Thunderbird for Buddy. He just passed all his exams and he's coming home for the weekend."

"Well, you know exactly what he wants, Mrs. Preston. Because he's been in here a couple times, looking at T-Birds. He's a very lucky boy."

"He's a good boy, Mark. Not a lucky boy."

"Yes, he's one of the best," said Mark McGranville.

"And you say you can have a car just like this in two hours? Where do you have to go for it?"

"Oh, all I have to do is pick up the phone, call the factory distributor, and tell him what I want."

"But how do you know he has what *I* want?"

"Because we dealers get a list of what was shipped to the factory distributor. I guarantee you I have just what you want. I'll bring it to your door this afternoon, personally, and be glad to take care of the registration, insurance, all the details. Would you want us to finance it for you?"

"I would not. You bring the car around and I'll give you a cheque for the whole thing, license and everything. I don't suppose you could have his initials put on today?"

"If you let me have the car overnight I can have his initials put on and bring it back to you before noon tomorrow. R. W. P.?"

"R. W. P. That's right. In yellow. Yellow would be better on red."

"About three quarters of an inch high? Or smaller? Maybe a half an inch. A half an inch in yellow shows up well. If he wants bigger initials later, that's easy to fix."

"I'll leave that to you, Mark. And you'll take care of everything? He gets home tomorrow afternoon."

"He couldn't have a nicer surprise. It is a surprise, isn't it?"

"It certainly is. It's a surprise to *me.* I wasn't going to buy him a car till he graduates. But he's been so good, and why not let him have the fun out of it?"

"You're right, Mrs. Preston."

"How's Jean? And the children?"

"They're fine, thank you. Very fine."

"You get credit for this sale, don't you?"

"You bet I do," he said. "Appreciate your asking for me."

"Well, you've always been a good boy, too, Mark. I'm sure your mother's very pleased with you."

"Thank you."

"Your mother's a fine woman, Mark. Any time she's thinking of going back to work again, I hope she lets me know first."

"She would, that's for sure. But I guess she likes keeping house for my sister. They have that little ranch-type out at Putnam Park, the two of them. Mary has her job at the Trust Company, and my mother has enough to keep her occupied."

"Very nice for both of them. Well, I mustn't keep you any longer. You have some telephoning to do."

"Thank you very much, Mrs. Preston," he said. He accompanied her to her ranch wagon, held the door open for her, and waited in the parking lot until she turned the corner.

The other transactions of the day were more typical, not sales that were dropped in his lap by a Mrs. Preston. But all three sales should have made him feel better than he felt on the way home, and he did not know why he should find himself wanting a drink and, what's more, heading for Ernie's to get it.

He locked his car and entered the taproom, hung his hat and coat on a clothestree, and took a seat in a booth. Ernie came to wait on him.

"Well, hi, stranger," said Ernie.

"Hello, Ernie," said Mark McGranville. "Quiet."

"Well, a little early. Never much action before six. The lunch trade till ha' past two, then maybe a few strays during the afternoon. How's it with you?"

"Not bad. Pretty good."

"Ed and Paul were in last night, them and their wives for dinner. Paul made a pretty good load. What's her name, his wife?"

"Charlotte."

"She snuck over and asked me to cut his drinks, but I couldn't do that. I said to her, what'd she want to do? Get me in trouble? You know Paul, he caught me watering his drinks and he'd have it all over town in no time. He's no bargain anyway, Paul."

"No, he's a noisy son of a bitch when he makes the load."

"But he's a friend of yours, though, isn't he?"

"I guess so," said Mark. "Let me have a bourbon and soda, will you, Ernie?"

"Why sure. Is there anything the matter, Mark?"

"No. Why?"

"I don't know. You want any particular bourbon?"

"I wouldn't be able to tell the difference. You know that."

"Okay, okay," said Ernie. He pantomimed getting a kick in the behind and went to the bar to get Mark's drink. He returned with a small

round tray on which were a highball glass, a shot glass with the bourbon, a small bottle of club soda. "There you are. That's Old Gutburner, the bar bourbon."

"Old what?"

"Gutburner. Old Gutburner. That's what Paul calls the bar bourbon. It ain't all that bad. You want some music?"

"Christ, no."

"You just want to sit here and nobody bother you. Okay," said Ernie. He walked away, spinning the inverted tray on his forefinger, and Mark had a couple of sips of his drink. He waited for some pleasant effect, and when none came, he finished the drink in a gulp. "Ernie? Bring me another shot, will you?"

"Right," said Ernie. He served a second shot glass of the bourbon. "You got enough soda there? Yeah, you got enough soda."

"I don't want any soda. I'm drinking this straight."

"Yeah, bourbon ought to be drunk straight. Bourbon has a flavor that if you ask me, you oughtn't to dilute it. That is, if you happen to like the taste of bourbon in the first place. Personally, I don't. I'll take a drink of bourbon, like if I'm at a football game to see the New York Giants. Or you take if I'm out in the woods, looking for deer, I usely take a pint of rye with me, or sometimes bourbon. It'll ward off the cold and the taste lasts longer. But for all-day drinking, I stick to scatch. You don't get tired of the taste of scatch. Your rye and your bourbon, they're too sweet if you're gonna drink all day. You know a funny thing about scatch, it's getting to be the most popular drink in France and Japan. That was in an article I read, this magazine I get. You know, in this business we get these magazines. I guess you have them in the car business. Trade publications, they're known as."

"Even the undertakers."

"Huh?"

"The undertakers have trade publications."

"They do, ah? Well, wuddia know. I guess every business has them."

"Every business is the same, when you come right down to it," said Mark McGranville.

"Well that's a new one on me. We're all in it for the money, but what's the same about selling cars and pushing Old Gutburner?"

"What you just said," said Mark McGranville. "We're all in it for the money. You. Me. Undertakers."

"You're talking like an I-don't-know-what," said Ernie.

"I know I am. What do I owe you?"

"Be—nothing," said Ernie.

"On the house?"

"Come in again when you'll get some enjoyment out of it. I don't want to take your money under these conditions."

"You, Ernie?"

"Yeah, me. You got sumpn eatin' you, boy, whatever it is."

"I know I have," said Mark McGranville. "Maybe it's the weather. I don't know."

"Well, my booze won't do it any good, Mark. I get days like this myself, once in a great while. The women get them all the time, but that's different. Take in a show tonight. You know this English fellow, with the big gap in his teeth. Terry?"

"Terry-Thomas."

"He's at the Carteret. He's always good for a laugh. You're not a booze man, Mark. Some are, but not you. You were taking it like medicine, for God's sake. Castor oil or something."

"Yeah. Well, thanks, Ernie. See you," said Mark McGranville.

He could not understand why he went through dinner and the entire evening without telling Jean about the T-Bird and the two Galaxies in one day. He knew that it was because he did not want to give her any good news; that much he understood. She would respond to the good news as she always did, enthusiastically and proudly, and he was in no mood to share her enthusiasm or accept the compliment of her pride in him. All that he understood, but he could not understand why he preferred to remain in this mood. She would cheer him up, and he did not want to be cheered up. He was perfunctory when the kids kissed him goodnight, and after the eleven o'clock news on the TV he rose, snapped the power dial, and went to the bedroom. He was in bed when Jean kissed him goodnight and turned out the light.

"Mark?" she said, from her bed.

"What?"

"Is there something the matter?"

"Nope."

"Goodnight," she said.

"Goodnight," said Mark McGranville.

Five, ten dark minutes passed.

"If you don't want to tell me," she said.

"How the hell can I tell you when I don't know myself?" he said.

"Oh," she said. "Shall I come over?"

"I just as soon you wouldn't," he said. "I don't know what it is."

"If I come over you'll sleep better," she said.

"Jean, please. It isn't that. Christ, I sold two Galaxies and a T-Bird today—"

"You *did?*"

"That ought to make me feel good, but I don't know what's the matter with me. I had a couple drinks at Ernie's, but nothing."

"I knew you had something to drink. It didn't show, but I could smell it."

"Oh, I'm not hiding anything."

"You hid it about the Galaxies and the T-Bird."

"I know I did. I'd have told you in the morning."

"All right. Goodnight."

"Goodnight," he said.

He thought his mind was busy, busy, busy, and that he had been unable to go to sleep, but at five minutes past two he looked at the radium hands of the alarm clock and realized that he must have slept for at least an hour, that some of the activity of his mind was actually dreams. They were not frightening dreams or lascivious ones; they were not much of anything but mental activity that had taken place while he thought he was awake but must have been asleep. Jean was asleep, breathing regularly. She made two musical notes in deep sleep, the first two notes of "Yes Sir That's My Baby"; the *yes* note as she exhaled, the *sir* as she drew breath. And yet he could tell, in spite of the dark, that she would be slightly frowning, dreaming or thinking, one or the other or both. He had so often watched her asleep, physically asleep, and making the musical notes of her regular breathing, but the slight frown revealing that her mind was at work, that her intelligence was functioning in ways that would always be kept secret from him, possibly even from herself. It was not that her sleeping face was a mask; far from it. The mask was her wakeful face, telling only her responses to things that happened and were said, the obvious responses to pleasant and unpleasant things in life. But in the frowning placidity of sleep her mind was naked. It did not matter that he could not read her thoughts; they were there, far more so than when she was awake.

He got out of bed and went to the warm livingroom and turned on one bulb in a table lamp. He lit a cigarette and took the first drag, but he let it go out. He was thirty years old, a good father, a good husband, and so well thought of that Mrs. Preston would make sure that he got credit for a sale. His sister had a good job, and his mother was taken care of. On the sales blackboard at the garage his name was always first or second, in two years had not been down to third. Nevertheless he went to the hall closet and got out his 20-gauge and broke it and inserted a shell.

He returned to his chair and re-lit the cigarette that had gone out, and this time he smoked rapidly. The shotgun rested with the butt on the floor, the barrel lying against his thigh, and he held the barrel loosely with the fingers of his left hand as he smoked. The cigarette was now down to an inch in length, and he crushed it carefully.

Her voice came softly. "Mark," she said.

He looked at the carpet. "What?" he said.

"Don't. Please?"

"I won't," he said.

J. F. Powers

Blue Island

On the day the Daviccis moved into their house, Ethel was visited by a Welcome Wagon hostess bearing small gifts from local merchants, but after that by nobody for three weeks, only Ralph's relatives and door-to-door salesmen. And then Mrs. Hancock came smiling. They sat on the matching green chairs which glinted with threads of what appeared to be gold. In the picture window, the overstimulated plants grew wild in pots.

Mrs. Hancock had guessed right about Ethel and Ralph, that they were newlyweds. "Am I right in thinking you're of Swedish descent, Mrs. Davicky? You, I mean?"

Ethel smiled, as if taking a compliment, and said nothing.

"I only ask because so many people in the neighborhood are. I'm not, myself," said Mrs. Hancock. She was unnaturally pink, with tinted blue hair. Her own sharp-looking teeth were transparent at the tips. "But you're so fair."

"My maiden name was Taylor," Ethel said. It was, and it wasn't—it was the name she'd got at the orphanage. Wanting a cigarette, she pushed the silver box on the coffee table toward Mrs. Hancock.

Mrs. Hancock used one of her purple claws to pry up the first cigarette from the top layer. "A good old American name like mine."

She was making too much of it, Ethel thought, and wondered about Mrs. Hancock's maiden name.

"Is your husband in business, Mrs. Davicky?"

"Yes, he is." Ethel put the lighter—a simple column of silver, the mate to the box—to Mrs. Hancock's cigarette and then to her own.

"Not here in Blue Island?"

"No." From here on, it could be difficult. Ralph was afraid that people in the neighborhood would disapprove of his business. "In Minneapolis." The Mohawk Inn, where Ethel had worked as a waitress, was first-class—thick steaks, dark lights, an electric organ—but Ralph's other places, for which his brothers were listed as the owners, were cut-rate bars on or near Washington Avenue. "He's a distributor," Ethel said, heading her off. "Non-alcoholic beverages mostly." It was true. Ralph had taken over his family's wholesale wine business, never much in Minneapolis, and got it to pay by converting to soft drinks.

Mrs. Hancock was noticing the two paintings which, because of their size and the lowness of the ceiling, hung two feet from the floor, but she didn't comment on them. "Lovely, lovely," she said, referring to the driftwood lamp in the picture window. A faraway noise came from her stomach. She raised her voice. "But you've been lonely, haven't you? I could see it when I came in. It's this neighborhood."

"It's very nice," said Ethel quickly. Maybe Mrs. Hancock was at war with the neighbors, looking for an ally.

"I suppose you know Mrs. Nilgren," said Mrs. Hancock, nodding to the left.

"No, but I've seen her. Once she waved."

"She's nice. Tied down with children, though." Mrs. Hancock nodded to the right. "How about old Mrs. Mann?"

"I don't think anybody's there now."

"The Manns are away! California. So you don't know anybody yet?"

"No."

"I'm surprised you haven't met some of them at the Cashway."

"I never go there," Ethel said. "Ralph—that's my husband—he wants me to trade at the home-owned stores."

"Oh?" Mrs. Hancock's stomach cut loose again. "I didn't know people still felt that way." Mrs. Hancock looked down the street, in the direction of the little corner store. "Do they do much business?"

"No," said Ethel. The old couple who ran it were suspicious of her, she thought, for buying so much from them. The worst of it was that Ralph had told her to open a charge account, and she hadn't, and she never knew when he'd stop there and try to use it. There was a sign up in the store that said: In God We Trust–All Others Pay Cash.

"I'll bet that's it," Mrs. Hancock was saying. "I'm afraid people are pretty clannish around here–and the Wagners have so many friends. They live one-two-three-five houses down." Mrs. Hancock had been counting the houses across the street. "Mr. Wagner's the manager of the Cashway."

Ethel was holding her breath.

"I'm afraid so," said Mrs. Hancock.

Ethel sighed. It was Ralph's fault. She'd always wanted to trade at the Cashway.

Mrs. Hancock threw back her head, inhaling, and her eyelids, like a doll's, came down. "I'm afraid it's your move, Mrs. Davicky."

Ethel didn't feel that it was her move at all and must have shown it.

Mrs. Hancock sounded impatient. "Invite 'em in. Have 'em in for a morning coffee."

"I couldn't do that," Ethel said. "I've never been to a coffee." She'd only read about coffees in the women's magazines to which Ralph had subscribed for her. "I wouldn't know what to do."

"Nothing to it. Rolls, coffee, and come as you are. Of course nobody really does, not really." Mrs. Hancock's stomach began again. "Oh, shut up," she said to it. "I've just come from one too many." Mrs. Hancock made a face, showing Ethel a brown mohair tongue. She laughed at Ethel. "Cheer up. It wasn't in this neighborhood."

Ethel felt better. "I'll certainly think about it," she said.

Mrs. Hancock rose, smiling, and went over to the telephone. "You'll do it right now," she said, as though being an older woman entitled her to talk that way to Ethel. "They're probably dying to get inside this lovely house."

After a moment, Ethel, who was already on her feet, having thought that Mrs. Hancock was leaving, went over and sat down to telephone. In the wall mirror she saw how she must appear to Mrs. Hancock. When the doorbell had rung, she'd been in too much of a hurry to see who it was to do anything about her lips and hair. "Will they know who I am?"

"Of course." Mrs. Hancock squatted on the white leather hassock with the phone book. "And you don't have to say I'm coming. Oh, I'll come. I'll be more than happy to. You don't need me, though. All you need is confidence."

And Mrs. Hancock was right. Ethel called eight neighbors, and six could come on Wednesday morning, which Mrs. Hancock had thought would be the best time for her. Two of the six even sounded anxious to meet Ethel, and, surprisingly, Mrs. Wagner was one of these.

"You did it all yourself," said Mrs. Hancock.

"With your help," said Ethel, feeling indebted to Mrs. Hancock, intimately so. It was as if they'd cleaned the house together.

They were saying good-by on the front stoop when Ralph rolled into the driveway. Ordinarily at noon he parked just outside the garage, but that day he drove in–without acknowledging them in any way. "Mr. Daveechee," Ethel commented. For Mrs. Hancock, after listening to Ethel pronounce her name for all the neighbors, was still saying "Davicky."

Mrs. Hancock stayed long enough to get the idea that Ralph wasn't going to show himself. She went down the front walk saying, " 'Bye now."

While Mrs. Hancock was getting into her car, which seemed a little old for the neighborhood, Ralph came out of the garage.

Mrs. Hancock waved and nodded–which, Ethel guessed, was for Ralph's benefit, the best Mrs. Hancock could do to introduce herself at the distance. She drove off. Too late, Ralph's hand moved up to wave. He stared after Mrs. Hancock's moving car with a look that just didn't belong to him, Ethel thought, a look that she hadn't seen on his face until they moved out to Blue Island.

During lunch, Ethel tried to reproduce her conversation with Mrs. Hancock, but she couldn't tell Ralph enough. He wanted to know the neighbors' names, and she could recall the names of only three. Mrs. Wagner, one of them, was very popular in the neighborhood, and her husband . . .

"You go to the Cashway then. Some of 'em sounded all right, huh?"

"Ralph, they all sounded all right, real friendly. The man next door sells insurance. Mr. Nilgren."

Ethel remembered that one of the husbands was a lawyer and told

Ralph that. He left the table. A few minutes later Ethel heard him driving away.

It had been a mistake to mention the lawyer to Ralph. It had made him think of the shooting they'd had at the Bow Wow, one of the joints. There had been a mix-up, and Ralph's home address had appeared in the back pages of one of the papers when the shooting was no longer news. Ethel doubted that the neighbors had seen the little item. Ralph might be right about the lawyer, though, who would probably have to keep up with everything like that.

Ralph wouldn't have worried so much about such a little thing in the old days. He was different now. It was hard to get him to smile. Ethel could remember how he would damn the Swedes for slapping higher and higher taxes on liquor and tobacco, but now, when she pointed out a letter some joker had written to the paper suggesting a tax on coffee, or when she showed him the picture of the wife of the Minnesota senator—the fearless one—christening an ore boat with a bottle of milk, which certainly should've given Ralph a laugh, he was silent.

It just made Ethel sick to see him at the windows, watching Mr. Nilgren, a sandy-haired, dim-looking man who wore plaid shirts and a red cap in the yard. Mr. Nilgren would be raking out his hedge, or wiring up the skinny little trees, or washing his car if it was Sunday morning, and there Ralph would be, behind a drape. One warm day Ethel had seen Mr. Nilgren in the yard with a golf club, and had said, "He should get some of those little balls that don't go anywhere." It had been painful to see Ralph then. She could almost *hear* him thinking. He would get some of those balls and give them to Mr. Nilgren as a present. No, it would look funny if he did. Then he got that sick look that seemed to come from wanting to do a favor for someone who might not let him do it.

A couple of days later Ethel learned that Ralph had gone to an indoor driving range to take golf lessons. He came home happy, with a club he was supposed to swing in his spare time. He'd made a friend, too, another beginner. They were going to have the same schedule and be measured for clubs. During his second lesson, however, he quit. Ethel wasn't surprised, for Ralph, though strong, was awkward. She was better than he was with a hammer and nails, and he mutilated the heads of screws. When he went back the second time, it must have been too much for him, finding out he wasn't any better, after carrying the club around the house for three days. Ethel asked about the other beginner, and at first Ralph acted as though she'd made him up, and then he hotly rejected the word "friend," which she'd used. Finally he said, "If you ask me, that bastard's played before!"

That was just like him. At the coffee, Ethel planned to ask the women to come over soon with their husbands, but she was afraid some of the husbands wouldn't take to Ralph. Probably he could buy insurance from Mr. Nilgren. He would want to do something for the ones who weren't selling anything, though–if there were any like that–and they might misunderstand Ralph. He was used to buying the drinks. He should relax and take the neighbors as they came. Or move.

She didn't know why they were there anyway. It was funny. After they were married, before they left on their honeymoon, Ralph had driven her out to Blue Island and walked her through the house. That was all there was to it. Sometimes she wondered if he'd won the house at cards. She didn't know why they were there when they could just as well be living at Minnetonka or White Bear, where they could keep a launch like the one they'd hired in Florida–and where the houses were far apart and neighbors wouldn't matter so much. What were they waiting for? Some of the things they owned, she knew, were for later. They didn't need sterling for eighteen in Blue Island. And the two big pictures were definitely for later.

She didn't know what Ralph liked about his picture, which was of an Indian who looked all in sitting on a horse that looked all in, but he had gone to the trouble of ordering it from a regular art store. Hers was more cheerful, the palace of the Doge of Venice, Italy. Ralph hadn't wanted her to have it at first. He was really down on anything foreign. (There were never any Italian dishes on the menu at the Mohawk.) But she believed he liked her for wanting that picture, for having a weakness for things Italian, for him–and even for his father and mother, whom he was always sorry to see and hadn't invited to the house. When they came anyway, with his brothers, their wives and children (and wine, which Ralph wouldn't touch), Ralph was in and out, upstairs and down, never long in the same room with them, never encouraging them to stay when they started to leave. They called him

"Rock" or "Rocky," but Ralph didn't always answer to that. To one of the little boys who had followed him down into the basement, Ethel had heard him growl, "The name's Ralph"–that to a nine-year-old. His family must have noticed the change in Ralph, but they were wrong if they blamed her, just because she was a little young for him, a blonde, and not a Catholic–not that Ralph went to church. In fact, she thought Ralph would be better off with his family for his friends, instead of counting so much on the neighbors. She liked Ralph's family and enjoyed having them in the house.

And if Ralph's family hadn't come around, the neighbors might even think they weren't properly married, that they had a love nest going there. Ethel didn't blame the neighbors for being suspicious of her and Ralph. Mr. Nilgren in his shirt and cap that did nothing for him, he belonged there, but not Ralph, so dark, with his dark blue suits, pearl-gray hats, white jacquard shirts–and with her, with her looks and platinum hair. She tried to dress down, to look like an older woman, when she went out. The biggest thing in their favor, but it wasn't noticeable yet, was the fact that she was pregnant.

Sometimes she thought Ralph must be worrying about the baby–as she was–about the kind of life a little kid would have in a neighborhood where his father and mother didn't know anybody. There were two pre-school children at the Nilgrens'. Would they play with the Davicci kid? Ethel didn't ever want to see that sick look of Ralph's on a child of hers.

That afternoon two men in white overalls arrived from Minneapolis in a white truck and washed the windows inside and out, including the basement and garage. Ralph had sent them. Ethel sat in the dining room and polished silver to the music of *Carmen* on records. She played whole operas when Ralph wasn't home.

In bed that night Ralph made her run through the neighbors again. Seven for sure, counting Mrs. Hancock. "Is that all?" Ethel said she was going to call the neighbor who hadn't been home. "When?" When she got the number from Mrs. Hancock. "When's that?" When Mrs. Hancock phoned, if she phoned . . . And that was where Ralph believed Ethel had really fallen down. She didn't have Mrs. Hancock's number–or address–and there wasn't a Hancock listed for Blue Island in the phone book. "How about next door?" Mrs. Nilgren was still coming. "The other side?" The Manns were still away, in California, and Ralph knew it. "They might come back. Ever think of that? You don't wanna leave them out." *Them,* he'd said, showing Ethel what was expected of her. He wanted those husbands. Ethel promised to watch for the return of the Manns. "They could come home in the night." Ethel reminded Ralph that a person in her condition needed a lot of sleep, and Ralph left her alone then.

Before Ralph was up the next morning, Ethel started to clean the house. Ralph was afraid the house cleaning wouldn't be done right (*he* spoke of her condition) and wanted to get another crew of professionals out from Minneapolis. Ethel said it wouldn't look good. She said the neighbors expected them to do their own house cleaning–*and window washing.* Ralph shut up.

When he came home for lunch, Ethel was able to say that Mrs. Hancock had called and that the neighbor who hadn't been home could come to the coffee. Ethel had talked to her, and she had sounded very friendly. "That's three of 'em, huh?" Ethel was tired of that one, but told him they'd *all* sounded friendly to her. "Mrs. Hancock okay?" Mrs. Hancock was okay. More than happy to be coming. Ralph asked if Ethel had got Mrs. Hancock's phone number and address. No. "Why not?" Mrs. Hancock would be there in the morning. That was why–and Ralph should get a hold on himself.

In the afternoon, after he was gone, Ethel put on one of her new conservative dresses and took the bus to Minneapolis to buy some Swedish pastry. She wanted something better than she could buy in Blue Island. In the window of the store where they'd bought Ralph's Indian, there were some little miniatures, lovely New England snow scenes. She hesitated to go in when she saw the sissy clerk was on duty again. He had made Ralph sore, asking how he'd like to have the Indian framed in birch bark. The Mohawk was plastered with birch bark, and Ralph thought the sissy recognized him and was trying to be funny. "This is going into my home!" Ralph had said, and ordered the gold frame costing six times as much as the Indian. However, he'd taken the sissy's advice about having a light put on it. Ethel hesitated, but she went in. In his way, the sissy was very nice, and Ethel went home with five little Old English prints. When she'd asked about the pictures in the window, the New England ones, calling them "landscapes," he'd said "snowscapes" and looked disgusted, as if they weren't what she should want.

When she got home, she hung the prints over the sofa where there was a blank space, and they looked fine in their shiny black frames. She didn't say anything to Ralph, hoping he'd notice them, but he didn't until after supper. "Hey, what *is* this?" he said. He bounced off the sofa, confronting her.

"Ralph, they're cute!"

"Not in my home!"

"Ralph, they're humorous!" The clerk had called them that. Ralph called them drunks and whores. He had Ethel feeling ashamed of herself. It was hard to believe that she could have felt they were just fat and funny and just what their living room needed, as the clerk had said. Ralph took them down. "Man or woman sell 'em to you?" Ethel, seeing what he had in mind, knew she couldn't tell him where she'd got them. She lied. "I was in Dayton's . . ."

"A woman—all right, then *you* can take 'em back!"

She was scared. Something like that was enough to make Ralph regret *marrying* her—and to remind her again that she couldn't have made him. If there had been a showdown between them, he would've learned about her first pregnancy. It would've been easy for a lawyer to find out about that. She'd listened to an old doctor who'd told her to go ahead and have it, that she'd love her little baby, who hadn't lived, but there would be a record anyway. She wasn't sorry about going to a regular hospital to have it, though it made it harder for her now, having that record. She'd done what she could for the baby. She hated to think of the whole thing, but when she did, as she did that evening, she knew she'd done her best.

It might have been a bad evening for her, with Ralph brooding on her faults, if a boy hadn't come to the door selling chances on a raffle. Ralph bought all the boy had, over five dollars' worth, and asked where he lived in the neighborhood. "I live in Minneapolis."

"Huh? Whatcha doin' way out here then?" The boy said it was easier to sell chances out there. Ethel, who had been doing the dishes, returned to the sink before Ralph could see her. He went back to his *Reader's Digest,* and she slipped off to bed, early, hoping his mind would be occupied with the boy if she kept out of sight.

He came to bed after the ten o'clock news. "You awake?" Ethel, awake, but afraid he wanted to talk neighbors, moaned remotely. "If anybody comes to the door sellin' anything, make sure it's somebody local."

In the morning, Ralph checked over the silver and china laid out in the dining room and worried over the pastry. "Fresh?" Fresh! She'd put it in the deep freeze right away and it hadn't even thawed out yet. "Is that *all?*" That was all, and it was more than enough. She certainly didn't need a whole quart of whipping cream. "Want me to call up for something to go with this?" No. "Turkey or a ham? I maybe got time to go myself if I go right now." He carried on like that until ten o'clock, when she got rid of him, saying, "You wouldn't want to be the only man, Ralph."

Then she was on her own, wishing Mrs. Hancock would come early and see her through the first minutes.

But Mrs. Wagner was the first to arrive. After that, the neighbors seemed to ring the bell at regular intervals. Ethel met them at the door, hung their coats in the hall closet, returning each time to Mrs. Wagner in the kitchen. They were all very nice, but Mrs. Wagner was the nicest.

"Now let's just let everything be," she said after they'd arranged the food in the dining room. "Let's go in and meet your friends."

They found the neighbors standing before the two pictures. Ethel snapped on the spotlights. She heard little cries of pleasure all around.

"Heirlooms!"

"Is Mr. Davitchy a collector?"

"Just likes good things, huh?"

"I just love this lamp."

"I just *stare* at it when I go by."

"So do I."

Ethel, looking at her driftwood lamp, her plants, and beyond, stood in a haze of pleasure. Earlier, when she was giving her attention to Mrs. Nilgren (who was telling about the trouble "Carl" had with his trees), Ethel had seen Ralph's car cruise by, she thought, and now again, but this time there was no doubt of it. She recognized the rather old one parked in front of Mrs. Hancock's, but where was Mrs. Hancock?

"Hello, everybody!"

Mrs. Hancock had let herself in, and was hanging up her coat.

Ethel disappeared into the kitchen. She carried the coffeepot, which had been on *low,* into the dining room, where they were supposed to come and help themselves. She stood by the pot, nervous, ready to pour, hoping that someone would look in and see that she was ready, but no one did.

She went to see what they were doing. They were still sitting down, listening to Mrs. Hancock. She'd had trouble with her car. That was why she was late. She saw Ethel. "I can see you want to get started," she said, rising. "So do I."

Ethel returned to the dining room and stood by the coffeepot.

Mrs. Hancock came first. "Starved," she said. She carried off her coffee, roll, and two of the little Swedish cookies, and Ethel heard her in the living room rallying the others.

They came then, quietly, and Ethel poured. When all had been served, she started another pot of coffee, and took her cup and a cookie–she wasn't hungry–into the living room.

Mrs. Hancock, sitting on the hassock, had a bottle in her hand. On the rug around her were some brushes and one copper pan. "Ladies," she was saying, "now here's something new." Noticing Ethel, Mrs. Hancock picked up the pan. "How'd you like to have this for your kitchen? Here."

Ethel crossed the room. She carried the pan back to where she'd been standing.

"This is no ordinary polish," continued Mrs. Hancock, shaking the bottle vigorously. "This is what is known as liquefied ointment. It possesses rare medicinal properties. It renews wood. It gives you a base for polishing–something to shine that simply wasn't there before. There's nothing like it on the market–not in the polish field. It's a Shipshape product, and you all know what that means." Mrs. Hancock opened the bottle and dabbed at the air. "Note the handy applicator." Snatching a cloth from her lap, she rubbed the leg of the coffee table–"remove all foreign matter first"–and dabbed at the leg with the applicator. "This does for wood what liniment does for horses. It relaxes the grain, injects new life, *soothes* the wood. Well, how do you like it?" she called over to Ethel.

Ethel glanced down at the pan, forgotten in her hand.

"Pass it around," said Mrs. Hancock.

Ethel offered the pan to Mrs. Nilgren, who was nearest.

"I've seen it, thanks."

Ethel moved to the next neighbor.

"I've seen it."

Ethel moved on. "Mrs. Wagner, have you?"

"Many times"—with a smile.

Ethel looked back where she'd been standing before she started out with the pan—and went the other way, finally stepping into the hallway. There she saw a canvas duffel bag on the side of which was embossed a pennant flying the word SHIPSHAPE. And hearing Mrs. Hancock—"And this is new, girls. Can you all see from where you're sitting?"—Ethel began to move again. She kept right on going.

Upstairs, in the bedroom, lying down, she noticed the pan in her hand. She shook it off. It hit the headboard of the bed, denting the traditional mahogany, and came to rest in the satin furrow between Ralph's pillow and hers. Oh, God! In a minute, she'd have to get up and go down to them and do *something*—but then she heard the coat hangers banging back empty in the closet downstairs, and the front door opening and, finally, closing. There was a moment of perfect silence in the house before her sudden sob, then another moment before she heard someone coming, climbing the carpeted stairs.

Ethel foolishly thought it would be Mrs. Wagner, but of course it was Mrs. Hancock, after her pan.

She tiptoed into the room, adjusted the venetian blind, and seated herself slightly on the edge of the bed. "Don't think I don't know how you feel," she said. "Not that it shows yet. I wasn't *sure,* dear." She looked into Ethel's eyes, frightening her.

As though only changing positions, Ethel moved the hand that Mrs. Hancock was after.

"My ointment would fix that, restore the surface," said Mrs. Hancock, her finger searching the little wound in the headboard. She began to explain, gently—like someone with a terrible temper warming up: "When we first started having these little Shipshape parties, they didn't tell each other. They do now, oh, yes, or they would if I'd let them. I'm on to them. They're just in it for the mops now. You get one, you know, for having the party in your home. It's collapsible, ideal for the small home or travel. But the truth is you let me down! Why, when you left the room the way you did, you didn't give them any choice. Why,

I don't think there's one of that crowd—with the exception of May Wagner—that isn't using one of my free mops! Why, they just walked out on me!"

Ethel, closing her eyes, saw Mrs. Hancock alone, on the hassock, with her products all around her.

"It's a lot of pan for the money," Mrs. Hancock was saying now. She reached over Ethel's body for it. "You'll love your little pan," she said, fondling it.

Ethel's eyes were resisting Mrs. Hancock, but her right hand betrayed her.

"Here?" Mrs. Hancock opened a drawer, took out a purse, and handed it over, saying, "Only $12.95."

Ethel found a five and a ten.

"You *do* want the ointment, don't you? The pan and the large bottle come to a little more than this, but it's not enough to worry about."

Mrs. Hancock got up, apparently to leave.

Ethel thought of something. "You do live in Blue Island, don't you?" Ralph would be sure to ask about that—if she had to tell him. And she would!

"Not any more, thank God."

Ethel nodded. She wasn't surprised.

Mrs. Hancock, at the door, peeked out—reminding Ethel of a bored visitor looking for a nurse who would tell her it was time to leave the patient. "You'll find your ointment and mop downstairs," she said. "I just know everything's going to be all right." Then she smiled and left.

When, toward noon, Ethel heard Ralph come into the driveway, she got out of bed, straightened the spread, and concealed the pan in the closet. She went to the window and gazed down upon the crown of his pearl-gray hat. He was carrying a big club of roses.

Christopher Zenowich

Think Big

Bob Bodewicz didn't want to be a Boy Scout. They were too groupie. But he loved their magazine, *Boys' Life,* and he asked his Boy Scout friends for their copies after they had finished with them.

He stacked these in a corner of the living room, and returned to them for tips on tying exotic knots and building shelters out of snow, for stories of wilderness survival and heroism during disaster, and for profiles of star athletes. Eventually his mother would insist that he clip and save the articles he wanted and throw away the rest.

It was during one of these purges that Bob noticed a small ad in the back pages of one issue.

MAKE MONEY IN YOUR SPARE TIME

> Make extra spending money in your free time by raising chinchillas. It's easy, fun, and guaranteed. Write for free information using the coupon below, and indicate how much extra income you desire. No obligation!

The possibility of freeing himself from allowances and their awful chores appealed to Bob. He didn't know what chinchillas were, but he filled in the coupon, pausing only to consider how much extra income he could use. There were three choices: "Between $1,000 and $2,000," "Between $4,000 and $6,000," and "Over $10,000." He checked the first option and left the coupon on the table for his father to mail the next day.

His father woke him with a shake early on Saturday morning.

"You want me to mail this," he said, holding out the coupon. His forehead was wrinkled and his voice was gruff.

Bob couldn't think of anything he'd done wrong, so he nodded.

"Where's the envelope?"

"Could you do it?"

His father looked at the coupon; then at Bob. "If you want me to fill out the envelope, I get to see what you want to mail, and I don't approve."

Bob couldn't imagine his father not approving. Money was money.

"What is this, anyway?" his father continued. "You want to make just a thousand? You can't live on a thousand. What do you think this is? The eighteen hundreds? For chrissake, if you're going to think at all, think big. That's what separates the winners from the losers in this world. As long as you've got winners and losers, you've got competition. Free enterprise. If there's no risk, there's no gain. So think big." He took a pen from his pocket and crossed out Bob's choice, and checked the box for "Over $10,000." Then he stared briefly at what he had done. "There, you see, that's the spirit."

Bob got up and watched his father leave. His father was big. Fat Frank, his friends called him.

A few weeks later on one of the first warm spring days, Bob's mother announced that a man had called.

"He said he'd received our coupon, and that he wanted to pay us a visit to discuss our interest in chinchillas," she said, giving her head a shake to knock her one gray bang to the side.

"I thought they were going to send information first," his father said. "What did you say?"

"I asked him when he wanted to drop by, and he said he'd be in the area just a couple more days and how about tomorrow night."

"Tomorrow? Not tomorrow, it's Friday, for chrissake. I bowl." His father mopped his plate clean with a piece of bread and then looked at Bob. "You finished with that?" He pointed to the remains of a pork chop on Bob's plate. Bob said nothing. His father took it and began gnawing at the bone, stripping off the last fibers of meat, his lips shiny.

"Who's coming?" Carl asked.

Bob glared at him. He was so stupid. Why hadn't he been listening?

"No one's coming," his father said. "Not tomorrow." When Bob's father made up his mind, that was usually the end of discussion.

"I'm afraid he's coming whether you go bowling or not," his mother said, holding three dirty plates on her way to the kitchen. His father handed her the pork chop bone, chewed clean.

"Call him back and cancel," he said, and then belched: "Bow-wow."

"Can't," his mother said from the kitchen. "No number." It wasn't like her to be so matter-of-fact in contradicting his father.

"Who doesn't have a number?" Carl asked.

"Ellie, you're not meeting with him without me here. I don't want you getting suckered into some deal by a slick talker."

"Who's coming?" Carl asked.

"Just go look at your bird books," Bob said.

He never saw the hand coming. It snapped his head back, stinging his cheek and sending white spots into his eyes.

"Watch your lip," his father said. "It was your idea, you know. And Carl could help you with it."

"Who's coming?" Carl asked, this time softer.

"The chinchilla guy, dammit," his father said. "Don't you listen?"

Carl kept his head down, and traced a wrinkle in the blue plastic tablecloth. Bob was close to not caring anymore. Getting smacked just for saying that, it wasn't fair. "So you're not going bowling?" his mother said, wiping her hands on her apron. She stared at Bob. He was fighting back tears. She turned to his father. "You'll be here?"

"What choice do I have? First, mister mail order sends off for information. And then you invite a stranger into our house. What choice do I have?"

"He said he rarely has someone as interested as we are. He asked if we live on a farm. What did you put on that coupon, anyway, Bob?"

Carl and his mother both stared at him. Bob felt like everyone was blaming him. He looked at his father, who was ignoring everyone. He didn't dare say anything about how the coupon had been changed. His father wiped his mouth and belched the words, "Scussi mwah."

* * *

The chinchilla man was due at seven, right after Walter Cronkite. Everyone sat in the living room, waiting. Carl was gluing together a model of a rose-breasted grosbeak. Bob's mother looked at a magazine in her chair. His father wrinkled his forehead and reread the sports page. Bob sat there, standing every few minutes when a car went down the road. The new electric coffeepot gurgled in the kitchen. There were small white donuts on a plate, too.

After twenty minutes, Bob's father began snapping the pages of the newspaper as he turned them. Finally, he tossed the paper on the floor.

"Please, Frank, I just picked up," his mother said.

"And I canceled my bowling night," he said, folding his arms across his chest. He did this whenever he was ready to argue.

Carl saw the car first. "Wow," he said. Everyone went to the door.

It was big. It barely fit on their dirt driveway.

"What is it?" Bob asked.

"One of those brand-new Caddys," his father said. "The guy must be rakin' it in."

The car was a well-polished powder blue, with shiny chrome, twin headlights, a fancy hood ornament and large fins with huge taillights shaped like flying saucers. It had New Jersey plates. Bob had never been to New Jersey, but for a brief moment, his spirits lifted at the prospect of making thousands of dollars in his spare time, it seemed to him like a land of great opportunity.

"He must be Italian," Bob's mother said, watching from the front door as the man got out of the driver's seat and waved to her.

"What's the matter," his father said. "He too successful for your tastes?"

Bob opened the door and stood on the steps, watching the man. He was big, too. He wore a blue suit just a bit darker than his Cadillac, and the tail of his white shirt dangled below his jacket at his back.

"Son," the man said, opening the trunk. "How about lending me a hand here?" The man smiled at Bob and waved him over. Seal, Bob's Lab, woofed from the steps.

"C'mere, lady," the man said to the dog. "How about one of these?" He handed her a biscuit.

The trunk was dark and deep like a cave, and packed with neatly organized boxes. Bob was certain this would be better than selling Christmas cards.

"Ivan Helgren," the man said, extending his hand. "And you are . . . ?"

"Bob," he said. The man squeezed his hand until it hurt. "The one who wrote."

"Oh," the man said. "You wrote, huh? You got an older brother?"

"Nope, I'm the oldest."

"That a fact," he said. He lifted a green case and a rolled-up movie screen out of the trunk. "I take it your dad's a farmer out here?"

"Naw, he works in a factory," Bob said, taking a heavy black case that the man handed to him.

Mr. Helgren looked at him for a second, then up at the front door where Bob's mother and father stood. He shook his head quickly and said, "Well, sport, let's get going. I'm heading out of state tonight, back home."

Mr. Helgren introduced himself to everyone else and accepted a cup of black coffee to which he added four teaspoons of sugar. He drank it straight down, then stood up and stretched himself.

"That certainly hits the spot," he said. "Now, where should I set up the movie?"

"Gee, I don't know," Bob's mother said. "We've never had a movie in the house before. Let me clear an area." She pushed the TV to one side of the living room and dragged the coffee table to the rear. It was warm and humid and Bob saw a trickle of sweat making its way down her forehead. She was exhaling deeply, and Bob wondered if she were trying to get his father's attention.

"You two get in there and help your mother," Bob's father said to Carl and him. They put down their half-finished second donuts and went into the living room.

"Good boys," Mr. Helgren said. "They look like the kind that would like to raise chinchillas."

Bob watched as Mr. Helgren looked out the rear window into the back field. He was helping his brother drag a chair across the living room into the dining room, and the slipcover started to pull off.

"Please, boys, let me do this," his mother said, picking up dust balls and two small plastic soldiers from where the chair had been. Bob and Carl returned to the dining room and took their seats at the table.

"I don't see a barn back here," Mr. Helgren said. "Maybe you could point me in the right direction."

"Not unless you've got a good imagination," Bob's father said. "We don't have one."

"But you were interested in making more than ten grand a year, if I recall," Mr. Helgren said.

"That's correct."

"Hmmm. How about your cellar? Maybe we could fit them in your cellar."

"If it means making ten grand a year, we could put 'em in our bedrooms," Bob's father said. He laughed at his own joke. Bob saw his mother stand up straight and smooth out her dress. She was listening intently now.

"Do you mind if I take a look at the basement?" Mr. Helgren asked.

"Not at all," Bob's father said.

"It's such a mess, though," Bob's mother said. "We're ready to see the movie."

"We'll be right back up," Mr. Helgren said. "I just want to size out your cellar. Bob, you've seen a movie screen set up in school, haven't you?"

Bob nodded.

"Good boy. Why don't you try to set up this one."

While Bob's father and Mr. Helgren were down in the cellar, Bob's mother helped him stand the screen and open it up.

"I'm getting madder by the minute," she was saying. "Your father needs to talk to me about this."

Carl was sliding a torn hassock from the bedroom down the hallway. Bob could hear fragments of the discussion in the cellar. He could make out a "considering" and "profit."

"Don't you bring that in here," Bob's mother said to Carl. "I want that out of sight. And, be quiet. Carry it, don't slide it." She was standing perfectly still between the living room and dining room, staring now into space and listening. Carl ignored her.

"Take that back to the bedroom," Bob whispered at Carl.

"Both of you, shhhh!"

The men were climbing the stairs. As they came up through the kitchen, Mr. Helgren was speaking and his father was nodding.

"As I was saying," he went on, "ten grand a year might be a little steep for the space you've got. But two hundred cages, about one per cinder block along the north wall, why that ought to generate close to six grand a year. I can get into the numbers and contractual arrangements in a few minutes after the movie. Before I show it, might I use your bathroom?"

Bob's father pointed him to the door and took a seat in the living room, right next to Carl on the couch. Bob's mother went over to him.

"What are you doing?" she whispered. "We don't even know what's involved with these things. Why are you acting like we're going to do this?" She went to the hutch and pulled out her silver horn-tipped glasses, which she wore only when a life insurance salesman was visiting.

"What's your problem," he said.

"Shhhh," she hissed as Mr. Helgren emerged from the bathroom, the toilet in the final throes of a flush. "Maybe we should take a seat at the table while we discuss this," she announced.

"We got a movie here, don't we, Ivan?" Bob's father said. "Let's watch the movie."

"That's right, Frank," Mr. Helgren said. "If you don't mind, ma'am, I thought we'd watch the movie first. That way, you'll have an accurate idea about what's involved with running a money-making chinchilla operation in a home like yours." He set up the projector and started the movie. It was called *The Chinchilla Story: There's Gold in Those There Furs.*

"Since the days of the earliest Spanish settlers in Chile and Peru," the movie began, "since the rise of the grand Incan empires, the chinchilla has been valued for its soft, pearly gray fur. . . ."

A small creature about the size of a squirrel was shown sipping water from a metal pan and nibbling on food.

"It looks like a rat," Bob's mother said.

Mr. Helgren chuckled. "Nothing like a rat, ma'am," he said. "Clean and friendly these things are."

The movie showed how thousands of Americans today made extra money by raising chinchillas in their spare time. "Today, Americans know, as did the ancient Incas, 'there's gold in those there furs,' " the movie concluded. The film clicked through the projector, and the screen went white.

In the glare of the screen Bob's mother appeared expressionless. She had her arms folded, and she was tapping her foot.

"What do you think?" Bob's father said to him, rubbing his head. "You want to try it?"

Bob looked at his mother, who pushed her glasses up the bridge of her nose and stared at him. He couldn't bring himself to speak. Not when he could see his mother was angry. First his father, now his mother. And all he wanted was a way to make money. How could things be going so wrong?

"Don't need to answer just yet, son," Mr. Helgren said. "Let me tell you a little more about them." He packed up the screen and the projector, leaving them by the front door, and then brought a briefcase over to the dining room table.

"Ellie, how about a little of that coffee," Bob's father said.

"That sounds good to me," Mr. Helgren said, opening the briefcase and pulling out some papers. He looked them over in silence, waiting for Bob's mother to return with a tray holding the coffeepot and cups. She dropped the tray on the table with a thwack, and Bob's father looked up at her in surprise. Mr. Helgren didn't seem to notice.

"First, I'd like to know, Bob," Mr. Helgren said, "what do you think? You still interested in making thousands of dollars a year raising chinchillas?"

Bob nodded. That was the whole point of the night. But he felt like there was something else going on, just beyond his knowing.

"You certain about that, Bob?" Mr. Helgren asked. "You don't seem too certain."

"I'm certain," Bob said.

"Of course you are," Mr. Helgren said. "In fact . . ."

"Just a second," Bob's mother said. "Let's talk over some of the details. How do we raise these things? Let 'em run around downstairs and throw the food to them? And what kind of time will it take? These boys want to go to college. They don't want to spend their evenings feeding these things when they should be studying."

"I was just getting to that, ma'am," Mr. Helgren said.

"C'mon, Ellie, give him a chance, will you?" Bob's father said. "It's for the kids."

For the first time that night, Bob felt like his father was on his side. It was for him. And for Carl, too. It would be their money, he hoped. In the bank for them.

"First, though, I'd like you to feel this," Mr. Helgren said, lifting a compartment in his briefcase and pulling out a gray fur. "Go ahead, feel it."

Everyone took turns feeling it. Carl took two turns.

"You ever feel anything so soft?" Mr. Helgren said.

"No," Carl said, rubbing it on his cheek.

Mr. Helgren reached inside his jacket and pulled out another gray fur. "And that's not even a chinchilla fur," he said. "Feel that against a real chinchilla fur."

"Wow," Carl said.

Everyone took turns feeling the real chinchilla fur.

"Huh," Bob's father said, the last to feel. "That's really something."

"You can say that again, Frank," Mr. Helgren said. "I know you can see why these chinchilla furs are so valuable. And why there's money to be made raising them."

"Make a nice pair of underwear," Bob's father said.

Mr. Helgren laughed. "Never thought of that, Frank. Maybe we should put you on the marketing council. But we do know they make a nice coat. Wouldn't you agree, Ellie?"

She didn't answer his question. There was a moment of silence. "Just how do we raise them?" she asked, pushing up her glasses.

"I was getting to that," Mr. Helgren said. "As you can see here"—he slid a piece of paper with a chart on it across the table—"you've got space for two hundred cages, and with one total turnover per year, that gives you four hundred pelts worth a minimum wholesale of ten-fifty per pelt. . . ."

Bob's father whistled.

"That's right, Frank, we're talking in the vicinity of forty-two hundred a year, gross. Now, don't stake me to this, but in my opinion, with the mink disease they're having out West, we could see these pelts going up another two bucks per year in the next year."

Bob tried to imagine what he could do with that much money.

He would be the most popular kid in the school. He'd be able to buy a car of his own when he was sixteen. He'd be able to buy presents whenever he wanted.

"Where do the cages come from?" Bob's mother asked as she inspected the chart.

"We supply 'em," Mr. Helgren said, pulling out several other sheets of paper. "Along with the food, the medicine, and all the technical support you need. You got a question, call us collect, twenty-four hours a day."

"That's sounds like a helluva support system to me," Bob's father said. He shifted in his chair.

"I'm glad you brought that up," Mr. Helgren said, "because that's what we're here for. As a support group for our growers. A resource for your every need."

"How do we pay for all this?" Bob's mother asked.

"As you can see from this," Mr. Helgren said, sliding another chart across the table, "there are several ways, the simplest being a fourteen-thousand-dollar up-front investment on your part for the cages and a four-year feed contract that calls for a specially developed, nutritionally balanced chinchilla feed not available anywhere else in this country."

"It seems like an awful lot of money," Bob's mother said.

"You've got to spend money to make money," Bob's father snapped. "Christ, I can see that at the plant."

"I'm glad you mentioned that, Frank," Mr. Helgren said. "You're right, too, Ellie, if I may. That's why we've developed a special four-year payment plan that enables you to keep ten percent of your gross revenue until the cages and feed contracts are all paid off. At that point, the profits are all yours, minus, of course, the feed, medicine, and litters that we keep you supplied with."

"And how much does that run?" she asked.

"Approximately fifteen hundred a year," Mr. Helgren said, taking out another chart with blanks and the heading "Profit Potential." He took a blue magic marker and deducted the number fifteen hundred from forty-eight hundred. He looked up at Bob's father and slid the chart slowly toward him. "That leaves you with a minimum of thirty-three hundred, free and clear. Your labor . . ." He looked at Bob and Carl. "Why, that's free and clear, too, isn't it? You boys are ready to make money, aren't you?"

Bob and Carl nodded. Bob picked up the chinchilla fur and felt it against the other gray fur. Ten-fifty per pelt. Just a small fur, no bigger than a squirrel's. His head was swimming with numbers. It was better than the frontier days. He knew his mother didn't like the idea, but she could get used to it. She'd gotten used to other things before, like the dog. She hadn't wanted Seal at first. But Bob promised to take care of it, and he had. He'd manage with the chinchillas. And, he'd keep up with his schoolwork, too. She'd see.

"How much work are these animals?" Bob's mother asked. Eyeing Frank, she added, "How clean are they?"

"That's a good question, and one I'm frequently asked by the lady of the house," Mr. Helgren said. "The truth is, if you keep their water and their cages clean every other day, they're cleaner than hamsters. And I'd be happy to supply you with the phone numbers of a few growers who do raise them in their cellars just like you will. Why, I've seen some shipments of pelts arrive that I felt didn't even need to be washed, although we clean each batch as a matter of principle."

"Who does the skinning?" Bob's mother asked.

"We supply you with a special skinning apparatus the size of a toaster," Mr. Helgren said. "Takes it off quicker than you can pull the skin off a chicken."

"And the bodies? What about the bodies?"

"Simply dispose of them, ma'am," Mr. Helgren said, shifting in his chair.

"Oh, no," she said. She shook her head quickly. "Hundreds of bloody chinchillas stuffed in the garbage cans. The stink would be unbearable."

"The stink wouldn't be that bad," Bob's father said, shaking his hand as if he were refusing a cup of coffee. "Not for that kind of money."

"We can do it, Mom," Bob said. "Right, Carl?"

This time, Carl said nothing. He looked at Bob, then at his mother, then back at Bob.

"I think we need some time to think about this," Bob's mother said. "Among ourselves."

"Of course," Mr. Helgren said. "It's a major decision you're talking about. I should tell you, though, that we are going to keep our membership restricted to maintain the quality and price of our pelts. Based on your interest, we've reserved a membership for you. However, we can honor this reservation only for a limited time. I think you understand. Now I'd be happy to wait in my car for a half hour or so if you'd like to discuss this, but I'm afraid that I'm going to have to ask that you answer us tonight."

"In that case, the answer is no," Bob's mother said.

"Oh no it isn't," Bob's father said. "We'll talk about it."

Bob's hopes fell and rose with each speaker. Things were too touchy to dare adding a word. He had seen his mother bring things to a halt before. Once she put her mind to it, she could overcome the momentum of almost anything.

"Who exactly is the 'we' you keep referring to," Bob's mother said to Mr. Helgren. She sounded suddenly calmer. That worried Bob more than her earlier uneasiness.

"I haven't told you? Why, please excuse my oversight." He pulled out a certificate from his briefcase. "I'm with the Chinchilla Growers Guild of America. The CGGA, more than thirteen hundred members, and, since nineteen fifty-seven, the voice of the chinchilla grower in Washington."

"I'd say we're very interested in reaching an agreement tonight," Bob's father said.

"Did you say 'guild'?" Bob's mother asked, calmer still and pushing up her glasses.

"Yes, I did," Mr. Helgren said. "Have you heard of us, the Chinchilla Growers Guild of America?"

"Not specifically of you," Bob's mother said. "But I have heard a thing or two about guilds."

"They're a marvelous concept in money-making for everyone involved," Mr. Helgren said.

"I don't know," Bob's mother said. "The whole thing sounds kind of foreign to me. The Incas, Chile, Peru, and now a guild. Let me think. . . ." She took off her glasses and stared at the ceiling. "Yes, I'm quite sure now, guild has something to do with the communists."

"What?" Mr. Helgren said. "Nothing could be . . ."

"Carl," Bob's mother said. "Go look up 'guild' in the dictionary and tell me what you find."

Carl ran into the living room.

"There's nothing even remotely communist about this organization, ma'am," Mr. Helgren said. "Why, we're dedicated to making money. You understand, don't you, Frank?"

"Sure, I guess," Bob's father said. But he turned his eyes away from

Mr. Helgren and stared down at the tablecloth. *Communism* was a powerful word in the house, something which instantly turned friendly conversations serious. "She knows a lot about them. The communists, that is. She's read Ayn Rand."

Carl returned holding the dictionary open. "It says an association of people bound by a common goal or shared interests, as in medieval guilds," he reported.

"See," Bob's mother said. "A common goal, shared interests, the whole thing goes against the individual."

Mr. Helgren brought his hand down on the table. "I don't know where you get your ideas, lady, but this is the last thing we're out to do."

"Look up China, Carl," Bob's mother said. "See if it says anything about guilds. Then check Russia."

Mr. Helgren was sweeping up his papers. "Lady, you don't have the slightest idea what you're talking about."

Bob's father stood up, knocking his chair over backward. "You're a guest in this house, mister, but that doesn't give you the right to talk to my wife like that. I suggest you leave."

"You won't have to ask me twice," Mr. Helgren said. "I've never been received like this before."

"China has guilds, too," Carl said, bringing in the encyclopedia.

Mr. Helgren began yanking up his papers and charts, stuffing them into his briefcase. "I can't believe I've wasted a call on rednecks like you."

"Now just a second," Bob's father said, poking his finger in Mr. Helgren's chest. "Where do you get off talking like that? I'm beginning to think my wife's right about you. What kind of name is that, anyway, 'Ivan'?"

"You want to know what kind of name that is? It goes with Patulsky, not Helgren. It's Polish."

"I knew it all the time," Bob's father said. "You can't hide it."

"People trust Scandinavians in the fur business, that's all," Mr. Helgren said. "Nothing more than that. I'm from Paterson. Christ, John Wayne is a made-up name."

"I've heard enough out of you," Bob's father said.

"You think it's a treat for me?" Mr. Helgren asked. "Just let me out of here."

Bob and Carl got out of the way as their father quickly followed Mr.

Helgren—the movie screen tucked under one arm, one hand holding the projector, the other his briefcase. He banged his way out the door. He opened the back door of the Cadillac and tossed everything across the seat. Bob's father stood on the front steps, his arms folded, as if supervising the exit to make sure everything proceeded according to orders. The engine of the Cadillac revved, its lights came on. Then it retreated quickly, kicking up dust and stones as it spun out of the driveway, its tires squealing when they hit the pavement. It paused there on the road, the idle of the engine gradually slowing until the hum of an electric window could be heard. Mr. Helgren's head appeared, a silhouette outlined by the glow of the dashboard lights.

"Never again will you have a chance with us," he shouted. "You're nothing. Not even prospects." The window hummed back up, the transmission popped into drive, and the Cadillac swooshed down the road, its ruby red brake lights casting a pink glow over the fins. Bob watched the lights, wanting them to somehow be clues to a new life, one away from the lawns he mowed and the rewinding tape of talk about bad supervisors and dumb bosses. How he wished there was a way to make money without giving in to all that.

Bob's mother was picking up the coffee cups when Mr. Helgren spoke his final words. She snorted as if clearing her sinuses.

"Tough darts to you, too," she said.

"I think you were onto something, Mom," Carl said. "You got under his skin."

"You think so, sweetie?" She hugged Carl and winked at Bob, and took the cups to the kitchen. Bob's father had retaken his seat on the couch, newspaper again in hand. His mother returned and pushed the TV back to its place, a neat square of dust on the floor at the center of the far wall.

"I'm glad that's behind us," she said.

"How did you know, Mom?" Carl asked.

"Oh, I guess I did what I had to."

"That's right," Bob's father said, setting down the paper. "And to think he drove a Caddy, too. Talk about a wolf in sheep's clothing."

"Exactly," she said. She hummed the first four notes of Beethoven's Fifth as she straightened out the living room.

"Let it be a lesson to you boys," Bob's father said. "Be prepared."

"Prepared!" Carl shouted.

"Drop!" Bob's father said.

And as if they had choreographed it, Bob and Carl hit the floor and began their push-ups. One after another, down and up, down and up. Carl weakened first. Bob could see his arms wobbling, his rear arching upward, his face contorted almost clownishly in agony.

"One more," Frank said with a military snap to his voice, and Carl sank again and barely rose, this time only to collapse in exhaustion.

Bob continued. Ten more. And another five. Until he too felt his arms burning, the heels of his hands aching, his sight dimming.

"One more," his father said again.

Bob sank and tried. He tried harder.

"C'mon, one more."

"Honestly, Frank," his mother said. "He's trying."

"Trying doesn't count."

Bob dipped. He felt his rear moving up, but nothing else.

"C'mon, defeatist, a Russian boy could do one more. You can't be weak."

No, Bob couldn't be weak. He closed his eyes, strained until he saw spots, and in his imagination, rose one last time.

JOHN UPDIKE

from *Rabbit Is Rich*

Running out of gas, Rabbit Angstrom thinks as he stands behind the summer-dusty windows of the Springer Motors display room watching the traffic go by on Route 111, traffic somehow thin and scared compared to what it used to be. The fucking world is running out of gas. But they won't catch him, not yet, because there isn't a piece of junk on the road gets better mileage than his Toyotas, with lower service costs. Read *Consumer Reports,* April issue. That's all he has to tell the people when they come in. And come in they do, the people out there are getting frantic, they know the great American ride is ending. Gas lines at ninety-nine point nine cents a gallon and ninety per cent of the stations to be closed for the weekend. The governor of the Commonwealth of Pennsylvania calling for five-dollar minimum sales to stop the panicky topping-up. And truckers who can't get diesel shooting at their own trucks, there was an incident right in Diamond County, along the Pottsville Pike. People are going wild, their dollars are going rotten, they shell out like there's no tomorrow. He tells them, when they buy a Toyota, they're turning their dollars into yen. And they believe them. A hundred twelve units new and used moved in the first five months of 1979, with eight Corollas, five Coronas including a Luxury Edition Wagon, and that Celica that Charlie said looked like a

Pimpmobile unloaded in these first three weeks of June already, at an average gross mark-up of eight hundred dollars per sale. Rabbit is rich.

He owns Springer Motors, one of the two Toyota agencies in the Brewer area. Or rather he co-owns a half-interest with his wife Janice, her mother Bessie sitting on the other half inherited when old man Springer died five years back. But Rabbit feels as though he owns it all, showing up at the showroom day after day, riding herd on the paperwork and the payroll, swinging in his clean suit in and out of Service and Parts where the men work filmed with oil and look up white-eyed from the bulb-lit engines as in a kind of underworld while he makes contact with the public, the community, the star and spearpoint of all these two dozen employees and hundred thousand square feet of working space, which seem a wide shadow behind him as he stands there up front. The wall of imitation boards, really sheets of random-grooved Masonite, around the door into his office is hung with framed old clippings and team portraits, including two all-county tens, from his days as a basketball hero twenty years ago—no, more than twenty years now. Even under glass, the clippings keep yellowing, something in the chemistry of the paper apart from the air, something like the deepening taint of sin people used to try to scare you with. ANGSTROM HITS FOR 42. *"Rabbit" Leads Mt. Judge Into Semi-Finals.* Resurrected from the attic where his dead parents had long kept them, in scrapbooks whose mucilage had dried so they came loose like snakeskins, these clippings thus displayed were Fred Springer's idea, along with that phrase about an agency's reputation being the shadow of the man up front. Knowing he was dying long before he did, Fred was getting Harry ready to be the man up front. When you think of the dead, you got to be grateful.

Ten years ago when Rabbit got laid off as a Linotyper and reconciled with Janice, her father took him on as salesman and when the time was ripe five years later had the kindness to die. Who would have thought such a little tense busy bird of a man could get it up for a massive coronary? Hypertense: his diastolic had been up around one-twenty for years. Loved salt. Loved to talk Republican, too, and when Nixon left him nothing to say he had kind of burst. Actually, he had lasted a year into Ford, but the skin of his face was getting tighter and the red spots where the cheek and jaw bones pressed from underneath redder. When

Harry looked down at him rouged in the coffin he saw it had been coming, Fred hadn't much changed. From the way Janice and her mother carried on you would have thought a mixture of Prince Valiant and Moses had bit the dust. Maybe having already buried both his own parents made Harry hard. He looked down, noticed that Fred's hair had been parted wrong, and felt nothing. The great thing about the dead, they make space.

While old man Springer was still prancing around life at the lot was hard. He kept long hours, held the showroom open on winter nights when there wasn't a snowplow moving along Route 111, was always grinding away in that little high-pitched grinder of a voice about performance guidelines and washout profits and customer servicing and whether or not a mechanic had left a thumbprint on some heap's steering wheel or a cigarette butt in the ashtray. When he was around the lot it was like they were all trying to fill some big skin that Springer spent all his time and energy imagining, the ideal Springer Motors. When he died that skin became Harry's own, to stand around in loosely. Now that he is king of the lot he likes it here, the acre of asphalt, the new-car smell present even in the pamphlets and pep talks Toyota mails from California, the shampooed carpet wall to wall, the yellowing basketball feats up on the walls along with the plaques saying Kiwanis and Rotary and C of C and the trophies on a high shelf won by the Little League teams the company sponsors, the ample square peace of this masculine place spiced by the girls in billing and reception that come and go under old Mildred Kroust, and the little cards printed with HAROLD C. ANGSTROM on them and CHIEF SALES REPRESENTATIVE. The man up front. A center of sorts, where he had been a forward. There is an airiness to it for Harry, standing there in his own skin, casting a shadow. The cars sell themselves, is his philosophy. The Toyota commercials on television are out there all the time, preying on people's minds. He likes being part of all that; he likes the nod he gets from the community, that had overlooked him like dirt ever since high school. The other men in Rotary and Chamber turn out to be the guys he played ball with back then, or their ugly younger brothers. He likes having money to float in, a big bland good guy is how he sees himself, six three and around two ten by now, with a forty-two waist the suit salesman at Kroll's tried to tell him until he sucked his gut in and the man's thumb grudgingly inched the tape tighter. He avoids mirrors, when he used to love them. The face far behind him, crew-cut and thin-jawed with sleepy predatory teen-age eyes in the glossy team portraits, exists in his present face like the chrome bones of a grille within the full front view of a car and its fenders. His nose is still small and straight, his eyes maybe less sleepy. An ample blown-dry-looking businessman's haircut masks his eartips and fills in where his temples are receding. He didn't much like the counterculture with all its drugs and draft-dodging but he does like being allowed within limits to let your hair grow longer than those old Marine cuts and to have it naturally fluff out. In the shaving mirror a chaos of wattles and slack cords blooms beneath his chin in a way that doesn't bear study. Still, life is sweet. That's what old people used to say and when he was young he wondered how they could mean it.

* * *

YOU ASKED FOR IT, WE GOT IT, the big paper banner on the showroom window cries, in tune with the current Toyota television campaign. The sign cuts a slice from the afternoon sun and gives the showroom a muted aquarium air, or that of a wide sunken ship wherein the two Coronas and the acid-green Corolla SR-5 liftback wait to be bought and hoisted into the air on the other side of the glass and set down safe on the surface of the lot and Route 111 and the world of asphalt beyond.

A car swings in from this world: a fat tired '71 or '2 Country Squire wagon soft on its shocks, with one dented fender hammered out semi-smooth but the ruddy rustproofing underpaint left to do for a finish. A young couple steps out, the girl milky-pale and bare-legged and blinking in the sunshine but the boy roughened and reddened by the sun, his jeans dirt-stiffened by actual work done in the red mud of the county. A kind of crate of rough green boards has been built into the Squire's chrome roof rack and from where Rabbit is standing, a soft wedge shot away, he can see how the upholstery and inner padding have been mangled by the station wagon's use as a farm truck. "Hicks," Charlie says from his desk. The pair comes in shyly, like elongated animals, sniffing the air-conditioned air.

Feeling protective, God knows why, Charlie's snipe ringing in his ears, Harry walks toward them, glancing at the girl's hand to see if she wears a wedding ring. She does not, but such things mean less than they used to. Kids shack up. Her age he puts at nineteen or twenty, the boy a bit older—the age of his own son. "Can I help you folks?"

The boy brushes back his hair, showing a low white forehead. His broad baked face gives him a look of smiling even when he isn't. "We chust came in for some information." His accent bespeaks the south of the county, less aggressively Dutch than the north, where the brick churches get spiky and the houses and barns are built of limestone instead of sandstone. Harry figures them for leaving some farm to come into the city, with no more need to haul fenceposts and hay bales and pumpkins and whatever else this poor heap was made to haul. Shack up, get city jobs, and spin around in a little Corolla. We got it. But the boy could be just scouting out prices for his father, and the girlfriend be riding along, or not even be a girlfriend, but a sister, or a hitchhiker. A little touch of the hooker about her looks. The way her soft body wants to spill from these small clothes, the faded denim shorts and purple Paisley halter. The shining faintly freckled flesh of her shoulders and top arms and the bushy wanton abundance of her browny-red many-colored hair, carelessly bundled. A buried bell rings. She has blue eyes in deep sockets and the silence of a girl from the country used to letting men talk while she holds a sweet-and-sour secret in her mouth, sucking it. An incongruous disco touch in her shoes, with their high cork heels and ankle straps. Pink toes, painted nails. This girl will not stick with this boy. Rabbit wants this to be so; he imagines he feels an unwitting swimming of her spirit upward toward his, while her manner is all stillness. He feels she wants to hide from him, but is too big and white, too suddenly womanly, too nearly naked. Her shoes accent the length of her legs; she is taller than average, and not quite fat, though tending toward chunky, especially around the chest. Her upper lip closes over the lower with a puffy bruised look. She is bruisable, he wants to protect her; he relieves her of the pressure of his gaze, too long by a second, and turns to the boy.

"This is a Corolla," Harry says, slapping orange tin. "The two-door model begins at thirty-nine hundred and will give you highway mileage up to forty a gallon and twenty to twenty-five city driving. I know some other makes advertise more but believe me you can't get a better buy in America today than this jalopy right here. Read *Consumer Reports,* April issue. Much better than average on maintenance and repairs through the first four years. Who in this day and age keeps a car much longer than four years? In four years we may all be pushing bicycles the way things are going. This particular car has four-speed synchromesh transmission, fully transistorized ignition system, power-assisted front disc brakes, vinyl reclining bucket seats, a locking gas cap. That last feature's getting to be pretty important. Have you noticed lately how all the auto-supply stores are selling out of their siphons? You can't buy a siphon in Brewer today for love nor money, guess why. My mother-in-law's old Chrysler over in Mt. Judge was drained dry the other day in front of the hairdresser's, she hardly ever takes the buggy out except to go to church. People are getting rough. Did you notice in the paper this morning where Carter is taking gas from the farmers and going to give it to the truckers? Shows the power of a gun, doesn't it?"

"I didn't see the paper," the boy says.

He is standing there so stolidly Harry has to move around him with a quick shuffle-step, dodging a cardboard cutout of a happy customer with her dog and packages, to slap acid-green. "Now if you want to replace your big old wagon, that's some antique, with another wagon that gives you almost just as much space for half the running expense, this SR-5 has some beautiful features—a *five*-speed transmission with an overdrive that really saves fuel on a long trip, and a fold-down split rear seat that enables you to carry one passenger back there and still have the long space on the other side for golf clubs or fenceposts or whatever. I don't know why Detroit never thought it, that split seat. Here we're supposed to be Automobile Heaven and the foreigners come up with all the ideas. If you ask me Detroit's let us all down, two hundred million of us. I'd much rather handle native American cars but between the three of us they're junk. They're cardboard. They're pretend."

"Now what are those over there?" the boy asks.

"That's the Corona, if you want to move toward the top of the line. Bigger engine—twenty-two hundred ccs, instead of sixteen. More of a European look. I drive one and love it. I get about thirty miles to the gallon on the highway, eighteen or so in Brewer. Depends on how you drive, of course. How heavy a foot you have. Those testers for *Consumer Reports,* they must really give it the gun, their mileage figures are the one place they seem off to me. This liftback here is priced at sixty-eight five, but remember you're buying yen for dollars, and when trade-in time comes you get your yen back."

The girl smiles at "yen." The boy, gaining confidence, says, "And this one here now." The young farmer has touched the Celica's suave black hood. Harry is running out of enthusiasm. Interested in that, the kid wasn't very interested in buying.

"You've just put your hand on one super machine," Harry tells him. "The Celica GT Sport Coupe, a car that'll ride with a Porsche or an MG any day. Steel-belted radials, quartz crystal clock, AM/FM stereo–all standard. *Standard.* You can imagine what the extras are. This one has power steering and a sun roof. Frankly, it's pricey, pretty near five figures, but like I say, it's an investment. That's how people buy cars now, more and more. That old Kleenex mentality of trade it in every two years is gone with the wind. Buy a good solid car now, you'll have something for a long while, while the dollars if you keep 'em will go straight to Hell. Buy good goods, that's my advice to any young man starting up right now."

He must be getting too impassioned, for the boy says, "We're chust looking around, more or less."

"I understand that," Rabbit says quickly, pivoting to face the silent girl. "You're under absolutely no pressure from me. Picking a car is like picking a mate–you want to take your time." The girl blushes and looks away. Generous paternal talkativeness keeps bubbling up in Harry. "It's still a free country, the Commies haven't gotten any further than Cambodia. No way I can make you folks buy until you're good and ready. It's all the same to me, this product sells itself. Actually you're lucky there's such a selection on the floor, a shipment came in two weeks ago and we won't have another until August. Japan can't make enough of these cars to keep the world happy. Toyota is number one import all over the globe." He can't take his eyes off this girl. Those chunky eyesockets reminding him of somebody. The milky flecked shoulders, the dent of flesh where the halter strap digs. Squeeze her and you'd leave thumbprints, she's that fresh from the oven. "Tell me," he says, "which size're you thinking of? You planning to cart a family around, or just yourselves?"

The girl's blush deepens. Don't marry this chump, Harry thinks. His brats will drag you down. The boy says, "We don't need another wagon. My dad has a Chevy pick-up, and he let me take the Squire over when I got out of high school."

"A great junk car," Rabbit concedes. "You can hurt it but you can't kill it. Even in '71 they were putting more metal in than they do now.

Detroit is giving up the ghost." He feels he is floating—on their youth, on his money, on the brightness of this June afternoon and its promise that tomorrow, a Sunday, will be fair for his golf game. "But for people planning to tie the knot and get serious you need something more than a nostalgia item, you need something more like this." He slaps orange tin again and reads irritation in the cool pallor of the girl's eyes as they lift to his. Forgive me, baby, you get so fucking bored standing around in here, when the time comes you tend to run off at the mouth.

Stavros, forgotten, calls from his desk, across the showroom space awash in sun shafts slowly approaching the horizontal, "Maybe they'd like to take a spin." He wants peace and quiet for his paperwork.

"Want to test drive?" Harry asks the couple.

"It's pretty late," the boy points out.

"It'll take a minute. You only pass this way once. Live it up. I'll get some keys and a plate. Charlie, are the keys to the blue Corolla outside hanging on the pegboard or in your desk?"

"I'll get 'em," Charlie grunts. He pushes up from his desk and, still bent, goes into the corridor behind the waist-high partition of frosted glass—a tacky improvement ordered by Fred Springer toward the end of his life. Behind it, three hollow flush doors in a wall of fake-walnut pressboard open into the offices of Mildred Kroust and the billing girl, whoever she is that month, with the office of the Chief Sales Representative between them. The doors are usually ajar and the girl and Mildred keep crossing back and forth to consult. Harry prefers to stand out here on the floor. In the old days there were just three steel desks and a strip of carpet; the one closed door marked the company toilet with its dispenser of powdered soap you turned upside down to get any out. Reception now is off in another separate cubicle, adjoining the waiting room where few customers ever wait. The keys Charlie needs hang, among many others, some no longer unlocking anything in this world, on a pegboard darkened by the touch of greasy fingertips beside the door on the way to Parts: Parts, that tunnel of loaded steel shelves whose sliding window overlooks the clangorous cavern of Service. No reason for Charlie to go except he knows where things are and you don't want to leave customers alone for a moment and feeling foolish, they're apt to sneak away. More timid than deer, customers. With nothing to say between them, the boy, the girl, and Harry can hear the faint strained wheeze of Charlie's breathing as he comes back with the demonstrator Corolla keys and the dealer's plate on its rusty spring clip. "Want me to take these youngsters out?" he asks.

"No, you sit and rest," Harry tells him, adding, "You might start locking up in back." Their sign claims they are open Saturdays to six but on this ominous June day of gas drought quarter of should be close enough. "Back in a minute."

The boy asks the girl, "Want to come or stay here?"

"Oh, *come,*" she says, impatience lighting up her mild face as she turns and names him. "Jamie, Mother expects me *back.*"

Harry reassures her, "It'll just take a minute." Mother. He wishes he could ask her to describe Mother.

Out on the lot, bright wind is bringing summer in. The spots of grass around the asphalt sport buttery dabs of dandelion. He clips the plate to the back of the Corolla and hands the boy the keys. He holds the seat on the passenger side forward so the girl can get into the rear; as she does so the denim of her shorts permits a peek of cheek of ass. Rabbit squeezes into the death seat and explains to Jamie the trinkets of the dashboard, including the space where a tape deck could go. They are, all three passengers, on the tall side, and the small car feels stuffed. Yet with imported spunk the Toyota tugs them into rapid motion and finds its place in the passing lane of Route 111. Like riding on the back of a big bumblebee; you feel *on top* of the buzzing engine. "Peppy," Jamie acknowledges.

"And smooth, considering," Harry adds, trying not to brake on the bare floor. To the girl he calls backwards, "You O.K.? Shall I slide my seat forward to give more room?" The way the shorts are so short now you wonder if the crotches don't hurt. The stitching, pinching up.

"No I'm all right, I'll sit sideways."

He wants to turn and look at her but at his age turning his head is not so easy and indeed some days he wakes with pains all through the neck and shoulders from no more cause than his dead weight on the bed all night. He tells Jamie, "This is the sixteen hundred cc., they make a twelve hundred base model but we don't like to handle it, I'd hate to have it on my conscience that somebody was killed because he didn't have enough pick-up to get around a truck or something on these American roads. Also we believe in carrying a pretty full complement of options; without 'em you'll find yourself short-changed on the trade-in when the time comes." He manages to work his body around to look at the girl. "These Japanese for all their virtues have pretty short legs," he tells her. The way she has to sit, her ass is nearly on the floor and her knees are up in the air, these young luminous knees inches from his face.

Unself-consciously she is pulling a few long hairs away from her mouth where they have blown and gazing through the side window at this commercial stretch of greater Brewer. Fast-food huts in eye-catching shapes and retail outlets of everything from bridal outfits to plaster birdbaths have widened the aspect of this, the old Weisertown Pike, with their parking lots, leaving the odd surviving house and its stump of a front lawn sticking out painfully. Competitors–Pike Porsche and Renault, Diefendorfer Volkswagen, Old Red Barn Mazda and BMW, Diamond County Automotive Imports–flicker their FUEL ECONOMY banners while the gasoline stations intermixed with their beckoning have shrouded pumps and tow trucks parked across the lanes where automobiles once glided in, were filled, and glided on. An effect of hostile barricade, late in the day. Where did the shrouds come from? Some of them quite smartly tailored, in squared-off crimson canvas. A new industry, gas pump shrouds. Among vacant lakes of asphalt a few small stands offer strawberries and early peas. A tall sign gestures to a cement-block building well off the road; Rabbit can remember when this was a giant Mister Peanut pointing toward a low shop where salted nuts were arrayed in glass cases, Brazil nuts and hazelnuts and whole cashews and for a lesser price broken ones, Diamond County a great area for nuts but not that great, the shop failed. Its shell was broken and doubled in size and made into a nightclub and the sign repainted, keeping the top hat but Mister Peanut becoming a human reveller in white tie and tails. Now after many mutilations this sign has been turned into an ill-fitted female figure, a black silhouette with no bumps indicating clothing, her head thrown back and the large letters DISCO falling in bubbles as if plucked one by one from her cut throat. Beyond such advertisements the worn green hills hold a haze of vapor and pale fields bake as their rows of corn thicken. The inside of the Corolla is warming with a mingled human smell. Harry thinks of the girl's long thigh as she stretched her way into the back seat and imagines he smells vanilla. Cunt would be a good flavor of ice cream, Sealtest ought to work on it.

The silence from the young people troubles him. He prods it. He says, "Some storm last night. I heard on the radio this morning the underpass at Eisenhower and Seventh was flooded for over an hour."

Then he says, "You know it seems gruesome to me, all these gas stations closed up like somebody has died."

Then he says, "Did you see in the paper where the Hershey company has had to lay off nine hundred people because of the truckers' strike? Next thing we'll be in lines for Hershey bars."

The boy is intently passing a Freihofer's Bakery truck and Harry answers for him: "The downtown stores are all pulling out. Nothing left in the middle of the city now but the banks and the post office. They put that crazy stand of trees in to make a mall but it won't do any good, the people are still scared to go downtown."

The boy is staying in the fast lane, and in third gear, either for the pep or because he's forgotten there is a fourth. Harry asks him, "Getting the feel of it, Jamie? If you want to turn around, there's an intersection coming up."

The girl understands. "Jamie, we better turn around. The man wants to get home for supper."

As Jamie slows to ease right at the intersection, a Pacer—silliest car on the road, looks like a glass bathtub upside-down—swings left without looking. The driver is a fat spic in a Hawaiian shirt. The boy slaps the steering wheel in vain search for the horn. Toyota indeed has put the horn in a funny place, on two little arcs a thumb's reach inside the steering-wheel rim; Harry reaches over quick and toots for him. The Pacer swerves back into its lane, with a dark look back above the Hawaiian shirt. Harry directs, "Jamie, I want you to take a left at the next light and go across the highway and take the next left you can and that'll bring us back." To the girl he explains, "Prettier this way." He thinks aloud, "What can I tell you about the car I haven't? It has a lot of locks. Those Japanese, they live on top of each other and are crazy about locks. Don't kid yourselves, we're coming to it, I won't be here to see it, but you will. When I was a kid nobody ever thought to lock their house and now everybody does, except my crazy wife. If she locked the door she'd lose the key. One of the reasons I'd like to go to Japan, Toyota asks some of their dealers but you got to have a bigger gross than I do, is to see how you lock up a paper house. At any rate. You can't get the key out of the ignition without releasing this catch down here. The trunk in back releases from this lever. The locking gas cap you already know about. Did either of you hear about the woman somewhere around Ardmore this week who cut into a gas line and the guy behind her got so mad he sneaked his own locking gas cap onto her tank so when she got to the pump the attendant couldn't remove it? They had to tow her away. Serve the bitch right, if you ask me."

They have taken their two lefts and are winding along a road where fields come to the edge so you can see the clumps of red earth still shiny from where the plow turned them, and where what businesses there are—LAWNMOWERS SHARPENED, PA. DUTCH QUILTS—seem to stem from an earlier decade than those along Route 111, which runs parallel. On the banks of the road, between mailboxes some of which are painted with a heart or hex design, crown vetch is in violet flower. At a crest the elephant-colored gas tanks of Brewer lift into view, and the brick-red rows as they climb Mt. Judge and smudge its side. Rabbit dares ask the girl, "You from around here?"

"More toward Galilee. My mother has a farm."

And is your mother's name Ruth? Harry wants to ask, but doesn't, lest he frighten her, and destroy for himself the vibration of excitement, of possibility untested. He tries to steal another peek at her, to see if her white skin is a mirror, and if the innocent blue in her eyes is his, but his bulk restrains him, and the tightness of the car. He asks the boy, "You follow the Phillies, Jamie? How about that seven-zip loss last night? You don't see Bowa commit an error that often."

"Is Bowa the one with the big salary?"

Harry will feel better when he gets the Toyota out of this moron's hands. Every turn, he can feel the tires pull and the sudden secret widen within him, circle upon circle, it's like seed: seed that goes into the ground invisible and if it takes hold cannot be stopped, it fulfills the shape it was programmed for, its destiny, sure as our death, and shapely. "I think you mean Rose," he answers. "He's not been that much help, either. They're not going anywhere this year, Pittsburgh's the team. Pirates or Steelers, they always win. Take this left, at the yellow blinker. That'll take you right across One Eleven and then you swing into the lot from the back. What's your verdict?"

From the side the boy has an Oriental look—a big stretch of skin between his red ear and red nose, puffy eyes whose glitter gives away nothing. People who gouge a living out of the dirt are just naturally mean, Harry has always thought. Jamie says, "Like I said we were looking around. This car seems pretty small but maybe that's chust what you're used to."

"Want to give the Corona a whirl? That interior feels like a palace after you've been in one of these, you wouldn't think it would, it's only about two centimeters wider and five longer." He marvels at himself, how centimeters trip off his tongue. Another five years with these cars and he'll be talking Japanese. "But you better get used," he tells Jamie, "to a little scaling down. The big old boats have had it. People trade 'em in and we can't give 'em away. Wholesale half of 'em, and the wholesalers turn 'em into windowboxes. The five hundred trade-in I'd allow you on yours is just a courtesy, believe me. We like to help young people out. I think it's a helluva world we're coming to, where a young couple like yourselves can't afford to buy a car or own a home. If you can't get your foot on even the bottom rung of a society geared like this, people are going to lose faith in the system. The Sixties were a lark in the park compared to what we're going to see if things don't straighten out."

Loose stones in the back section of the lot crackle. They pull into the space the Corolla came from and the boy can't find the button to release the key until Harry shows him again. The girl leans forward, anxious to escape, and her breath stirs the colorless hairs on Harry's wrist. His shirt is stuck to his shoulder blades, he discovers standing to his height in the air. All three of them straighten slowly. The sun is still bright but horsetails high in the sky cast doubt upon the weather for tomorrow's golf game after all. "Good driving," he says to Jamie, having given up on any sale. "Come back in for a minute and I'll give you some literature." Inside the showroom the sun strikes the paper banner and makes the letters TI TOↃ ƎW show through. Stavros is nowhere to be seen. Harry hands the boy his CHIEF card and asks him to sign the customer register.

"Like I said—" the boy begins.

Harry has lost patience with this escapade. "It doesn't commit you to a blessed thing," he says. "Toyota'll send you a Christmas card is all it means. I'll do it for you. First name James—?"

"Nunemacher," the boy says warily, and spells it. "R. D. number two, Galilee."

Harry's handwriting has deteriorated over the years, gained a twitch at the end of his long arm, which yet is not long enough for him to see clearly what he writes. He owns reading glasses but it is his vanity never to wear them in public. "Done," he says, and all too casually turns to the girl. "O.K. young lady, how about you? Same name?"

"No way," she says, and giggles. "You don't want me."

A boldness sparks in the cool flat eyes. In that way of women she has gone all circles, silly, elusive. When her gaze levels there is something sexy in the fit of her lower lids, and the shadow of insufficient sleep below them. Her nose is slightly snub. "Jamie's our neighbor, I just came along for the ride. I was going to look for a sundress at Kroll's if there was time."

Something buried far back glints toward the light. Today's slant of sun has reached the shelf where the trophies Springer Motors sponsors wait to be awarded; oval embossments on their weightless white-metal surfaces shine. Keep your name, you little cunt, it's still a free country. But he has given her his. She has taken his card from Jamie's broad red hand and her eyes, childishly alight, slip from its lettering to his face to the section of far wall where his old headlines hang yellowing, toasted brown by time. She asks him, "Were you ever a famous basketball player?"

The question is not so easy to answer, it was so long ago. He tells her, "In the dark ages. Why do you ask, you've heard the name?"

"Oh no," this visitant from lost time gaily lies. "You just have that look."

THOMAS WOLFE

The Company

George considered himself lucky to have the little room over the Shepperton garage. He was also glad that his visit had overlapped that of Mr. David Merrit, and that Mr. Merrit had been allowed to enjoy undisturbed the greater comfort of the Shepperton guest room, for Mr. Merrit had filled him with a pleasant glow at their first meeting. He was a ruddy, plump, well-kept man of forty-five or so, always ready with a joke and immensely agreeable, with pockets bulging with savory cigars which he handed out to people on the slightest provocation. Randy had spoken of him as "the Company's man," and although George did not know what the duties of a "Company's man" were, Mr. Merrit made them seem very pleasant.

George knew, of course, that Mr. Merrit was Randy's boss, and he learned that Mr. Merrit was in the habit of coming to town every two or three months. He would arrive like a benevolent, pink-cheeked Santa Claus, making his jolly little jokes, passing out his fat cigars, putting his arm around people's shoulders, and, in general, making everyone feel good. As he said himself:

"I've got to turn up now and then just to see that the boys are behaving themselves, and not taking in any wooden nickels."

Here he winked at George in such a comical way that all of them had to grin. Then he gave George a big cigar.

His functions seemed to be ambassadorial. He was always taking Randy and the salesmen of the Company out to lunch or dinner, and, save for brief visits to the office, he seemed to spend most of his time inaugurating an era of good feeling and high living. He would go around town and meet everybody, slapping people on the back and calling them by their first names, and for a week after he had left the business men of Libya Hill would still be smoking his cigars. When he came to town he always stayed "out at the house," and one knew that Margaret would prepare her best meals for him, and that there would be some good drinks. Mr. Merrit supplied the drinks himself, for he always brought along a plentiful store of expensive beverages. George could see at their first meeting that he was the kind of man who exudes an aura of good fellowship, and that was why it was so pleasant to have Mr. Merrit staying in the house.

Mr. Merrit was not only a nice fellow. He was also "with the Company," and George soon realized that "the Company" was a vital and mysterious force in all their lives. Randy had gone with it as soon as he left college. He had been sent to the main office, up North somewhere, and had been put through a course of training. Then he had come back South and had worked his way up from salesman to district agent–an important member of the sales organization.

"The Company," "district agent," "the sales organization"–mysterious titles all of them, but most comforting. During the week George was in Libya Hill with Randy and Margaret, Mr. Merrit was usually on hand at meal times, and at night he would sit out on the front porch with them and carry on in his jolly way, joking and laughing and giving them all a good time. Sometimes he would talk shop with Randy, telling stories about the Company and about his own experiences in the organization, and before long George began to pick up a pretty good idea of what it was all about.

The Federal Weight, Scales, and Computing Company was a far-flung empire which had a superficial aspect of great complexity, but in its essence it was really beautifully simple. Its heart and soul–indeed, its very life–was its sales organization.

The entire country was divided into districts, and over each district an agent was appointed. This agent, in turn, employed salesmen to cover the various portions of his district. Each district also had an "office man" to attend to any business that might come up while the agent and his salesmen were away, and a "repair man" whose duty it was to overhaul damaged or broken-down machines. Together, these comprised the agency, and the country was so divided that there was, on the average, an agency for every unit of half a million people in the total population. Thus there were two hundred and sixty or seventy agencies through the nation, and the agents with their salesmen made up a working force of from twelve to fifteen hundred men.

The higher purposes of this industrial empire, which the employees almost never referred to by name, as who should speak of the deity with coarse directness, but always with a just perceptible lowering and huskiness of the voice as "the Company"–these higher purposes were also beautifully simple. They were summed up in the famous utterance of the Great Man himself, Mr. Paul S. Appleton, III, who invariably repeated it every year as a peroration to his hour-long address before the assembled members of the sales organization at their national convention. Standing before them at the close of each year's session, he would sweep his arm in a gesture of magnificent command toward an enormous map of the United States of America that covered the whole wall behind him, and say:

"There's your market! Go out and sell them!"

What could be simpler and more beautiful than this? What could more eloquently indicate that mighty sweep of the imagination which has been celebrated in the annals of modern business under the name of "vision"? The words had the spacious scope and austere directness that have characterized the utterances of great leaders in every epoch of man's history. It is Napoleon speaking to his troops in Egypt: "Soldiers, from the summit of yonder pyramids, forty centuries look down upon you." It is Captain Perry: "We have met the enemy, and they are ours." It is Dewey at Manila Bay: "You may fire when ready, Gridley." It is Grant before Spottsylvania Court House: "I propose to fight it out on this line, if it takes all summer."

So when Mr. Paul S. Appleton, III, waved his arm at the wall and said: "There's your market! Go out and sell them!"–the assembled captains, lieutenants, and privates in the ranks of his sales organization knew that there were still giants in the earth, and that the age of romance was not dead.

True, there had once been a time when the aspirations of the Company had been more limited. That was when the founder of the institution, the grandfather of Mr. Paul S. Appleton, III, had expressed his modest hopes by saying: "I should like to see one of my machines in every store, shop, or business that needs one, and that can afford to pay for one." But the self-denying restrictions implicit in the founder's statement had long since become so out of date as to seem utterly mid-Victorian. Mr. David Merrit admitted it himself. Much as he hated to speak ill of any man, and especially the founder of the Company, he had to confess that by the standards of 1929 the old gentleman had lacked vision.

"That's old stuff now," said Mr. Merrit, shaking his head and winking at George, as though to take the curse off of his treason to the founder by making a joke of it. "We've gone way beyond that!" he exclaimed with pardonable pride. "Why, if we waited nowadays to sell a machine to someone who *needs one,* we'd get nowhere." He was nodding now at Randy, and speaking with the seriousness of deep conviction. "We don't wait until he *needs* one. If he says he's getting along all right without one, we make him buy one anyhow. We make him *see* the need, don't we, Randy? In other words, we *create* the need."

This, as Mr. Merrit went on to explain, was what is known in more technical phrase as "creative salesmanship" or "creating the market." And this poetic conception was the inspired work of one man—none other than the present head of the Company, Mr. Paul S. Appleton, III, himself. The idea had come to him in a single blinding flash, born full-blown like Pallas Athene from the head of Zeus, and Mr. Merrit still remembered the momentous occasion as vividly as if it had been only yesterday. It was at one of the meetings of the assembled parliaments of the Company that Mr. Appleton, soaring in an impassioned flight of oratory, became so intoxicated with the grandeur of his own vision that he stopped abruptly in the middle of a sentence and stood there as one entranced, gazing out dreamily into the unknown vistas of magic Canaan; and when he at last went on again, it was in a voice surcharged with quivering emotion:

"My friends," he said, "the possibilities of the market, now that we see how to create it, are practically unlimited!" Here he was silent for a moment, and Mr. Merrit said that the Great Man actually paled and seemed to stagger as he tried to speak, and that his voice faltered and sank to an almost inaudible whisper, as if he himself could hardly comprehend the magnitude of his own conception. "My friends—" he muttered thickly, and was seen to clutch the rostrum for support—"my friends, seen properly—" he whispered, and moistened his dry lips—"seen properly—the market we shall create being what it is—" his voice grew stronger, and the clarion words now rang forth—"there is no reason why one of our machines should not be in the possession of every man, woman, and child in the United States!" Then came the grand, familiar gesture to the map: "There's your market, boys! Go out and sell them!"

Henceforth this vision became the stone on which Mr. Paul S. Appleton, III, erected the magnificent edifice of the true church and living faith which was called "the Company." And in the service of this vision Mr. Appleton built up an organization which worked with the beautiful precision of a locomotive piston. Over the salesman was the agent, and over the agent was the district supervisor, and over the district supervisor was the district manager, and over the district manager was the general manager, and over the general manager was—if not God himself, then the next thing to it, for the agents and salesmen referred to him in tones of proper reverence as "P.S.A."

Mr. Appleton also invented a special Company Heaven known as the Hundred Club. Its membership was headed by P.S.A., and all the ranks of the sales organization were eligible, down to the humblest salesman. The Hundred Club was a social order, but it was also a good deal more than that. Each agent and salesman had a "quota"—that is to say, a certain amount of business which was assigned to him as the normal average of his district and capacity. A man's quota differed from another's according to the size of his territory, its wealth, and his own experience and ability. One man's quota would be sixty, another's eighty, another's ninety or one hundred, and if he was a district agent, his quota would be higher than that of a mere salesman. Each man, however, no matter how small or how large his quota might be, was eligible for membership in the Hundred Club, the only restriction being that he must average one hundred per cent of his quota. If he averaged more—if he got, say, one hundred and twenty per cent of his quota—there were appropriate honors and rewards, not only social but financial as well. One could be either high up or low down in the Hundred Club, for it had almost as many degrees of merit as the Masonic order.

The unit of the quota system was "the point," and a point was forty dollars' worth of business. So if a salesman had a quota of eighty, this meant that he had to sell the products of the Federal Weight, Scales, and Computing Company to the amount of at least $3200 every month, or almost $40,000 a year. The rewards were high. A salesman's commission was from fifteen to twenty per cent of his sales; an agent's, from twenty to twenty-five per cent. Beyond this there were bonuses to be earned by achieving or surpassing his quota. Thus it was possible for an ordinary salesman in an average district to earn from $6000 to $8000 a year, while an agent could earn from $12,000 to $15,000, and even more if his district was an exceptionally good one.

So much for the rewards of Mr. Appleton's Heaven. But what would Heaven be if there were no Hell? So Mr. Appleton was forced by the logic of the situation to invent a Hell, too. Once a man's quota was fixed at any given point, the Company never reduced it. Moreover, if a salesman's quota was eighty points and he achieved it during the year, he must be prepared at the beginning of the new year to find that his quota had been increased to ninety points. One had to go onward and upward constantly, and the race was to the swift.

While it was quite true that membership in the Hundred Club was not compulsory, it was also true that Mr. Paul S. Appleton, III, was a theologian who, like Calvin, knew how to combine free will and predestination. If one did *not* belong to the Hundred Club, the time was not far distant when one would not belong to Mr. Appleton. Not to belong to it was, for agent or salesman, the equivalent of living on the other side of the railroad tracks. If one failed of admission to the Company Heaven, or if one dropped out, his fellows would begin to ask guardedly: "Where's Joe Klutz these days?" The answers would be vague, and in the course of time Joe Klutz would be spoken of no more. He would fade into oblivion. He was "no longer with the Company."

Mr. Paul S. Appleton, III, never had but the one revelation–the one which Mr. Merrit so movingly described–but that was enough, and he never let its glories and allurements grow dim. Four times a year, at the beginning of each quarter, he would call his general manager before him and say: "What's the matter, Elmer? You're not getting the business! The market is *there!* You know what you can do about it–or else . . . !" Thereupon the general manager would summon the district managers one by one and repeat to them the words and manner of P. S. A., and the district managers would reenact the scene before each of the district supervisors, who would duplicate it to the agents, who would pass it on to the salesmen, who, since they had no one below them, would "get out and hustle—or else!" This was called "keeping up the morale of the organization."

As Mr. David Merrit sat on the front porch and told of his many experiences with the Company, his words conveyed to George Webber a great deal more than he actually said. For his talk went on and on in its vein of mellow reminiscence, and Mr. Merrit made his little jokes and puffed contentedly at one of his own good cigars, and everything he said carried an overtone of "What a fine and wonderful thing it is to be connected with the Company!"

He told, for example, about the splendid occasion every year when all the members of the Hundred Club were brought together for what was known as "The Week of Play." This was a magnificent annual outing conducted "at the Company's expense." The meeting place might be in Philadelphia or Washington, or in the tropic opulence of Los Angeles or Miami, or it might be on board a chartered ship—one of the small but luxurious twenty-thousand-tonners that ply the transatlantic routes—bound to Bermuda or Havana. Wherever it was, the Hundred Club was given a free sweep. If the journey was by sea, the ship was theirs—for a week. All the liquor in the world was theirs, if they could drink it—and Bermuda's coral isles, or the unlicensed privilege of gay Havana. For that one week everything on earth that money could buy was at the command of the members of the Hundred Club, everything was done on the grand scale, and the Company—the immortal, paternal, and great-hearted Company—"paid for everything."

But as Mr. Merrit painted his glowing picture of the fun they had on these occasions, George Webber saw quite another image. It was an image of twelve or fifteen hundred men—for on these pilgrimages, by general consent, women (or, at any rate, wives) were debarred—twelve or fifteen hundred men, Americans, most of them in their middle years, exhausted, overwrought, their nerves frayed down and stretched to the breaking point, met from all quarters of the continent "at the Company's expense" for one brief, wild, gaudy week of riot. And George thought grimly what this tragic spectacle of business men at play meant in terms of the entire scheme of things and the plan of life that had produced it. He began to understand, too, the changes which time had brought about in Randy.

The last day of his week in Libya Hill, George had gone to the station to buy his return ticket and he stopped in at Randy's office a little before one o'clock to go home to lunch with him. The outer salesroom, with its shining stock of scales and computing machines imposingly arrayed on walnut pedestals, was deserted, so he sat down to wait. On one wall hung a gigantic colored poster. "August Was the Best Month in Federal History," it read. *"Make September a Better One!* The Market's There, Mr. Agent. The Rest Is Up to You!"

Behind the salesroom was a little partitioned space which served Randy as an office. As George waited, gradually he became aware of mysterious sounds emanating from beyond the partition. First there was the rustle of heavy paper, as if the pages of a ledger were being turned, and occasionally there would be a quick murmur of hushed voices, confidential, ominous, interspersed with grunts and half-suppressed exclamations. Then all at once there were two loud bangs, as of a large ledger being slammed shut and thrown upon a desk or table, and after a moment's silence the voices rose louder, distinct, plainly audible. Instantly he recognized Randy's voice—low, grave, hesitant, and deeply troubled. The other voice he had never heard before.

But as he listened to that voice he began to tremble and grow white about the lips. For its very tone was a foul insult to human life, an ugly sneer whipped across the face of decent humanity, and as he realized that that voice, these words, were being used against his friend, he had a sudden blind feeling of murder in his heart. And what was so perplexing and so troubling was that this devil's voice had in it as well a curiously familiar note, as of someone he had known.

Then it came to him in a flash—it was Merrit speaking! The owner of that voice, incredible as it seemed, was none other than that plump, well-kept, jolly-looking man who had always been so full of hearty cheerfulness and good spirits every time he had seen him.

Now, behind that little partition of glazed glass and varnished wood, this man's voice had suddenly become fiendish. It was inconceivable, and as George listened he grew sick, as one does in some awful nightmare when he visions someone he knows doing some perverse and abominable act. But what was more dreadful of all was Randy's voice, humble, low, submissive, modestly entreating. Merrit's voice would cut across the air like a gob of rasping phlegm, and then Randy's voice—gentle, hesitant, deeply troubled—would come in from time to time in answer.

"Well, what's the matter? Don't you want the job?"

"Why—why, yes, you know I do, Dave—haw-w—" and Randy's voice lifted a little in a troubled and protesting laugh.

"What's the matter that you're not getting the business?"

"Why—haw-w!—" again the little laugh, embarrassed and troubled—"I *thought* I was—"

"Well, you're not!" that rasping voice cut in like a knife. "This district ought to deliver thirty per cent more business than you're getting from it, and the Company is going to have it, too—or else! You deliver or you go right out on your can! See? The Company doesn't give a damn about you! It's after the business! You've been around a long time, but you don't mean a damn bit more to the Company than anybody else! And you know what's happened to a lot of other guys who got to feeling they were too big for their job—don't you?"

"Why—why, yes, Dave—but—haw-w!" the little laugh again—"but—honestly, I never thought—"

"We don't give a damn what you never thought!" the brutal voice ripped in. "I've given you fair warning now! You get the business or out you go!"

The glazed glass door burst open violently and Merrit came striding out of the little partitioned office. When he saw George, he looked startled. Then he was instantly transformed. His plump and ruddy face became wreathed in smiles, and he cried out in a hearty tone:

"Well, well, well! Look who's here! If it's not the old boy himself!"

Randy had followed him out, and Merrit now turned and winked humorously at him, in the manner of a man who is carrying on a little bantering byplay:

"Randy," he said, "I believe George gets better looking from day to day. Has he broken any hearts yet?"

Randy tried to smile, grey-faced and haggardly.

"I bet you're burning them up in the Big Town," said Merrit, turning back to George. "And, say, I read that piece in the paper about your book. Great stuff, son! We're all proud of you!"

He gave George a hearty slap on the back and turned away with an air of jaunty readiness, picked up his hat, and said cheerfully:

"Well, what d'ya say, folks? What about one of Margaret's famous meals, out at the old homestead? Well, you can't hurt my feelings. I'm ready if you are. Let's go!"

And, smiling, ruddy, plump, cheerful, a perverted picture of amiable good will to all the world, he sauntered through the door. For a moment the two old friends just stood there looking at each other, white and haggard, with a bewildered expression in their eyes. In Randy's eyes there was also a look of shame. With that instinct for loyalty which was one of the roots of his soul, he said:

"Dave's a good fellow. . . . You–you see, he's got to do these things. . . . He–he's with the Company."

George didn't say anything. For as Randy spoke, and George remembered all that Merrit had told him about the Company, a terrific picture flashed through his mind. It was a picture he had seen in a gallery somewhere, portraying a long line of men stretching from the Great Pyramid to the very portals of great Pharaoh's house, and great Pharaoh stood with a thonged whip in his hand and applied it unmercifully to the bare back and shoulders of the man in front of him, who was great Pharaoh's chief overseer, and in the hand of the overseer was a whip of many tails which he unstintedly applied to the quivering back of the wretch before him, who was the chief overseer's chief lieutenant, and in the lieutenant's hand a whip of rawhide which he laid vigorously on the quailing body of his head sergeant, and in the sergeant's hand a wicked flail with which he belabored a whole company of groaning corporals, and in the hands of every corporal a knotted lash with which to whack a whole regiment of slaves, who pulled and hauled and bore burdens and toiled and sweated and built the towering structure of the pyramid.

So George didn't say anything. He couldn't. He had just found out something about life that he had not known before.

Eudora Welty

Death of a Traveling Salesman

R. J. Bowman, who for fourteen years had traveled for a shoe company through Mississippi, drove his Ford along a rutted dirt path. It was a long day! The time did not seem to clear the noon hurdle and settle into soft afternoon. The sun, keeping its strength here even in winter, stayed at the top of the sky, and every time Bowman stuck his head out of the dusty car to stare up the road, it seemed to reach a long arm down and push against the top of his head, right through his hat—like the practical joke of an old drummer, long on the road. It made him feel all the more angry and helpless. He was feverish, and he was not quite sure of the way.

This was his first day back on the road after a long siege of influenza. He had had very high fever, and dreams, and had become weakened and pale, enough to tell the difference in the mirror, and he could not think clearly. . . . All afternoon, in the midst of his anger, and for no reason, he had thought of his dead grandmother. She had been a comfortable soul. Once more Bowman wished he could fall into the big feather bed that had been in her room. . . . Then he forgot her again.

This desolate hill country! And he seemed to be going the wrong way—it was as if he were going back, far back. There was not a house in sight. . . . There was no use wishing he were back in bed, though. By paying the hotel doctor his bill he had proved his recovery. He had not even been sorry when the pretty trained nurse said good-bye. He did not like illness, he distrusted it, as he distrusted the road without signposts. It angered him. He had given the nurse a really expensive bracelet, just because she was packing up her bag and leaving.

But now—what if in fourteen years on the road he had never been ill before and never had an accident? His record was broken, and he had even begun almost to question it. . . . He had gradually put up at better hotels, in the bigger towns, but weren't they all, eternally, stuffy in summer and drafty in winter? Women? He could only remember little rooms within little rooms, like a nest of Chinese paper boxes, and if he thought of one woman he saw the worn loneliness that the furniture of that room seemed built of. And he himself—he was a man who always wore rather wide-brimmed black hats, and in the wavy hotel mirrors had looked something like a bullfighter, as he paused for that inevitable instant on the landing, walking downstairs to supper. . . . He leaned out of the car again, and once more the sun pushed at his head.

Bowman had wanted to reach Beulah by dark, to go to bed and sleep off his fatigue. As he remembered, Beulah was fifty miles away from the last town, on a graveled road. This was only a cow trail. How had he ever come to such a place? One hand wiped the sweat from his face, and he drove on.

He had made the Beulah trip before. But he had never seen this hill or this petering-out path before—or that cloud, he thought shyly, looking up and then down quickly—any more than he had seen this day before. Why did he not admit he was simply lost and had been for miles? . . . He was not in the habit of asking the way of strangers, and these people never knew where the very roads they lived on went to; but then he had not even been close enough to anyone to call out. People standing in the fields now and then, or on top of the haystacks, had been too far away, looking like leaning sticks or weeds, turning a little at the solitary rattle of his car across their countryside, watching the pale sobered winter dust where it chunked out behind like big squashes down the road. The stares of these distant people had followed him solidly like a wall, impenetrable, behind which they turned back after he had passed.

The cloud floated there to one side like the bolster on his grandmother's bed. It went over a cabin on the edge of a hill, where two bare chinaberry trees clutched at the sky. He drove through a heap of dead oak leaves, his wheels stirring their weightless sides to make a silvery melancholy whistle as the car passed through their bed. No car had been along this way ahead of him. Then he saw that he was on the edge of a ravine that fell away, a red erosion, and that this was indeed the road's end.

He pulled the brake. But it did not hold, though he put all his strength into it. The car, tipped toward the edge, rolled a little. Without doubt, it was going over the bank.

He got out quietly, as though some mischief had been done him and he had his dignity to remember. He lifted his bag and sample case out, set them down, and stood back and watched the car roll over the edge. He heard something—not the crash he was listening for, but a slow, unuproarious crackle. Rather distastefully he went to look over, and he saw that his car had fallen into a tangle of immense grapevines as thick as his arm, which caught it and held it, rocked it like a grotesque child in a dark cradle, and then, as he watched, concerned somehow that he was not still inside it, released it gently to the ground.

He sighed.

Where am I? he wondered with a shock. Why didn't I do something? All his anger seemed to have drifted away from him. There was the house, back on the hill. He took a bag in each hand and with almost childlike willingness went toward it. But his breathing came with difficulty, and he had to stop to rest.

It was a shotgun house, two rooms and an open passage between, perched on the hill. The whole cabin slanted a little under the heavy heaped-up vine that covered the roof, light and green, as though forgotten from summer. A woman stood in the passage.

He stopped still. Then all of a sudden his heart began to behave strangely. Like a rocket set off, it began to leap and expand into uneven patterns of beats which showered into his brain, and he could not think. But in scattering and falling it made no noise. It shot up with great power, almost elation, and fell gently, like acrobats into nets. It began to pound profoundly, then waited irresponsibly, hitting in some sort of inward mockery first at his ribs, then against his eyes, then under his shoulder blades, and against the roof of his mouth when he tried to say, "Good afternoon, madam." But he could not hear his heart—it was as quiet as ashes falling. This was rather comforting; still, it was shocking to Bowman to feel his heart beating at all.

Stock-still in his confusion, he dropped his bags, which seemed to drift in slow bulks gracefully through the air and to cushion themselves on the gray prostrate grass near the doorstep.

As for the woman standing there, he saw at once that she was old. Since she could not possibly hear his heart, he ignored the pounding and now looked at her carefully, and yet in his distraction dreamily, with his mouth open.

She had been cleaning the lamp, and held it, half blackened, half clear, in front of her. He saw her with the dark passage behind her. She was a big woman with a weather-beaten but unwrinkled face; her lips were held tightly together, and her eyes looked with a curious dulled brightness into his. He looked at her shoes, which were like bundles. If it were summer she would be barefoot. . . . Bowman, who automatically judged a woman's age on sight, set her age at fifty. She wore a formless garment of some gray coarse material, rough-dried from a washing, from which her arms appeared pink and unexpectedly round. When she never said a word, and sustained her quiet pose of holding the lamp, he was convinced of the strength in her body.

"Good afternoon, madam," he said.

She stared on, whether at him or at the air around him he could not tell, but after a moment she lowered her eyes to show that she would listen to whatever he had to say.

"I wonder if you would be interested—" He tried once more. "An accident—my car . . ."

Her voice emerged low and remote, like a sound across a lake. "Sonny he ain't here."

"Sonny?"

"Sonny ain't here now."

Her son—a fellow able to bring my car up, he decided in blurred relief. He pointed down the hill. "My car's in the bottom of the ditch. I'll need help."

"Sonny ain't here, but he'll be here."

She was becoming clearer to him and her voice stronger, and Bowman saw that she was stupid.

He was hardly surprised at the deepening postponement and tedium of his journey. He took a breath, and heard his voice speaking over the silent blows of his heart. "I was sick. I am not strong yet. . . . May I come in?"

He stooped and laid his big black hat over the handle on his bag. It was a humble motion, almost a bow, that instantly struck him as absurd and betraying of all his weakness. He looked up at the woman, the wind blowing his hair. He might have continued for a long time in this unfamiliar attitude; he had never been a patient man, but when he was sick he had learned to sink submissively into the pillows, to wait for his medicine. He waited on the woman.

Then she, looking at him with blue eyes, turned and held open the door, and after a moment Bowman, as if convinced in his action, stood erect and followed her in.

Inside, the darkness of the house touched him like a professional hand, the doctor's. The woman set the half-cleaned lamp on a table in the center of the room and pointed, also like a professional person, a guide, to a chair with a yellow cowhide seat. She herself crouched on the hearth, drawing her knees up under the shapeless dress.

At first he felt hopefully secure. His heart was quieter. The room was enclosed in the gloom of yellow pine boards. He could see the other room, with the foot of an iron bed showing, across the passage. The bed had been made up with a red-and-yellow pieced quilt that looked like a map or a picture, a little like his grandmother's girlhood painting of Rome burning.

He had ached for coolness, but in this room it was cold. He stared at the hearth with dead coals lying on it and iron pots in the corners. The hearth and smoked chimney were of the stone he had seen ribbing the hills, mostly slate. Why is there no fire? he wondered.

And it was so still. The silence of the fields seemed to enter and move familiarly through the house. The wind used the open hall. He felt that he was in a mysterious, quiet, cool danger. It was necessary to do what? . . . To talk.

"I have a nice line of women's low-priced shoes . . ." he said.

But the woman answered, "Sonny 'll be here. He's strong. Sonny'll move your car."

"Where is he now?"

"Farms for Mr. Redmond."

Mr. Redmond. Mr. Redmond. That was someone he would never

have to encounter, and he was glad. Somehow the name did not appeal to him. . . . In a flare of touchiness and anxiety, Bowman wished to avoid even mention of unknown men and their unknown farms.

"Do you two live here alone?" He was surprised to hear his old voice, chatty, confidential, inflected for selling shoes, asking a question like that—a thing he did not even want to know.

"Yes. We are alone."

He was surprised at the way she answered. She had taken a long time to say that. She had nodded her head in a deep way too. Had she wished to affect him with some sort of premonition? he wondered unhappily. Or was it only that she would not help him, after all, by talking with him? For he was not strong enough to receive the impact of unfamiliar things without a little talk to break their fall. He had lived a month in which nothing had happened except in his head and his body—an almost inaudible life of heartbeats and dreams that came back, a life of fever and privacy, a delicate life which had left him weak to the point of—what? Of begging. The pulse in his palm leapt like a trout in a brook.

He wondered over and over why the woman did not go ahead with cleaning the lamp. What prompted her to stay there across the room, silently bestowing her presence upon him? He saw that with her it was not a time for doing little tasks. Her face was grave; she was feeling how right she was. Perhaps it was only politeness. In docility he held his eyes stiffly wide; they fixed themselves on the woman's clasped hands as though she held the cord they were strung on.

Then, "Sonny's coming," she said.

He himself had not heard anything, but there came a man passing the window and then plunging in at the door, with two hounds beside him. Sonny was a big enough man, with his belt slung low about his hips. He looked at least thirty. He had a hot, red face that was yet full of silence. He wore muddy blue pants and an old military coat stained and patched. World War? Bowman wondered. Great God, it was a Confederate coat. On the back of his light hair he had a wide filthy black hat which seemed to insult Bowman's own. He pushed down the dogs from his chest. He was strong, with dignity and heaviness in his way of moving. . . . There was the resemblance to his mother.

They stood side by side. . . . He must account again for his presence here.

"Sonny, this man, he had his car to run off over the prec'pice an' wants to know if you will git it out for him," the woman said after a few minutes.

Bowman could not even state his case.

Sonny's eyes lay upon him.

He knew he should offer explanations and show money—at least appear either penitent or authoritative. But all he could do was to shrug slightly.

Sonny brushed by him going to the window, followed by the eager dogs, and looked out. There was effort even in the way he was looking, as if he could throw his sight out like a rope. Without turning Bowman felt that his own eyes could have seen nothing: it was too far.

"Got me a mule out there an' got me a block an' tackle," said Sonny meaningfully. "I *could* catch me my mule an' git me my ropes, an' before long I'd git your car out the ravine."

He looked completely around the room, as if in meditation, his eyes roving in their own distance. Then he pressed his lips firmly and yet shyly together, and with the dogs ahead of him this time, he lowered his head and strode out. The hard earth sounded, cupping to his powerful way of walking—almost a stagger.

Mischievously, at the suggestion of those sounds, Bowman's heart leapt again. It seemed to walk about inside him.

"Sonny's goin' to do it," the woman said. She said it again, singing it almost, like a song. She was sitting in her place by the hearth.

Without looking out, he heard some shouts and the dogs barking and the pounding of hoofs in short runs on the hill. In a few minutes Sonny passed under the window with a rope, and there was a brown mule with quivering, shining, purple-looking ears. The mule actually looked in the window. Under its eyelashes it turned target-like eyes into his. Bowman averted his head and saw the woman looking serenely back at the mule, with only satisfaction in her face.

She sang a little more, under her breath. It occurred to him, and it seemed quite marvelous, that she was not really talking to him, but rather following the thing that came about with words that were unconscious and part of her looking.

So he said nothing, and this time when he did not reply he felt a curious and strong emotion, not fear, rise up in him.

This time, when his heart leapt, something—his soul—seemed to leap too, like a little colt invited out of a pen. He stared at the woman while the frantic nimbleness of his feeling made his head sway. He could not move; there was nothing he could do, unless perhaps he might embrace this woman who sat there growing old and shapeless before him.

But he wanted to leap up, to say to her, I have been sick and I found out then, only then, how lonely I am. Is it too late? My heart puts up a struggle inside me, and you may have heard it, protesting against emptiness. . . . It should be full, he would rush on to tell her, thinking of his heart now as a deep lake, it should be holding love like other hearts. It should be flooded with love. There would be a warm spring day . . . Come and stand in my heart, whoever you are, and a whole river would cover your feet and rise higher and take your knees in whirlpools, and draw you down to itself, your whole body, your heart too.

But he moved a trembling hand across his eyes, and looked at the placid crouching woman across the room. She was still as a statue. He felt ashamed and exhausted by the thought that he might, in one more moment, have tried by simple words and embraces to communicate some strange thing–something which seemed always to have just escaped him . . .

Sunlight touched the furthest pot on the hearth. It was late afternoon. This time tomorrow he would be somewhere on a good graveled road, driving his car past things that happened to people, quicker than their happening. Seeing ahead to the next day, he was glad, and knew that this was no time to embrace an old woman. He could feel in his pounding temples the readying of his blood for motion and for hurrying away.

"Sonny's hitched up your car by now," said the woman. "He'll git it out the ravine right shortly."

"Fine!" he cried with his customary enthusiasm.

Yet it seemed a long time that they waited. It began to get dark. Bowman was cramped in his chair. Any man should know enough to get up and walk around while he waited. There was something like guilt in such stillness and silence.

But instead of getting up, he listened. . . . His breathing restrained, his eyes powerless in the growing dark, he listened uneasily for a warning sound, forgetting in wariness what it would be. Before long he heard something–soft, continuous, insinuating.

"What's that noise?" he asked, his voice jumping into the dark. Then wildly he was afraid it would be his heart beating so plainly in the quiet room, and she would tell him so.

"You might hear the stream," she said grudgingly.

Her voice was closer. She was standing by the table. He wondered why she did not light the lamp. She stood there in the dark and did not light it.

Bowman would never speak to her now, for the time was past. I'll sleep in the dark, he thought, in his bewilderment pitying himself.

Heavily she moved on to the window. Her arm, vaguely white, rose straight from her full side and she pointed out into the darkness.

"That white speck's Sonny," she said, talking to herself.

He turned unwillingly and peered over her shoulder; he hesitated to rise and stand beside her. His eyes searched the dusky air. The white speck floated smoothly toward her finger, like a leaf on a river, growing whiter in the dark. It was as if she had shown him something secret, part of her life, but had offered no explanation. He looked away. He was moved almost to tears, feeling for no reason that she had made a silent declaration equivalent to his own. His hand waited upon his chest.

Then a step shook the house, and Sonny was in the room. Bowman felt how the woman left him there and went to the other man's side.

"I done got your car out, mister," said Sonny's voice in the dark. "She's settin' a-waitin' in the road, turned to go back where she come from."

"Fine!" said Bowman, projecting his own voice to loudness. "I'm surely much obliged–I could never have done it myself–I was sick. . . ."

"I could do it easy," said Sonny.

Bowman could feel them both waiting in the dark, and he could hear the dogs panting out in the yard, waiting to bark when he should go. He felt strangely helpless and resentful. Now that he could go, he longed to stay. From what was he being deprived? His chest was rudely shaken by the violence of his heart. These people cherished something here that he could not see, they withheld some ancient promise of food and warmth and light. Between them they had a conspiracy. He thought of the way she had moved away from him and gone to Sonny, she had flowed toward him. He was shaking with cold, he was tired, and it was not fair. Humbly and yet angrily he stuck his hand into his pocket.

"Of course I'm going to pay you for everything—"

"We don't take money for such," said Sonny's voice belligerently.

"I want to pay. But do something more . . . Let me stay—tonight. . . ." He took another step toward them. If only they could see him, they would know his sincerity, his real need! His voice went on, "I'm not very strong yet, I'm not able to walk far, even back to my car, maybe, I don't know—I don't know exactly where I am—"

He stopped. He felt as if he might burst into tears. What would they think of him!

Sonny came over and put his hands on him. Bowman felt them pass (they were professional too) across his chest, over his hips. He could feel Sonny's eyes upon him in the dark.

"You ain't no revenuer come sneakin' here, mister, ain't got no gun?"

To this end of nowhere! And yet *he* had come. He made a grave answer. "No."

"You can stay."

"Sonny," said the woman, "you'll have to borry some fire."

"I'll go git it from Redmond's," said Sonny.

"What?" Bowman strained to hear their words to each other.

"Our fire, it's out, and Sonny's got to borry some, because its dark an' cold," she said.

"But matches—I have matches—"

"We don't have no need for 'em," she said proudly. "Sonny's goin' after his own fire."

"I'm goin' to Redmond's," said Sonny with an air of importance, and he went out.

After they had waited a while, Bowman looked out the window and saw a light moving over the hill. It spread itself out like a little fan. It zigzagged along the field, darting and swift, not like Sonny at all. . . . Soon enough, Sonny staggered in, holding a burning stick behind him in tongs, fire flowing in his wake, blazing light into the corners of the room.

"We'll make a fire now," the woman said, taking the brand.

When that was done she lit the lamp. It showed its dark and light. The whole room turned golden-yellow like some sort of flower, and the walls smelled of it and seemed to tremble with the quiet rushing of the fire and the waving of the burning lampwick in its funnel of light.

The woman moved among the iron pots. With the tongs she dropped hot coals on top of the iron lids. They made a set of soft vibrations, like the sound of a bell far away.

She looked up and over at Bowman, but he could not answer. He was trembling. . . .

"Have a drink, mister?" Sonny asked. He had brought in a chair from the other room and sat astride it with his folded arms across the back. Now we are all visible to one another, Bowman thought, and cried, "Yes sir, you bet, thanks!"

"Come after me and do just what I do," said Sonny.

It was another excursion into the dark. They went through the hall, out to the back of the house, past a shed and a hooded well. They came to a wilderness of thicket.

"Down on your knees," said Sonny.

"What?" Sweat broke out on his forehead.

He understood when Sonny began to crawl through a sort of tunnel that the bushes made over the ground. He followed, startled in spite of himself when a twig or a thorn touched him gently without making a sound, clinging to him and finally letting him go.

Sonny stopped crawling and, crouched on his knees, began to dig with both his hands into the dirt. Bowman shyly struck matches and made a light. In a few minutes Sonny pulled up a jug. He poured out some of the whisky into a bottle from his coat pocket, and buried the jug again. "You never know who's liable to knock at your door," he said, and laughed. "Start back," he said, almost formally. "Ain't no need for us to drink outdoors, like hogs."

At the table by the fire, sitting opposite each other in their chairs, Sonny and Bowman took drinks out of the bottle, passing it across. The dogs slept; one of them was having a dream.

"This is good," said Bowman. "This is what I needed." It was just as though he were drinking the fire off the hearth.

"He makes it," said the woman with quiet pride.

She was pushing the coals off the pots, and the smells of corn bread and coffee circled the room. She set everything on the table before the men, with a bone-handled knife stuck into one of the potatoes, splitting out its golden fiber. Then she stood for a minute looking at them, tall and full above them where they sat. She leaned a little toward them.

"You all can eat now," she said, and suddenly smiled.

Bowman had just happened to be looking at her. He set his cup back on the table in unbelieving protest. A pain pressed at his eyes. He saw that she was not an old woman. She was young, still young. He could think of no number of years for her. She was the same age as Sonny, and she belonged to him. She stood with the deep dark corner of the room behind her, the shifting yellow light scattering over her head and her gray formless dress, trembling over her tall body when it bent over them in its sudden communication. She was young. Her teeth were shining and her eyes glowed. She turned and walked slowly and heavily out of the room, and he heard her sit down on the cot and then lie down. The pattern on the quilt moved.

"She's goin' to have a baby," said Sonny, popping a bite into his mouth.

Bowman could not speak. He was shocked with knowing what was really in this house. A marriage, a fruitful marriage. That simple thing. Anyone could have had that.

Somehow he felt unable to be indignant or protest, although some sort of joke had certainly been played upon him. There was nothing remote or mysterious here—only something private. The only secret was the ancient communication between two people. But the memory of the woman's waiting silently by the cold hearth, of the man's stubborn journey a mile away to get fire, and how they finally brought out their food and drink and filled the room proudly with all they had to show, was suddenly too clear and too enormous within him for response. . . .

"You ain't as hungry as you look," said Sonny.

The woman came out of the bedroom as soon as the men had finished, and ate her supper while her husband stared peacefully into the fire.

Then they put the dogs out, with the food that was left.

"I think I'd better sleep here by the fire, on the floor," said Bowman.

He felt that he had been cheated, and that he could afford now to be generous. Ill though he was, he was not going to ask them for their bed. He was through with asking favors in this house, now that he understood what was there.

"Sure, mister."

But he had not known yet how slowly he understood. They had not meant to give him their bed. After a little interval they both rose and looking at him gravely went into the other room.

He lay stretched by the fire until it grew low and dying. He watched every tongue of blaze lick out and vanish. "There will be special reduced prices on all footwear during the month of January," he found himself repeating quietly, and then he lay with his lips tight shut.

How many noises the night had! He heard the stream running, the fire dying, and he was sure now that he heard his heart beating, too, the sound it made under his ribs. He heard breathing, round and deep, of the man and his wife in the room across the passage. And that was all. But emotion swelled patiently within him, and he wished that the child were his.

He must get back to where he had been before. He stood weakly before the red coals and put on his overcoat. It felt too heavy on his shoulders. As he started out he looked and saw that the woman had never got through with cleaning the lamp. On some impulse he put all the money from his billfold under its fluted glass base, almost ostentatiously.

Ashamed, shrugging a little, and then shivering, he took his bags and went out. The cold of the air seemed to lift him bodily. The moon was in the sky.

On the slope he began to run, he could not help it. Just as he reached the road, where his car seemed to sit in the moonlight like a boat, his heart began to give off tremendous explosions like a rifle, bang bang bang.

He sank in fright onto the road, his bags falling about him. He felt as if all this had happened before. He covered his heart with both hands to keep anyone from hearing the noise it made.

But nobody heard it.

PERMISSIONS

Excerpt from *The Competitor,* by Thomas J. Bontly. Copyright © 1966 by Thomas J. Bontly. Reprinted by permission of Curtis Brown Ltd. All rights reserved.

"Handsome Brown's Day Off" is from *Georgia Boy,* by Erskine Caldwell. Copyright © 1943, 1971 by Erskine Caldwell. Reprinted by permission of McIntosh and Otis, Inc.

"The Autobiography of a Drummer" is from *Thirteen Uncollected Stories,* by John Cheever. Copyright © 1994 by Academy Chicago Publishers.

Excerpt from *The Mulching of America,* by Harry Crews. Copyright © 1995 by Harry Crews. Reprinted with the permission of Simon & Schuster.

"The Smile of a Turtle" is from *Under the Wheat,* by Rick DeMarinis. Copyright © 1986 by Rick DeMarinis. Reprinted by permission of the University of Pittsburgh Press.

"Through a Glass Darkly" is from *The New Yorker,* December 31, 1949. Copyright © 1949 by New Yorker Magazine, Inc. Reprinted by permission of the Estate of Peter De Vries and the Watkins Loomis Agency.

"Harry" is from *The Daring Young Man on the Flying Trapeze,* by William Saroyan. Copyright © 1934 by William Saroyan. Reprinted by permission of the Board of Trustees of Leland Stanford Junior University.

"Collectors" is from *Will You Please Be Quiet, Please?,* by Raymond Carver. Copyright © 1986, 1987, 1988 by Raymond Carver. Reprinted by permission of Grove/Atlantic, Inc.

"Sales Pitch" is from *The Collected Stories of Philip K. Dick,* by Philip K. Dick. Copyright © 1987. Reprinted by permission of Scovil Chichak Galen Literary Agency, Inc.

"Jeopardy" is from *Working Men,* by Michael Dorris. Copyright © 1993 by Michael Dorris. Reprinted by permission of Henry Holt and Company, Inc.

"My Brother's Keeper" is from *A Penny for Charity,* by Seymour Epstein. Copyright © 1965 by Seymour Epstein. Reprinted by permission of Little Brown and Company.

"Simply Skirts" is from *Roast Beef Medium: The Business Adventures of Emma McChesney,* by Edna Ferber. Copyright © 1913.

"The Unswept Emptiness" is from *Sister Age,* by M. F. K. Fisher. Copyright © 1983 by M. F. K. Fisher. Reprinted by permission of Alfred A. Knopf, Inc.

Excerpt from *Independence Day,* by Richard Ford. Copyright © 1995 by Richard Ford. Reprinted by permission of Alfred A. Knopf, Inc.

Excerpt from *Glengarry Glen Ross,* by David Mamet. Copyright © 1982, 1983 by David Mamet. Used by permission of Grove/Atlantic, Inc.

"Can I Just Sit Here For a While?" is from *Nebraska Stories,* by Ron Hansen. Copyright © 1989 by Ron Hansen. Used by permission of Grove/Atlantic, Inc.

Excerpt from *Ladies' Man,* by Richard Price. Copyright © 1978 by Richard Price. Reprinted by permission of Houghton Mifflin Company. All rights reserved.

Excerpt from *Elmer Gantry,* by Sinclair Lewis. Copyright © 1927 by Sinclair Lewis. Reprinted by permission of McIntosh and Otis, Inc.

Excerpt from *The Rug Merchant,* by Phillip Lopate. Copyright © 1987 by Phillip Lopate. Used by permission of Viking Penguin, a division of Penguin Books USA, Inc.

"200,000 Dozen Pairs of Socks" is from *Southern Fried Plus Six,* by William Price Fox. Copyright © 1968 by William Price Fox. Reprinted by permission of the author.

"The Story Mac Told" is from *Ghostly Populations,* by Jack Matthews. Copyright © 1986 by Jack Matthews. Reprinted by permission of The Johns Hopkins University Press.

Excerpt from *Death of a Salesman,* by Arthur Miller. Copyright © 1949, renewed © 1977 by Arthur Miller. Used by permission of Viking Penguin, a division of Penguin Books USA, Inc.

"Likely Houses" is from *Star Game,* by Lucia Nevai. Copyright © 1983 by Lucia Nevai. Reprinted by permission of Don Congdon Associates, Inc.

"Good Country People" is from *A Good Man Is Hard to Find and Other Stories,* by Flannery O'Connor. Copyright © 1955 by Flannery O'Connor and renewed 1983 by Regina O'Connor. Reprinted by permission of Harcourt Brace & Company.

"How Can I Tell You?" is from *The Hat on the Bed,* by John O'Hara. Copyright © 1963 by John O'Hara. Reprinted by permission of Random House, Inc.

"Blue Island" is from *The Presence of Grace and Other Stories,* by J. F. Powers. Copyright © 1956 by J. F. Powers. Reprinted by permission of the author.

"Think Big" is from *Economies of the Heart,* by Christopher Zenowich. Copyright © 1990 by Christopher Zenowich. Reprinted by permission of the author.

Excerpt from *Rabbit Is Rich,* by John Updike. Copyright © 1987 by John Updike. Reprinted by permission of Alfred A. Knopf, Inc.

"The Company" is from *Our Lives: American Labor Stories,* by Thomas Wolfe. Copyright © 1948. Reprinted by permission of the Estate of Thomas Wolfe, Paul Gitlin, Administrator, C.T.A.

"Death of a Traveling Salesman" is from *A Curtain of Green and Other Stories,* by Eudora Welty. Copyright © 1941 and renewed 1969 by Eudora Welty. Reprinted by permission of Harcourt Brace & Company.